Voltaire's l

Complete in (

Voltaire

Alpha Editions

This edition published in 2024

ISBN : 9789364738705

Design and Setting By
Alpha Editions
www.alphaedis.com
Email - info@alphaedis.com

As per information held with us this book is in Public Domain.
This book is a reproduction of an important historical work. Alpha Editions uses the best technology to reproduce historical work in the same manner it was first published to preserve its original nature. Any marks or number seen are left intentionally to preserve its true form.

Contents

PUBLISHER'S PREFACE ....- 1 -
THE WHITE BULL. ....- 15 -
ZADIG; OR FATE. ....- 58 -
THE SAGE AND THE ATHEIST. ....- 143 -
PRINCESS OF BABYLON ....- 193 -
THE MAN OF FORTY CROWNS. ....- 267 -
THE HURON; OR, PUPIL OF NATURE.[1] ....- 313 -
MICROMEGAS: ....- 385 -
THE WORLD AS IT GOES. ....- 407 -
THE BLACK AND THE WHITE. ....- 422 -
MEMNON THE PHILOSOPHER. ....- 436 -
ANDRÉ DES TOUCHES AT SIAM. ....- 443 -
BABABEC...- 449 -
THE STUDY OF NATURE. ....- 457 -
A CONVERSATION WITH A CHINESE. ....- 468 -
PLATO'S DREAM. ....- 477 -
PLEASURE IN HAVING NO PLEASURE. ....- 481 -
AN ADVENTURE IN INDIA..- 487 -
JEANNOT AND COLIN. ....- 492 -
THE HISTORY OF THE TRAVELS OF
SCARMENTADO. [1] ....- 501 -
THE GOOD BRAMIN. ....- 509 -
THE TWO COMFORTERS. ....- 513 -
ANCIENT FAITH AND FABLE..- 515 -

PUBLISHER'S PREFACE

Voltaire wrote what the people thought, and consequently his writings were universally read. He wittily ridiculed established abuses, and keenly satirized venerable absurdities. For this he was consigned to the Bastile, and this distinction served to increase his popularity and extend his influence. He was thus enabled to cope successfully with the papal hierarchy, and laugh at the murmurs of the Vatican. The struggle commenced in his youth, and continued till his death. It was a struggle of light against darkness—of freedom against tyranny; and it ended in the triumph of truth over error and of toleration over bigotry.

Educated by the Jesuits, he early learned their methods, and his great ability enabled him to circumvent their wiles. The ceremonious presentation of his tragedy of *Mahomet*[1] to Pope Benedict XIV., is an example of his daring audacity;—his success with the "head of the church" shows his intellectual superiority—whilst the gracious reply of "his Holiness" fitly illustrates the pontiff's vanity. From priest to bishop, from cardinal to pope, all felt his intellectual power and all dreaded his merciless satire.

Voltaire at seventy.

He was famous as poet, dramatist, historian, and philosopher. An experienced courtier and polished writer, he gracefully and politely conquered his clerical opponents, and with courteous irony overthrew his literary critics. From his demeanor you could not judge of his thoughts or intentions, and while listening to his compliments, you instinctively dreaded his sarcasms. But venture to approach this grand seigneur, this keen man of the world, this intellectual giant, and plead in favor of human justice—appeal to his magnanimity and love of toleration—and you then had no cause to question his earnestness, no reason to doubt his sincerity. His blood boiled, says Macaulay,[2] at the sight of cruelty and injustice, and in an age of religious persecution, judicial torture, and arbitrary imprisonment, he made manful war, with every faculty he possessed, on what he considered as abuses; and on many signal occasions, placed himself gallantly between the powerful and the oppressed. "When an innocent man was broken on the wheel at Toulouse, when a youth, guilty only of an indiscretion, was beheaded at Abbéville, when a brave officer, borne down by public injustice, was dragged, with a gag in his mouth, to die on the Place de Grêve, a voice instantly went forth from the banks of Lake Leman, which made itself heard from Moscow to Cadiz, and which sentenced the unjust judges to the contempt and detestation of all Europe."

"None can read these stories of the horrible religious bigotry of the day," says Alex. A. Knox, in *The Nineteenth Century*,[3] "without feeling for Voltaire reverence and respect."

The following extract from the above named Review will explain the religious cruelty to which Macaulay refers:

> "Jean Calas, a Protestant, kept a small shop in Toulouse. He had a scape-grace of a son, Marc Antoine by name, who hanged himself in his father's shop. The poor father and mother were up stairs at the time, at supper, in company with the second son. The evidence was so clear that a coroner's jury at a public-house would not have turned round upon it. The priests and the priest party got hold of it, and turned it into a religious crime. The Protestant, or Huguenot parents were charged with murdering their son for fear he should turn Catholic. The body was taken to the Hôtel de Ville, and then escorted by priests to the cathedral. The religious orders—White Penitents and others—held solemn ceremonies for the repose of Marc Antoine's soul. The churches resounded with the exhortations of the priests, informing the people what evidence was required to procure the condemnation of the Calas, and directing them to come forward as witnesses. Upon such assumptions as

these horrible people could devise, the poor old man was stretched till his limbs were torn out of the sockets. He was then submitted to the *question extraordinaire*. This consisted in pouring water into his mouth from a horn till his body was swollen to twice its size. The man had been drowned a hundred times over, but he was still alive. He was then carried to the scaffold and his limbs were broken with an iron bar, and he was left for two hours to die. He did not then die, and so the executioner strangled him at last; but he died without confessing his crime. The man was innocent; he had no confession to make. The poor creature by his unutterable agony thus saved the lives of his wife and family, all as innocent as himself. Two daughters were thrust into a convent: a son shammed conversion to Catholicism and was released. The servant escaped into a convent. The property of the family was confiscated. The poor mother slipped away unseen. Finally, another son, who had been apprenticed to a watchmaker of Nismes, escaped to Geneva. This is a picture of France in the eighteenth century.

"Voltaire took poor young Calas into his family. He tried at once to interest the Cardinal de Bernis, the Duc de Choiseul, and others in this horrible story. He found for the widow a comfortable retreat at Paris; he employed the best lawyers he could find to give practical form to the business; he sent the daughters to join the mother. He paid all the expenses out of his own pocket. He reached the Chancellor; he made his appeal to Europe. He employed a clever young advocate M. Elie de Beaumont, to conduct the cast. The Queen of England, Frederick the Great, Catharine of Russia, were induced by Voltaire to help the Calas.

"The case of the Sirvens was well-nigh as bad as that of the Calas. Sirven lived with his wife and three daughters, all Protestants, near Toulouse. The story is so illustrative of the France of the eighteenth century, and of what Voltaire was about, that it deserves a few lines. Sirven's housekeeper, a Roman Catholic, with the assent of the Bishop of Castres, spirited away the youngest daughter, and placed her in a convent of the Black Ladies with a view to her conversion. She returned to her parents in a state of insanity, her body covered with the marks of the whip. She never recovered from the cruelties she had endured at the convent. One day, when her father was absent on his professional duties, she threw herself into a well, at the bottom of which she was found drowned. It was obvious to the authorities that the parents had murdered their child because she wished to become a Roman Catholic. They most wisely did not appear, and were sentenced to be hanged when they could be caught. In their flight the married daughter gave premature birth to a child; and Madame Sirven died in despair. It took Voltaire ten years to get this abominable sentence reversed, and to turn wrong into right.

"A Protestant gentleman, M. Espinasse, had been condemned to the galleys for life and his estate confiscated because he had given supper and lodging to a Protestant clergyman. He served twenty-three years; but in 1763 Voltaire obtained his release, and ultimately obtained back for the family a portion of their property.

"The Chevalier de la Barre was another victim. Some person or persons unknown had hacked with a knife a wooden crucifix which stood on a bridge at Abbéville over the Somme. The same night a crucifix on one of the cemeteries was bespattered with mud. The bishop of the place set to work to stir up excitement, praying for punishment 'on those who had rendered themselves worthy of the severest punishment known to the world's law.' Young De la Barre was arrested. The evidence against him was that he, with certain companions, had been known to pass within thirty yards of a procession bearing the Sacrament without taking off their hats. It was further proved in evidence that he and his friends had sung certain objectionable songs, and that not only some novels had been found in his rooms, but also two small volumes of Voltaire's *Dictionnaire Philosophique*. On this evidence he was sentenced to be subjected to the torture, ordinary and extraordinary; to have his tongue torn out by the roots with pincers of iron, to have his right hand cut off at the door of the principal church at Abbéville, to be drawn in a cart to the market-place, and there to be burned to death by a slow fire. The sentence was mitigated so far that he was allowed to be beheaded before he was burned. This sentence was carried out on the 1st of July, 1766. These are samples of what was occurring in France. Was there not enough to rouse indignation to fever-heat?

"When one reads such stories, even at this distance of time, he understands the French Revolution and Voltaire."

In all his writings Voltaire claimed to be religious, and was as ready to oppose with his sarcasms the agnostic or atheist, as the catholic. In speaking of Tully as a doubter, he makes Pococurante exclaim: "I once had some liking for his philosophical works; but when I found he doubted of everything, I thought I knew as much as himself, and had no need of a guide to learn ignorance."

But while Voltaire was a Theist—as Lord Brougham says,[4] "without any hesitation or any intermission, a Theist"—and was a firm believer in the existence of a Creator and ruler of the universe,—he was also an avowed opponent of Catholicism; and when not engaged in the production of works which have added dignity to the literature of France, his life was passed in open warfare with the church of Rome. To this church he was as sincerely opposed as Martin Luther, and although his methods of attack and opposition differed entirely from that of the great German reformer, who shall say that his efforts have not proved even more successful? Macaulay has shown[5] that no Catholic nation has become Protestant since the period of the Reformation; while on the other hand, no nation once Protestant, has returned to Catholicism. Each party has retained its own territory, and the only gain has been in favor of religious freedom. The sincere and earnest appeals of Luther, which convulsed Germany, produced but little or no effect on the versatile mind of France. But the brilliant writings of Voltaire were welcomed by his countrymen, and have not been without their influence on French civilization. And although France has not been claimed as a protestant nation, yet freethinkers have there attained great power and influence, whilst Germany, once the stronghold of Protestantism, is now the chosen and hospitable home of freethought.

Voltaire in his day was an acknowledged leader of public opinion. His thoughts engrossed the attention of the world. "Whole nations," says Quinet,[6] "emulously repeat every syllable that falls from his pen:" and the lapse of time has but confirmed the verdict of his cotemporaries, that of all the great reformers, his writings are the most useful to mankind.

"If we judge of men by what they have *done*" says Lamartine,[7] "then Voltaire is incontestably the greatest writer of modern Europe. No one has caused, through the powerful influence of his genius alone, and the perseverance of his will, so great a commotion in the minds of men; his pen aroused a world, and has shaken a far mightier empire than that of Charlemagne, the European empire of a theocracy. His genius was not *force* but *light*. Heaven had destined him not to destroy but to illuminate, and wherever he trod light followed him, for reason (which is *light*) had destined him to be first her poet, then her apostle, and lastly her idol."

At seventeen years of age Voltaire wrote *Œdipus*, at eighty-three he wrote *Irène*. During the intervening years he enriched the world of thought with seventy volumes of irresistible humor—of brilliant and caustic wit,—in truth, a mine of literary gems undimmed with mediocrity's prosy dullness. In fact, it was this quality of humor and mirth that made Voltaire's writings so distasteful to his opponents—so welcome to mankind. Other writers, who went far beyond Voltaire, were not considered dangerous, because they were never read. They were sincere and learned, but tedious and austere. Their disbelief was condoned by its metaphysical obscurity—their skepticism was redeemed by its unmitigated dullness. But with Voltaire the case was very different. His writings were read and appreciated by old or young, grave or gay, sage or sophist, prince or peasant. To answer him was impossible—to abuse him was thought commendable.

"Napoleon, during fifteen years," says Lamartine,[8] "paid writers who degrade, vilify, and deny the genius of Voltaire; he hated his name as *might* must ever *hate intellect*; and so long as men yet cherished the memory of Voltaire—so long he felt his position was not secure." The church voluntarily joined in this work of aspersion. To the priests it was no hardship,—it was a welcome task—a labor of love. They hated the writings they could not answer—the genius they could not destroy.

"The church," says Macaulay,[9] "made no defense, except by acts of power. Censures were pronounced; books were seized; insults were offered to the remains of infidel writers but no Bossuet, no Pascal, came forth to encounter Voltaire. There appeared not a single defense of the catholic doctrine which produced any considerable effect, or which is even now remembered."

"His element," says Schlosser,[10] "was the lighter kind of poetry, and his fugitive verses, his sharp wit, his bold opinions, produced effects in his time, like flashes of lightning, for they illuminated at the same time the night of Jesuitical superstition, and struck and shivered to pieces the majestic towers and gothic domes of the middle ages.

"The so-called fugitive pieces alone, if he had written nothing else, would have been sufficient to secure Voltaire's immortality; for in these he is altogether in his sphere; he has only to think of the people whom he calls exclusively the world, and he can direct every spark of his genius to the production of instantaneous effect, delight his reader by his fancy, and surprise him by his wit.

"The chief aim of each one of Voltaire's small novels is the overthrow and refutation of some ruling opinion, and this object is admirably attained by the story itself, and by weaving in sarcasms, because this rendered all reply and refutation impossible. Seriousness could never have reached the readers of these novels, or would immediately weary them; and every attempt to rival Voltaire in a strain of pleasantry and satire, would have been a folly.

"In *Zadig* he shows palpably and obviously how entirely devoid of reason and taste the usual moral and edifying considerations upon the way of Providence, upon a God who thinks, counsels, acts, and conducts the affairs of the world as a man, must appear to the bold scoffer. Voltaire, we would say, confined and limited the doctrine of an immediate guidance of human affairs by the hand of Divine Providence, wholly to the church and to the faith of the people; he roofed it out of higher life and out of science by means of his dreadful ridicule. By his narratives he made that obvious, which indeed is easily made palpable enough, because it is undeniable, that the theory of a palpable guidance of human affairs by an ever-manifesting interposing Providence, may be just as easily refuted as proved by history and experience. In *Memnon* is shown, in an admirable manner, how the multitude are enamoured of their prudence, and laugh at nature and its feelings. In the *Ingenu*, the witty man yields himself up wholly to his humor and to accident, and brings forth a rich abundance of wit and flashes of genius with respect to the most various subjects."

"Voltaire had the genius of criticism," says Lamartine,[1] "that power of raillery which withers all it overthrows. He had made human nature laugh at itself, had felled it low in order to raise it, had laid bare before it all errors, prejudices, iniquities, and crimes of ignorance; he had urged it to rebellion against consecrated ideas, not by the ideal but by sheer contempt. Destiny gave him eighty years of existence, that he might slowly decompose the decayed age; he had the time to combat against time, and when he fell he was the conqueror.

"Such were the elements of the revolution in religious matters. Voltaire laid hold of them, at the precise moment, with that *coup d'œil* of strong instinct which sees clearer than genius itself. To an age young, fickle, and unreflecting, he did not present reason under the form of an austere philosophy, but beneath the guise of a facile freedom of ideas, and a scoffing irony. He would not have succeeded in making his age think, he did succeed in making it smile. He never attacked it in front, nor with his face uncovered, in order that he might not set the laws in array against him; and to avoid the fate of Servetus, he, the modern Æsop, attacked under imaginary names the tyranny which he wished, to destroy. He concealed his hate in history, the drama, light poetry, romance, and even in jests. His genius was a perpetual allusion, comprehending all his age, but impossible to be seized on by his enemies. He struck, but his hand was concealed. Yet the struggle of a man against a priesthood, an individual against an institution, a life against eighteen centuries, was by no means destitute of courage.

"There is an incalculable power of conviction and devotion of idea, in the daring of one against all. To brave at once, with no other power than individual reason, with no other support than conscience, human consideration, that cowardice of the mind, masked under respect for error; to dare the hatred of earth and the anathema of heaven, is the heroism of the writer. Voltaire was not a martyr in his body, but he consented to be one in his name, and devoted it during his life and after his death. He condemned his own ashes to be thrown to the winds, and not to have either an asylum or a tomb. He resigned himself even to lengthened exile in exchange for the liberty of a free combat. He isolated himself voluntarily from men, in order that their too close contact might not interfere with his thoughts.

"At eighty years of age, feeble, and feeling his death nearly approaching, he several times made his preparations hastily, in order to go and struggle still, and die at a distance from the roof of his old age. The unwearied activity of his mind was never checked for a moment. He carried his gaiety even to genius, and under that pleasantry of his whole life we may perceive a grave power of perseverance and conviction. Such was the character of this great man. The enlightened serenity of his mind concealed the depth of its workings: under the joke and laugh his constancy of purpose was hardly sufficiently recognized. He suffered all with a laugh, and was willing to endure all, even in absence from his native land, in his lost friendships, in his refused fame, in his blighted name, in his memory accursed. He took all—bore all—for the sake of the triumph of the independence of human reason."

The manners and customs of the eighteenth century differ widely from those of the nineteenth. Certain words and phrases that were then in common use are now wisely suppressed. Lecky says very truly,[112] that "a Roman of the age of Pliny, an Englishman of the age of Henry VIII., and an Englishman of our own day, would all agree in regarding humanity as a virtue, and its opposite as a vice; but their judgments of the acts which are compatible with a humane disposition would be widely different."

The enemies of freethought have taken advantage of this fact—this change in modes of expression—this refinement in literature—to defame the memory of Voltaire. They denounce *La Pucelle* or *The Maid of Orleans* for language and expressions, formerly popular in court circles and sanctioned by the nobility and ladies of fashion, but which, happily, have now become obsolete. They judge the license of the eighteenth century—the license and profligacy which accompany ecclesiasticism and monasticism—by nineteenth century standards. If the same rule were applied to other writers, none would have cause to complain. But, unfortunately, an exception has been unjustly made in favor of the language employed by historians like Moses and Solomon, by poets like Shakspeare and Pope, by theologians like Rabelais and Swift, by novelists like Fielding and Smollett. In short, immodest language cannot be redeemed by wit, by learning, or by pretended revelation, and should always and invariably be suppressed; but writers should be judged by the manners and customs of their age, and not by modern standards. There are many passages in the old classic authors that were formerly considered in good taste, which cannot now be commended. Still, the gold outweighs the dross, and we should remember the laxity and licentiousness of the times in which those books were written.

The romances and tales in this publication have been selected for their graceful and sprightly wit, as well as genial humor and keen satire; and further, because they are free from even a suspicion of impropriety. They each teach a lesson of wisdom and morality—they teach courage, fortitude and resignation, and, what is perhaps of even greater importance, they also tend to free the mind from the baneful errors of priestcraft and superstition.

"The most interesting adventures are related to no sort of purpose," says Voltaire in one of his essays, "if they do not convey, at the same time, a description of manners. And even this is but a frivolous amusement, if that description does not contribute to inspire us with sentiments of virtue. I dare assert that, from the *Henriade* to *Zara* and down to the Chinese tragedy of *The Orphan of Tchao* such was always the aim I proposed, and the principle that conducted me. In the history of the age of Louis the fourteenth, I have celebrated my king and country, without flattering either. In these endeavors have I spent above forty years. But here is the advice of a Chinese philosopher, whose writings are translated into Spanish, by the famous *Navarette*:

"'If you write a book, show it only to your friends. Dread the public and your brother authors. They will embitter your expressions, misrepresent your meaning, and impute to you, what you never thought of. Calumny, which has an hundred mouths, will open them against you; and truth, which is silent, will remain with you.'"

It has been said of Voltaire that he was "not only just, but generous in his dealings with others. With open purse and open heart, helpful to all who approached him. Collini, his secretary, said he was a miser *only of his time*, which was always usefully employed. But we are also told that there was one person to whom he could not even deny his time—it was Mademoiselle de Varicourt—*Belle-et-Bonne*—whom he had adopted, and who was afterward married to the Marquis de Villette. "She could never disturb him," says A.A. Knox, "not even when he was giving the last touches to *Irène*. If he were in a passion with anybody else, and she appeared in the room, he was at once gentle and calm. There is something very affecting in the old man's love and tenderness for this young girl."

After the success of the French Revolution, to which the writings of Voltaire had so greatly contributed, when the National Assembly ordered the removal of his remains to the Pantheon, to repose between the ashes of Descartes and Mirabeau—when France honored herself in honoring the great philosopher—it was *Belle-et-Bonne*—in the full splendor of her majestic beauty—her heart overflowing with tenderness and gratitude—her eyes dimmed with pathetic tears—who placed with loving hands on the bier of her noble benefactor the wreath of filial affection—the grandest tribute that humanity can bestow.

PETER ECKLER.

New York, Jan. 28, 1885.

---

[1] This work, says Prof. F.C. Schlosser in his *History of the Eighteenth Century*, (vol. ii, p. 122.) "was sent to the pope, and very favorably received by him; although it could not possibly escape the notice of the pope, that the piece was indebted for its chief effect upon the public, to the vehement expressions against religious fanaticism which it contained. The pope felt himself flattered by the transmission of the *Mahomet*, and notified his approbation, of which Voltaire cunningly enough availed himself, for the advantage of his new principles."

[2] *Critical and Historical Essays*, page 553.

[3] Vol. iv, No. 39.

[4] *Men of Letters of the time of George III.*

[5] *Critical & Historical Essays*, p. 553.

[6] *Lectures on the Romish Church.*

[7] *History of the Girondists*, vol. i, p. 152.

[8] *History of the Girondists*, vol. i, p. 152.

[9] *Critical and Historical Essays*, p. 553.

[10] *History of the Eighteenth Century*, vol. i, pp. 263-269.

[11] *History of the Girondists*, vol. i, pp. 15, 154, 155, 156.

[12] *History of European Morals*, vol. i, page iii.

The illustrations in this work and a few notes have been added by the publisher. The head of Voltaire in the frontispiece is from a bust by Houdon, and is copied from an engraving published by Messrs. J. & H.L. Hunt, London, 1824. It represents the gifted author as he appeared in his eighty-third year. The full-length portrait of Voltaire on page iii, shows him in his seventieth year, and the remaining portrait, on page xii, gives his likeness in early manhood; it is from a French edition of his works published in 1746.

Voltaire in early manhood.

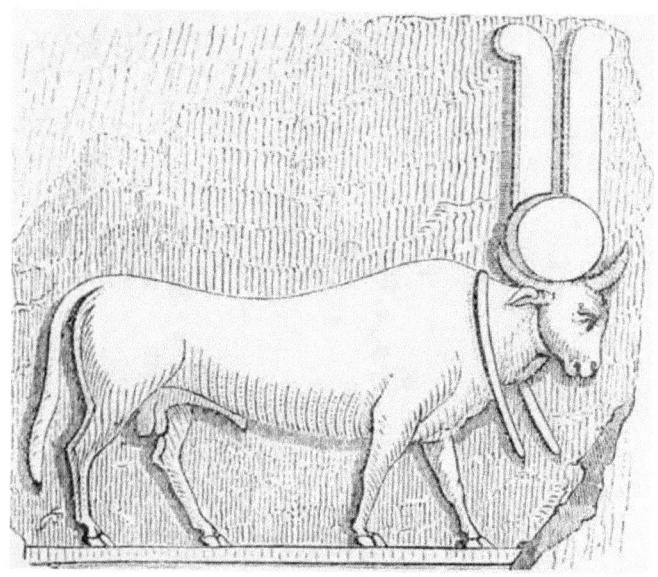

The white bull. A satyrical romance.—"*Daniel changed a monarch into this bull, and I have changed this bull into a god!*"

TAURUS.

The object and significance of ancient Tauric and Phallic worship have been clearly set forth by Dupuis, Payne Knight, and other learned authors, and we have, even at the present day, a survival of the ancient faith, in the Mayday festivals of India and Britain, which were originally instituted to celebrate the entrance of the sun into the zodiacal sign Taurus, at the vernal equinox, when the god Osiris was worshiped in Egypt under the form of a bull called Apis.

"The general devotion of the ancients to the worship of the BULL," says the Rev. Mr. Maurice in his learned work on the *Antiquities of India*, "I have had frequent occasion to remark, and more particularly in the Indian history, by their devotion to it at that period 'when the Bull with his horns opened the Vernal year.' I observed that all nations seem anciently to have vied with each other in celebrating that blissful epoch; and that the moment the sun entered the sign Taurus, were displayed the signals of triumph and the incentives to passion; that memorials of the universal festivity indulged at that season, are to be found in the records and customs of people otherwise the most opposite in manners and most remote in situation;... that the Apis, or Sacred Bull of Egypt, was only the symbol of the sun in the vigor of vernal youth; and that the Bull of Japan, breaking with his horn the mundane egg, was evidently connected with the same bovine species of superstition, founded on the mixture of astronomy and mythology."

"In many of the most ancient temples or India," says Godfrey Higgins in the *Anacalypsis*, "the Bull, as an object of adoration makes a most conspicuous figure. A gigantic image of one protrudes from the front of the temple of *the Great Creator*, called in the language of the country, Jaggernaut, in Orissa. This is the Bull of the Zodiac,—the emblem of the sun when the equinox took place in the first degree of the sign of the Zodiac, Taurus. In consequence of the precession of the equinoxes, the sun at the vernal equinox left Taurus, and took place in Aries, which it has left also for a great number of years, and it now takes place in Aquarius. Thus it keeps receding about one degree in seventy-two years, and about a whole *sign* in 2,160 years. M. Dupuis has demonstrated that the labors of Hercules are nothing but a history of the passage of the sun through the signs of the zodiac; and that Hercules is the sun in Aries or the Ram, Bacchus the sun in Taurus or the Bull. The adoration of the Bull of the zodiac is to be met with everywhere throughout the world, in the most opposite climes. The examples of it are innumerable and incontrovertable; they admit of no dispute.

"It appears from the book or history of the Exod, that it was on the leaving of Egypt that Moses changed the object of adoration from Taurus to Aries. It appears that the change took place on the mountain of *Sin*, or Nisi, or Bacchus, which was evidently its old name before Moses arrived there. The Israelites were punished for adhering to the old worship, that of the Calf, in opposition to the paschal Lamb, which Moses had substituted—'the Lamb which taketh away the sins of the world,'—in place of the Bull or Calf which took away the sins of the world.

"The planets were in later times all called by names appropriated to the days of the week, which were dedicated by astrologers to the gods who were typified by the Bull: Monday to the horned *Isis*; Tuesday to Mercury, the same as Hermes and Osiris; Wednesday to Woden, Fo, Buddha, and Surya; Thursday or Thor-day, or *Tur*, or Taurus, or Bull-day, to Jove or Jupiter, who, as a Bull, stole Europa; Friday was dedicated to Venus, Ashteroth or beeve-horned Astarte; Saturday to Saturn, identified by Mr. Faber with Moloch and the *Centaur Cronus* or Taschter; Sunday to the Sun, everywhere typified by Taurus. All these, I think, must have taken their names after the entrance of the Sun into Taurus; and before this date all history and even mythology fails us.

"In ancient collections we often meet with a person in the prime of life killing a young bull. He is generally accompanied with a number of astrological emblems. This Bull was the mediatorial Mithra, slain to make atonement for, and to take away the sins of the world. This was the God Bull, to whom the prayers were addressed which we find in Bryant and Faber, and in which he is expressly called the Mediator. This is the Bull of Persia, which Sir. William Jones and Mr. Faber identify with Buddha or Mahabad. The sacrifice of the Bull, which taketh away the sins of the world, was succeeded by the sacrifice of the Agni or of Fire, by our Indians in, comparatively speaking, modern times; it was closely connected with the two principles spoken of above. While the sun was in Taurus, the Bull was slain as the vicarious sacrifice; when it got into Aries, the Ram or Lamb was substituted.

"M. Dupuis observes, that the lamb was a symbol or mark of initiation into the Christian mysteries, a sort of proof of admission into the societies of the initiated of the lamb, like the private sign of the free-masons. It follows, then, that the mysteries of Christ are the mysteries of the Lamb, and that the mysteries of the Lamb are mysteries of the same nature as those of the Mithraitic Bull to which they succeeded by the effect of the precession of the equinoxes, which substituted the slain *lamb* for the slain *bull*."—E.

THE WHITE BULL.

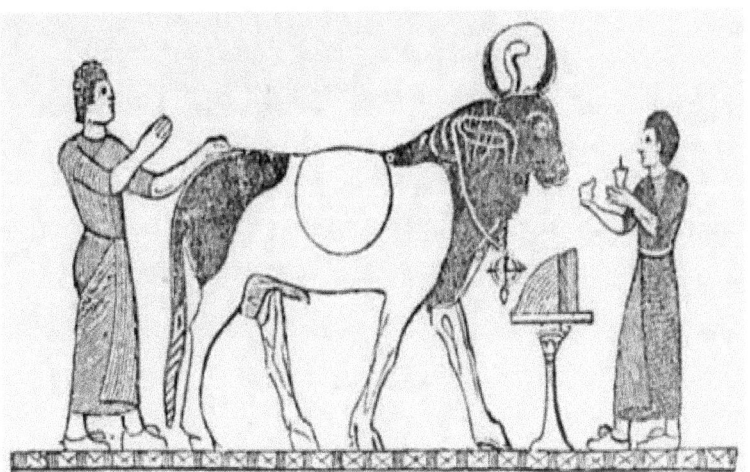

Apis. [1]

CHAPTER I.

HOW THE PRINCESS AMASIDIA MEETS A BULL.

The princess Amasidia, daughter of Amasis, King of Tanis in Egypt, took a walk upon the highway of Peluaium with the ladies of her train. She was sunk in deep melancholy. Tears gushed from her beautiful eyes. The cause of her grief was known, as well as the fears she entertained lest that grief should displease the king, her father. The old man, Mambres, ancient magician and eunuch of the Pharoahs, was beside her, and seldom left her. He was present at her birth. He had educated her, and taught her all that a fair princess was allowed to know of the sciences of Egypt. The mind of Amasidia equaled her beauty. Her sensibility and tenderness rivaled the charms of her person; and it was this sensibility which cost her so many tears.

The princess was twenty-four years old, the magician, Mambres, about thirteen hundred. It was he, as every one knows, who had that famous dispute with Moses, in which the victory was so long doubtful between these two profound philosophers. If Mambres yielded, it was owing to the visible protection of the celestial powers, who favored his rival. It required gods to overcome Mambres!

Amasis made him superintendent of his daughter's household, and he acquitted himself in this office with his usual prudence. His compassion was excited by the sighs of the beautiful Amasidia.

"O, my lover!" said she to herself, "my young, my dear lover! O, greatest of conquerors, most accomplished, most beautiful of men! Almost seven years hast thou disappeared from the world. What God hath snatched thee from thy tender Amasidia? Thou art not dead. The wise Egyptian prophets confess this. But thou art dead to me. I am alone in the world. To me it is a desert. By what extraordinary prodigy hast thou abandoned thy throne and thy mistress?—thy throne, which was the first in the world—however, that is a matter of small consequence; but to abandon me, who adores thee! O, my dear Ne—"

She was going on.

"Tremble to pronounce that fatal name," said Mambres, the ancient eunuch and magician of the Pharoahs. "You would perhaps be discovered by some of the ladies of your court. They are all very much devoted to you, and all fair ladies certainly make it a merit to serve the noble passions of fair princesses. But there may be one among them indiscreet, and even treacherous. You know that your father, although he loves you, has sworn to put you to death, should you pronounce the terrible name always ready to escape your lips. This law is severe; but you have not been educated in Egyptian wisdom to be ignorant of the government of the tongue. Remember that Hippocrates, one of our greatest gods, has always his finger upon his mouth."

The beautiful Amasidia wept, and was silent.

As she pensively advanced toward the banks of the Nile she perceived at a distance, under a thicket watered by the river, an old woman in a tattered gray garment, seated on a hillock. This old woman had beside her a she-ass, a dog, and a he-goat. Opposite to her was a serpent, which was not like the common serpents; for its eyes were mild, its physiognomy noble and engaging, while its skin shone with the liveliest and brightest colors. A huge fish, half immersed in the river, was not the least astonishing figure in the group; and on a neighboring tree were perched a raven and a pigeon. All these creatures seemed to carry on a very animated conversation.

Amasidia—"*O, my lover! my young, my dear lover! O, greatest of conquerors, most accomplished, most beautiful of men!*"

"Alas!" said the princess in a low tone, "these animals undoubtedly speak of their loves, and it is not so much as allowed me to mention the name of mine."

The old woman held in her hand a slender steel chain a hundred fathoms long, to which was fastened a bull who fed in the meadow. This bull was white, perfectly well-made, plump, and at the same time agile, which is a thing seldom to be found. He was indeed the most beautiful specimen that was ever seen of his kind. Neither the bull of Pasiphæ, nor that in whose shape Jupiter appeared when he carried off Europa, could be compared to this noble animal. The charming young heifer into which Isis was changed, would have scarce been worthy of his company.

As soon as the bull saw the princess he ran toward her with the swiftness of a young Arabian horse, who pricks up his ears and flies over the plains and rivers of the ancient Saana to approach the lovely consort whose image reigns in his heart. The old woman used her utmost efforts to restrain the bull. The serpent wanted to terrify him by its hissing. The dog followed him and bit his beautiful limbs. The she-ass crossed his way and kicked him to make him return. The great fish remounted the Nile and, darting himself out of the water, threatened to devour him. The he-goat remained immovable, apparently struck with fear. The raven fluttered round his head as if it wanted to tear out his eyes. The pigeon alone accompanied him from curiosity, and applauded him by a sweet murmur.

So extraordinary a sight threw Mambres into serious reflections. In the meanwhile, the white bull, dragging after him his chain and the old woman, had already reached the princess, who was struck with astonishment and fear. He threw himself at her feet. He kissed them. He shed tears. He looked upon her with eyes in which there was a strange mixture of grief and joy. He dared not to low, lest he should terrify the beautiful Amasidia. He could not speak. A weak use of the voice, granted by Heaven to certain animals, was denied him; but all his actions were eloquent. The princess was delighted by him. She perceived that a trifling amusement could suspend for some moments even the most poignant grief.

"Here," said she, "is a most amiable animal. I could wish much to have him in my stable."

At these words he bull bent himself on his knees and kissed the ground.

"He understands me," cried the princess. "He shows me that he wants to be mine. Ah, heavenly magician! ah, divine eunuch! Give me this consolation. Purchase this beautiful bovine. Settle the price with the old woman, to whom he no doubt belongs. This animal must be mine. Do not refuse me this innocent comfort."

All the ladies joined their requests to the entreaties of the princess. Mambres yielded to them, and immediately went to speak to the old woman.

[1] According to Eschenburg, Apis is the name of the ox in which Osiris was supposed to reside, rather than a distinct deity. The ox thus honored was known by certain marks; his body was all black, excepting a square spot of white on his forehead, and a white crescent or sort of half-moon on his right side; on his back was the figure of an eagle; under his tongue a sort of knot resembling a beetle (*cantharus*), and two sorts of hair upon his tail. This ox was permitted to live twenty-five years. His body was then embalmed, placed

in a chest, and buried with many solemnities. A season of mourning then followed, until a new Apis, or ox properly marked, was discovered.—E.

CHAPTER II.

HOW THE WISE MAMBRES, FORMERLY MAGICIAN OF PHAROAH, KNEW AGAIN THE OLD WOMAN, AND WAS KNOWN BY HER.

"Madam," said Mambres to her, "you know that ladies, and particularly princesses, have need of amusement. The daughter of the king is distractedly fond of your bull. I beg that you will sell him to us. You shall be paid in ready money."

"Sir," answered the old woman, "this precious animal does not belong to me. I am charged, together with all the beasts which you see, to keep him with care, to watch all his motions, and to give an exact account of them. God forbid that I should ever have any inclination to sell this invaluable animal."

The remarkable witch of Endor.—"*What, is it indeed you,*" cried Mambres, "*who are so famous upon the banks of your little Jordan, and the first person in the world for raising apparitions?*"

Mambres, upon this discourse, began to have a confused remembrance of something which he could not yet properly distinguish. He eyed the old woman in the gray cloak with greater attention.

"Respectable lady," said he to her, "I either mistake, or I have seen you formerly."

"I make no mistake, sir," replied the old woman. "I have seen you seven hundred years ago, in a journey which I made from Syria into Egypt some months after the destruction of Troy, when Hiram the second reigned at Tyre, and Nephel Keres in ancient Egypt."

"Ah! madam," cried the old man, "you are the remarkable witch of Endor."

"And you, sir," said the sorceress, embracing him, "are the great Mambres of Egypt."

"O, unforeseen meeting! memorable day! eternal decrees!" said Mambres. "It certainly is not without permission of the universal providence that we meet again in this meadow upon the banks of the Nile near the noble city of Tanis. What, is it indeed you," continued Mambres, "who are so famous upon the banks of your little Jordan, and the first person in the world for raising apparitions?"

"What, is it you, sir," replied Miss Endor, "who are so famous for changing rods into serpents, the day into darkness, and rivers into blood?"

"Yes, madam, but my great age has in part deprived me of my knowledge and power. I am ignorant from whence you have this beautiful bull, and who these animals are that, together with you, watch round him."

The old woman, recollecting herself, raised her eyes to heaven, and then replied.

"My dear Mambres. We are of the same profession, but it is expressly forbidden me to tell you who this bull is. I can satisfy you with regard to the other animals. You will easily know them by the marks which characterize them. The serpent is that which persuaded Eve to eat an apple, and to make her husband partake of it. The ass, that which spoke to your contemporary, Balaam, in a remarkable discourse. The fish, which always carries its head above water, is that which swallowed Jonah a few years ago. The dog is he who followed Raphael and the young Tobit in their journey to Ragusa in Media, in the time of the great Salamanzar. This goat is he who expiates all the sins of your nation. The raven and the pigeon, those which were in the ark of Noah. Great event! universal catastrophe! of which almost all the world is still ignorant. You are now informed. But of the bull you can know nothing."

Mambres, having listened with respect, said:

"The Eternal, O illustrious witch! reveals and conceals what he thinks proper. All these animals who, together with you, are entrusted with the custody of the white bull, are only known to your generous and agreeable nation, which is itself unknown to almost all the world. The miracles which you and yours, I and mine, have performed, shall one day be a great subject of doubt and scandal to inquisitive philosophers. But happily these miracles shall find belief with the devout sages, who shall prove submissive to the enlightened in one corner of the world; and this is all that is necessary."

As he spoke these words, the princess pulled him by the sleeve, and said to him,—

"Mambres, will you not buy my bull?"

The magician, plunged into a deep reverie, made no reply, and Amasidia poured forth her tears.

She then addressed herself to the old woman.

"My good woman," said she, "I conjure you, by all you hold most dear in the world, by your father, by your mother, by your nurse, who are certainly still alive, to sell me not only your bull, but likewise your pigeon, which seems very much attached to him.

"As for the other animals, I do not want them; but I shall catch the vapors if you do not sell me this charming bull, who will be all the happiness of my life."

The old woman respectfully kissed the fringe of her gauze robe, and replied,—

"Princess, my bull is not to be sold. Your illustrious magician is acquainted with this. All that I can do for your service is, to permit him to feed every day near your palace. You may caress him, give him biscuits, and make him dance about at your pleasure; but he must always be under the eyes of all these animals who accompany me, and who are charged with the keeping of him. If he does not endeavor to escape from them, they will prove peaceable; but if he attempt once more to break his chain, as he did upon seeing you, woe be unto him. I would not then answer for his life. This large fish, which you see, will certainly swallow him, and keep him longer than *three* days in his belly; or this serpent, who appears to you so mild, will give him a mortal sting."

The white bull, who understood perfectly the old woman's conversation, but was unable to speak, humbly accepted all the proposals. He laid himself down at her feet; he lowed softly, and, looking tenderly at Amasidia, seemed to say to her,

"Come and see me sometimes upon the lawn."

The serpent now took up the conversation:

"Princess," said he, "I advise you to act implicitly, as mademoiselle of Endor has told you."

The she-ass likewise put in her word, and was of the opinion of the serpent.

Amasidia was afflicted that this serpent and this ass should speak so well; while a beautiful bull, who had such noble and tender sentiments, was unable to express them.

"Alas," said she, in a low voice, "nothing is more common at court. One sees there every day fine lords who cannot converse, and contemptible wretches who speak with assurance."

"This serpent," said Mambres, "is not a contemptible wretch. He is perhaps the personage of the greatest importance."

The day now declined, and the princess was obliged to return home, after having promised to come back next day at the same hour. Her ladies of the palace were astonished, and understood nothing of what they had seen or heard. Mambres made reflections. The princess recollecting that the serpent called the old woman Miss, concluded at random that she was still unmarried, and felt some affliction that such was also her own condition. Respectable affliction! which she concealed, however, with as much care as the name of her lover.

CHAPTER III.

HOW THE BEAUTIFUL AMASIDIA HAD A SECRET CONVERSATION WITH A BEAUTIFUL SERPENT.

The beautiful princess recommended secrecy to her ladies with regard to what they had seen. They all promised it, and kept their promise for a whole day.

We may believe that Amasidia slept little that night. An inexplicable charm continually recalled the idea of her beautiful bull. As soon, therefore, as she was at freedom with her wise Mambres, she said to him:

"O, sage! this animal turns my head."

"He employs mine very much," said Mambres. "I see plainly that this bovine is very much superior to those of his species. I see that there is a great mystery, and I suspect a fatal event. Your father Amasis is suspicious and violent; and this affair requires that you conduct yourself with the greatest precaution."

"Ah!" said the princess, "I have too much curiosity to be prudent. It is the only sentiment which can unite in my heart with that which preys upon me on account of the lover I have lost. Can I not know who this white bull is that gives me such strange disquiet?"

Mambres replied,—

"I have already confessed to you, frankly, that my knowledge declines in proportion as my age advances; but I mistake much if the serpent is not informed of what you are so very desirous of knowing. He does not want sense. He expresses himself with propriety. He has been long accustomed to interfere in the affairs of the ladies."

"Ah! undoubtedly," said Amasidia, "this is the beautiful serpent of Egypt, who, by fixing his tail into his mouth, becomes the emblem of eternity; who enlightens the world when he opens his eyes, and darkens it when he shuts them?"

"No, Miss."

"It is then the serpent of Æsculapius?"

"Still less."

"It is perhaps Jupiter under the figure of a serpent?"

"Not at all."

"Ah, now I see, I see. It is the rod which you formerly changed into a serpent?"

"No, indeed, it is not; but all these serpents are of the same family. This one has a very high character in his own country. He passes there for the most extraordinary serpent that was ever seen. Address yourself to him. However, I warn you it is a dangerous undertaking. Were I in your place, I would hardly trouble myself either with the bull, the she-ass, the he-goat, the serpent, the fish, the raven, or the pigeon. But passion hurries you on; and all I can do is to pity you, and tremble."

The princess conjured him to procure her a tête-à-tête with the serpent. Mambres, who was obliging, consented, and making profound reflections, he went and communicated to the witch in so insinuating a manner the whim of the princess, that the old woman told him Amasidia might lay her commands upon her; that the serpent was perfectly well bred, and so polite to the ladies, that he wished for nothing more than to oblige them, and would not fail to keep the princess's appointment.

The ancient magician returned to inform the princess of this good news; but he still dreaded some misfortune, and made reflections.

"You desire to speak with the serpent, mademoiselle. This you may accomplish whenever your highness thinks proper. But remember you must flatter him; for every animal has a great deal of self-love, and the serpent in particular. It is said he was formerly driven out of heaven for excessive pride."

"I have never heard of it," replied the princess.

"I believe it," said the old man.

He then informed her of all the reports which had been spread about this famous serpent.

"But, my dear princess, whatever singular adventures may have happened to him, you never can extort these secrets from him but by flattery. Having formerly deceived women, it is equitable that a woman in her turn should deceive him."

"I will do my utmost," said the princess; and departed with her maids of honor. The old woman was feeding the bull at a considerable distance.

Mambres left Amasidia to herself, and went and discoursed with the witch. One lady of honor chatted with the she-ass, the others amused themselves with the goat, the dog, the raven, and the pigeon. As for the large fish that frightened every body, he plunged himself into the Nile by order of the old woman.

The serpent then attended the beautiful Amasidia into the grove, where they had the following conversation.

SERPENT.—You cannot imagine, mademoiselle, how much I am flattered with the honor which your highness deigns to confer upon me.

PRINCESS.—Your great reputation, sir, the beauty of your countenance, and the brilliancy of your eyes, have emboldened me to seek for this conversation. I know by public report (if it be not false) that you were formerly a very great lord in the empyrean heaven.

SERPENT.—It is true, miss, I had there a very distinguished place. It is pretended I am a disgraced favorite. This is a report which once went abroad in India. The Brahmins were the first who gave a history of my adventures. And I doubt not but one day or other the poets of the north will make them the subject of an extravagant epic poem;[1] for in truth it is all that can be made of them. Yet I am not so much fallen, but that I have left in this globe a very extensive dominion. I might venture to assert that the whole earth belongs to me.

PRINCESS.—I believe it; for they tell me that your powers of persuasion are irresistible, and to please is to reign.

SERPENT.—I feel, mademoiselle, while I behold and listen to you, that you have over me the same power which you ascribe to me over so many others.

PRINCESS.—You are, I believe, an amiable conqueror. It is said that your conquests among the fair sex have been numerous, and that you began with our common mother, whose name I have unfortunately forgotten.

SERPENT.—They do me injustice. She honored me with her confidence, and I gave her the best advice. I desired that she and her husband should eat heartily of the fruit of the tree of knowledge. I imagined in doing this that I should please the ruler of all things. It seemed to me that a tree so necessary to the human race was not planted to be entirely useless. Would the supreme being have wished to have been served by fools and idiots? Is not the mind formed for the acquisition of knowledge and for improvement? Is not the knowledge of good and evil necessary for doing the one and avoiding the other? I certainly merited their thanks.

PRINCESS.—Yet, they tell me that you have suffered for it. Probably it is since this period that so many ministers have been punished for giving good advice, and so many real philosophers and men of genius persecuted for their writings that were useful to mankind.

SERPENT.—It is my enemies who have told you these stories. They say that I am out of favor at court. But a proof that my influence there has not declined, is their own confession that I entered into the council when it was in agitation to try the good man Job; and I was again called upon when the resolution was taken to deceive a certain petty king called Ahab. I alone was charged with this honorable commission.

PRINCESS.—Ah, sir! I do not believe that you are formed to deceive. But since you are always in the ministry, may I beg a favor of you? I hope so amiable a lord will not deny me.

SERPENT.—Mademoiselle, your requests are laws; name your commands.

PRINCESS.—I intreat that you will tell me who this white bull is, for whom I feel such extraordinary sentiments, which both affect and alarm me. I am told that you would deign to inform me.

SERPENT.—Curiosity is necessary to human nature, and especially to your amiable sex. Without it they would live in the most shameful ignorance. I have always satisfied, as far as lay in my power, the curiosity of the ladies. I am accused indeed of using this complaisance only to vex the ruler of the world. I swear to you, that I could propose nothing more agreeable to myself than to obey you; but the old woman must have informed you that the revealing of this secret will be attended with some danger to you.

PRINCESS.—Ah! it is that which makes me still more curious.

SERPENT.—In this I discover the sex to whom I have formerly done service.

PRINCESS.—If you possess any feeling; if rational beings should mutually assist each other; if you have compassion for an unfortunate creature, do not refuse my request.

SERPENT.—You affect me. I must satisfy you; but do not interrupt me.

PRINCESS.—I promise you I will not.

SERPENT.—There was a young king, beautiful, charming, in love, beloved—

PRINCESS.—A young king! beautiful, charming, in love, beloved! And by whom? And who was this king? How old was he? What has become of him? Where is his kingdom? What is his name?

SERPENT.—See, I have scarce begun, and you have already interrupted me. Take care. If you have not more command over yourself, you are undone.

PRINCESS.—Ah, pardon me, sir. I will not repeat my indiscretion. Go on, I beseech you.

SERPENT.—This great king, the most valiant of men, victorious wherever he carried his arms, often dreamed when asleep, and forgot his dreams when awake. He wanted his magicians to remember and inform him what he had dreamed, otherwise he declared he would hang them; for that nothing was more equitable. It is now near seven years since he dreamed a fine dream, which he entirely forgot when he awoke; and a young Jew, full of experience, having revealed it to him, this amiable king was immediately changed into an ox for—

PRINCESS.—Ah! it is my dear Neb——

She could not finish, she fainted away. Mambres, who listened at a distance, saw her fall, and believed her dead.

[1] A prophetic reference by the serpent to Milton's *Paradise Lost*.—E.

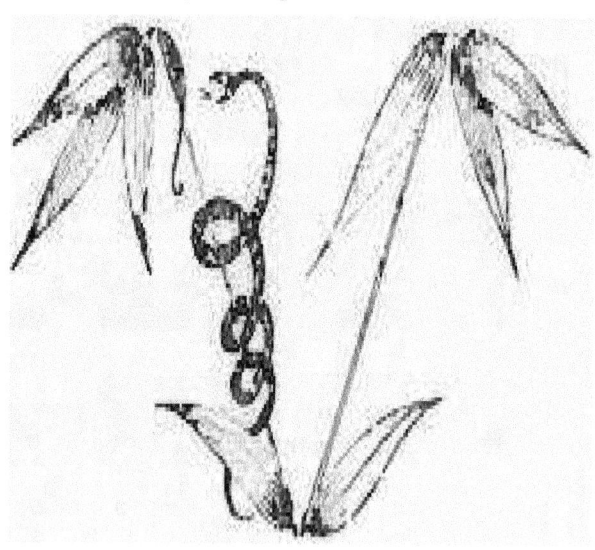

Nebuchadnezzar.—Nebuchadnezzar, transformed into a white bull, is recognized by Amasidia.

CHAPTER IV.

HOW THEY WANTED TO SACRIFICE THE BULL, AND EXORCISE THE PRINCESS.

Mambres runs to her weeping. The serpent is affected. He, alas, cannot weep; but he hisses in a mournful tone. He cries out, "She is dead." The ass repeats, "She is dead." The raven tells it over again. All the other animals appeared afflicted, except the fish of Jonah, which has always been merciless. The lady of honor, the ladies of the court, arrive and tear their hair. The white bull, who fed at a distance and heard their cries, ran to the grove dragging the old woman after him, while his loud bellowings made the neighboring echoes resound. To no purpose did the ladies pour upon the expiring Amasidia their bottles of rose-water, of pink, of myrtle, of benzoin, of balm of Gilead, of amomum, of gilly-flower, of nutmeg, of ambergris. She had not as yet given the smallest signs of life. But as soon as she perceived that the beautiful white bull was beside her, she came to herself, more blooming, more beautiful and lively than ever. A thousand times did she kiss this charming animal, who languishingly leaned his head on her snowy bosom. She called him, "My master, my king, my dear, my life!" She throws her fair arms around his neck, which was whiter than the snow. The light straw does not adhere more closely to the amber, the vine to the elm, nor the ivy to the oak. The sweet murmur of her sighs was heard. Her eyes were seen, now sparkling with a tender flame, and now obscured by those precious tears which love makes us shed.

We may easily judge into what astonishment the lady of honor and ladies of her train were thrown. As soon as they entered the palace, they related to their lovers this extraordinary adventure, and every one with different circumstances, which increased its singularity, and which always contributes to the variety of all histories.

No sooner was Amasis, king of Tanis, informed of these events, than his royal breast was inflamed with just indignation. Such was the wrath of Minos, when he understood that his daughter Pasiphæ lavished her tender favors upon the father of the Minotaur. Thus raged Juno, when she beheld Jupiter caressing the beautiful cow Io, daughter of the river Inachus. Following the dictates of passion, the stern Amasis imprisoned his unhappy daughter, the beautiful Amasidia, in her chamber and placed over her a guard of black eunuchs. He then assembled his privy council.

The grand magician presided there, but had no longer the same influence as formerly. All the ministers of state concluded that this white bull was a sorcerer. It was quite the contrary. He was bewitched. But in delicate affairs they are always mistaken at court.

It was carried by a great majority that the princess should be exorcised, and the old woman and the bull sacrificed.

The wise Mambres contradicted not the opinion of the king and council. The right of exorcising belonged to him. He could delay it under some plausible pretence. The god Apis had lately died at Memphis. A god ox dies just like another ox. And it was not allowed to exorcise any person in Egypt until a new ox was found to replace the deceased.

It was decreed in the council to wait until the nomination should be made of a new god at Memphis.

The good old man, Mambres, perceived to what danger his dear princess was exposed. He knew who her lover was. The syllables NEBU———, which had escaped her, laid open the whole mystery to the eyes of this sage.

The dynasty of Memphis belonged at that time to the Babylonians. They preserved this remainder of the conquests they had gained under the greatest king of the world, to whom Amasis was a mortal enemy. Mambres had occasion for all his wisdom to conduct himself properly in the midst of so many difficulties. If the king Amasis should discover the lover of his daughter, her death would be inevitable. He had sworn it. The great, the young, the beautiful king of whom she was enamored, had dethroned the king her father, and Amasis had only recovered his kingdom about seven years. From that time it was not known what had become of the adorable monarch—the conqueror and idol of the nations—the tender and generous lover of the charming Amasidia. Sacrificing the white bull would eventually occasion the death of the beautiful princess.

Lot and his wayward daughters leaving Sodom.—From a celebrated picture in S. Marks, Florence, by Domenico Cresti, named il Passigiano.

DESTRUCTION OF SODOM AND GOMORRAH.
A STRANGE METAMORPHOSIS.

In the preceding engraving the artist has pictured the "Cities of the Plain" in flames, ignited by a shower of "fire and brimstone out of heaven." Warned by an angel, Lot and his family are fleeing from the conflagration. The madame has, however, unfortunately changed her mind, and is seen returning toward the doomed locality. She dearly loves her home, and braves danger—even death—in its protection. Her husband and her children heartlessly forsake her. Lot does not look like the coward he is represented to have been, who basely offered to surrender his daughters to the horrible abuse of a Sodomite mob; and the daughters—innocent and beautiful—seem incapable of the depravity with which they are charged in the nineteenth chapter of Genesis.

The comical statement that Madame Lot was transformed into "a pillar of salt" for merely *looking back* toward her old home in Sodom, rests on bible authority, and is believed by all the world excepting intelligent clergymen, scientists, philosophers and reasonable people.

The assertion of Mambres, (page 15), that this estimable "pillar" has become "very sharp tasted," rests on the authority of certain eastern travelers who claim to have examined and tasted the saline remains of this unfortunate female. But as this last claim is based on a French romance and not on Hebrew revelation, readers may be pardoned for receiving it with the greatest caution. Indeed, all that is absolutely necessary for even the orthodox to believe is that, "once upon a time," a Sodomite matron was chemically changed into pure chloride of sodium, and not that said sodium still retains its sharp and acrid flavor.—E.

What could Mambres do in such critical circumstances? He went, after the council had broken up, to find his dear foster daughter.

"My dear child," he says, "I will serve you; but I repeat it, they will behead you if ever you pronounce the name of your lover."

"Ah! what signifies my neck," replied the beautiful Amasidia, "if I cannot embrace that of Nebu—? My father is a cruel man. He not only refuses to give me a charming prince whom I adore, but he declares war against him; and after he was conquered by my lover, he has found the secret of changing him into an ox. Did one ever see more frightful malice? If my father were not my father, I do not know what I should do to him."

"It was not your father who played him this cruel trick," said the wise Mambres. "It was a native of Palestine, one of our ancient enemies, an inhabitant of a little country comprehended in that crowd of kingdoms which your lover subdued in order to polish and refine them.

"Such metamorphoses must not surprise you. You know that formerly I performed more extraordinary. Nothing was at that time more common than those changes which at present astonish philosophers. True history, which we have read together, informs us that Lycaon, king of Arcadia, was changed into a wolf; the beautiful Calista, his daughter, into a bear; Io, the daughter of Inachus, our venerable Isis, into a cow; Daphne into a laurel; Sirinx into a flute; the fair Edith, wife of Lot—the best and most affectionate husband and father ever known in the world—has she not become, in our neighborhood, a pillar of salt, very sharp tasted, which has preserved both her likeness and form, as the great men attest who have seen it? I was witness to this change in my youth. I saw seven powerful cities in the most dry and parched situation in the world, all at once transformed into a beautiful lake. In the early part of my life, the whole world was full of metamorphoses.

"In fine, madam, if examples can soothe your grief, remember that Venus changed Cerastes into an ox."

"I do not know," said the princess, "that examples comfort us. If my lover were dead, could I comfort myself by the idea that all men die?"

"Your pain may at least be alleviated," replied the sage; "and since your lover has become an ox, it is possible from an ox he may become a man. As for me, I should deserve to be changed into a tiger or a crocodile, if I did not employ the little power I have in the service of a princess worthy of the adoration of the world,—if I did not labor for the beautiful Amasidia, whom I have nursed upon my knees, and whom fatal destiny exposes to such rude trials."

CHAPTER V.

HOW THE WISE MAMBRES CONDUCTED HIMSELF WISELY.

The sage Mambres having said every thing he could to comfort the princess, but without succeeding in so doing, ran to the old woman.

"My companion," said he to her, "ours is a charming profession, but a very dangerous one. You run the risk of being hanged, and your ox of being burned, drowned or devoured, I don't know what they will do with your other animals; for, prophet as I am, I know very little; but do you carefully conceal the serpent, and the fish. Let not the one show his head above water, nor the other venture out of his hole. I will place the ox in one of my stables in the country. You shall be there with him, since you say that you are not allowed to abandon him. The good scape-goat may upon this occasion serve as an expiation. We will send him into the desert loaded with the sins of all the rest. He is accustomed to this ceremony, which does him no harm; and every one knows that sin is expiated by means of a he-goat, who walks about for his own amusement. I only beg of you to lend me immediately Tobit's dog, who is a very swift greyhound; Balaam's ass, who runs better than a dromedary; the raven and the pigeon of the ark, who fly with amazing swiftness. I want to send them on an embassy to Memphis. It is an affair of great consequence."

The old woman replied to the magician:

"You may dispose as you please of Tobit's dog,[1] of Balaam's ass, of the raven and the pigeon of the ark, and of the scape-goat; but my ox cannot enter into a stable. It is said, Daniel, v:21,—That he must be always made fast to an iron chain, be always wet with the dew of heaven, and eat the grass of the field, and his portion be with the wild beasts.

"He is entrusted to me, and I must obey. What would Daniel, Ezekiel, and Jeremiah, think of me, if I trusted my ox to any other than to myself? I see you know the secret of this extraordinary animal, but I have not to reproach myself with having revealed it to you. I am going to conduct him far from this polluted land, toward the lake Sirbon, where he will be sheltered from the cruelties of the king of Tanis. My fish and my serpent will defend me. I fear nobody when I serve my master."

"My good woman," answered the wise Mambres, "let the will of God be done! Provided I can find your white bull again, the lake Sirbon, the lake Maris, or the lake of Sodom, are to me perfectly indifferent. I want to do nothing but good to him and to you. But why have you spoken to me of Daniel, Ezekiel, and Jeremiah?"

"Ah! sir," answered the old woman, "you know as well as I what concern they have in this important affair. But I have no time to lose. I don't desire to be hanged. I want not that my bull should be burned, drowned, or devoured. I go to the lake Sirbon by Canopus, with my serpent and my fish. Adieu."

The bull followed her pensively, after having testified his gratitude to the beneficent Mambres.

The wise Mambres was greatly troubled. He saw that Amasis, king of Tanis, distracted by the strange passion of his daughter for this animal, and believing her bewitched, would pursue everywhere the unfortunate bull, who would infallibly be burned as a sorcerer in the public place of Tanis, or given to the fish of Jonah, or be roasted and served up for food. Mambres wanted at all events to save the princess from this cruel disaster.

He wrote a letter in sacred characters, to his friend, the high priest of Memphis, upon the paper of Egypt, which was not yet in use. Here are the identical words of this letter:

> "Light of the world, lieutenant of Isis, Osiris, and Horus, chief of the circumcised, you whose altar is justly raised above all thrones! I am informed that your god, the ox Apis, is dead. I have one at your service. Come quickly with your priests to acknowledge, to worship him, and to conduct him into the stable of your temple. May Isis, Osiris, and Horus, keep you in their holy and worthy protection, and likewise the priests of Memphis in their holy care.
>
> Your affectionate friend,
> Mambres."

He made four copies of this letter for fear of accidents, and enclosed them in cases of the hardest ebony. Then calling to him his four couriers, whom he had destined for this employment, (these were the ass, the dog, the raven, and the pigeon,) he said to the ass:

"I know with what fidelity you served Balaam my brother. Serve me as faithfully. There is not an unicorn who equals you in swiftness. Go, my dear friend, and deliver this letter to the person himself to whom it is directed, and return."

The ass answered:

"Sir, as I served Balaam, I will serve you. I will go, and I will return."

The sage put the box of ebony into her mouth, and she swiftly departed. He then called Tobit's dog.

"Faithful dog," said Mambres, "more speedy in thy course than the nimble-footed Achilles, I know what you performed for Tobit, son of Tobit, when you and the angel Raphael accompanied him from Nineveh to Ragusa in Medea, and from Ragusa to Nineveh, and that he brought back to his father ten talents, which the slave Tobit, the father, had lent to the slave Gabellus; for the slaves at that time were very rich. Carry this letter as it is directed. It is much more valuable than ten talents of silver."

The dog then replied:

"Sir, if I formerly followed the messenger Raphael, I can with equal ease execute your commission."

Mambres put the letter into his mouth.

He next spoke in the same manner to the pigeon, who replied.

"Sir, if I brought back a bough into the ark, I will likewise bring you back an answer."

She took the letter in her bill, and the three messengers were out of sight in a moment. Then Mambres addressed the raven,

"I know that you fed the great prophet Elijah, when he was concealed near the torrent of Cherith, so much celebrated in the world. You brought him every day good bread and fat pullets. I only ask of you to carry this letter to Memphis."

The raven answered in these words:

"It is true, sir, that I carried every day a dinner to the great prophet Elijah the Tishbite. I saw him mount in a chariot of fire drawn by fiery horses, although this is not the usual method of traveling. But I always took care to eat half the dinner myself. I am very well pleased to carry your letter, provided you make me certain of two good meals every day, and that I am paid money in advance for my commission."

Mambres, angry, replied:

"Gluttonous and malicious creature, I am not astonished that Apollo has made you black as a mole, after being white as a swan, as you was formerly before you betrayed in the plains of Thessaly the beautiful Coronis, the unfortunate mother of Æsculapius. Tell me, did you eat ribs of beef and pullets every day when you was ten whole months in the ark?"

"Sir," said the raven, "we had there very good cheer. They served up roast meat twice a day to all the fowls of my species who live upon nothing but flesh, such as the vultures, kites, eagles, buzzards, sparrow-hawks, owls, tarsels, falcons, great owls, and an innumerable crowd of birds of prey. They furnished, with the most plentiful profusion, the tables of the lions, leopards, tigers, panthers, hyænas, wolves, bears, foxes, polecats, and all sorts of carnivorous quadrupeds. There were in the ark eight persons of distinction, (and the only ones who were then in the world,) continually employed in the care of our table and our wardrobe; Noah and his wife, who were about six hundred years old, their three sons and their three wives. It was charming to see with what care, what dexterity, what cleanliness, our eight domestics served four thousand of the most ravenous guests, without reckoning the amazing trouble which about ten or twelve thousand other animals required, from the elephant and the giraffe, to the silk-worm and fly. What astonishes me is, that our purveyor Noah is unknown to all the nations of whom he is the stem, but I don't much mind it. I had already been present at a similar entertainment with Xesustres king of Thrace. Such things as these happen from time to time for the instruction of ravens. In a word, I want to have good cheer, and to be paid in ready money."

The wise Mambres took care not to give his letter to such a discontented and babbling animal; and they separated very much dissatisfied with each other.

But it is necessary to know what became of the white bull, and not to lose sight of the old woman and the serpent. Mambres ordered his intelligent and faithful domestics to follow them; and as for himself, he advanced in a litter by the side of the Nile, always making reflections.

Daniel, Ezekiel, and Jeremiah.—"A boatman singing a jovial song, made fast a small boat by the side of the river, and three grave personages, half clothed in dirty, tattered garments, landed from it; but preserved, under the garb of poverty the most majestic and august air. These strangers were Daniel, Ezekiel, and Jeremiah."

"How is it possible," said he to himself, "that a serpent should be master of almost all the world, as he boasts, and as so many learned men acknowledge, and that he nevertheless obeys an old woman? How is it, that he is sometimes called to the council of the Most High, while he creeps upon earth? In what manner can he enter by his power alone into the bodies of men, and that so many men pretend to dislodge him by means of words? In short, why does he pass with a small neighboring people, for having ruined the human race? And how is it that the human race are entirely ignorant of this? I am old, I have studied all my life, but I see a crowd of inconsistencies which I cannot reconcile. I cannot account for what has happened to myself, neither for the great things which I long ago performed, nor those of which I have been witness. Every thing well considered, I begin to think that this world subsists by contradictions, *rerum concordia discors*, as my master Zoroaster formerly said."

While he was plunged in this obscure metaphysical reasoning,—obscure like all metaphysics,—a boatman singing a jovial song, made fast a small boat by the side of the river, and three grave personages, half clothed in dirty tattered garments, landed from it; but preserved, under the garb of poverty, the most majestic and august air. These strangers were Daniel, Ezekiel, and Jeremiah.

[1] "Histories," says Pope, in his *Poetical Works*, vol. 4, p. 245, "are more full of examples of the fidelity of dogs than of friends, but: I will only say for the honor of dogs, that the two most ancient and estimable books, sacred and profane, extant, viz. the Scripture and Homer, have shown a particular regard to these animals. That of Tobit is the most remarkable, because there seemed no manner of reason to take notice of the dog, besides the great humanity of the author. ['And the dog went after them,' *Tobit*, xi: 4.] Homer's account of Ulysses's dog, Argus, is the most pathetic imaginable, all the circumstances considered, and an excellent proof of the old bard's good nature.... Plutarch, relating how the Athenians were obliged to abandon Athens in the time of Themistocles, steps back again out of the way of his history, purely to describe the lamentable cries and howlings of the poor dogs they left behind. He makes mention of one that followed his master across the sea to Salamis, where he died, and was honored with a tomb by the Athenians, who gave the name of the Dog's Grave to that part of the island where he was buried. This respect to a dog, in the most polite people of the world, is very observable. A modern instance of gratitude to a dog is, that the chief order of Denmark, (now injuriously called the order of the elephant), was instituted in memory of the fidelity of a dog, named Wildbrat, to one of their kings who had been deserted by his subjects. He gave his order this motto, or to this effect, (which still remains), 'Wildbrat was faithful.' Sir William Trumbull has told me a story, which he heard from one that was present. King Charles I. being with some of his Court, during his troubles, a discourse arose what sort of dogs deserved pre-eminence, and it being on all hands agreed to belong either to the spaniel or greyhound, the King gave his opinion on the part of the greyhound, because (said he) it has all the good-nature of the other without the fawning."

This satire upon fawning would no doubt have been as applicable to the court of king Amasis as to that of Charles I., for fawning has ever been the besetting sin of dogs and courtiers.

It is indeed a grand testimonial to the value of the greyhound, that his fleetness and fidelity were appreciated by Mambres, the great Egyptian magician, five thousand years before they were endorsed by the unfortunate English king. Miss Endor, Homer, Ulysses, Mambres, Tobit, Plutarch, the polite Athenians, Charles I., and Alexander Pope are certainly as respectable a list of references as the most aristocratic greyhound could desire.—E.

CHAPTER VI.

HOW MAMBRES MET THREE PROPHETS, AND GAVE THEM A GOOD DINNER.

These three great men who had the prophetic light in their countenance, knew the wise Mambres to be one of their brethren, by some marks of the same light which he had still remaining, and prostrated themselves before his litter. Mambres likewise knew them to be prophets, more by their uncouth dress, than by those gleams of fire which proceeded from their august heads. He conjectured that they came to learn news of the white bull; and conducting himself with his usual propriety, he alighted from his carriage and advanced a few steps toward them, with dignified politeness. He raised them up, caused tents to be erected, and prepared a dinner, of which he rightly judged that the prophets had very great need.

He invited the old woman to it, who was only about five hundred paces from them. She accepted the invitation, and arrived leading her white bull.

Two soups were served up, one *de Bisque*, and the other *a la Reine*. The first course consisted of a carp's tongue pie, livers of eel-pouts, and pikes; fowls dressed with pistachios, pigeons with truffles and olives; two young turkeys with gravy of cray fish, mushrooms, and morels; and a chipotata. The second course was composed of pheasants, partridges, quails, and ortalons, with four salads; the epergne was in the highest taste; nothing could be more delicious than the side dishes, nothing more brilliant and more ingenious than the dessert. But the wise Mambres took great care to have no boiled beef, nor short ribs, nor tongue, nor palate of an ox, nor cows' udder, lest the unfortunate monarch near at hand should think that they insulted him.

This great and unfortunate prince was feeding near the tent; and never did he feel in a more cruel manner the fatal revolution which had deprived him of his throne for seven long years.

"Alas!" said he, to himself, "this Daniel who has changed me into a bull, and this sorceress my keeper, make the best cheer in the world; while I, the sovereign of Asia, am reduced to the necessity of eating grass, and drinking water."

When they had drank heartily of the wine of Engaddi, of Tadmor, and of Sebiras, the prophets and the witch conversed with more frankness than at the first course.

"I must acknowledge," said Daniel, "that I did not live so well in the lion's den."

"What, sir," said Mambres, "did they put you into a den of lions? How came you not to be devoured?"

"Sir," said Daniel, "you know very well that lions never eat prophets."

"As for me," said Jeremiah, "I have passed my whole life starving of hunger. This is the only day I ever ate a good meal; and were I to spend my life over again, and had it in my power to choose my condition, I must own I would much rather be comptroller-general or bishop of Babylon, than prophet at Jerusalem."

Ezekiel cried, "I was once ordered to sleep three hundred and ninety days upon my left side, and to eat all that time bread of wheat, and barley, and beans, and lentiles, cooked in the strangest manner. Still I must own that the cookery of Seigneur Mambres is much more delicate. However, the prophetic trade has its advantages, and the proof is, that there are many who follow it."

After they had spoken thus freely, Mambres entered upon business. He asked the three pilgrims the reason of their journey into the dominions of the king of Tanis. Daniel replied, "That the kingdom of Babylon had been all in a flame since Nebuchadnezzar had disappeared: that according to the custom of the court, they had persecuted all the prophets, who passed their lives in sometimes seeing kings humbled at their feet, and sometimes receiving a hundred lashes from them; that at length they had been obliged to take refuge in Egypt for fear of being starved."

Ezekiel and Jeremiah likewise spoke a long time in such fine terms, that it was almost impossible to understand them. As for the witch, she had always a strict eye over her charge. The fish of Jonah continued in the Nile, opposite to the tent, and the serpent sported upon the grass. After drinking coffee, they took a walk by the side of the Nile; and the white bull, perceiving the three prophets, his enemies, bellowed most dreadfully, ran furiously at them, and gored them with his horns. As prophets never have anything but skin upon their bones, he would certainly have run them through; but the ruler of the world, who sees all and remedies all, changed them immediately into magpies; and they continued to chatter as before. The same thing happened since to the Pierides;[11] so much has fable always imitated sacred history.

This incident caused new reflections in the mind of Mambres.

"Here," said he, "are three great prophets changed into magpies. This ought to teach us never to speak too much, and always to observe a suitable discretion."

He concluded that wisdom was better than eloquence, and thought profoundly as usual; when a great and terrible spectacle presented itself to his eyes.

[1] The nine daughters of Pierus, king of Emathia, were called Pierides. They entered into a contest with the Muses, and being conquered were metamorphosed into birds.—E.

CHAPTER VII.

HOW KING AMASIS WANTED TO GIVE THE WHITE BULL TO BE DEVOURED BY THE FISH OF JONAH, AND DID NOT DO IT.

Clouds of dust floated from south to north. The noise of drums, fifes, psalteries, harps, and sackbuts was heard. Several squadrons and battalions advanced, and Amasis, king of Tanis, was at their head upon an Arabian horse caparisoned with scarlet trappings embroidered with gold. The heralds proclaimed that they should seize the white bull, bind him, and throw him into the Nile, to be devoured by the fish of Jonah; "for the king our lord, who is just, wants to revenge himself upon the white bull, who has bewitched his daughter."

The good old man Mambres made more reflections than ever. He saw very plainly that the malicious raven had told all to the king, and that the princess ran a great risk of being beheaded.

"My dear friend," said he to the serpent, "go quickly and comfort the fair Amasidia, my foster daughter. Bid her fear nothing whatever may happen, and tell her stories to alleviate her inquietude; for stories always amuse the ladies, and it is only by interesting them that one can succeed in the world."

Mambres next prostrated himself before Amasis, king of Tanis, and thus addressed him:

"O king, live for ever! The white bull should certainly be sacrificed, for your majesty is always in the right, but the ruler of the world has said, this bull must not be swallowed up by the fish of Jonah till Memphis shall have found a god to supply the place of him who is dead. Then thou shalt be revenged, and thy daughter exorcised, for she is possessed. Your piety is too great not to obey the commands of the ruler of the universe."

Amasis, king of Tanis, remained for some time silent and in deep thought.

"The god Apis," said he, at length, "is dead! God rest his soul! When do you think another ox will be found to reign over the fruitful Egypt?"

"Sire," replied Mambres, "I ask but eight days."

"I grant them to you," replied the king, who was very religious, "and I will remain here the eight days. At the expiration of that time I will sacrifice the enemy of my daughter."

Amasis immediately ordered that his tents, cooks, and musicians should be brought, and remained here eight days, as it is related in Manethon.

The old woman was in despair that the bull she had in charge had but eight days to live. She raised phantoms every night, in order to dissuade the king from his cruel resolution; but Amasis forgot in the morning the phantoms he had seen in the night; similar to Nebuchadnezzar, who had always forgotten his dreams.

CHAPTER VIII.

HOW THE SERPENT TOLD STORIES TO THE PRINCESS TO COMFORT HER.

Meanwhile the serpent told stories to the fair Amasidia to soothe her. He related to her how he had formerly cured a whole nation of the bite of certain little serpents, only by showing himself at the end of a staff. (*Num. xx:9.*) He informed her of the conquests of a hero who made a charming contrast with Amphion, architect of Thebes. Amphion assembled hewn stones by the sound of his violin. To build a city he had only to play a rigadoon and a minuet; but the other hero destroyed them by the sound of rams' horns. He executed thirty-one powerful kings in a country of four leagues in length and four in breadth. He made stones rain down from heaven upon a battalion of routed Amorites; and having thus exterminated them, he stopped the sun and moon at noon-day between Gibeon and Ajalon, in the road to Beth-horon, to exterminate them still more, after the example of Bacchus, who had stopped the sun and the moon in his journey to the Indies.

The prudence which every serpent ought to have, did not allow him to tell the fair Amasidia of the powerful Jephthah, who made a vow and beheaded his daughter, because he had gained a battle. This would have struck terror into the mind of the fair princess. But he related to her the adventures of the great Sampson, who killed a thousand Philistines with the jaw-bone of an ass, who tied together three hundred foxes by the tail, and who fell into the snares of a lady, less beautiful, less tender, and less faithful than the charming Amasidia.

He related to her the story of the unfortunate Sechem and Dinah, as well as the more celebrated adventures of Ruth and Boaz; those of Judah and Tamar; those even of Lot's two daughters; those of Abraham and Jacob's servant maids; those of Reuben and Bilhah; those of David and Bath-sheba; and those of the great king Solomon. In short, every thing which could dissipate the grief of a fair princess.

CHAPTER IX.

HOW THE SERPENT DID NOT COMFORT THE PRINCESS.

"All these stories tire me," said Amasidia, for she had understanding and taste. "They are good for nothing but to be commented upon among the Irish by that madman Abbadie, or among the Welsh by that prattler d'Houteville. Stories which might have amused the great, great, great grandmother of my grandmother, appear insipid to me who have been educated by the wise Mambres, and who have read *Human Understanding* by the Egyptian philosopher named Locke[1] and the *Matron of Ephesus*. I choose that a story should be founded on probability, and not always resemble a dream. I desire to find nothing in it trivial or extravagant; and I desire above all, that under the appearance of fable there may appear some latent truth, obvious to the discerning eye, though it escape the observation of the vulgar."

"I am weary of a sun and of a moon which an old beldam disposes of at her pleasure, of mountains which dance, of rivers which return to their sources, and of dead men who rise again; but I am above measure disgusted when such insipid stories are written in a bombastic and unintelligible manner. A lady who expects to see her lover swallowed up by a great fish, and who is apprehensive of being beheaded by her own father, has need of amusement; but suit amusement to my taste."

"You impose a difficult task upon me," replied the serpent. "I could have formerly made you pass a few hours agreeably enough, but for some time past I have lost both my imagination and memory. Alas! what has become of those faculties with which I formerly amused the ladies? Let me try, however, if I can recollect one moral tale for your entertainment.

"Five and twenty thousand years ago king Gnaof and queen Patra reigned in Thebes with its hundred gates. King Gnaof was very handsome, and queen Patra still more beautiful. But their home was unblest with children, and no heirs were born to continue the royal race.

"The members of the faculty of medicine and of the academy of surgery wrote excellent treatises upon this subject. The queen was sent to drink mineral waters; she fasted and prayed; she made magnificent presents to the temple of Jupiter Ammon, but all was to no purpose. At length a———"

"Mon Dieu!" said the princess, "but I see where this leads. This story is too common, and I must likewise tell you that it offends my modesty. Relate some very true and moral story, which I have never yet heard, to complete the improvement of my understanding and my heart, as the Egyptian professor Lenro says."

- 50 -

"Here then, madam," said the beautiful serpent, "is one most incontestably authentic.

"There were three prophets all equally ambitious and discontented with their condition. They had in common the folly to wish to be kings: for there is only one step from the rank of a prophet to that of a monarch, and man always aspires to the highest step in the ladder of fortune. In other respects, their inclinations and their pleasures were totally different. The first preached admirably to his assembled brethren, who applauded him by clapping their hands; the second was distractedly fond of music; and the third was a passionate lover of the fair sex.

"The angel Ithuriel presented himself one day to them when they were at table discoursing on the sweets of royalty.

"'The ruler of the world,' said the angel to them, 'sends me to you to reward your virtue. Not only shall you be kings, but you shall constantly satisfy your ruling passions. Your first prophet, I make king of Egypt, and you shall continually preside in your council, who shall applaud your eloquence and your wisdom; and you, second prophet, I make king over Persia, and you shall continually hear most heavenly music; and you, third prophet, I make king of India, and I give you a charming mistress who shall never forsake you.'

"He to whose lot Egypt fell, began his reign by assembling his council, which was composed only of two hundred sages. He made them a long and eloquent speech, which was very much applauded, and the monarch enjoyed the pleasing satisfaction of intoxicating himself with praises uncorrupted by flattery.

"The council for foreign affairs succeeded to the privy council. This was much more numerous; and a new speech received still greater encomiums. And it was the same in the other councils. There was not a moment of intermission in the pleasures and glory of the prophet king of Egypt. The fame of his eloquence filled the world.

"The prophet king of Persia began his reign by an Italian opera, whose choruses were sung by fifteen hundred eunuchs. Their voices penetrated his soul even to the very marrow of the bones, where it resides. To this opera succeeded another, and to the second a third, without interruption.

"The king of India shut himself up with his mistress, and enjoyed perfect pleasure in her society. He considered the necessity of always flattering her as the highest felicity, and pitied the wretched situation of his two brethren, of whom one was obliged always to convene his council, and the other to be continually at an opera.

"It happened at the end of a few days, that each of these kings became disgusted with his occupation, and beheld from his window, certain woodcutters who came from an ale-house, and who were going to work in a neighboring forest. They walked arm in arm with their sweet-hearts, with whom they were happy. The kings begged of the angel Ithuriel, that he would intercede with the ruler of the world, and make them wood-cutters."

"I do not know whether the ruler of the world granted their request or not," interrupted the tender Amasidia, "and I do not care much about it; but I know very well that I should ask for nothing of any one, were I with my lover, with my dear NEBUCHADNEZZAR!"

The vaults of the palace resounded this mighty name. At first Amasidia had only pronounced Ne—, afterwards Neb—, then Nebu———. At length passion hurried her on, and she pronounced entire the fatal name, notwithstanding the oath she had sworn to the king, her father. All the ladies of the court repeated Nebuchadnezzar, and the malicious raven did not fail to carry the tidings to the king. The countenance of Amasis, king of Tanis, sunk, because his heart was troubled. And thus it was that the serpent, the wisest and most subtle of animals, always beguiled the women, thinking to do them service.

Amasis, in a fury, sent twelve alguazils for his daughter. These men are always ready to execute barbarous orders, because they are paid for it.

[1] The doctrine of metempsychosis must be relied upon to explain this seeming anachronism.—E.

CHAPTER X.

HOW THEY WANTED TO BEHEAD THE PRINCESS, AND DID NOT DO IT.

No sooner had the princess entered the camp of the king, than he said to her: "My daughter, you know that all princesses who disobey their fathers are put to death; without which it would be impossible that a kingdom could be well governed. I charged you never to mention the name of your lover, Nebuchadnezzar, my mortal enemy, who dethroned me about seven years ago, and disappeared. In his place, you have chosen a white bull, and you have cried Nebuchadnezzar. It is just that I behead you."

The princess replied: "My father, thy will be done: but grant me some time to bewail my sad fate."

"That is reasonable," said King Amasis; "and it is a rule established among the most judicious princes. I give you a whole day to bewail your destiny, since it is your desire. To-morrow, which is the eighth day of my encampment, I will cause the white bull to be swallowed up by the fish, and I will behead you precisely at nine o'clock in the morning."

The beautiful Amasidia then went forth in sorrow, to bewail her father's cruelty, and wandered by the side of the Nile, accompanied with the ladies of her train.

The wise Mambres pondered beside her, and reckoned the hours and the moments.

"Well! my dear Mambres," said she to him, "you have changed the waters of the Nile into blood, according to custom, and cannot you change the heart of Amasis, king of Tanis, my father? Will you suffer him to behead me to-morrow, at nine o'clock in the morning?"

"That depends," replied the reflecting Mambres, "upon the speed and diligence of my couriers."

The next day, as soon as the shadows of the obelisks and pyramids marked upon the ground the ninth hour of the day, the white bull was securely bound, to be thrown to the fish of Jonah; and they brought to the king his large sabre.

"Alas! alas!" said Nebuchadnezzar to himself, "I, a king, have been a bull for near seven years; and scarcely have I found the mistress I had lost when I am condemned to be devoured by a fish."

Never had the wise Mambres made such profound reflections; and he was quite absorbed in his melancholy thoughts when he saw at a distance all he expected. An innumerable crowd drew nigh. Three figures of Isis, Osiris, and Horus, joined together, advanced, drawn in a carriage of gold and precious stones, by a hundred senators of Memphis, preceded by a hundred girls, playing upon the sacred sistrums. Four thousand priests, with their heads shaved, were each mounted upon a hippopotamus.

At a great distance, appeared with the same pomp, the sheep of Thebes, the dog of Babastes, the cat of Phoebe, the crocodile of Arsinoe, the goat of Mendez, and all the inferior gods of Egypt, who came to pay homage to the great ox, to the mighty Apis, as powerful as Isis, Osiris, and Horus, united together.

In the midst of the demi-gods, forty priests carried an enormous basket, filled with sacred onions. These were, it is true, gods, but they resembled onions very much.

On both sides of this aisle of gods, followed by an innumerable crowd of people, marched forty thousand warriors, with helmets on their heads, scimitars upon their left thighs, quivers at their shoulders, and bows in their hands.

All the priests sang in chorus, with a harmony which ravished the soul, and which melted it.

"Alas! alas! our ox is dead—
We'll have a finer in its stead."

And at every pause was heard the sound of the sistrums, of cymbals, of tabors, of psalteries, of bagpipes, harps, and sackbuts.

Amasis, king of Tanis, astonished at this spectacle, beheaded not his daughter. He sheathed his scimitar.

CHAPTER XI.

APOTHEOSIS OF THE WHITE BULL. TRIUMPH OF THE WISE MAMBRES. THE SEVEN YEARS PROCLAIMED BY DANIEL ARE ACCOMPLISHED. NEBUCHADNEZZAR RESUMES THE HUMAN FORM, MARRIES THE BEAUTIFUL AMASIDIA, AND ASCENDS THE THRONE OF BABYLON.

"Great king," said Mambres to him, "the order of things is now changed. Your majesty must set the example. O king! quickly unbind the white bull, and be the first to adore him."

Amasis obeyed, and prostrated himself with all his people. The high priest of Memphis presented to the new god Apis the first handful of hay; the Princess Amasidia tied to his beautiful horse festoons of roses, anemonies, ranunculuses, tulips, pinks, and hyacinths. She took the liberty to kiss him, but with a profound respect. The priests strewed palms and flowers on the road by which they were to conduct him to Memphis. And the wise Mambres, still making reflections, whispered to his friend, the serpent:

"Daniel changed this monarch into a bull, and I have changed this bull into a god!"

They returned to Memphis in the same order, and the king of Tanis, in some confusion, followed the band. Mambres, with a serene and diplomatic air, walked by his side. The old woman came after, much amazed. She was accompanied by the serpent, the dog, the she-ass, the raven, the pigeon, and the scape-goat. The great fish mounted up the Nile. Daniel, Ezekiel, and Jeremiah, changed into magpies, brought up the rear.

When they had reached the frontiers of the kingdom, which are not far distant, King Amasis took leave of the bull Apis, and said to his daughter:

"My daughter, let us return into my dominions, that I may behead you, as it has been determined in my royal breast, because you have pronounced the name of Nebuchadnezzar, my enemy, who dethroned me seven years ago. When a father has sworn to behead his daughter, he must either fulfill his oath, or sink into hell for ever; and I will not damn myself out of love for you."

The fair princess Amasidia replied to the King Amasis:

"My dear father, whom it pleases you go and behead, but it shall not be me. I am now in the territories of Isis, Osiris, Horus, and Apis. I will never forsake my beautiful white bull, and I will continue to kiss him, till I have seen his apotheosis in his stable in the holy city of Memphis. It is a weakness pardonable in a young lady of high birth."

Scarce had she spoken these words, when the ox Apis cried out:

"My dear Amasidia, I will love you whilst I live!"

This was the first time that the god Apis had been heard to speak during the forty thousand years that he had been worshiped.

The serpent and the she-ass cried out, "the seven years are accomplished!" And the three magpies repeated, "the seven years are accomplished!"

All the priests of Egypt raised their hands to heaven.

The god on a sudden was seen to lose his two hind legs, his two fore legs were changed into two human legs; two white strong muscular arms grew from his shoulders; his taurine visage was changed to the face of a charming hero; and he once more became the most beautiful of mortals.

"I choose," cried he, "rather to be the lover of the beautiful Amasidia than a god. I am NEBUCHADNEZZAR, KING OF KINGS!"

This metamorphosis astonished all the world, except the wise Mambres. But what surprised nobody was, that Nebuchadnezzar immediately married the fair Amasidia in presence of this assembly.

He left his father-in-law in quiet possession of the kingdom of Tanis; and made noble provision for the she-ass, the serpent, the dog, the pigeon, and even for the raven, the three magpies, and the large fish; showing to all the world that he knew how to forgive as well as to conquer.

The old woman had a considerable pension placed at her disposal.

The scape-goat was sent for a day into the wilderness, that all past sins might be expiated; and had afterwards twelve sprightly goats for his companions.

The wise Mambres returned to his palace, and made reflections.

Nebuchadnezzar, after having embraced the magician, his benefactor, governed in tranquillity the kingdoms of Memphis, Babylon, Damascus, Balbec, Tyre, Syria, Asia Minor, Scythia, the countries of Thiras, Mosok, Tubal, Madai, Gog, Magog, Javan, Sogdiana, Aroriana, the Indies, and the Isles; and the people of this vast empire cried out aloud every morning at the rising of the sun:

"Long live great Nebuchadnezzar, king of kings, who is no longer an ox!"

Since which time it has been a custom in Babylon, when the sovereign, deceived by his satraps, his magicians, treasurers or wives, at length acknowledges his errors, and amends his conduct, for all the people to cry out at his gate:

Long live our great king, who is no longer an ox.

The scape-goat

ZADIG; OR FATE.

AN ORIENTAL HISTORY.

APPROBATION.

I, the underwritten, who have obtained the character of a learned, and even of an ingenious man, have read this manuscript, which, in spite of myself, I have found to be curious, entertaining, moral, philosophical, and capable of affording pleasure even to those who hate romances. I have therefore decried it; and have assured the cadi-lesquier that it is an abominable performance.

EPISTLE DEDICATORY TO THE SULTANA SERAA.

The 18th of the month Schewal, in the 837th year of the Hegira.

Delight of the eyes, torment of the heart, and light of the mind, I kiss not the dust of thy feet, because thou never walkest; or walkest only on the carpets of Iran, or in paths strewn with roses.

I offer thee the translation of a book, written by an ancient sage, who, having the happiness to have nothing to do, amused himself in composing the *History of Zadig*; a work which performs more than it promises.

I beseech thee to read and examine it; for, though thou art in the spring of life, and every pleasure courts thee to its embrace; though thou art beautiful, and thy beauty be embellished by thy admirable talents; though thou art praised from morning to evening, and, on all these accounts, hast a right to be devoid of common sense, yet thou hast a sound judgment and a fine taste; and I have heard thee reason with more accuracy than the old dervises, with their long beards and pointed bonnets.

Thou art discreet without being distrustful; gentle without weakness; and beneficent with discernment. Thou lovest thy friends, and makest thyself no enemies. Thy wit never borrows its charms from the shafts of detraction. Thou neither sayest nor doest any ill, notwithstanding that both are so much in thy power.

In a word, thy soul hath always appeared to me to be as pure and unsullied as thy beauty. Besides, thou hast some little knowledge in philosophy, which makes me believe that thou wilt take more pleasure than others of thy sex in perusing the work of this venerable sage.

It was originally written in the ancient Chaldee, a language which neither thou nor I understand. It was afterward translated into the Arabic, to amuse the famous sultan Oulougbeg, much about the time that the Arabians and the Persians began to write the *Thousand and One Nights*, the *Thousand and One Days*, etc.

Ouloug was fond of reading *Zadig*, but the sultanas were fonder of the *Thousand and One*. "How can you prefer," said the wise Ouloug to them, "those stories which have neither sense nor meaning?" "It is for that very reason," replied the sultanas, "that we prefer them."

I flatter myself that thou wilt not resemble these, thy predecessors; but that thou wilt be a true Ouloug. I even hope, that when thou art tired with those general conversations, which differ from the *Thousand and One* in nothing but in being less agreeable, I shall have the honor to entertain thee for a moment with a rational discourse.

Hadst thou been Thalestris in the time of Scander, the son of Philip; hadst thou been the Queen of Sheba in the time of Solomon; these are the very kings that would have paid thee a visit.

I pray the heavenly powers, that thy pleasures may be unmixed, thy beauty never fading, and thy happiness without end.

SADI.

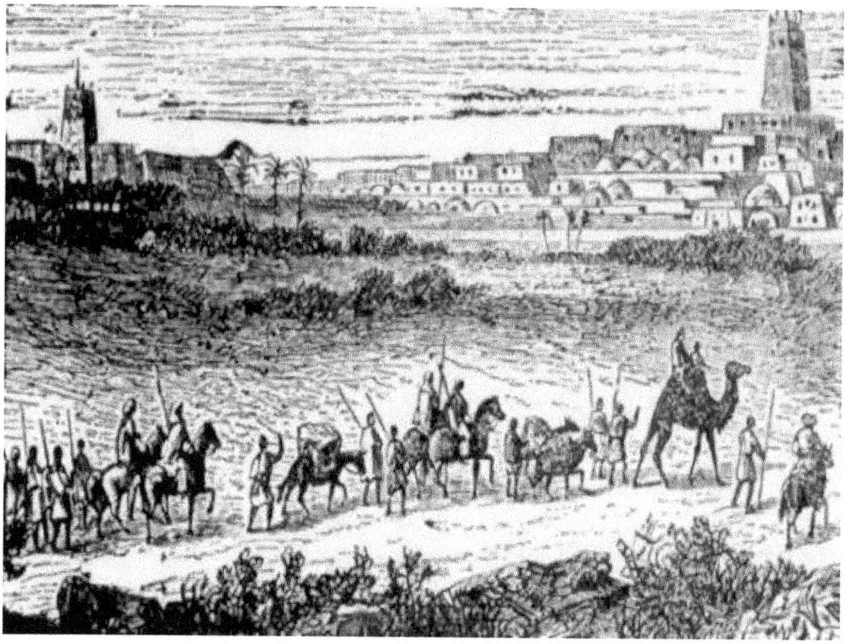

ZADIG: OR, FATE

I.

THE BLIND OF ONE EYE.

There lived at Babylon, in the reign of King Moabdar, a young man, named Zadig, of a good natural disposition, strengthened and improved by education. Though rich and young, he had learned to moderate his passions. He had nothing stiff or affected in his behavior. He did not pretend to examine every action by the strict rules of reason, but was always ready to make proper allowances for the weakness of mankind. It was a matter of surprise, that, notwithstanding his sprightly wit, he never exposed by his raillery those vague, incoherent, and noisy discourses; those rash censures, ignorant decisions, coarse jests, and all that empty jingle of words which at Babylon went by the name of conversation. He had learned, in the first book of Zoroaster, that self-love is a foot-ball swelled with wind, from which, when pierced, the most terrible tempests issue forth. Above all, Zadig never boasted of his conquests among the women, nor affected to entertain a contemptible opinion of the fair sex. He was generous, and was never afraid of obliging the ungrateful; remembering the grand precept of Zoroaster, "When thou eatest, give to the dogs, should they even bite thee." He was as wise as it is possible for man to be, for he sought to live with the wise. Instructed in the sciences of the ancient Chaldeans, he understood the principles of natural philosophy, such as they were then supposed to be; and knew as much of metaphysics as hath ever been known in any age, that is, little or nothing at all. He was firmly persuaded, notwithstanding the new philosophy of the times, that the year consisted of three hundred and sixty-five days and six hours, and that the sun was the centre of the solar system. When the principal magi told him, with a haughty and contemptuous air, that his sentiments were of a dangerous tendency, and that it was to be an enemy to the state to believe that the sun revolved round its own axis, and that the year had twelve months, he held his tongue with great modesty and meekness.

Possessed as he was of great riches, and consequently of many friends, blessed with a good constitution, a handsome figure, a mind just and moderate, and a heart noble and sincere, he fondly imagined that he might easily be happy. He was going to be married to Semira, who, in point of beauty, birth, and fortune, was the first match in Babylon. He had a real and virtuous affection for this lady, and she loved him with the most passionate fondness. The happy moment was almost arrived that was to unite them for ever in the bands of wedlock, when happening to take a walk together toward one of the gates of Babylon, under the palm-trees that adorn the banks of the Euphrates, they saw some men approaching, armed with sabres and arrows. These were the attendants of young Orcan, the minister's nephew, whom his uncle's creatures had flattered into an opinion that he might do everything with impunity. He had none of the graces nor virtues of Zadig; but thinking himself a much more accomplished man, he was enraged to find that the other was preferred before him. This jealousy, which was merely the effect of his vanity, made him imagine that he was desperately in love with Semira; and accordingly he resolved to carry her off. The ravishers seized her; in the violence of the outrage, they wounded her, and made the blood flow from a person, the sight of which would have softened the tigers of mount Imaus. She pierced the heavens with her complaints. She cried out: "My dear husband! they tear me from the man I adore!"

Regardless of her own danger, she was only concerned for the fate of her dear Zadig, who, in the meantime, defended himself with all the strength that courage and love could inspire. Assisted only by two faithful slaves, he put the cowardly ravishers to flight, and carried home Semira, insensible and bloody as she was.

"O Zadig," said she, on opening her eyes, and beholding her deliverer, "I loved thee formerly as my intended husband, I now love thee as the preserver of my honor and my life!"

Never was heart more deeply affected than that of Semira. Never did a more charming mouth express more moving sentiments, in those glowing words inspired by a sense of the greatest of all favors, and by the most tender transports of a lawful passion. Her wound was slight, and was soon cured. Zadig was more dangerously wounded. An arrow had pierced him near his eye, and penetrated to a considerable depth, Semira wearied heaven with her prayers for the recovery of her lover. Her eyes were constantly bathed in tears; she anxiously waited the happy moment when those of Zadig should be able to meet hers; but an abscess growing on the wounded eye, gave everything to fear. A messenger was immediately dispatched to Memphis, for the great physician Hermes, who came with a numerous retinue. He visited the patient, and declared that he would lose his eye. He even foretold the day and hour when this fatal event would happen.

"Had it been the right eye," said he, "I could easily have cured it; but the wounds of the left eye are incurable."

All Babylon lamented the fate of Zadig, and admired the profound knowledge of Hermes. In two days the abscess broke of its own accord, and Zadig was perfectly cured. Hermes wrote a book, to prove that it ought not to have been cured. Zadig did not read it: but, as soon as he was able to go abroad, he went to pay a visit to her in whom all his hopes of happiness were centered, and for whose sake alone he wished to have eyes. Semira had been in the country for three days past. He learned on the road, that that fine lady, having openly declared that she had an unconquerable aversion to one-eyed men, had the night before given her hand to Orcan. At this news he fell speechless to the ground. His sorrows brought him almost to the brink of the grave. He was long indisposed; but reason at last got the better of his affliction; and the severity of his fate served even to console him.

"Since," said he, "I have suffered so much from the cruel caprice of a woman educated at court, I must now think of marrying the daughter of a citizen."

He pitched upon Azora, a lady of the greatest prudence, and of the best family in town. He married her, and lived with her for three months in all the delights of the most tender union. He only observed that she had a little levity; and was too apt to find that those young men who had the most handsome persons were likewise possessed of the most wit and virtue.

II.

THE NOSE.

One morning Azora returned from a walk in a terrible passion and uttering the most violent exclamations.

"What aileth thee," said he, "my dear spouse? What is it that can thus have disturbed thee?"

"Alas!" said she, "thou wouldst have been as much enraged as I am, hadst thou seen what I have just beheld. I have been to comfort the young widow Cosrou, who, within these two days, hath raised a tomb to her young husband, near the rivulet that washes the skirts of this meadow. She vowed to heaven, in the bitterness of her grief, to remain at this tomb whilst the water of the rivulet should continue to run near it."

"Well," said Zadig, "she is an excellent woman, and loved her husband with the most sincere affection."

"Ah!" replied Azora, "didst thou but know in what she was employed when I went to wait upon her!"

"In what, pray tell me, beautiful Azora? Was she turning the course of the rivulet?"

Azora broke out into such long invectives, and loaded the young widow with such bitter reproaches, that Zadig was far from being pleased with this ostentation of virtue.

Zadig had a friend named Cador; one of those young men in whom his wife discovered more probity and merit than in others. He made him his confidant, and secured his fidelity as much as possible by a considerable present. Azora, having passed two days with a friend in the country, returned home on the third. The servants told her, with tears in their eyes, that her husband died suddenly the night before; that they were afraid to send her an account of this mournful event; and that they had just been depositing his corpse in the tomb of his ancestors, at the end of the garden. She wept, she tore her hair, and swore she would follow him to the grave. In the evening, Cador begged leave to wait upon her, and joined his tears with hers. Next day they wept less, and dined together. Cador told her, that his friend had left him the greater part of his estate; and that he should think himself extremely happy in sharing his fortune with her. The lady wept, fell into a passion, and at last became more mild and gentle. They sat longer at supper than at dinner. They now talked with greater confidence. Azora praised the deceased; but owned that he had many failings from which Cador was free.

During supper, Cador complained of a violent pain in his side. The lady, greatly concerned, and eager to serve him, caused all kinds of essences to be brought, with which she anointed him, to try if some of them might not possibly ease him of his pain. She lamented that the great Hermes was not still in Babylon. She even condescended to touch the side in which Cador felt such exquisite pain.

"Art thou subject to this cruel disorder?" said she to him, with a compassionate air.

"It sometimes brings me," replied Cador, "to the brink of the grave; and there is but one remedy that can give me relief—and that is, to apply to my side the nose of a man who is lately dead."

"A strange remedy, indeed!" said Azora.

"Not more strange," replied he, "than the satchels of Arnou, against the apoplexy."

This reason, added to the great merit of the young man, at last determined the lady.

"After all," says she, "when my husband shall cross the bridge Tchinavar in his journey to the other world, the angel Asrael will not refuse him a passage because his nose is a little shorter in the second life than it was in the first."

She then took a razor, went to her husband's tomb, bedewed it with her tears, and drew near to cut off the nose of Zadig, whom she found extended at full length in the tomb. Zadig arose, holding his nose with one hand, and putting back the razor with the other.

"Madam," said he, "don't exclaim so violently against the widow Cosrou. The project of cutting off my nose is equal to that of turning the course of a rivulet."

III.

THE DOG AND THE HORSE.

Zadig found by experience, that the first month of marriage, as it is written in the book of Zend, is the moon of honey, and that the second is the moon of wormwood. He was some time after obliged to repudiate Azora, who became too difficult to be pleased; and he then sought for happiness in the study of nature.

"No man," said he, "can be happier than a philosopher, who reads in this great book, which God hath placed before our eyes. The truths he discovers are his own; he nourishes and exalts his soul; he lives in peace; he fears nothing from men; and his tender spouse will not come to cut off his nose."

Possessed of these ideas, he retired to a country house on the banks of the Euphrates. There he did not employ himself in calculating how many inches of water flow in a second of time under the arches of a bridge, or whether there fell a cube-line of rain in the month of the mouse more than in the month of the sheep. He never dreamed of making silk of cobwebs, or porcelain of broken bottles: but he chiefly studied the properties of plants and animals; and soon acquired a sagacity that made him discover a thousand differences where other men see nothing but uniformity.

One day, as he was walking near a little wood, he saw one of the queen's eunuchs running toward him, followed by several officers, who appeared to be in great perplexity, and who ran to and fro like men distracted, eagerly searching for something they had lost of great value.

"Young man," said the first eunuch, "hast thou seen the queen's dog?"

"It is a bitch," replied Zadig, with great modesty, "and not a dog."

"Thou art in the right," returned the first eunuch.

"It is a very small she-spaniel," added Zadig; "she has lately whelped; she limps on the left fore-foot, and has very long ears."

"Thou hast seen her," said the first eunuch, quite out of breath.

"No," replied Zadig, "I have not seen her, nor did I so much as know that the queen had a bitch."

Exactly at the same time, by one of the common freaks of fortune, the finest horse in the king's stable had escaped from the jockey in the plains of Babylon. The principal huntsman, and all the other officers, ran after him with as much eagerness and anxiety as the first eunuch had done after the bitch. The principal huntsman addressed himself to Zadig, and asked him if he had not seen the king's horse passing by.

"He is the fleetest horse in the king's stable," replied Zadig, "he is five feet high, with very small hoofs, and a tail three feet and an half in length; the studs on his bit are gold, of twenty-three carats, and his shoes are silver of eleven penny-weights."

"What way did he take? where is he?" demanded the chief huntsman.

"I have not seen him," replied Zadig, "and never heard talk of him before."

The principal huntsman and the first eunuch never doubted but that Zadig had stolen the king's horse and the queen's bitch. They therefore had him conducted before the assembly of the grand desterham, who condemned him to the knout, and to spend the rest of his days in Siberia. Hardly was the sentence passed, when the horse and the bitch were both found. The judges were reduced to the disagreeable necessity of reversing their sentence; but they condemned Zadig to pay four hundred ounces of gold for having said that he had not seen what he had seen. This fine he was obliged to pay; after which, he was permitted to plead his cause before the counsel of the grand desterham, when he spoke to the following effect.

"Ye stars of justice, abyss of sciences, mirrors of truth, who have the weight of lead, the hardness of iron, the splendor of the diamond, and many of the properties of gold; since I am permitted to speak before this august assembly, I swear to you by Oromazes, that I have never seen the queen's respectable bitch, nor the sacred horse of the king of kings. The truth of the matter is as follows: I was walking toward the little wood, where I afterward met the venerable eunuch, and the most illustrious chief huntsman. I observed on the sand the traces of an animal, and could easily perceive them to be those of a little dog. The light and long furrows impressed on little eminences of sand between the marks of the paws, plainly discovered that it was a bitch, whose dugs were hanging down, and that therefore she must have whelped a few days before. Other traces of a different kind, that always appeared to have gently brushed the surface of the sand near the marks of the fore-feet, showed me that she had very long ears; and as I remarked that there was always a slighter impression made on the sand by one foot than by the other three, I found that the bitch of our august queen was a little lame, if I may be allowed the expression. With regard to the horse of the king of kings, you will be pleased to know, that walking in the lanes of this wood, I observed the marks of a horse's shoes, all at equal distances. This must be a horse, said I to myself, that gallops excellently. The dust on the trees in a narrow road that was but seven feet wide, was a little brushed off, at the distance of three feet and a half from the middle of the road. This horse, said I, has a tail three feet and a half long, which, being whisked to the right and left, has swept away the dust. I observed under the trees that formed an arbor five feet in height, that the leaves of the branches were newly fallen, from whence I inferred that the horse had touched them, and that he must therefore be five feet high. As to his bit, it must be gold of twenty-three carats, for he had rubbed its bosses against a stone which I knew to be a touchstone, and which I have tried. In a word, from a mark made by his shoes on flints of another kind, I concluded that he was shod with silver eleven deniers fine."

All the judges admired Zadig for his acute and profound discernment. The news of this speech was carried even to the king and queen. Nothing was talked of but Zadig in the anti-chambers, the chambers, and the cabinet; and though many of the magi were of opinion that he ought to be burnt as a sorcerer, the king ordered his officers to restore him the four hundred ounces of gold which he had been obliged to pay. The register, the attorneys, and bailiffs, went to his house with great formality to carry him back his four hundred ounces. They only retained three hundred and ninety-eight of them to defray the expenses of justice; and then their servants demanded their fees.

Zadig saw how extremely dangerous it sometimes is to appear too knowing, and therefore resolved, that on the next occasion of the like nature he would not tell what he had seen.

Such an opportunity soon offered. A prisoner of state made his escape and passed under the windows of Zadig's house. Zadig was examined and made no answer. But it was proved that he had looked at the prisoner from this window. For this crime he was condemned to pay five hundred ounces of gold; and, according to the polite custom of Babylon, he thanked his judges for their indulgence.

"Great God!" said he to himself, "what a misfortune it is to walk in a wood through which the queen's bitch or the king's horse have passed! how dangerous to look out at a window! and how difficult to be happy in this life!"

IV.

THE ENVIOUS MAN.

Zadig resolved to comfort himself by philosophy and friendship for the evils he had suffered from fortune. He had in the suburbs of Babylon a house elegantly furnished, in which he assembled all the arts and all the pleasures worthy the pursuit of a gentleman. In the morning his library was open to the learned. In the evening his table was surrounded by good company. But he soon found what very dangerous guests these men of letters are. A warm dispute arose on one of Zoroaster's laws, which forbids the eating of a griffin.

"Why," said some of them, "prohibit the eating of a griffin, if there is no such animal in nature?"

"There must necessarily be such an animal," said the others, "since Zoroaster forbids us to eat it."

Zadig would fain have reconciled them by saying:

"If there are no griffins, we cannot possibly eat them; and thus either way we shall obey Zoroaster."

A learned man, who had composed thirteen volumes on the properties of the griffin, and was besides the chief theurgite, hasted away to accuse Zadig before one of the principal magi, named Yebor, the greatest blockhead, and therefore the greatest fanatic among the Chaldeans. This man would have empaled Zadig to do honor to the sun, and would then have recited the breviary of Zoroaster with greater satisfaction. The friend Cador (a friend is better than a hundred priests) went to Yebor, and said to him:

"Long live the sun and the griffins; beware of punishing Zadig; he is a saint; he has griffins in his inner court, and does not eat them; and his accuser is an heretic, who dares to maintain that rabbits have cloven feet, and are not unclean."

"Well," said Yebor, shaking his bald pate, "we must empale Zadig for having thought contemptuously of griffins, and the other party for having spoken disrespectfully of rabbits."

Cador hushed up the affair by appealing to a person who had great interest in the college of the magi. Nobody was empaled. This lenity occasioned a great murmuring among some of the doctors, who from thence predicted the fall of Babylon.

"Upon what does happiness depend?" said Zadig; "I am persecuted by everything in the world, even on account of beings that have no existence."

He cursed those men of learning, and resolved for the future to live with none but good company.

He assembled at his house the most worthy men, and the most beautiful ladies of Babylon. He gave them delicious suppers, often preceded by concerts of music, and always animated by polite conversation, from which he knew how to banish that affectation of wit, which is the surest method of preventing it entirely, and of spoiling the pleasure of the most agreeable society. Neither the choice of his friends, nor that of the dishes, was made by vanity; for in everything he preferred the substance to the shadow; and by these means he procured that real respect to which he did not aspire.

Opposite to his house lived one Arimazes, a man whose deformed countenance was but a faint picture of his still more deformed mind. His heart was a mixture of malice, pride, and envy. Having never been able to succeed in any of his undertakings, he revenged himself on all around him, by loading them with the blackest calumnies. Rich as he was, he found it difficult to procure a set of flatterers. The rattling of the chariots that entered Zadig's court in the evening, filled him with uneasiness; the sound of his praises enraged him still more. He sometimes went to Zadig's house, and sat down at table without being desired; where he spoiled all the pleasure of the company, as the harpies are said to infect the viands they touch.

It happened that one day he took it in his head to give an entertainment to a lady, who, instead of accepting it, went to sup with Zadig. At another time, as he was talking with Zadig at court, a minister of state came up to them, and invited Zadig to supper, without inviting Arimazes. The most implacable hatred has seldom a more solid foundation. This man, who in Babylon was called the *envious*, resolved to ruin Zadig, because he was called the *happy*. "The opportunity of doing mischief occurs a hundred times in a day, and that of doing good but once a year, as sayeth the wise Zoroaster."

The envious man went to see Zadig, who was walking in his garden with two friends and a lady, to whom he said many gallant things, without any other intention than that of saying them. The conversation turned upon a war which the king had just brought to a happy conclusion against the prince of Hircania, his vassal. Zadig, who had signalized his courage in this short war, bestowed great praises on the king, but greater still on the lady. He took out his pocket-book, and wrote four lines extempore, which he gave to this amiable person to read. His friends begged they might see them; but modesty, or rather a well-regulated self-love, would not allow him to grant their request. He knew that extemporary verses are never approved by any but by the person in whose honor they are written. He therefore tore in two the leaf on which he had written them, and threw both the pieces into a thicket of rose bushes where the rest of the company sought for them in vain. A slight shower falling soon after, obliged them to return to the house.

The envious man, who remained in the garden, continued to search, till at last he found a piece of the leaf. It had been torn in such a manner, that each half of a line formed a complete sense, and even a verse of a shorter measure; but what was still more surprising, these short verses were found to contain the most injurious reflections on the king. They ran thus:

To flagrant crimes
His crown he owes,
To peaceful times
The worst of foes.

The envious man was now happy for the first time in his life. He had it in his power to ruin a person of virtue and merit. Killed with this fiend-like joy, he found means to convey to the king the satire written by the hand of Zadig, who was immediately thrown into prison, together with the lady and Zadig's two friends.

His trial was soon finished without his being permitted to speak for himself. As he was going to receive his sentence, the envious man threw himself in his way, and told him with a loud voice, that his verses were good for nothing. Zadig did not value himself on being a good poet; but it filled him with inexpressible concern to find that he was condemned for high treason; and that the fair lady and his two friends were confined in prison for a crime of which they were not guilty. He was not allowed to speak, because his writing spoke for him. Such was the law of Babylon. Accordingly he was conducted to the place of execution through an immense crowd of spectators, who durst not venture to express their pity for him, but who carefully examined his countenance to see if he died with a good grace. His relations alone were inconsolable; for they could not succeed to his estate. Three-fourths of his wealth were confiscated into the king's treasury, and the other fourth was given to the envious man.

Just as he was preparing for death, the king's parrot flew from its cage, and alighted on a rose bush in Zadig's garden. A peach had been driven thither by the wind from a neighboring tree, and had fallen on a piece of the written leaf of the pocket-book to which it stuck. The bird carried off the peach and the paper, and laid them on the king's knee. The king took up the paper with great eagerness, and read the words, which formed no sense, and seemed to be the endings of verses. He loved poetry; and there is always some mercy to be expected from a prince of that disposition. The adventure of the parrot caused him to reflect.

The queen, who remembered what had been written on the piece of Zadig's pocket-book, ordered it to be brought. They compared the two pieces together, and found them to tally exactly. They then read the verses as Zadig had written them.

Tyrants are prone to flagrant crimes;
To clemency his crown he owes;
To concord and to peaceful times
Love only is the worst of foes.

The king gave immediate orders that Zadig should be brought before him, and that his two friends and the lady should be set at liberty. Zadig fell prostrate on the ground before the king and queen, humbly begged their pardon for having made such bad verses, and spoke with so much propriety, wit, and good sense, that their majesties desired they might see him again. He did himself that honor, and insinuated himself still farther into their good graces. They gave him all the wealth of the envious man; but Zadig restored him back the whole of it; and this instance of generosity gave no other pleasure to the envious man than that of having preserved his estate. The king's esteem for Zadig increased every day. He admitted him into all his parties of pleasure, and consulted him in all affairs of state. From that time the queen began to regard him with an eye of tenderness, that might one day prove dangerous to herself, to the king her august consort, to Zadig, and to the kingdom in general. Zadig now began to think that happiness was not so unattainable as he had formerly imagined.

V.

THE GENEROUS.

The time had now arrived for celebrating a grand festival, which returned every five years. It was a custom in Babylon solemnly to declare, at the end of every five years, which of the citizens had performed the most generous action. The grandees and the magi were the judges. The first satrap, who was charged with the government of the city, published the most noble actions that had passed under his administration. The competition was decided by votes; and the king pronounced the sentence. People came to this solemnity from the extremities of the earth. The conqueror received from the monarch's hands a golden cup adorned with precious stones, his majesty at the same time making him this compliment: "Receive this reward of thy generosity, and may the gods grant me many subjects like to thee."

This memorable day having come, the king appeared on his throne, surrounded by the grandees, the magi, and the deputies of all the nations that came to these games, where glory was acquired not by the swiftness of horses, nor by strength of body, but by virtue. The first satrap recited, with an audible voice, such actions as might entitle the authors of them to this invaluable prize. He did not mention the greatness of soul with which Zadig had restored the envious man his fortune, because it was not judged to be an action worthy of disputing the prize.

He first presented a judge, who having made a citizen lose a considerable cause by a mistake, for which, after all, he was not accountable, had given him the whole of his own estate, which was just equal to what the other had lost.

He next produced a young man, who being desperately in love with a lady whom he was going to marry, had yielded her up to his friend, whose passion for her had almost brought him to the brink of the grave, and at the same time had given him the lady's fortune.

He afterwards produced a soldier, who, in the wars of Hircania, had given a still more noble instance of generosity. A party of the enemy having seized his mistress, he fought in her defence with great intrepidity. At that very instant he was informed that another party, at the distance of a few paces, were carrying off his mother; he therefore left his mistress with tears in his eyes, and flew to the assistance of his mother. At last he returned to the dear object of his love, and found her expiring. He was just going to plunge his sword in his own bosom; but his mother remonstrating against such a desperate deed, and telling him that he was the only support of her life, he had the courage to endure to live.

The judges were inclined to give the prize to the soldier. But the king took up the discourse, and said:

"The action of the soldier, and those of the other two, are doubtless very great, but they have nothing in them surprising. Yesterday, Zadig performed an action that filled me with wonder. I had a few days before disgraced Coreb, my minister and favorite. I complained of him in the most violent and bitter terms; all my courtiers assured me that I was too gentle, and seemed to vie with each other in speaking ill of Coreb. I asked Zadig what he thought of him, and he had the courage to commend him. I have read in our histories of many people who have atoned for an error by the surrender of their fortune; who have resigned a mistress; or preferred a mother to the object of their affection, but never before did I hear of a courtier who spoke favorably of a disgraced minister, that labored under the displeasure of his sovereign. I give to each of those whose generous actions have been now recited, twenty thousand pieces of gold; but the cup I give to Zadig."

"May it please your majesty," said Zadig, "thyself alone deservest the cup. Thou hast performed an action of all others the most uncommon and meritorious, since, notwithstanding thy being a powerful king, thou wast not offended at thy slave, when he presumed to oppose thy passion."

The king and Zadig were equally the object of admiration. The judge who had given his estate to his client; the lover who had resigned his mistress to his friend, and the soldier, who had preferred the safety of his mother to that of his mistress, received the king's presents, and saw their names enrolled in the catalogue of generous men. Zadig had the cup, and the king acquired the reputation of a good prince, which he did not long enjoy. The day was celebrated by feasts that lasted longer than the law enjoined; and the memory of it is still preserved in Asia. Zadig said: "Now I am happy at last." But he found himself fatally deceived.

VI.

THE MINISTER.

The king had lost his first minister, and chose Zadig to supply his place. All the ladies in Babylon applauded the choice; for, since the foundation of the empire, there had never been such a young minister. But all the courtiers were filled with jealousy and vexation. The envious man, in particular, was troubled with a spitting of blood, and a prodigious inflammation in his nose. Zadig, having thanked the king and queen for their goodness, went likewise to thank the parrot.

"Beautiful bird," said he, "tis thou that hast saved my life, and made me first minister. The queen's bitch and the king's horse did me a great deal of mischief; but thou hast done me much good. Upon such slender threads as these do the fates of mortals hang! but," added he, "this happiness perhaps will vanish very soon."

The cup.—"*May it please your majesty*," said Zadig, "*thyself alone deservest the cup.*"

"Soon," replied the parrot.

Zadig was somewhat startled at this word. But as he was a good natural philosopher, and did not believe parrots to be prophets, he quickly recovered his spirits, and resolved to execute his duty to the best of his power.

He made every one feel the sacred authority of the laws, but no one felt the weight of his dignity. He never checked the deliberations of the divan; and every vizier might give his opinion without fear of incurring the minister's displeasure. When he gave judgment, it was not he that gave it; it was the law; the rigor of which, however, whenever it was too severe, he always took care to soften; and when laws were wanting, the equity of his decisions was such as might easily have made them pass for those of Zoroaster.

It is to him that the nations are indebted for this grand principle, to wit, that it is better to run the risk of sparing the guilty than to condemn the innocent. He imagined that laws were made as well to secure the people from the suffering of injuries as to restrain them from the commission of crimes. His chief talent consisted in discovering the truth, which all men seek to obscure. This great talent he put in practice from the very beginning of his administration.

A famous merchant of Babylon, who died in the Indies, divided his estate equally between his two sons, after having disposed of their sister in marriage, and left a present of thirty thousand pieces of gold to that son who should be found to have loved him best. The eldest raised a tomb to his memory; the youngest increased his sister's portion, by giving her a part of his inheritance. Every one said that the eldest son loved his father best, and the youngest his sister; and that the thirty thousand pieces belonged to the eldest.

Zadig sent for both of them, the one after the other. To the eldest he said:

"Thy father is not dead; but has survived his last illness, and is returning to Babylon."

"God be praised," replied the young man; "but his tomb cost me a considerable sum."

Zadig afterwards repeated the same story to the youngest son.

"God be praised," said he; "I will go and restore to my father all that I have; but I could wish that he would leave my sister what I have given her."

"Thou shalt restore nothing," replied Zadig, "and thou shalt have the thirty thousand pieces, for thou art the son who loves his father best."

A widow, having a young son, and being possessed of a handsome fortune, had given a promise of marriage to two magi; who were both desirous of marrying her.

"I will take for my husband," said she, "the man who can give the best education to my beloved son."

The two magi contended who should bring him up, and the cause was carried before Zadig. Zadig summoned the two magi to attend him.

"What will you teach your pupil?" said he to the first.

"I will teach him," said the doctor, "the eight parts of speech, logic, astrology, pneumatics, what is meant by substance and accident, abstract and concrete, the doctrine of the monades, and the pre-established harmony."

"For my part," said the second, "I will endeavor to give him a sense of justice, and to make him worthy the friendship of good men."

Zadig then cried:

"Whether thou art the child's favorite or not, thou shalt have his mother."

VII.

THE DISPUTES AND THE AUDIENCES.

In this manner he daily discovered the subtlety of his genius and the goodness of his heart. The people at once admired and loved him. He passed for the happiest man in the world. The whole empire resounded with his name. All the ladies ogled him. All the men praised him for his justice. The learned regarded him as an oracle; and even the priests confessed that he knew more than the old arch-magi Yebor. They were now so far from prosecuting him on account of the griffins, that they believed nothing but what he thought credible.

There had continued at Babylon, for the space of fifteen hundred years, a violent contest that had divided the empire into two sects. The one pretended that they ought to enter the temple of Mithra with the left foot foremost; the other held this custom in detestation, and always entered with the right foot first. The people waited with great impatience for the day on which the solemn feast of the sacred fire was to be celebrated, to see which sect Zadig would favor. All the world had their eyes fixed on his two feet, and the whole city was in the utmost suspense and perturbation. Zadig jumped into the temple with his feet joined together; and afterward proved, in an eloquent discourse, that the Sovereign of heaven and earth, who accepteth not the persons of men, maketh no distinction between the right and the left foot. The envious man and his wife alleged that his discourse was not figurative enough, and that he did not make the rocks and mountains dance with sufficient agility.

"He is dry," said they, "and void of genius. He does not make the sea to fly, and stars to fall, nor the sun to melt like wax. He has not the true oriental style."

Zadig contented himself with having the style of reason. All the world favored him, not because he was in the right road, or followed the dictates of reason, or was a man of real merit, but because he was prime vizier.

He terminated with the same happy address the grand dispute between the black and the white magi. The former maintained that it was the height of impiety to pray to God with the face turned toward the east in winter; the latter asserted that God abhorred the prayers of those who turned toward the west in summer. Zadig decreed that every man should be allowed to turn as he pleased.

Thus he found out the happy secret of finishing all affairs, whether of a private or a public nature, in the morning. The rest of the day he employed in superintending and promoting the embellishments of Babylon. He exhibited tragedies that drew tears from the eyes of the spectators, and comedies that shook their sides with laughter,—a custom which had long been disused, and which his good taste now induced him to revive. He never affected to be more knowing in the polite arts than the artists themselves. He encouraged them by rewards and honors, and was never jealous of their talents. In the evening the king was highly entertained with his conversation, and the queen still more.

"Great minister!" said the king.

"Amiable minister!" said the queen; and both of them added, "It would have been a great loss to the state had such a man been hanged."

Meanwhile Zadig perceived that his thoughts were always distracted, as well when he gave audience as when he sat in judgment. He did not know to what to attribute this absence of mind, and that was his only sorrow.

He had a dream, in which he imagined that he laid himself down upon a heap of dry herbs, among which there were many prickly ones that gave him great uneasiness, and that he afterward reposed himself on a soft bed of roses, from which there sprung a serpent that wounded him to the heart with its sharp venomed fangs. "Alas," said he, "I have long lain on these dry and prickly herbs, I am now on the bed of roses; but what shall be the serpent?"

VIII.

JEALOUSY.

Zadig's calamities sprung even from his happiness, and especially from his merit. He every day conversed with the king and his august consort. The charms of Zadig's conversation were greatly heightened by that desire of pleasing which is to the mind what dress is to beauty. His youth and graceful appearance insensibly made an impression on Astarte, which she did not at first perceive. Her passion grew and flourished in the bosom of innocence. Without fear or scruple, she indulged the pleasing satisfaction of seeing and hearing a man who was so dear to her husband, and to the empire in general. She was continually praising him to the king. She talked of him to her women, who were always sure to improve on her praises. And thus everything contributed to pierce her heart with a dart, of which she did not seem to be sensible. She made several presents to Zadig, which discovered a greater spirit of gallantry than she imagined. She intended to speak to him only as a queen satisfied with his services; and her expressions were sometimes those of a woman in love.

Astarte was much more beautiful than that Semira who had such a strong aversion to one-eyed men, or that other woman who had resolved to cut off her husband's nose. Her unreserved familiarity, her tender expressions, at which she began to blush; and her eyes, which, though she endeavored to divert them to other objects, were always fixed upon his, inspired Zadig with a passion that filled him with astonishment. He struggled hard to get the better of it. He called to his aid the precepts of philosophy, which had always stood him in stead; but from thence, though he could derive the light of knowledge, he could procure no remedy to cure the disorders of his love-sick heart. Duty, gratitude, and violated majesty, presented themselves to his mind, as so many avenging gods. He struggled, he conquered. But this victory, which he was obliged to purchase afresh every moment, cost him many sighs and tears. He no longer dared to speak to the queen with that sweet and charming familiarity which had been so agreeable to them both. His countenance was covered with a cloud. His conversation was constrained and incoherent. His eyes were fixed on the ground; and when, in spite of all his endeavors to the contrary, they encountered those of the queen, they found them bathed in tears, and darting arrows of flame. They seemed to say, We adore each other, and yet are afraid to love; we are consumed with a passion which we both condemn.

Zadig left the royal presence full of perplexity and despair, and having his heart oppressed with a burden which he was no longer able to bear. In the violence of his perturbation he involuntarily betrayed the secret to his friend

Cador, in the same manner as a man, who, having long endured a cruel disease, discovers his pain by a cry extorted from him by a more severe attack, and by the cold sweat that covers his brow.

"I have already discovered," said Cador, "the sentiments which thou wouldst fain conceal from thyself. The symptoms by which the passions show themselves are certain and infallible. Judge, my dear Zadig, since I have read thy heart, whether the king will not discover something in it that may give him offence. He has no other fault but that of being the most jealous man in the world. Thou canst resist the violence of thy passion with greater fortitude than the queen, because thou art a philosopher, and because thou art Zadig. Astarte is a woman. She suffers her eyes to speak with so much the more imprudence, as she does not as yet think herself guilty. Conscious of her own innocence, she unhappily neglects those external appearances which are so necessary. I shall tremble for her so long as she has nothing wherewithal to reproach herself. A growing passion which we endeavor to suppress, discovers itself in spite of all our efforts to the contrary.

Meanwhile, the queen mentioned the name of Zadig so frequently, and with such a blushing and downcast look. She was sometimes so lively, and sometimes so perplexed, when she spoke to him in the king's presence, and was seized with such a deep thoughtfulness at his going away, that the king began to be troubled. He believed all that he saw, and imagined all that he did not see. He particularly remarked, that his wife's shoes were blue, and that Zadig's shoes were blue; that his wife's ribbons were yellow, and that Zadig's bonnet was yellow, and these were terrible symptoms to a prince of so much delicacy. In his jealous mind suspicion was turned into certainty.

All the slaves of kings and queens are so many spies over their hearts. They soon observed that Astarte was tender, and that Moabdar was jealous. The envious man persuaded his wife to send anonymously to the king her garter, which resembled those of the queen; and to complete the misfortune, this garter was blue. The monarch now thought of nothing but in what manner he might best execute his vengeance. He one night resolved to poison the queen, and in the morning to put Zadig to death by the bowstring. The orders were given to a merciless eunuch, who commonly executed his acts of vengeance.

There happened at that time to be in the king's chamber a little dwarf, who, though dumb, was not deaf. He was allowed, on account of his insignificance, to go wherever he pleased; and, as a domestic animal, was a witness of what passed in the most profound secrecy.

This little mute was strongly attached to the queen and Zadig. With equal horror and surprise, he heard the cruel orders given; but how could he prevent the fatal sentence that in a few hours was to be carried into execution? He could not write, but he could paint; and excelled particularly in drawing a striking resemblance. He employed a part of the night in sketching out with his pencil what he meant to impart to the queen. The piece represented the king in one corner, boiling with rage, and giving orders to the eunuch; a blue bowstring, and a bowl on a table, with blue garters and yellow ribbons; the queen in the middle of the picture, expiring in the arms of her woman, and Zadig strangled at her feet. The horizon represented a rising sun, to express that this shocking execution was to be performed in the morning. As soon as he had finished the picture, he ran to one of Astarte's women, awoke her, and made her understand that she must immediately carry it to the queen.

At midnight a messenger knocks at Zadig's door, awakes him, and gives him a note from the queen. He doubts whether it is not a dream; and opens the letter with a trembling hand. But how great was his surprise, and who can express the consternation and despair into which he was thrown upon reading these words? "Fly, this instant, or thou art a dead man! Fly, Zadig, I conjure thee by our mutual love and my yellow ribbons. I have not been guilty, but I find that I must die like a criminal."

Zadig was hardly able to speak. He sent for Cador, and, without uttering a word, gave him the note. Cador forced him to obey, and forthwith to take the road to Memphis.

"Shouldst thou dare," said he, "to go in search of the queen, thou wilt hasten her death. Shouldst thou speak to the king, thou wilt infallibly ruin her. I will take upon me the charge of her destiny; follow thy own. I will spread a report that thou hast taken the road to India. I will soon follow thee, and inform thee of all that shall have passed in Babylon."

At that instant, Cador caused two of the swiftest dromedaries to be brought to a private gate of the palace. Upon one of these he mounted Zadig, whom he was obliged to carry to the door, and who was ready to expire with grief. He was accompanied by a single domestic, and Cador, plunged in sorrow and astonishment, soon lost sight of his friend.

This illustrious fugitive arriving on the side of a hill, from whence he could take a view of Babylon, turned his eyes toward the queen's palace, and fainted away at the sight; nor did he recover his senses but to shed a torrent of tears, and to wish for death. At length, after his thoughts had been long engrossed in lamenting the unhappy fate of the loveliest woman and the greatest queen in the world, he for a moment turned his views on himself, and cried:

"What then is human life? O virtue, how hast thou served me? Two women have basely deceived me; and now a third, who is innocent, and more beautiful than both the others, is going to be put to death! Whatever good I have done hath been to me a continual source of calamity and affliction; and I have only been raised to the height of grandeur, to be tumbled down the most horrid precipice of misfortune."

Filled with these gloomy reflections, his eyes overspread with the veil of grief, his countenance covered with the paleness of death, and his soul plunged in an abyss of the blackest despair, he continued his journey toward Egypt.

IX.

THE WOMAN BEATER.

Zadig directed his course by the stars. The constellation of Orion, and the splendid Dogstars, guided his steps toward the pole of Canopæa. He admired those vast globes of light which appear to our eyes as so many little sparks, while the earth, which in reality is only an imperceptible point in nature, appears to our fond imaginations as something so grand and noble. He then represented to himself the human species, as it really is, as a parcel of insects devouring one another on a little atom of clay. This true image seemed to annihilate his misfortunes, by making him sensible of the nothingness of his own being, and that of Babylon. His soul launched out into infinity, and detached from the senses, contemplated the immutable order of the universe. But when afterward, returning to himself, and entering into his own heart, he considered that Astarte had perhaps died for him, the universe vanished from his sight, and he beheld nothing in the whole compass of nature but Astarte expiring, and Zadig unhappy.

While he thus alternately gave up his mind to this flux and reflux of sublime philosophy and intolerable grief, he advanced toward the frontiers of Egypt; and his faithful domestic was already in the first village, in search of a lodging.

Meanwhile, as Zadig was walking toward the gardens that skirted the village, he saw, at a small distance from the highway, a woman bathed in tears and calling heaven and earth to her assistance, and a man in a furious passion pursuing her.

This madman had already overtaken the woman, who embraced his knees, notwithstanding which he loaded her with blows and reproaches. Zadig judged by the frantic behavior of the Egyptian, and by the repeated pardons which the lady asked him, that the one was jealous, and the other unfaithful. But when he surveyed the woman more narrowly, and found her to be a lady of exquisite beauty, and even to have a strong resemblance to the unhappy Astarte, he felt himself inspired with compassion for her, and horror toward the Egyptian.

"Assist me," cried she to Zadig, with the deepest sighs, "deliver me from the hands of the most barbarous man in the world. Save my life."

Moved by these pitiful cries, Zadig ran and threw himself between her and the barbarian. As he had some knowledge of the Egyptian language, he addressed him in that tongue.

"If," said he, "thou hast any humanity, I conjure thee to pay some regard to her beauty and weakness. How canst thou behave in this outrageous manner to one of the masterpieces of nature, who lies at thy feet, and hath no defence but her tears?"

"Ah, ah!" replied the madman, "thou art likewise in love with her. I must be revenged on thee too."

So saying, he left the lady, whom he had hitherto held with his hand twisted in her hair, and taking his lance attempted to stab the stranger. Zadig, who was in cold blood, easily eluded the blow aimed by the frantic Egyptian. He seized the lance near the iron with which it was armed. The Egyptian strove to draw it back; Zadig to wrest it from the Egyptian; and in the struggle it was broken in two. The Egyptian draws his sword; Zadig does the same. They attack each other. The former gives a hundred blows at random; the latter wards them off with great dexterity. The lady, seated on a turf, readjusts her head-dress, and looks at the combatants. The Egyptian excelled in strength: Zadig in address. The one fought like a man whose arm was directed by his judgment; the other like a madman, whose blind rage made him deal his blows at random. Zadig closes with him, and disarms him; and while the Egyptian, now become more furious, endeavors to throw himself upon him, he seizes him, presses him close, and throws him down; and then holding his sword to his breast, offers him his life. The Egyptian, frantic with rage, draws his poniard, and wounds Zadig at the very instant that the conqueror was granting a pardon. Zadig, provoked at such brutal behavior, plunged his sword in the bosom of the Egyptian, who giving a horrible shriek and a violent struggle, instantly expired. Zadig then approached the lady, and said to her with a gentle tone:

"He hath forced me to kill him. I have avenged thy cause. Thou art now delivered from the most violent man I ever saw. What further, madam, wouldest thou have me do for thee?

"Die, villain," replied she, "thou hast killed my lover. O that I were able to tear out thy heart!"

"Why truly, madam," said Zadig, "thou hadst a strange kind of a man for a lover; he beat thee with all his might, and would have killed thee, because thou hadst entreated me to give thee assistance."

"I wish he were beating me still," replied the lady with tears and lamentation. "I well deserved it; for I had given him cause to be jealous. Would to heaven that he was now beating me, and that thou wast in his place."

Zadig, struck with surprise, and inflamed with a higher degree of resentment than he had ever felt before, said:

"Beautiful as thou art, madam, thou deservest that I should beat thee in my turn for thy perverse and impertinent behavior. But I shall not give myself the trouble."

So saying, he remounted his camel, and advanced toward the town. He had proceeded but a few steps, when he turned back at the noise of four Babylonian couriers, who came riding at full gallop. One of them, upon seeing the woman, cried:

"It is the very same. She resembles the description that was given us."

They gave themselves no concern about the dead Egyptian, but instantly seized the lady. She called out to Zadig:

"Help me once more, generous stranger. I ask pardon for having complained of thy conduct. Deliver me again, and I will be thine for ever."

Zadig was no longer in the humor of fighting for her.

"Apply to another," said he, "thou shalt not again ensnare me in thy wiles."

Besides, he was wounded; his blood was still flowing, and he himself had need of assistance: and the sight of four Babylonians, probably sent by King Moabdar, filled him with apprehension. He therefore hastened toward the village, unable to comprehend why four Babylonian couriers should come and seize this Egyptian woman, but still more astonished at the lady's behavior.

X.

SLAVERY.

As he entered the Egyptian village, he saw himself surrounded by the people. Every one said:

"This is the man who carried off the beautiful Missouf, and assassinated Clitofis."

"Gentleman," said he, "God preserve me from carrying off your beautiful Missouf. She is too capricious for me. And with regard to Clitofis, I did not assassinate him, I only fought with him in my own defence. He endeavored to kill me, because I humbly interceded for the beautiful Missouf, whom he beat most unmercifully. I am a stranger, come to seek refuge in Egypt; and it is not likely, that in coming to implore your protection, I should begin by carrying off a woman, and assassinating a man."

The Egyptians were then just and humane. The people conducted Zadig to the town-house. They first of all ordered his wound to be dressed, and then examined him and his servant apart, in order to discover the truth. They found that Zadig was not an assassin; but as he was guilty of having killed a man, the law condemned him to be a slave. His two camels were sold for the benefit of the town: all the gold he had brought with him was distributed among the inhabitants; and his person, as well as that of the companion of his journey, was exposed for sale in the market-place. An Arabian merchant, named Setoc, made the purchase; but as the servant was fitter for labor than the master, he was sold at a higher price. There was no comparison between the two men. Thus Zadig became a slave subordinate to his own servant. They were linked together by a chain fastened to their feet, and in this condition they followed the Arabian merchant to his house.

By the way Zadig comforted his servant, and exhorted him to patience; but he could not help making, according to his usual custom, some reflections on human life. "I see," said he, "that the unhappiness of my fate hath an influence on thine. Hitherto everything has turned out to me in a most unaccountable manner. I have been condemned to pay a fine for having seen the marks of a bitch's feet. I thought that I should once have been empaled alive on account of a griffin. I have been sent to execution for having made some verses in praise of the king. I have been on the point of being strangled, because the queen had yellow ribbons; and now I am a slave with thee, because a brutal wretch beat his mistress. Come, let us keep a good heart; all this will perhaps have an end. The Arabian merchants must necessarily have slaves; and why not me as well as another, since, as well as another, I am a man? This merchant will not be cruel. He must treat his slaves well if he expects any advantage from them."

But while he spoke thus, his heart was entirely engrossed by the fate of the queen of Babylon.

Two days after, the merchant Setoc set out for Arabia Deserta, with his slaves and his camels. His tribe dwelt near the desert of Oreb. The journey was long and painful. Setoc set a much greater value on the servant than the master, because the former was more expert in loading the camels, and all the little marks of distinction were shown to him. A camel having died within two days journey of Oreb, his burden was divided and laid on the backs of the servants; and Zadig had his share among the rest. Setoc laughed to see all his slaves walking with their bodies inclined. Zadig took the liberty to explain to him the cause, and inform him of the laws of the balance. The merchant was astonished, and began to regard him with other eyes. Zadig, finding he had raised his curiosity, increased it still further by acquainting him with many things that related to commerce; the specific gravity of metals and commodities under an equal bulk; the properties of several useful animals; and the means of rendering those useful that are not naturally so.

At last Setoc began to consider Zadig as a sage, and preferred him to his companion, whom he had formerly so much esteemed. He treated him well, and had no cause to repent of his kindness.

As soon as Setoc arrived among his own tribe he demanded the payment of five hundred ounces of silver, which he had lent to a Jew in presence of two witnesses; but as the witnesses were dead, and the debt could not be proved, the Hebrew appropriated the merchant's money to himself, and piously thanked God for putting it in his power to cheat an Arabian. Setoc imparted this troublesome affair to Zadig, who had now become his counsel.

"In what place," said Zadig, "didst thou lend the five hundred ounces to this infidel?"

"Upon a large stone," replied the merchant, "that lies near the mountain of Oreb."

"What is the character of thy debter?" said Zadig.

"That of a knave," returned Setoc.

"But I ask thee, whether he is lively or phlegmatic; cautious or imprudent?"

"He is, of all bad payers," said Setoc, "the most lively fellow I ever knew."

"Well," resumed Zadig, "allow me to plead thy cause."

In effect, Zadig having summoned the Jew to the tribunal, addressed the judge in the following terms:

"Pillow of the throne of equity, I come to demand of this man, in the name of my master, five hundred ounces of silver, which he refuses to repay."

"Hast thou any witnesses?" said the judge.

"No, they are dead; but there remains a large stone upon which the money was counted; and if it please thy grandeur to order the stone to be sought for, I hope that it will bear witness. The Hebrew and I will tarry here till the stone arrives. I will send for it at my master's expense."

"With all my heart," replied the judge, and immediately applied himself to the discussion of other affairs.

When the court was going to break up, the judge said to Zadig:

"Well, friend, hath not thy stone yet arrived?"

The Hebrew replied with a smile:

"Thy grandeur may stay here till to-morrow, and after all not see the stone. It is more than six miles from hence and it would require fifteen men to move it."

"Well," cried Zadig, "did I not say that the stone would bear witness? Since this man knows where it is, he thereby confesses that it was upon it that the money was counted."

The Hebrew was disconcerted, and was soon after obliged to confess the truth. The judge ordered him to be fastened to the stone, without meat or drink, till he should restore the five hundred ounces, which were soon after paid.

The slave Zadig and the stone were held in great repute in Arabia.

XI.

THE FUNERAL PILE.

Setoc, charmed with the happy issue of this affair, made his slave his intimate friend. He had now conceived as great an esteem for him as ever the king of Babylon had done; and Zadig was glad that Setoc had no wife. He discovered in his master a good natural disposition, much probity of heart, and a great share of good sense; but he was sorry to see that, according to the ancient custom of Arabia, he adored the host of heaven; that is, the sun, moon, and stars. He sometimes spoke to him on this subject with great prudence and discretion. At last he told him that these bodies were like all other bodies in the universe, and no more deserving of our homage than a tree or a rock.

"But," said Setoc, "they are eternal beings; and it is from them we derive all we enjoy. They animate nature; they regulate the seasons; and, besides, are removed at such an immense distance from us, that we cannot help revering them."

"Thou receivest more advantage," replied Zadig, "from the waters of the Red Sea, which carry thy merchandize to the Indies. Why may not it be as ancient as the stars? and if thou adorest what is placed at a distance from thee, thou shouldest adore the land of the Gangarides, which lies at the extremity of the earth."

"No," said Setoc, "the brightness of the stars commands my adoration."

At night Zadig lighted up a great number of candles in the tent where he was to sup with Setoc; and the moment his patron appeared, he fell on his knees before these lighted tapers, and said:

"Eternal and shining luminaries! be ye always propitious to me."

Having thus said, he sat down at the table, without taking the least notice of Setoc.

"What art thou doing?" said Setoc in amaze.

"I act like thee," replied Zadig, "I adore these candles, and neglect their master and mine."

Setoc comprehended the profound sense of this apologue. The wisdom of his slave sunk deep into his soul. He no longer offered incense to the creatures, but he adored the eternal Being who made them.

There prevailed at that time in Arabia a shocking custom, sprung originally from Scythia, and which, being established in the Indies by the credit of the Brahmins, threatened to over-run all the East. When a married man died, and his beloved wife aspired to the character of a saint, she burned herself publicly on the body of her husband. This was a solemn feast, and was called the Funeral Pile of Widowhood; and that tribe in which most women had been burned was the most respected. An Arabian of Setoc's tribe being dead, his widow, whose name was Almona, and who was very devout, published the day and hour when she intended to throw herself into the fire, amidst the sound of drums and trumpets.

Zadig remonstrated against this horrible custom. He showed Setoc how inconsistent it was with the happiness of mankind to suffer young widows to burn themselves—widows who were capable of giving children to the state, or at least of educating those they already had; and he convinced him that it was his duty to do all that lay in his power to abolish such a barbarous practice.

"The women," said Setoc, "have possessed the right of burning themselves for more than a thousand years; and who shall dare to abrogate a law which time hath rendered sacred? Is there anything more respectable than ancient abuses?"

"Reason is more ancient," replied Zadig: "meanwhile, speak thou to the chiefs of the tribes, and I will go to wait on the young widow."

Accordingly, he was introduced to her, and after having insinuated himself into her good graces by some compliments on her beauty, and told her what a pity it was to commit so many charms to the flames, he at last praised her for her constancy and courage.

"Thou must surely have loved thy husband," said he to her, "with the most passionate fondness."

"Who, I?" replied the lady, "I loved him not at all. He was a brutal, jealous, and insupportable wretch; but I am firmly resolved to throw myself on his funeral pile."

The funeral pyre.—"*The women,*" said Setoc, "*have possessed the right of burning themselves for more than a thousand years; and who shall dare to abrogate a law which time hath rendered sacred? Is there anything more respectable than ancient abuses?*"

"It would appear then," said Zadig, "that there must be a very delicious pleasure in being burnt alive."

"Oh! it makes me shudder," replied the lady, "but that must be overlooked. I am a devotee; I should lose my reputation; and all the world would despise me, if I did not burn myself."

Zadig having made her acknowledge that she burned herself to gain the good opinion of others, and to gratify her own vanity, entertained her with a long discourse calculated to make her a little in love with life, and even went so far as to inspire her with some degree of good will for the person who spoke to her.

"And what wilt thou do at last," said he, "if the vanity of burning thyself should not continue?"

"Alas!" said the lady, "I believe I should desire thee to marry me."

Zadig's mind was too much engrossed with the idea of Astarte not to elude this declaration; but he instantly went to the chiefs of the tribes, told them what had passed, and advised them to make a law by which a widow should not be permitted to burn herself, till she had conversed privately with a young man for the space of an hour. Since that time not a single widow hath burned herself in Arabia. They were indebted to Zadig alone for destroying in one day a cruel custom that had lasted for so many ages; and thus he became the benefactor of Arabia.

XII.

THE SUPPER.

Setoc, who could not separate himself from this man in whom dwelt wisdom, carried Zadig to the great fair of Balzora, whither the richest merchants of the earth resorted. Zadig was highly pleased to see so many men of different countries united in the same place. He considered the whole universe as one large family assembled at Balzora. The second day he sat at table with an Egyptian, an Indian, an inhabitant of Cathay, a Greek, a Celtic, and several other strangers, who, in their frequent voyages to the Arabian Gulf, had learned enough of the Arabic to make themselves understood.

The Egyptian seemed to be in a violent passion. "What an abominable country," said he, "is Balzora! They refuse me a thousand ounces of gold on the best security in the world."

"How!" said Setoc. "On what security have they refused thee this sum?"

"On the body of my aunt," replied the Egyptian. "She was the most notable woman in Egypt; she always accompanied me in my journeys; she died on the road. I have converted her into one of the nest mummies in the world; and in my own country I could obtain any amount by giving her as a pledge. It is very strange that they will not here lend me a thousand ounces of gold on such a solid security."

Angry as he was, he was going to help himself to a bit of excellent boiled fowl, when the Indian, taking him by the hand, cried out in a sorrowful tone, "Ah! what art thou going to do?"

"To eat a bit of this fowl," replied the man who owned the mummy.

"Take care that thou dost not," replied the Indian. "It is possible that the soul of the deceased may have passed into this fowl; and thou wouldst not, surely, expose thyself to the danger of eating thy aunt? To boil fowls is a manifest outrage on nature."

"What dost thou mean by thy nature and thy fowls?" replied the choleric Egyptian. "We adore a bull, and yet we eat heartily of beef."

"You adore a bull! is it possible?" said the Indian.

"Nothing is more possible," returned the other; "we have done so for these hundred and thirty-five thousand years; and nobody amongst us has ever found fault with it."

"A hundred and thirty-five thousand years!" said the Indian. "This account is a little exaggerated. It is but eighty thousand years since India was first peopled, and we are surely more ancient than you are. Brahma prohibited our eating of ox-flesh before you thought of putting it on your spits or altars."

Oannes—the Fish God.—"*Thou art mistaken,*" *said a Chaldean.* "*It is to the fish Oannes that we owe these great advantages; and it is just that we should render homage to none but him. All the world will tell thee, that he is a divine being, with a golden tail, and a beautiful human head; and that for three hours every day he left the water to preach on dry land.*"

OANNES—THE FISH AVATAR.

"The accompanying engraving of the fish-god is from a drawing by Gentil, given in *Calmet's Dictionary*. The god was worshiped under the name of Dagon by the Syrians, and Oannes by the Chaldeans. The image represented the body of a fish with the head and arms of a man; and while all figures of the god are not exactly alike, they all combine a human form with that of a fish.

"Owing to the precession of the equinoxes," says the Rev. Mr. Maurice in the *Antiquities of India*, "after the rate of seventy-two years to a degree, a total alteration has taken place through all the signs of the ecliptic, insomuch that those stars which formerly were in Aries have now got into Taurus, and those of Taurus into Gemini. Now the vernal equinox, after the rate of that precession, could not have coincided with the first of May less than 4000 years before Christ."

An Avatar in the form of the celestial *Taurus* (♉) then occurred, and Osiris was worshiped in the form of a bull, by credulous believers. Next in the course of revolving years, we have the celestial *Aries*, (♈) and the god then became incarnate in the form of a lamb, and in that form received the adoration of devout multitudes. Later still the Zodiacal sign had progressed to *Pisces*, (♓) and mankind were then called upon to worship the astrological emblem of the amphibious being called Oannes—the sacred god of the land and the sea—whose representative on earth still claims to be the *Great Fisherman*, and who has entangled in the meshes of his net of faith the intellects and consciences of innumerable devotees.

"In Berosus and other authors," says Godfrey Higgins in the *Anacalypsis*, "the being half man, half fish, called Oannes, is said to have come out of the Erythræan Sea, and to have taught the Babylonians all kinds of useful knowledge. This is clearly the fish Avatar of India; whether or not it be the I-oannes of Jonas I leave to the reader. I apprehend it is the same as the Dagon of Pegu and the fish sign of the Zodiac. Very little is known about it, but it exactly answers the description of an Avatar.

"The apostles of Jesus, I believe, were most of them fishermen. There are many stories of miraculous draughts of fish, and other matters connected with fishes, in the Gospel histories; and Peter, the son of John, I-oannes or Oannes, the great fisherman, inherited the power of ruling the church from the Lamb of God. The fisherman succeeded to the shepherd. The Pope calls himself the great fisherman, and boasts of the contents of his Poitrine.

"In the Pentateuch, which is the sacred book of the Israelites, we meet with no Dagon, Fish or God. But we do meet with it in the book of Judges. I believe this Dagon to be the fish Avatar of India—the Dagon of Syrian in Pegu; in fact the emblem of the entrance of the sun into Pisces.

"In the earliest time, perhaps, of which we have any history, God the creator was adored under the form or emblem of a Bull. After that, we read of him under the form of a calf or two calves, afterward in the form of the Ram and the Lamb, and the devotees were called lambs: then came the fish or two fishes. It is a fact, not a theory, that he was called a fish, and that the devotees were called Pisciculi or little fishes. I suppose few persons will attribute these appearances of system to accident. As we have *lambs* and *little fishes* in the followers of the Ram, Aries, and the constellation Pisces, it is only in character to have the followers of the Bull called *calves*, and I am by no means certain that we have not them in the Cyclops.

"At first, no doubt, my reader will be very much surprised at the idea of the devotees having converted Jesus into the *fish* Avatar: but why was he called the lamb? And why were his followers called his flock, and his sheep, and his lambs? Not many circumstances are more striking than that of Jesus Christ being originally worshiped under the form of a Lamb—the actual lamb of God which taketh away the sins of the world. It does not appear to me to be more extraordinary that his followers, as it is admitted that they did, should call him a *fish* and the believers in him pisciculi, than that they should call him a lamb, and his followers lambs. He was originally represented as a lamb until one of the popes changed his effigy to that of a man on a cross. Applying the astronomical emblem of Pisces ($\mathcal{H}$) to Jesus, does not s seem more absurd than applying the astronomical symbol of the Lamb (Υ). They applied to him the monogram of Bacchus, IHΣ; the astrological and alchymical mark or sign of Aries, or the Ram (Υ) and, in short, what was there that was Heathenish that they have not applied to him? They have actually loaded his simple and sublime religion with every absurdity of Gentilism. I know not one absurdity that can be excepted."

In one of the windows of the Magnificent Cathedral of the Incarnation, erected by Mrs. A.T. Stewart, at Garden City, N.Y., is a painting representing the Sea of Tiberias. The "risen Lord," clothed in rich robes of green, scarlet, and gold, is standing on the seashore, with four of the apostles. Prominent among them is the *great fisherman* St. Peter, who is grasping the end of a seine. In the background is seen the mast and rigging of a fishing boat. At the feet of Christ a fire is burning, and on the coals are *two fishes*, like the two fishes in the Zodiacal sign *Pisces* (♓). The artist has thus reproduced the ancient myth, regardless of its astrological origin, and the mythical fishes of the zodiac, with other ancient Pagan emblems, now symbolize Christian faith in the so-called Cathedral of the Incarnation.—E.

"This Brahma of yours," said the Egyptian, "is a pleasant sort of an animal, truly, to compare with our Apis. What great things hath your Brahma done?"

"It was he," replied the Brahmin, "that taught mankind to read and write, and to whom the world is indebted for the game of chess."

"Thou art mistaken," said a Chaldean who sat near him. "It is to the fish Oannes that we owe these great advantages; and it is just that we should render homage to none but him. All the world will tell thee, that he is a divine being, with a golden tail, and a beautiful human head; and that for three hours every day he left the water to preach on dry land. He had several children, who were kings, as every one knows. I have a picture of him at home, which I worship with becoming reverence. We may eat as much beef as we please; but it is surely a great sin to dress fish for the table. Besides, you are both of an origin too recent and ignoble to dispute with me. The Egyptians reckon only a hundred and thirty-five thousand years, and the Indians but eighty thousand, while we have almanacs of four thousand ages. Believe me; renounce your follies; and I will give to each of you a beautiful picture of Oannes."

The man of Cathay took up the discourse, and said:

"I have a great respect for the Egyptians, the Chaldeans, the Greeks, the Celtics, Brahma, the bull Apis, and the beautiful fish Oannes; but I could think that Li, or Tien, as he is commonly called, is superior to all the bulls on the earth, or all the fish in the sea. I shall say nothing of my native country; it is as large as Egypt, Chaldea, and the Indies put together. Neither shall I dispute about the antiquity of our nation; because it is of little consequence whether we are ancient or not; it is enough if we are happy. But were it necessary to speak of almanacs, I could say that all Asia takes ours, and that we had very good ones before arithmetic was known in Chaldea."

"Ignorant men, as ye all are," said the Greek; "do you not know that Chaos is the father of all; and that form and matter have put the world into its present condition?"

The Greek spoke for a long time, but was at last interrupted by the Celtic, who, having drank pretty deeply while the rest were disputing, imagined he was now more knowing than all the others, and said, with an oath, that there were none but Teutat and the mistletoe of the oak that were worth the trouble of a dispute; that, for his own part, he had always some mistletoe in his pocket, and that the Scythians, his ancestors, were the only men of merit that had ever appeared in the world; that it was true they had sometimes eaten human flesh, but that, notwithstanding this circumstance, his nation deserved to be held in great esteem; and that, in fine, if any one spoke ill of Teutat, he would teach him better manners.

The quarrel had now become warm, and Setoc feared the table would be stained with blood.

Zadig, who had been silent during the whole dispute, arose at last. He first addressed himself to the Celtic, as the most furious of the disputants. He told him that he had reason on his side, and begged a few mistletoes. He then praised the Greek for his eloquence, and softened all their exasperated spirits. He said but little to the man of Cathay, because he had been the most reasonable of them all. At last he said:

"You were going, my friends, to quarrel about nothing; for you are all of one mind."

At this assertion they all cried out in dissent.

"Is it not true," said he to the Celtic, "that you adore not this mistletoe, but him that made both the mistletoe and the oak?"

"Most undoubtedly," replied the Celtic.

"And thou, Mr. Egyptian, dost not thou revere, in a certain bull, him who created the bulls?"

"Yes," said the Egyptian.

"The fish Oannes," continued he, "must yield to him who made the sea and the fishes. The Indian and the Cathaian," added he, "acknowledge a first principle. I did not fully comprehend the admirable things that were said by the Greek; but I am sure he will admit a superior being on whom form and matter depend."

The Greek, whom they all admired, said that Zadig had exactly taken his meaning.

"You are all then," replied Zadig, "of one opinion and have no cause to quarrel."

All the company embraced him.

Setoc, after having sold his commodities at a very high price, returned to his own tribe with his friend Zadig; who learned, upon his arrival, that he had been tried in his absence and was now going to be burned by a slow fire.

XIII.

THE RENDEZVOUS.

During his journey to Balzora the priests of the stars had resolved to punish Zadig. The precious stones and ornaments of the young widows whom they sent to the funeral pile belonged to them of right; and the least they could now do was to burn Zadig for the ill office he had done them. Accordingly they accused him of entertaining erroneous sentiments of the heavenly host. They deposed against him, and swore that they had heard him say that the stars did not set in the sea. This horrid blasphemy made the judges tremble; they were ready to tear their garments upon hearing these impious words; and they would certainly have torn them had Zadig had wherewithal to pay them for new ones. But, in the excess of their zeal and indignation, they contented themselves with condemning him to be burnt by a slow fire. Setoc, filled with despair at this unhappy event, employed all his interest to save his friend, but in vain. He was soon obliged to hold his peace. The young widow, Almona, who had now conceived a great fondness for life, for which she was obliged to Zadig, resolved to deliver him from the funeral pile, of the abuse of which he had fully convinced her. She resolved the scheme in her own mind, without imparting it to any person whatever. Zadig was to be executed the next day. If she could save him at all, she must do it that very night; and the method taken by this charitable and prudent lady was as follows:

She perfumed herself, she heightened her beauty by the richest and gayest apparel, and went to demand an audience of the chief priest of the stars. As soon as she was introduced to the venerable old man, she addressed him in these terms:

"Eldest son of the great bear, brother of the bull, and cousin of the great dog, (such were the titles of this pontiff,) I come to acquaint thee with my scruples. I am much afraid that I have committed a heinous crime in not burning myself on the funeral pile of my dear husband; for, indeed, what had I worth preserving? Perishable flesh, thou seest, that is already entirely withered." So saying, she drew up her long sleeves of silk, and showed her naked arms, which were of an elegant shape and a dazzling whiteness. "Thou seest," said she, that these are little worth. The priest found in his heart that they were worth a great deal. He swore that he had never in his life seen such beautiful arms. "Alas!" said the widow, "my arms, perhaps, are not so bad as the rest; but thou wilt confess that my neck is not worthy of the least regard." She then discovered the most charming neck that nature had ever formed. Compared to it a rose-bud on an apple of ivory would have appeared like madder on the box-tree, and the whiteness of new-washed lambs would have seemed of a dusky yellow. Her large black eyes, languishing with the gentle lustre of a tender fire; her cheeks animated with the finest pink, mixed with the whiteness of milk; her nose, which had no resemblance to the tower of Mount Lebanon; her lips, like two borders of coral, inclosing the nest pearls in the Arabian Sea; all conspired to make the old man fancy and believe that he was young again. Almona, seeing his admiration, now entreated him to pardon Zadig. "Alas!" said he, "my charming lady, should I grant thee his pardon, it would be of no service, as it must necessarily be signed by three others, my brethren." "Sign it, however," said Almona. "With all my heart," said the priest. "Be pleased to visit me," said Almona, "when the bright star of Sheat shall appear in the horizon."

Almona then went to the second pontiff. He assured her that the sun, the moon, and all the luminaries of heaven, were but glimmering meteors in comparison to her charms. She asked the same favor of him, and he also granted it readily. She then appointed the second pontiff to meet her at the rising of the star Algenib. From thence she went to the third and fourth priest, always taking their signatures, and making an appointment from star to star. She then sent a message to the judges, entreating them to come to her house on an affair of great importance. They obeyed her summons. She showed them the four names, and told them that the priests had granted the pardon of Zadig. Each of the pontiffs arrived at the hour appointed. Each was surprised at finding his brethren there, but still more at seeing the judges also present. Zadig was saved; and Setoc was so charmed with the skill and address of Almona that he at once made her his wife.

Almona.—Almona, seeing his admiration, now entreated him to pardon Zadig. "*Alas!*" said he, "*my charming lady, should I grant thee his pardon, it would be of no service, as it must necessarily be signed by three others, my brethren. Sign it, however,*" said Almona.

Business affairs now required Setoc's presence in the island of Serendib; but during the first month of his marriage—the month which is called the honeymoon—he could not permit himself to leave Almona, nor even to think he could ever leave her, and he requested Zadig to make the journey in his place. "Alas!" said Zadig, "must I put a still greater distance between the beautiful Astarte and myself? But it would be ungrateful not to serve my friend, and I will endeavor to do my duty."

Setoc and Zadig now took leave of each other with tears in their eyes, both swearing an eternal friendship, and promising to always share their fortunes with each other. Zadig then, after having thrown himself at the feet of his fair deliverer, set out on his journey to Serendib, still musing on the unhappy Astarte, and meditating on the severity of fortune, which seemed to persistently make him the sport of her cruelty and the object of her persecution.

"What!" said he to himself, "fined four hundred ounces of gold for having observed a bitch! condemned to lose my head for four bad verses in praise of the king! sentenced to be strangled because the queen had shoes the color of my turban! reduced to slavery for having succored a woman who was beaten! and on the point of being burned for having saved the lives of all the young widows of Arabia!"

XIII.(1)

THE DANCE.

Arriving in due time at the island of Serendib, Zadig's merits were at once recognized, and he was popularly regarded as an extraordinary man. He became the friend of the wise and learned, the arbitrator of disputes, and the advisor of the small number of those who were willing to take advice. He was duly presented to the king, who was pleased with his affability, and soon chose him for his friend. But this royal favor caused Zadig to tremble; for he well remembered the misfortunes which the kindness of king Moabdar had formerly brought upon him. "I please the king," said he; "shall I not therefore be lost?" Still he could not refuse the king's friendship, for it must be confessed that Nabussan, king of Serendib, son of Nassanab, son of Nabassun, son of Sanbusna, was one of the most amiable princes in Asia.

But this good prince was always flattered, deceived, and robbed. It was a contest who should most pillage the royal treasury. The example set by the receiver-general of Serendib was universally followed by the inferior officers.

This the king knew. He had often changed his treasurers, but had never been able to change the established custom of dividing the revenues into two unequal parts, of which the smaller came to his majesty, and the larger to his officers.

This custom Nabussan explained to Zadig. "You, whose knowledge embraces so many subjects," said he, "can you not tell me how to select a treasurer who will not rob me?" "Assuredly," said Zadig; "I know a sure method for finding you a man who will keep his hands clean."

The king was charmed, and asked, while he embraced him, how this was to be done.

"You have only," said Zadig, "to cause all those who apply for the office of treasurer to dance. He who dances the lightest will surely prove to be the most honest man."

"You jest," said the king. "A strange way, certainly, of choosing a receiver of my revenues. What! do you pretend that he who cuts the neatest caper will be the most just and skillful financier?"

"I will not answer," returned Zadig, "for his being the most skillful, but I assure you he will be the most honest."

Zadig spoke with so much confidence that the king imagined he had some supernatural test for selecting honest financiers.

"I do not like the supernatural," said Zadig: "people and books dealing in prodigies have always displeased me. If your majesty will permit me to make the test, you will be convinced it is the easiest and simplest thing possible."

Nabussan consented, and was more astonished to hear that the test was simple, than if it had been claimed as a miracle.

"Leave all the details to me," said Zadig: "You will gain more by this trial than you imagine."

The same day he made proclamation in the king's name, that all candidates for the office of receiver-in-chief of the revenues of his gracious majesty Nabussan, son of Nussanab, must present themselves in dresses of light silk, on the first day of the month of the crocodile, in the king's anti-chamber. The candidates came, accordingly, to the number of sixty-four. Musicians were placed in an adjoining room, and all was prepared for the dance. As the door of the saloon was closed, it was necessary, in order to enter it, to pass through a small gallery which was slightly darkened. An usher directed each candidate in succession through this obscure passage, in which he was left alone for some moments. The king, being aware of the plan, had temptingly spread out in this gallery many of his choicest treasures. When all the candidates were assembled in the saloon, the king ordered the band to play and the dance to begin. Never had dancers performed more unwillingly or with less grace. Their heads were down, their backs bent, their hands pressed to their sides.

"What rascals!" murmured Zadig.

One alone danced with grace and agility,—his head up, his look assured, his body erect, his arms free, his motions natural.

"Ah, the honest man, the excellent man!" cried Zadig.

The king embraced this upright dancer, appointed him treasurer, and punished all the others with the utmost justice, for each one had, while passing through the gallery, filled his pockets till he could hardly walk. His majesty was distressed at this exhibition of dishonesty, and regretted that among these sixty-four dancers there should be sixty-three thieves. This dark gallery was then named the Corridor of Temptation.

In Persia these sixty-three lords would have been impaled; in other countries a chamber of justice would have consumed in costs three times the money stolen, replacing nothing in the king's coffers; in yet another kingdom they would have been honorably acquitted, and the light dancer disgraced; in Serendib they were only sentenced to add to the public treasure, for Nabussan was very indulgent.

He was also very grateful, and willingly gave Zadig a larger sum than any treasurer had ever stolen from the revenue. This wealth Zadig used to send a courier to Babylon to learn the fate of queen Astarte. His voice trembled when directing the courier. His blood seemed to stagnate in his veins. His heart almost ceased to beat. His eyes were suffused with tears.

XIII.(2)

BLUE EYES.

After the courier had gone, Zadig returned to the palace; and forgetting that he was not in his own room, almost unconsciously uttered the word LOVE.

"Ah! love," exclaimed the king, "that is indeed the cause of my unhappiness. You have divined what it is that causes me pain. You are indeed a great man. I hope you will assist me in my search for a woman, perfect in all respects, and of whose affection I may feel assured. You have proved your ability for this service by selecting for me an honest financier, and I have entire confidence in your success."

Zadig, having recovered his composure, promised to serve the king in love as he had in finance, although the task seemed to him far more difficult.

"The body and the heart," said the king.

At these words Zadig could not refrain from interrupting his majesty: "You show good taste," said he, "by not saying the mind and the heart; for we hear nothing but these words in the talk of Babylon. We see nothing but books which treat of the heart and mind, written by people who have neither the one nor the other: but pardon me, sire, and deign to continue."

"I have in my palace," said the king, "one hundred women who are all called charming, graceful, beautiful, affectionate even, or pretending to be so when in my company; but I have too often realized that it is to the king of Serendib they pay court, and that they care very little for Nabussan. This pretended affection does not satisfy my desires. I would find a consort that loves me for myself, and who would willingly be all my own. For such a treasure I would joyfully barter the hundred beauties whose forced smiles afford me no delight. Let us see if out of these hundred queens you can select one true woman to bless me with her love."

Zadig replied to him as he had previously done in regard to the finances: "Sire, allow me to make the attempt, and permit me to again use the treasure formerly displayed in the Corridor of Temptation. I will render you a faithful account."

The king willingly acceded to this request, and permitted Zadig to do as he desired. He first chose thirty-three of the ugliest little hunchbacks that could be procured in Serendib, then thirty-three of the handsomest pages to be found, and, lastly, thirty-three bonzes, (priests), the most eloquent and robust he could select. He gave them all liberty to enter the king's private apartments in the palace, and secure a partner if they so desired. Each little hunchback had four thousand gold pieces given to him: and on the first day each had secured a companion. The pages, who had nothing to give but themselves, did not succeed in many cases until the end of two or three days. The priests had still more trouble in obtaining partners, but, finally, thirty-three devotees joined their fortunes with these pious suitors. The king, through the blinds which opened into his apartments, saw all these trials, and was astounded. Of these hundred women, ninety-nine discarded his protection. There still remained one, however, still quite young, with whom his majesty had never conversed. They sent to her one, two, three hunchbacks, who displayed before her twenty thousand pieces of gold. She still remained firm, and could not refrain from laughing at the idea of these cripples, that wealth could change their appearance. They then presented before her the two most beautiful pages. She said she thought the king was still more beautiful. They attacked her with the most eloquent of the priests, and afterward with the most audacious. She found the first a prattler, and could not perceive any merit in the second.

"The heart," said she, "is everything. I will never yield to the hunchbacks' gold, the pages' vanity, or the pompous prattle of the priests. I love only Nabussan, son of Nussanab, and I will wait until he condescends to love me in return."

The king was transported with joy, astonishment, and love. He took back all the money that had brought success to the hunchbacks, and made a present of it the beautiful Falide, which was the name of this charming lady. He gave her his heart, which she amply deserved, for never were glances from female eyes more brilliant than her own, nor the charms of youthful beauty more enchanting. Envy, it is true, asserted that she courtesied awkwardly; but candor compels the admission that she danced like the fairies, acted like the graces, sang like the sirens, and that she was in truth the very embodiment of intelligence and virtue. Nabussan loved and adored her; but, alas! she had BLUE EYES, and this apparently trivial fact was the cause of the gravest misfortunes.

There was an old law in Serendib forbidding the kings to marry those to whom the Greeks applied the word *Boῶπις*. [1] A high-priest had established this law thousands of years ago. He had anathematized blue eyes in order that he might secure for himself the hand of the king's favorite. The various orders of the empire now remonstrated with Nabussan for disregarding this organic law and loving the beautiful Falide. They publicly asserted that the last days of the kingdom had arrived—that this act of royal love was the height of sacrilege—that all nature was threatened with a sinister ending— and all because Nabussan, son of Nussanab, loved two magnificent blue eyes. The cripples, the capitalists, the bonzes and the brunettes filled the kingdom with their complaints.

The barbarians of the northern provinces profited by the general discontent. They invaded the territory of the good Nabussan and demanded a tribute from his subjects. The priests, who possessed half the revenues of the state, contented themselves with raising their hands to heaven, and refused to put them in their coffers to aid the king. They chanted beautiful prayers, and left the state a prey to the invaders.

"Oh! my dear Zadig," sadly cried Nabussan, "can you not rescue me from this impending danger?"

"Very willingly," replied Zadig: "you shall have for your defence as much money from the priests as you may desire. Leave, I pray you, without guard the property of the bonzes, and defend only your own possessions."

Nabussan wisely followed this advice. The priests became alarmed, threw themselves at his feet and implored his protection. The king replied with agreeable music, and chanted forth prayers and invocations to heaven with much sweetness and melody; finally, the priests reluctantly contributed the money, and the king brought the war to a happy termination.

Thus Zadig by his sensible advice and judicious services drew upon himself the enmity of the most powerful parties in the state. The bonzes and the brunettes swore to destroy him; the capitalists and the cripples did not spare him. They caused the good Nabussan to suspect him. "Services rendered often remain in the anti-chamber, and distrust enters into the cabinet." So said Zoroaster. Every day there were fresh accusations: the first is repelled; the second is lightly thought of; the third wounds; the fourth kills.

Zadig was dismayed, and having now satisfactorily arranged Setoc's affairs, he only thought of leaving the island in safety.

"But where shall I go?" said he. "If I remain in Serendib the priests will doubtless have me impaled; in Egypt I would probably be enslaved, burnt, according to all appearances, in Arabia; strangled in Babylon. However, I must learn what has become of Queen Astarte, and will go on and see what sad fate destiny has still in store for me."

[1] Having large, full, finely rounded eyes. In Homer, always applied to females, and most frequently to the goddess Juno, as a point of majestic beauty.—E.

XIV.

THE ROBBER.

Arriving on the frontiers which divide Arabia Petræa from Syria, he passed by a very strong castle from which a party of armed Arabians sallied forth. They instantly surrounded him and cried:

"All thou hast belongs to us, and thy person is the property of our master."

Zadig replied by drawing his sword; his servant, who was a man of courage, did the same. They killed the first Arabians that presumed to lay hands on them; and though the number was redoubled, they were not dismayed, but resolved to perish in the conflict. Two men defended themselves against a multitude; but such combat could not last long, the master of the castle, whose name was Arbogad, having observed from a window the prodigies of valor performed by Zadig, conceived a high esteem for this heroic stranger. He descended in haste, and went in person to call off his men and deliver the two travelers.

"All that passes over my lands," said he, "belongs to me, as well as what I find upon the lands of others; but thou seemest to be a man of such undaunted courage, that I will exempt thee from the common law."

He then conducted him to his castle, ordering his men to treat him well; and in the evening Arbogad supped with Zadig. The lord of the castle was one of those Arabians who are commonly called robbers; but he now and then performed some good actions amidst a multitude of bad ones. He robbed with a furious rapacity, and granted favors with great generosity. He was intrepid in action; affable in company; a debauchee at table, but gay in his debauchery; and particularly remarkable for his frank and open behavior. He was highly pleased with Zadig, whose lively conversation lengthened the repast. At last Arbogad said to him:

"I advise thee to enroll thy name in my catalogue. Thou canst not do better. This is not a bad trade, and thou mayest one day become what I am at present."

"May I take the liberty of asking thee," said Zadig, "how long thou hast followed this noble profession?"

"From my most tender youth," replied the lord, "I was servant to a petty, good-natured Arabian, but could not endure the hardships of my situation. I was vexed to find that fate had given me no share of the earth which equally belongs to all men. I imparted the cause of my uneasiness to an old Arabian, who said to me:

"'My son, do not despair; there was once a grain of sand that lamented that it was no more than a neglected atom in the deserts; at the end of a few years it became a diamond, and it is now the brightest ornament in the crown of the king of the Indies.'

Zadig and the brigand.—"*I advise thee to enroll thy name in my catalogue. Thou canst not do better,*" said the robber, "*This is not a bad trade, and thou mayest one day become what I am at present.*"

"This discourse made a deep impression on my mind. I was the grain of sand, and I resolved to become the diamond. I began by stealing two horses. I soon got a party of companions. I put myself in a condition to rob small caravans; and thus, by degrees, I destroyed the difference which had formerly subsisted between me and other men. I had my share of the good things of this world; and was even recompensed with usury for the hardships I had suffered. I was greatly respected, and became the captain of a band of robbers. I seized this castle by force. The satrap of Syria had a mind to dispossess me of it; but I was too rich to have any thing to fear. I gave the satrap a handsome present, by which means I preserved my castle, and increased my possessions. He even appointed me treasurer of the tributes which Arabia Petræa pays to the king of kings. I perform my office of receiver with great punctuality; but take the freedom to dispense with that of paymaster.

"The grand Desterham of Babylon sent hither a petty satrap in the name of king Moabdar, to have me strangled. This man arrived with his orders. I was apprised of all. I caused to be strangled in his presence the four persons he had brought with him to draw the noose; after which I asked him how much his commission of strangling me might be worth. He replied, that his fees would amount to above three hundred pieces of gold. I then convinced him that he might gain more by staying with me. I made him an inferior robber; and he is now one of my best and richest officers. If thou wilt take my advice, thy success may be equal to his. Never was there a better season for plunder, since king Moabdar is killed, and all Babylon thrown into confusion."

"Moabdar killed!" said Zadig, "and what has become of queen Astarte?"

"I know not," replied Arbogad. "All I know is, that Moabdar lost his senses and was killed; that Babylon is a scene of disorder and bloodshed; that all the empire is desolated; that there are some fine strokes to be made yet; and that, for my own part, I have struck some that are admirable."

"But the queen," said Zadig; "for heaven's sake, knowest thou nothing of the queen's fate?"

"Yes," replied he, "I have heard something of a prince of Plircania. If she was not killed in the tumult, she is probably one of his concubines. But I am much fonder of booty than news. I have taken several women in my excursions, but I keep none of them. I sell them at a high price when they are beautiful, without enquiring who they are. In commodities of this kind rank makes no difference, and a queen that is ugly will never find a merchant. Perhaps I may have sold queen Astarte; perhaps she is dead; but, be it as it will, it is of little consequence to me, and I should imagine of as little to thee."

So saying, he drank a large draught, which threw all his ideas into such confusion that Zadig could obtain no farther information.

Zadig remained for some time without speech, sense, or motion. Arbogad continued drinking, constantly repeated that he was the happiest man in the world; and exhorted Zadig to put himself in the same condition. At last the soporiferous fume of the wine lulled him into a gentle repose. Zadig passed the night in the most violent perturbation.

"What," said he, "did the king lose his senses? and is he killed? I cannot help lamenting his fate. The empire is rent in pieces: and this robber is happy. O fortune! O destiny! A robber is happy, and the most beautiful of nature's works hath perhaps perished in a barbarous manner, or lives in a state worse than death. O Astarte! what has become of thee?"

At day break, he questioned all those he met in the castle; but they were all busy and he received no answer. During the night they had made a new capture, and they were now employed in dividing the spoil. All he could obtain in this hurry and confusion was an opportunity of departing, which he immediately embraced, plunged deeper than ever in the most gloomy and mournful reflections.

Zadig proceeded on his journey with a mind full of disquiet and perplexity, and wholly employed on the unhappy Astarte on the king of Babylon, on his faithful friend Cador, on the happy robber Arbogad, on that capricious woman whom the Babylonians had seized on the frontiers of Egypt. In a word, on all the misfortunes and disappointments he had hitherto suffered.

XV.

THE FISHERMAN.

At few leagues distance from Arbogad's castle he came to the banks of a small river, still deploring his fate, and considering himself as the most wretched of mankind. He saw a fisherman lying on the bank of the river, scarcely holding in his weak and feeble hand a net which he seemed ready to drop, and lifting up his eyes to heaven.

"I am certainly," said the fisherman, "the most unhappy man in the world. I was universally allowed to be the most famous dealer in cream-cheese in Babylon, and yet I am ruined. I had the most handsome wife that any man in my situation could have; and by her I have been betrayed. I had still left a paltry house, and that I have seen pillaged and destroyed. At last I took refuge in this cottage, where I have no other resource than fishing, and yet I cannot catch a single fish. Oh, my net! no more will I throw thee into the water; I will throw myself in thy place."

So saying, he arose and advanced forward, in the attitude of a man ready to throw himself into the river, and thus to finish his life.

"What," said Zadig, "are there men as wretched as I?"

His eagerness to save the fisherman's life was as sudden as this reflection. He runs to him, stops him, and speaks to him with a tender and compassionate air. It is commonly supposed that we are less miserable when we have companions in our misery. This, according to Zoroaster, does not proceed from malice, but necessity. We feel ourselves insensibly drawn to an unhappy person as to one like ourselves. The joy of the happy would be an insult; but two men in distress are like two slender trees, which, mutually supporting each other, fortify themselves against the tempest.

"Why," said Zadig to the fisherman, "dost thou sink under thy misfortunes?"

"Because," replied he, "I see no means of relief. I was the most considerable man in the village of Derlback, near Babylon, and with the assistance of my wife I made the best cream-cheese in the empire. Queen Astarte, and the famous minister, Zadig, were extremely fond of them. I had sent them six hundred cheeses, and one day went to the city to receive my money; but, on my arrival at Babylon, was informed that the queen and Zadig had disappeared. I ran to the house of Lord Zadig, whom I had never seen; and found there the inferior officers of the grand Desterham, who being furnished with a royal license, were plundering it with great loyalty and order. From thence I flew to the queen's kitchen, some of the lords of which told me that the queen was dead; some said she was in prison; and others pretended that she had made her escape; but they all agreed in assuring me that I would not be paid for my cheese. I went with my wife to the house of Lord Orcan, who was one of my customers, and begged his protection in my present distress. He granted it to my wife, but refused it to me. She was whiter than the cream-cheeses that began my misfortune, and the lustre of the Tyrian purple was not more bright than the carnation which animated this whiteness. For this reason Orcan detained her, and drove me from his house. In my despair I wrote a letter to my dear wife. She said to the bearer, 'Ha, ha! I know the writer of this a little. I have heard his name mentioned. They say he I makes excellent cream-cheeses. Desire him to send me some and he shall be paid.'

"In my distress I resolved to apply to justice. I had still six ounces of gold remaining. I was obliged to give two to the lawyer whom I consulted, two to the procurator who undertook my cause, and two to the secretary of the first judge. When all this was done, my business was not begun; and I had already expended more money than my cheese and my wife were worth. I returned to my own village, with an intention to sell my house, in order to enable me to recover my wife.

"My house was well worth sixty ounces of gold; but as my neighbors saw that I was poor and obliged to sell it, the first to whom I applied offered me thirty ounces, the second twenty, and the third ten. Bad as these offers were, I was so blind that I was going to strike a bargain, when a prince of Hircania came to Babylon, and ravaged all in his way. My house was first sacked and then burned.

"Having thus lost my money, my wife, and my house, I retired into this country, where thou now seest me. I have endeavored to gain a subsistence by fishing; but the fish make a mock of thee as well as the men. I catch none; I die with hunger; and had it not been for thee, august comforter, I should have perished in the river."

The fisherman was not allowed to give this long account without interruption; at every moment, Zadig, moved and transported, said:

"What! knowest thou nothing of the queen's fate?"

"No my lord," replied the fisherman; "but I know that neither the queen nor Zadig have paid me for my cream-cheeses; that I have lost my wife, and am now reduced to despair."

"I flatter myself," said Zadig, "that thou wilt not lose all thy money. I have heard of this Zadig; he is an honest man; and if he return to Babylon, as he expects, he will give thee more than he owes thee. But with regard to thy wife, who is not so honest, I advise thee not to seek to recover her. Believe me, go to Babylon; I shall be there before thee, because I am on horseback, and thou art on foot. Apply to the illustrious Cador. Tell him thou hast met his friend. Wait for me at his house. Go, perhaps thou wilt not always be unhappy.

"O powerful Oromazes!" continued he, "thou employest me to comfort this man. Whom wilt thou employ to give me consolation?"

So saying, he gave the fisherman half the money he had brought from Arabia. The fisherman, struck with surprise and ravished with joy, kissed the feet of the friend of Cador, and said:

"Thou art surely an angel sent from heaven to save me!" Meanwhile Zadig continued to make fresh inquiries and to shed tears. "What! my lord," cried the fisherman, "and art thou then so unhappy, thou who bestowest favors?"

"A hundred times more unhappy than thee," replied Zadig.

"But how is it possible," said the good man, "that the giver can be more wretched than the receiver?"

"Because," replied Zadig, "thy greatest misery arose from poverty, and mine is seated in the heart."

"Did Orcan take thy wife from thee?" said the fisherman.

This word recalled to Zadig's mind the whole of his adventures. He repeated the catalogue of his misfortunes, beginning with the queen's bitch and ending with his arrival at the castle of the robber Arbogad.

"Ah!" said he to the fisherman, "Orcan deserves to be punished: but it is commonly such men as those that are the favorites of fortune. However, go thou to the house of Lord Cador, and there await my arrival."

They then parted: the fisherman walked, thanking heaven for the happiness of his condition; and Zadig rode, accusing fortune for the hardness of his lot.

XVI.

THE BASILISK.

Arriving in a beautiful meadow, he there saw several women, who were searching for something with great application. He took the liberty to approach one of them, and to ask if he might have the honor to assist them in their search.

"Take care that thou dost not," replied the Syrian. "What we are searching for can be touched only by women."

"Strange," said Zadig. "May I presume to ask thee what it is that women only are permitted to touch?"

"It is a basilisk," said she.

"A basilisk, madam! and for what purpose, pray, dost thou seek for a basilisk?"

"It is for our lord and master, Ogul, whose castle thou seest on the bank of that river, at the end of that meadow. We are his most humble slaves. The lord Ogul is sick. His physician hath ordered him to eat a basilisk, stewed in rose-water; and as it is a very rare animal, and can only be taken by women, the lord Ogul hath promised to choose for his well-beloved wife the woman that shall bring him a basilisk. Let me go on in my search; for thou seest what I shall lose if I am forestalled by my companions."

The basilisk.

THE BASILISK, OR COCKATRICE.

The Basilisk, called "Cockatrice" in "holy writ," was first described by certain ancient historians of unquestioned imaginative ability, but of very doubtful veracity; and they have also enriched the popular mythology with minute descriptions of the Phoenix, the Griffin, the Centaur, the

Chimera, the Unicorn, and many other fanciful and mythical creations.

The learned and pious naturalist, Charles Owen, D.D., of London, England, (from whose celebrated *Essay Towards a Natural History of Serpents*, published in 1742, the preceding engraving has been copied), tells us that "the Basilisk is a serpent of the Draconick line—the property of Africa; that in shape it resembles a cock, the tail excepted; that the Egyptians say it springs from the egg of the bird Ibis, and others, from eggs of a cock; that it is gross in body, of fiery eyes and sharp head, on which it wears a crest like a cock's comb; that it has the honor to be styled Regulus by the Latins—*the little king of serpents*; that it is terrible to them, and its voice puts them to flight, that, as tradition adds, its eyes and breath are killing; that dreadful things are attributed to it by the poets; and that, according to Pliny, the venom of the Basilisk is said to be so exalted, that if it bites a staff 'twill kill the person that makes use of it; but this," continues the reverend doctor of divinity, "is tradition without a voucher."

The "inspired" prophet Isaiah, whose writings are venerated by both Jews and Christians, and whose prophetic utterances have so long been discussed with more zeal than discretion by the sectarians, tells us, (Isaiah xiv. 29), that "Out of the serpent's root shall come forth a Cockatrice, and his fruit *shall be* a fiery, flying serpent." This somewhat incoherent prediction has never been satisfactorily explained by the learned commentators who are specially educated in our colleges for solving theological enigmas, and who have failed to show, to the confusion of scientists and the admiration of a believing world, how a Cockatrice may emerge from a "serpent's root," and why a Cockatrice's "fiery and flying fruit" should have formed a theme for prophetic inspiration.—E.

Zadig discovers Queen Astarte.--"In her hand she held a small rod with which she was tracing characters on the fine sand that lay between the turf and the brook."

Zadig left her and the other Assyrians to search for their basilisk, and continued his journey through the meadow; when coming to the brink of a small rivulet, he found a lady lying on the grass, and who was not searching for any thing. Her person seemed majestic; but her face was covered with a veil. She was inclined toward the rivulet, and profound sighs proceeded from her bosom. In her hand she held a small rod with which she was tracing characters on the fine sand that lay between the turf and the brook.

Zadig had the curiosity to examine what this woman was writing. He drew near. He saw the letter Z, then an A; he was astonished: then appeared a D; he started. But never was surprise equal to his, when he saw the two last letters of his name. He stood for some time immovable. At last breaking silence with a faltering voice:

"Oh! generous lady!" pardon a stranger, an unfortunate man, for presuming to ask thee by what surprising adventure I here find the name of Zadig traced out by thy divine hand?'

At this voice and these words, the lady lifted up the veil with a trembling hand, looked at Zadig, sent forth a cry of tenderness, surprise, and joy, and sinking under the various emotions which at once assaulted her soul fell speechless into his arms. It was Astarte herself; it was the queen of Babylon; it was she whom Zadig adored, and whom he had reproached himself for adoring; it was she whose misfortunes he had so deeply lamented, and for whose fate he had been so anxiously concerned. He was for a moment deprived of the use of his senses, when he had fixed his eyes on those of Astarte, which now began to open again with a languor mixed with confusion and tenderness:

"O ye immortal powers!" cried he, "who preside over the fates of weak mortals; do ye indeed restore Astarte to me? At what a time, in what a place, and in what a condition do I again behold her?"

He fell on his knees before Astarte, and laid his face in the dust at her feet. The queen of Babylon raised him up, and made him sit by her side on the brink of the rivulet. She frequently wiped her eyes, from which the tears continued to flow afresh. She twenty times resumed her discourse, which her sighs as often interrupted. She asked by what strange accident they were brought together, and suddenly prevented his answer by other questions. She waived the account of her own misfortunes, and desired to be informed of those of Zadig. At last, both of them having a little composed the tumult of their souls, Zadig acquainted her in a few words by what adventure he was brought into that meadow.

"But, O unhappy and respectable queen! by what means do I find thee in this lonely place, clothed in the habit of a slave, and accompanied by other female slaves, who are searching for a basilisk, which, by order of the physician, is to be stewed in rose-water?"

"While they are searching for their basilisk," said the fair Astarte, "I will inform thee of all I have suffered, for which heaven has sufficiently recompensed me, by restoring thee to my sight. Thou knowest that the king, my husband, was vexed to see thee, the most amiable of mankind; and that for this reason he one night resolved to strangle thee and poison me. Thou knowest how heaven permitted my little mute to inform me of the orders of his sublime majesty. Hardly had the faithful Cador obliged thee to depart, in obedience to my command, when he ventured to enter my apartment at midnight by a secret passage. He carried me off, and conducted me to the temple of Oromazes, where the magi, his brother, shut me up in that huge statue, whose base reaches to the foundation of the temple, and whose top rises to the summit of the dome. I was there buried in a manner; but was served by the magi, and supplied with all the necessaries of life. At break of day his majesty's apothecary entered my chamber with a potion composed of a mixture of henbane, opium, hemlock, black hellebore, and aconite; and another officer went to thine with a bowstring of blue silk. Neither of us were to be found. Cador, the better to deceive the king, pretended to come and accuse us both. He said that thou hadst taken the road to the Indies, and I that to Memphis; on which the king's guards were immediately dispatched in pursuit of us both.

Cador concealing Astarte in the temple of Oromazes.

"The couriers who pursured me did not know me. I had hardly ever shown my face to any but thee, and to thee only in the presence and by the order of my husband. They conducted themselves in the pursuit by the description that had been given of my person. On the frontiers of Egypt they met with a woman of the same stature with me, and possessed perhaps of greater charms. She was weeping and wandering. They made no doubt but that this woman was the queen of Babylon, and accordingly brought her to Moabdar. Their mistake at first threw the king into a violent passion; but having viewed this woman more attentively, he found her extremely handsome, and was comforted. She was called Missouf. I have since been informed that this name in the Egyptian language signifies the capricious fair one. She was so in reality; but she had as much cunning as caprice. She pleased Moabdar, and gained such an ascendency over him as to make him choose her for his wife.

Her character then began to appear in its true colors. She gave herself up, without scruple, to all the freaks of a wanton imagination. She would have obliged the chief of the magi, who was old and gouty, to dance before her; and on his refusal, she persecuted him with the most unrelenting cruelty. She ordered her master of the horse to make her a pie of sweetmeats. In vain did he represent that he was not a pastry-cook. He was obliged to make it, and lost his place because it was baked a little too hard. The post of master of the horse she gave to her dwarf, and that of Chancellor to her page. In this manner did she govern Babylon. Every body regretted the loss of me. The king, who till the moment of his resolving to poison me and strangle thee had been a tolerably good kind of man, seemed now to have drowned all his virtues in his immoderate fondness for this capricious fair one. He came to the temple on the great day of the feast held in honor of the sacred fire. I saw him implore the gods in behalf of Missouf, at the feet of the statue in which I was inclosed. I raised my voice; I cried out:

"'The gods reject the prayers of a king who is now become a tyrant, and who attempted to murder a reasonable wife, in order to marry a woman remarkable for nothing but her folly and extravagance.'

"At these words Moabdar was confounded and his head became disordered. The oracle I had pronounced, and the tyranny of Missouf, conspired to deprive him of his judgment, and in a few days his reason entirely forsook him.

"His madness, which seemed to be the judgment of heaven, was the signal for a revolt. The people rose, and ran to arms; and Babylon, which had been so long immersed in idleness and effeminacy, became the theatre of a bloody civil war. I was taken from the heart of my statue and placed at the head of a party. Cador flew to Memphis to bring thee back to Babylon. The prince of Hircania, informed of these fatal events, returned with his army and made a third party in Chaldea. He attacked the king, who fled before him with his capricious Egyptian. Moabdar died pierced with wounds. Missouf fell into the hands of the conqueror. I myself had the misfortune to be taken by a party of Hircanians, who conducted me to their prince's tent, at the very moment that Missouf was brought before him. Thou wilt doubtless be pleased to hear that the prince thought me more beautiful than the Egyptian; but thou wilt be sorry to be informed that he designed me for his seraglio. He told me, with a blunt and resolute air, that as soon as he had finished a military expedition, which he was just going to undertake, he would come to me. Judge how great must have been my grief. My ties with Moabdar were already dissolved; I might have been the wife of Zadig; and I was fallen into the hands of a barbarian. I answered him with all the pride which my high rank and noble sentiment could inspire. I had always heard it affirmed that heaven stamped on persons of my condition a mark of grandeur, which, with a single word or glance, could reduce to the lowliness of the most profound respect those rash and forward persons who presume to deviate from the rules of politeness. I spoke like a queen, but was treated like a maid-servant. The Hircanian, without even deigning to speak to me, told his black eunuch that I was impertinent, but that he thought me handsome. He ordered him to take care of me and to put me under the regimen of favorites, that, so my complexion being improved, I might be the more worthy of his favors when he should be at leisure to honor me with them. I told him, that, rather than submit to his desires, I would put an end to my life. He replied with a smile, that women, he believed, were not so blood-thirsty, and that he was accustomed to such violent expressions; and then left me with the air of a man who had just put another parrot into his aviary. What a state for the first queen in the universe, and, what is more, for a heart devoted to Zadig!"

At these words Zadig threw himself at her feet, and bathed them with his tears. Astarte raised him with great tenderness, and thus continued her story:

"I now saw myself in the power of a barbarian, and rival to the foolish woman with whom I was conned. She gave me an account of her adventures in Egypt. From the description she gave of your person, from the time, from the dromedary on which you were mounted, and from every other circumstance, I inferred that Zadig was the man who had fought for her. I doubted not but that you were at Memphis, and therefore resolved to repair thither. 'Beautiful Missouf,' said I, 'thou art more handsome than I, and will please the prince of Hircania much better. Assist me in contriving the means of my escape. Thou wilt then reign alone. Thou wilt at once make me happy and rid thyself of a rival.'

"Missouf concerted with me the means of my flight; and I departed secretly with a female slave. As I approached the frontiers of Arabia, a famous robber, named Arbogad, seized me and sold me to some merchants who brought me to this castle where ford Ogul resides. He bought me without knowing who I was. He is a voluptuary, ambitious of nothing but good living, and thinks that God sent him into the world for no other purpose than to sit at table. He is so extremely corpulent, that he is always in danger of suffocation. His physician, who has but little credit with him when he has a good digestion, governs him with a despotic sway when he has eaten too much. He has persuaded him that a basilisk stewed in rose-water will effect a complete cure. The ford Ogul hath promised his hand to the female slave that brings him a basilisk. Thou seest that I leave them to vie with each other in meriting this honor; and never was I less desirous of finding the basilisk than since heaven hath restored thee to my sight."

This account was succeeded by a long conversation between Astarte and Zadig, consisting of every thing that their long suppressed sentiments, their great sufferings, and their mutual love, could inspire into hearts the most noble and tender, and the genii who preside over love carried their words to the sphere of Venus.

The women returned to Ogul without having found the basilisk. Zadig was introduced to this mighty lord, and spoke to him in the following terms:

"May immortal health descend from heaven to bless all thy days! I am a physician. At the first report of thy indisposition I flew to thy castle, and have now brought thee a basilisk stewed in rose-water. Not that I pretend to marry thee. All I ask is the liberty of a Babylonian slave, who hath been in thy possession for a few days; and, if I should not be so happy as to cure thee, magnificent Lord Ogul, I consent to remain a slave in her place."

The proposal was accepted. Astarte set out for Babylon with Zadig's servant, promising, immediately upon her arrival, to send a courier to inform him of all that had happened. Their parting was as tender as their meeting. The moment of meeting, and that of parting are the two greatest epochs of life as sayeth the great book of Zend. Zadig loved the queen with as much ardor as he professed; and the queen loved Zadig more than she thought proper to acknowledge.

Meanwhile Zadig spoke thus to Ogul:

"My lord, my basilisk is not to be eaten; all its virtues must enter through thy pores. I have inclosed it in a little ball, blown up and covered with a fine skin. Thou must strike this ball with all thy might, and I must strike it back for a considerable time; and by observing this regimen for a few days, thou wilt see the effects of my art."

The first day Ogul was out of breath, and thought he should have died with fatigue. The second, he was less fatigued, and slept better. In eight days he recovered all the strength, all the health, all the agility and cheerfulness of his most agreeable years.

"Thou hast played at ball, and hast been temperate," said Zadig. "Know that there is no such thing in nature as a basilisk; that temperance and exercise are the two great preservatives of health; and that the art of reconciling intemperance and health is as chimerical as the philosopher's stone, judicial astrology, or the theology of the magi."

Ogul's first physician observing how dangerous this man might prove to the medical art, formed a design, in conjunction with the apothecary, to send Zadig to search for a basilisk in the other world. Thus, after having suffered such a long train of calamities on account of his good actions, he was now upon the point of losing his life for curing a gluttonous lord. He was invited to an excellent dinner, and was to have been poisoned in the second course; but, during the first, he happily received a courier from the fair Astarte.

"When one is beloved by a beautiful woman," says the great Zoroaster, "he hath always the good fortune to extricate himself out of every kind of difficulty and danger."

XVII.

THE COMBATS.

The queen was received at Babylon with all those transports of joy which are ever felt on the return of a beautiful princess who hath been involved in calamities. Babylon was now in greater tranquillity. The prince of Hircania had been killed in battle. The victorious Babylonians declared that the queen should marry the man whom they should choose for their sovereign. They were resolved that the first place in the world, that of being husband to Astarte and king of Babylon, should not depend on cabals and intrigues. They swore to acknowledge for king the man who, upon trial, should be found to be possessed of the greatest valor and the greatest wisdom. Accordingly, at the distance of a few leagues from the city, a spacious place was marked out for the list, surrounded with magnificent amphitheatres. Thither the combatants were to repair in complete armor. Each of them had a separate apartment behind the amphitheatres, where they were neither to be seen nor known by any one. Each was to encounter four knights; and those that were so happy as to conquer four, were then to engage with one another: so that he who remained the last master of the field, would be proclaimed conqueror at the games. Four days after he was to return to the same place, and to explain the enigmas proposed by the magi. If he did not explain the enigmas, he was not king; and the running at the lances was to begin afresh, till a man should be found who was conqueror in both these combats; for they were absolutely determined to have a king possessed of the greatest wisdom and the most invincible courage. The queen was all the while to be strictly guarded. She was only allowed to be present at the games, and even there she was to be covered with a veil; but was not allowed to speak to any of the competitors, that so they might neither receive favor, nor suffer injustice.

These particulars Astarte communicated to her lover, hoping that, in order to obtain her, he would show himself possessed of greater courage and wisdom than any other person.

Zadig set out on his journey, beseeching Venus to fortify his courage and enlighten his understanding. He arrived on the banks of the Euphrates on the eve of this great day. He caused his device to be inscribed among those of the combatants, concealing his face and his name, as the law ordained; and then went to repose himself in the apartment that fell to him by lot. His friend, Cador, who after the fruitless search he had made for him in Egypt, had now returned to Babylon, sent to his tent a complete suit of armor, which was a present from the queen; as also from himself, one of the finest horses in Persia. Zadig presently perceived that these presents were sent by Astarte;

and from thence his courage derived fresh strength, and his love the most animating hopes.

Next day, the queen being seated under a canopy of jewels, and the amphitheatres filled with all the gentlemen and ladies of rank in Babylon, the combatants appeared in the circus. Each of them came and laid his device at the feet of the grand magi. They drew their devices by lot; and that of Zadig was the last. The first who advanced was a certain lord, named Itobad, very rich and very vain, but possessed of little courage, of less address, and scarcely of any judgment at all. His servants had persuaded him that such a man as he ought to be king. He had said in reply, "Such a man as I ought to reign;" and thus they had armed him cap-a-pie. He wore an armor of gold enameled with green, a plume of green feathers, and a lance adorned with green ribbons. It was instantly perceived by the manner in which Itobad managed his horse, that it was not for such a man as him that heaven reserved the sceptre of Babylon. The first knight that ran against him threw him out of his saddle: the second laid him flat on his horse's buttocks, with his legs in the air, and his arms extended. Itobad recovered himself, but with so bad a grace, that the whole amphitheatre burst out a laughing. The third knight disdained to make use of his lance; but, making a pass at him, took him by the right leg, and wheeling him half round, laid him prostrate on the sand. The squires of the games ran to him laughing, and replaced him in his saddle. The fourth combatant took him by the left leg, and tumbled him down on the other side. He was conducted back with scornful shouts to his tent, where, according to the law, he was to pass the night; and as he limped along with great difficulty, he said: "What an adventure for such a man as I!"

The combats.

The other knights acquitted themselves with greater ability and success. Some of them conquered two combatants; a few of them vanquished three; but none but prince of Otamus conquered four. At last Zadig fought in his turn. He successively threw four knights off their saddles with all the grace imaginable. It then remained to be seen who should be conqueror, of Otamus or Zadig. The arms of the first were gold and blue, with a plume of the same color; those of the last were white. The wishes of all the spectators were divided between the knight in blue and the knight in white. The queen, whose heart was in a violent palpitation, offered prayers to heaven for the success of the white color.

The two champions made their passes and vaults with so much agility, they mutually gave and received such dexterous blows with their lances, and sat so firmly in their saddles, that every body but the queen wished there might be two kings in Babylon. At length, their horses being tired and their lances broken, Zadig had recourse to this stratagem: He passed behind the blue prince; springs upon the buttocks of his horse; seizes him by the middle; throws him on the earth; places himself in the saddle, and wheels around Otamus as he lay extended on the ground. All the amphitheatre cried out, "Victory to the white knight!" Otamus rises in a violent passion, and draws his sword; Zadig leaps from his horse with his sabre in his hand. Both of them are now on the ground, engaged in a new combat, where strength and agility triumph by turns. The plumes of their helmets, the studs of their bracelets, and the rings of their armor are driven to a great distance by the violence of a thousand furious blows. They strike with the point and the edge; to the right, to the left; on the head, on the breast; they retreat; they advance; they measure swords; they close; they seize each other; they bend like serpents; they attack like lions; and the fire every moment flashes from their blows. At last Zadig, having recovered his spirits, stops; makes a feint; leaps upon Otamus; throws him on the ground and disarms him; and Otamus cries out:

"It is thou alone, O white knight, that oughtest to reign over Babylon!"

The queen was now at the height of her joy. The knight in blue armor, and the knight in white, were conducted each to his own apartment, as well as all the others, according to the intention of the law. Mutes came to wait upon them, and to serve them at table. It may be easily supposed that the queen's little mute waited upon Zadig. They were then left to themselves to enjoy the sweets of repose till next morning, at which time the conqueror was to bring his device to the grand magi, to compare it with that which he had left, and make himself known.

Zadig, though deeply in love, was so much fatigued that he could not help sleeping. Itobad, who lay near him, never closed his eyes. He arose in the night, entered his apartment, took the white arms and the device of Zadig, and put his green armor in their place. At break of day, he went boldly to the grand magi, to declare that so great a man as he was conqueror. This was little expected; however, he was proclaimed while Zadig was still asleep. Astarte, surprised and filled with despair, returned to Babylon. The amphitheatre was almost empty when Zadig awoke; he sought for his arms but could find none but the green armor. With this he was obliged to cover himself, having nothing else near him. Astonished and enraged, he put it on in a furious passion and advanced in this equipage.

The people that still remained in the amphitheatre and the circus received him with hoofs and hisses. They surrounded him, and insulted him to his face. Never did man suffer such cruel mortifications. He lost his patience; with his sabre he dispersed such of the populace as dared to affront him; but he knew not what course to take. He could not see the queen; he could not claim the white armor she had sent him without exposing her; and thus, while she was plunged in grief, he was filled with fury and distraction. He walked on the banks of the Euphrates, fully persuaded that his star had destined him to inevitable misery; and revolving in his mind all his misfortunes, from the adventure of the woman who hated one-eyed men, to that of his armor:

"This," said he, "is the consequence of my having slept too long. Had I slept less, I should now have been king of Babylon, and in possession of Astarte. Knowledge, virtue, and courage, have hitherto served only to make me miserable."

He then let fall some secret murmurings against providence, and was tempted to believe that the world was governed by a cruel destiny, which oppressed the good, and prospered knights in green armor.

XVIII.

THE HERMIT.

One of Zadig's greatest mortifications was his being obliged to wear that green armor which had exposed him to such contumelious treatment. A merchant happening to pass by, he sold it to him for a trifle, and bought a gown and a long bonnet. In this garb he proceeded along the banks of the Euphrates, filled with despair, and secretly accusing providence, which thus continued to persecute him with unremitting severity.

While he was thus sauntering along, he met a hermit whose white and venerable beard hung down to his girdle. He held a book in his hand, which he read with great attention. Zadig stopped, and made him a profound obeisance. The hermit returned the compliment with such a noble and engaging air, that Zadig had the curiosity to enter into conversation with him. He asked him what book it was that he had been reading.

"It is the book of destinies," said the hermit. "Wouldst thou choose to look into it?"

He put the book into the hands of Zadig, who, thoroughly versed as he was in several languages, could not decipher a single character of it. This only redoubled his curiosity.

"Thou seemest," said the good father, "to be in great distress."

"Alas!" replied Zadig, "I have but too much reason."

"If thou wilt permit me to accompany thee," resumed the old man, "perhaps I may be of some service to thee. I have often poured the balm of consolation into the bleeding heart of the unhappy."

Zadig felt himself inspired with respect for the dignity, the beard, and the book of the hermit. He found, in the course of the conversation, that he was possessed of superior degrees of knowledge. The hermit talked of fate, of justice, of morals, of the chief good, of human weakness, and of virtue and vice, with such a spirited and moving eloquence, that Zadig felt himself drawn toward him by an irresistible charm. He earnestly entreated the favor of his company till their return to Babylon.

"I ask the same favor of thee," said the old man. "Swear to me by Oromazes that, whatever I do, thou wilt not leave me for some days."

Zadig swore, and they set out together. In the evening the two travelers arrived at a superb castle. The hermit entreated a hospitable reception for himself and the young man who accompanied him. The porter, whom one might have mistaken for a great lord, introduced them with a kind of disdainful civility. He presented them to a principal domestic, who showed them his master's magnificent apartments. They were admitted to the lower end of the table, without being honored with the least mark of regard by the lord of the castle; but they were served, like the rest, with delicacy and profusion. They were then presented, in a golden basin adorned with emeralds and rubies, with water to wash their hands. At last they were conducted to bed in a beautiful apartment; and in the morning a domestic brought each of them a piece of gold, after which they took their leave and departed.

"The master of the house," said Zadig, as they were proceeding on the journey, "appears to be a generous man, though somewhat too proud. He nobly performs the duties of hospitality."

At that instant he observed that a kind of large pocket, which the hermit had, was filled and distended; and upon looking more narrowly, he found that it contained the golden basin adorned with precious stones, which the hermit had stolen. He durst not then take any notice of it; but he was filled with a strange surprise.

About noon the hermit came to the door of a paltry house, inhabited by a rich miser, and begged the favor of an hospitable reception for a few hours. An old servant, in a tattered garb, received them with a blunt and rude air, and led them into the stable, where he gave them some rotten olives, sour wine, and mouldy bread. The hermit ate and drank with as much seeming satisfaction as he had done the evening before, and then addressing himself to the old servant who watched them both to prevent them stealing anything, and had rudely pressed them to depart, he gave him the two pieces of gold he had received in the morning, and thanked him for his great civility.

"Pray," added he, "allow me to speak to thy master."

The servant, filled with astonishment, introduced the two travelers.

"Magnificent lord!" said the hermit, "I cannot but return thee my most humble thanks for the noble manner in which thou hast entertained us. Be pleased to accept of this golden basin as a small mark of my gratitude."

The miser started, and was ready to fall backwards; but the hermit, without giving him time to recover from his surprise, instantly departed with his young fellow traveler.

"Father," said Zadig, "what is the meaning of all this? Thou seemest to me to be entirely different from other men. Thou stealest a golden basin adorned with precious stones, from a lord who received thee magnificently, and givest it to a miser who treats thee with indignity."

"Son," replied the old man, "this magnificent lord, who receives strangers only from vanity and ostentation, will hereby be rendered more wise; and the miser will learn to practice the duties of hospitality. Be surprised at nothing, but follow me."

Zadig knew not as yet whether he was in company with the most foolish or the most prudent of mankind' but the hermit spoke with such an ascendency that Zadig, who was moreover bound by his oath, could not refuse to follow him.

In the evening they arrived at a house built with equal elegance and simplicity, where nothing savored either of prodigality or avarice. The master of it was a philosopher who had retired from the world, and who cultivated in peace the study of virtue and wisdom, without any of that rigid and morose severity so commonly found in men of his character. He had chosen to build this fine house in which he received strangers with a generosity free from ostentation. He went himself to meet the two travelers, whom he led into a commodious apartment, and desired them to repose themselves. Soon after he came and invited them to a decent and well ordered repast, during which he spoke with great judgment of the last revolutions in Babylon. He seemed to be strongly attached to the queen, and wished that Zadig had appeared in the lists to contend for the crown.

"But the people," added he, "do not deserve to have such a king as Zadig."

Zadig blushed and felt his griefs redoubled. They agreed, in the course of the conversation, that the things of this world did not always answer the wishes of the wise. The hermit maintained that the ways of providence were inscrutable; and that men were in the wrong to judge of a whole, of which they understood but the smallest part. They talked of the passions.

"Ah," said Zadig, "how fatal are their effects!"

"They are the winds," replied the hermit, "that swell the sails of the ship; it is true, they sometimes sink her, but without them she could not sail at all. The bile makes us sick and choleric but without the bile we could not live. Everything in this world is dangerous, and yet everything in it is necessary."

The conversation turned on pleasure; and the hermit proved that it was a present bestowed by the deity.

"For," said he, "man cannot either give himself sensations or ideas: he receives all; and pain and pleasure proceed from a foreign cause as well as his being."

Zadig was surprised to see a man who had been guilty of such extravagant actions, capable of reasoning with so much judgment and propriety. At last, after a conversation equally entertaining and instructive, the host led back his two guests to their apartment, blessing heaven for having sent him two men possessed of so much wisdom and virtue. He offered them money with such an easy and noble air that it could not possibly give any offence. The hermit refused it, and said that he must now take his leave of him, as he proposed to set out for Babylon in the morning before it was light. Their parting was tender. Zadig especially felt himself filled with esteem and affection for a man of such an amiable character.

When he and the hermit were alone in their apartment they spent a long time in praising their host. At break of day the old man awakened his companion.

"We must now depart," said he; "but while all the family are still asleep, I will leave this man a mark of my esteem and affection."

So saying he took a candle and set fire to the house. Zadig, struck with horror, cried aloud, and endeavored to hinder him from committing such a barbarous action; but the hermit drew him away by a superior force, and the house was soon in flames. The hermit, who, with his companion, was already at a considerable distance, looked back to the conflagration with great tranquillity.

"Thanks be to God," said he, "the house of my dear host is entirely destroyed! Happy man!"

At these words Zadig was at once tempted to burst out in laughing, to reproach the reverend father, to beat him, and to run away. But he did none of all these; for still subdued by the powerful ascendancy of the hermit, he followed him, in spite of himself, to the next stage.

This was at the house of a charitable and virtuous widow, who had a nephew fourteen years of age, a handsome and promising youth, and her only hope. She performed the honors of the house as well us she could. Next day, she ordered her nephew to accompany the strangers to a bridge, which being lately broken down, was become extremely dangerous in passing. The young man walked before them with great alacrity. As they were crossing the bridge, the hermit said to the youth:

"Come, I must show my gratitude to thy aunt."

He then took him by the hair, and plunged him into the river. The boy sank, appeared again on the surface of the water, and was swallowed up by the current.

"O monster! O thou most wicked of mankind!" cried Zadig.

"Thou promised to behave with greater patience," said the hermit, interrupting him. "Know, that under the ruins of that house which providence hath set on fire, the master hath found an immense treasure I know, that this young man, whose life providence hath shortened, would have assassinated his aunt in the space of a year, and thee in that of two."

"Who told thee so, barbarian?" cried Zadig, "and though thou hadst read this event in thy book of destinies, art thou permitted to drown a youth who never did thee any harm?"

While the Babylonian was thus exclaiming, he observed that the old man had no longer a beard, and that his countenance assumed the features and complexion of youth. The hermit's habit disappeared, and four beautiful wings covered a majestic body resplendent with light.

"O sent of heaven! O divine angel!" cried Zadig, humbly prostrating himself on the ground, "Hast thou then descended from the empyrean to teach a weak mortal to submit to the eternal decrees of providence?"

"Men," said the angel Jesrad, "judge of all without knowing any thing; and, of all men, thou best deservest to be enlightened."

Zadig begged to be permitted to speak:

"I distrust myself," said he, "but may I presume to ask the favor of thee to clear up one doubt that still remains in my mind. Would it not have been better to have corrected this youth, and made him virtuous, than to have drowned him?"

The hermit.

> The poem, called *The Hermit*, by Thomas Parnell, D.D., expresses views in regard to providence similar to those of Voltaire. The same thoughts may also be found in the *Divine Dialogues* of Henry Moore. Indeed this "tale to prose-men known to verse-men fam'd," has been used by many authors. Pope says "the story was written originally in Spanish;" Goldsmith, in his *Life of Parnell*, intimates that it was originally of Arabian invention, while, in fact, it seems to bear internal evidence of Persian or Hindoo origin.—E.

"Had he become virtuous," replied Jesrad, "and enjoyed a longer life, it would have been his fate to have been assassinated himself, together with the wife he would have married, and the child he would have had by her."

"But why," said Zadig, "is it necessary that there should be crimes and misfortunes, and that these misfortunes should fall on the good?"

"The wicked," replied Jesrad, "are always unhappy. They serve to prove and try the small number of the just that are scattered through the earth; and there is no evil that is not productive of some good."

"But," said Zadig, "suppose there was nothing but good and no evil at all."

"Then," replied Jesrad, "this earth would be another earth: the chain of events would be ranged in another order and directed by wisdom. But this other order, which would be perfect, can exist only in the eternal abode of the Supreme Being, to which no evil can approach. The Deity hath created millions of worlds, among which there is not one that resembles another. This immense variety is the effect of his immense power. There are not two leaves among the trees of the earth, nor two globes in the unlimited expanse of heaven, that are exactly similar; and all that thou seest on the little atom in which thou art born, ought to be, in its proper time and place, according to the immutable decrees of him who comprehends all. Men think that this child, who hath just perished, is fallen into the water by chance; and that it is by the same chance that this house is burned. But there is no such thing as chance. All is either a trial, or a punishment, or a reward, or a foresight. Remember the fisherman, who thought himself the most wretched of mankind. Oromazes sent thee to change his fate. Cease then, frail mortal, to dispute against what thou oughtest to adore."

"But," said Zadig—

As he pronounced the word "But," the angel took his flight toward the tenth sphere. Zadig on his knees adored providence, and submitted. The angel cried to him from on high:

"Direct thy course toward Babylon."

XIX.

THE ENIGMAS.

Zadig, entranced as it were, and like a man about whose head the thunder had burst, walked at random. He entered Babylon on the very day when those who had fought at the tournaments were assembled in the grand vestibule of the palace to explain the enigmas, and to answer the questions of the grand magi. All the knights were already present, except the knight in green armor. As soon as Zadig appeared in the city, the people crowded around him; every eye was fixed on him, every mouth blessed him, and every heart wished him the empire. The envious man saw him pass; he frowned and turned aside. The people conducted him to the place where the assembly was held. The queen, when informed of his arrival, became a prey to the most violent agitations of hope and fear. She was filled with anxiety and apprehension. She could not comprehend why Zadig was without arms, nor why Itobad wore the white armor.

When the knights who had fought were directed to appear in the assembly, Zadig said. "I have fought as well as the other knights, but another here wears my arms; and while I wait for the honor of proving the truth of my assertion, I demand the liberty of presenting myself to explain the enigmas."

The question was put to vote, and his reputation for probity was so well established, that they admitted him without scruple.

The first question proposed by the grand magi, was: "What, of all things in the world, is the longest and the shortest, the swiftest and the slowest, the most divisible and the most extended, the most neglected and the most regretted, without which nothing can be done, which devours all that is little, and enlivens all that is great?"

Itobad was to speak. He replied, that so great a man as he did not understand enigmas; and that it was sufficient for him to have conquered by his strength and valor. Some said that the meaning of the enigma was fortune; some, the earth; and others, the light. Zadig said that it was time.

"Nothing," added he, "is longer, since it is the measure of eternity. Nothing is shorter, since it is insufficient for the accomplishment of our projects. Nothing more slow to him that expects, nothing more rapid to him that enjoys. In greatness it extends to infinity, in smallness it is infinitely divisible. All men neglect it, all regret the loss of it; nothing can be done without it. It consigns to oblivion whatever is unworthy of being transmitted to posterity, and it immortalizes such actions as are truly great."

The assembly acknowledged that Zadig was in the right.

The next question was: "What is the thing which we receive without thanks, which we enjoy without knowing how, and which we lose without perceiving it?"

Every one gave his own explanation. Zadig alone guessed that it was life; and he explained all the other enigmas with the same facility. Itobad always said that nothing was more easy, and that he could have answered them with the same readiness, had he chosen to have given himself the trouble. Questions were then proposed on justice, on the sovereign good, and on the art of government. Zadig's answers were judged to be the most solid, and the people exclaimed:

"What a pity it is, that so great a genius should be so bad a knight!"

"Illustrious lords," said Zadig, "I have had the honor of conquering in the tournaments. It is to me that the white armor belongs. Lord Itobad took possession of it during my sleep. He probably thought it would fit him better than the green. I am now ready to prove in your presence, with my gown and sword, against all that beautiful white armor which he took from me, that it is I who have had the honor of conquering the brave of Otamus."

Itobad accepted the challenge with the greatest confidence. He never doubted but that, armed as he was with a helmet, a cuirass, and brassarts, he would obtain an easy victory over a champion in a cap and a night-gown. Zadig drew his sword, saluting the queen, who looked at him with a mixture of fear and joy. Itobad drew his, without saluting any one. He rushed upon Zadig, like a man who had nothing to fear; he was ready to cleave him in two. Zadig knew how to ward off his blows, by opposing the strongest part of his sword to the weakest of that of his adversary, in such a manner that Itobad's sword was broken. Upon which Zadig, seizing his enemy by the waist, threw him on the ground; and fixing the point of his sword at the extremity of his breast-plate, exclaimed: "Suffer thyself to be disarmed, or thou art a dead man."

Itobad greatly surprised at the disgrace that happened to such a man as he, was obliged to yield to Zadig, who took from him with great composure, his magnificent helmet, his superb cuirass, his fine brassarts, his shining cuisses; clothed himself with them, and in this dress ran to throw himself at the feet of Astarte. Cador easily proved that the armor belonged to Zadig. He was acknowledged king by the unanimous consent of the whole nation, and especially by that of Astarte, who, after so many calamities, now tasted the exquisite pleasure of seeing her lover worthy, in the eyes of the world, to be her husband. Itobad went home to be called lord in his own house. Zadig was king, and was happy. He recollected what the angel Jesrad had said to him. He even remembered the grain of sand that became a diamond. He sent in search of the robber Arbogad, to whom he gave an honorable post in his army, promising to advance him to the first dignities, if he behaved like a true warrior; and threatening to hang him, if he followed the profession of a robber.

Setoc, with the fair Almona, was called from the heart of Arabia, and placed at the head of the commerce of Babylon. Cador was preferred and distinguished according to his great services. He was the friend of the king; and the king was then the only monarch on earth that had a friend. The little mute was not forgotten. A fine house was given to the fisherman; and Orcan was condemned to pay him a large sum of money, and to restore him his wife; but the fisherman, who had now become wise, took only the money.

The beautiful Semira could not be comforted for having believed that Zadig would be blind of an eye; nor did Azora cease to lament her attempt to cut off his nose: their griefs, however, he softened by his presents. The capricious beauty, Missouf, was left unnoticed. The envious man died of rage and shame. The empire enjoyed peace, glory, and plenty. This was the happiest age of the earth. It was governed by love and justice. The people blessed Zadig, and Zadig blessed heaven.

THE SAGE AND THE ATHEIST.

INTRODUCTION.

You request me, sir, to give you some account of our worthy friend, and his singular son. The leisure that the retirement of Lord Peterborough now affords me, places it in my power to oblige you. You will be as astonished as I was, and perhaps adopt my opinion on the subject.

You scarcely knew the young and unfortunate Johnny, Freind's only son, whom his father took with him to Spain when he received the appointment of chaplain to our armies, in 1705. You started for Aleppo, before my lord besieged Barcelona; yet you were right when you said, John's countenance was amiable and interesting, and that he gave proofs of intelligence and courage. It was quite true. Every one who knew him, loved him. At first he was intended for the church; but, as he manifested much aversion for that profession, which, indeed, requires great skill, management, and finesse, his prudent father considered it a folly and a crime to oppose his inclination.

John was not twenty years old when he assisted, as a volunteer, at the attack on Mont-Joui, which was captured, and where the Prince of Hesse lost his life. Our poor Johnny was wounded, taken prisoner, and carried into the town. The following is an account of his adventures from the attack of Mont-Joui till the taking of Barcelona. It is as told by a Catalonian lady, a little too free and too simple. Such stories do not find a way to the hearts of your wise men. I received it from her when I entered Barcelona in the suite of Lord Peterborough. You must read it without offence, as a true description of the manners of the country.

CHAPTER I.

ADVENTURES OF JOHNNY, A YOUNG ENGLISHMAN. WRITTEN BY DONNA LAS NALGAS.

When we were informed that the same savages who came through the air to seize on Gibraltar, were come to besiege our beautiful Barcelona, we began to offer prayers at Notre Dame de Manreze—assuredly the best mode of defence.

These people, who come from so far, are called by a name very hard to pronounce, that is, English. Our reverend father inquisitor, Don Jeronimo Bueno Caracucarador, preached against these brigands. He anathematized them in Notre Dame d'Elpino. He assured us that the English had monkey-tails, bears' paws, and parrot-heads; that they sometimes spoke like men, but invariably made a great hissing; that they were moreover notorious heretics; that though the Blessed Virgin was often indulgent to poor sinners, she never forgave heretics, and that consequently they would all be infallibly exterminated, especially if they presumed to appear before Mont-Joui. He had scarcely finished his sermon when he heard that Mont-Joui was taken by storm.

The same evening we learned that a young Englishman, who had been wounded in the assault, was our prisoner. Throughout the town arose cries of victory! victory! And the illuminations were very general.

Donna Boca Vermeja, who had the honor to be the reverend inquisitor's favorite, was very desirous to see what the English animal and heretic was like. She was my intimate friend. I shared her curiosity. We were oblished to wait till his wound was cured; and this did not take very long.

Don Jeronimo Bueno Caracucarador.

Soon after, we learned that he was in the habit of visiting daily at the residence of Elbob, my cousin german, who, as every one knows, is the best surgeon in the town. My friend Boca Vermeja's impatience to see this singular monster increased two-fold. We had no rest ourselves, and gave none to our cousin, the surgeon, till he allowed us to conceal ourselves in a small closet, which we entered on tiptoe without saying a word and scarcely venturing to breathe, just as the Englishman arrived. His face was not turned toward us. He took off a small cap which enclosed his light hair, which then fell in thick curls down the finest neck I ever beheld. His form presented a plumpness, a finish, an elegance, approaching, in my opinion, the Apollo Belvidere at Rome—a copy of which my uncle the sculptor possesses.

Donna Boca Vermeja was transported with surprise, and delighted. I shared her ecstacy, and could not forbear exclaiming: "O che hermoso Muchacho!"

These words made the young man turn round. We then saw the face of an Adonis on the body of a young Hercules. Donna Boca Vermeja nearly fell backwards at the sight:

"St. James!" she exclaimed, "Holy Virgin! is it possible heretics are such fine men? How we have been deceived about them."

Donna Boca was soon violently in love with the heretical monster. She is handsomer than I am, I must confess; and I must also confess that I became doubly jealous of her on that account. I took care to show her that to forsake the reverend father inquisitor, Don Jeronimo Bueno Caracucarador, for an Englishman, would be a crime falling nothing short of damnation.

"Ah! my dear Las Nalgas," she said, (Las Nalgas is my name) "I would forsake Melchizedek himself for so fine a young man."

One of the inquisitors who attended four masses daily, to obtain from Our Lady of Manreze the destruction of the English, heard of our admiration. The Reverend Father Don Caracucarador whipped us both, and had our dear Englishman arrested by twenty-four Alguazils of St. Hermandad. Johnny killed four; and was at length captured by the remaining twenty. He was confined in a very damp cellar, and sentenced to be burnt the following Sunday, in full ceremony, clothed in a San-bénito, wearing a sugar-loaf cap, in honor of our Savior and the Virgin Mary, his mother. Don Caracucarador prepared a fine sermon, but had no occasion for it, as the town was taken at four o'clock on the Sunday morning.

Here Donna Las Nalgas's tale terminates. This lady was not without a description of wit, which in Spain we call agudéza.

CHAPTER II.

CONTINUATION OF THE ADVENTURES OF JOHN, THE YOUNG ENGLISHMAN; ALSO THOSE OF HIS WORTHY FATHER, D.D., M.P., AND F.R.S.

You know the skillful conduct of the Earl of Peterborough after he took Barcelona, how successfully he prevented pillage, restored order, and rescued the Duchess of Popoli from the hands of some drunken Germans, who robbed and abused her. Conceive the surprise, grief, rage, and tears, of our friend Freind, on learning that John was confined in the dungeons of the holy inquisition, and condemned to the stake. You know that cold temperaments are frequently most energetic when great events call them into action. You should have seen this distracted father, whom you were accustomed to think imperturbable, fly to the dungeon of his son more rapidly than the horses at Newmarket hasten to the goal. The fifty soldiers who went with him were soon out of breath, and always a hundred paces behind. At length he reached the cell and entered it. What a scene! what tears! what joy! Twenty victims, devoted to the same ceremony, are delivered. All the prisoners take arms and fight with our soldiers. The buildings of the holy office are destroyed in ten minutes, and they breakfasted beside the ruins, on the wine and ham of the inquisitors.

Condemned by the Inquisition.—He was confined to a very damp cellar, and sentenced to be burnt the following Sunday, in full ceremony, clothed in a San-bénito, wearing a sugar-loaf cap, in honor of our Savior and the Virgin Mary, his mother.

In the midst of the roar of cannon, the sound of trumpets and drums, announcing our victory to Catalonia, our friend Freind recovered his accustomed tranquillity of manner. He was as calm as the sky after a day of storm. He was raising to God a heart as serene as his countenance, when he perceived a black spectral figure, clad in a surplice, issue from a vault, and fall at his feet, crying for mercy.

"Who are you?" said our friend. "Do you come from Hades?"

"Almost," rejoined the other. "I am Don Jeronimo Bueno Caracucarador, inquisitor. I solicit most humbly your forgiveness for wishing to roast your son in public. I took him for a Jew."

"Supposing that to be the case," said our friend with his customary sang froid, "does it become you, Señor Caracucarador, to roast people alive because they are descended from a sect that formerly inhabited a rocky canton near the Syrian desert? What does it matter to you whether a man is circumcised or not? that he observe Easter at the full of the moon, or on the following Sunday? It is very bad reasoning to say, 'That man is a Jew; therefore I must have him burnt, and take his property.' The Royal Society of London do not reason in that way.

"Do you know, Señor Caracucarador, that Jesus Christ was a Jew—that he was born, lived, and died a Jew? that he observed the passover like a Jew, at the full of the moon? that all his apostles were Jews? that they went to the temple after his death, as we are expressly told? that the first fifteen secret bishops of Jerusalem were Jews? But my son is no Jew; he belongs to the established church. How came it into your head to burn him alive?"

The inquisitor, overawed by the learning of Monsieur Freind, and still prostrate at his feet, replied:

"Alas! sir, we know nothing about this at the University of Salamanca. Forgive me, once more. The true reason is, your son took from me my favorite, Donna Boca Vermeja."

"Ah! if he took your favorite, that's another thing. We should never take 'our neighbor's goods.' That is not, however, a sufficient reason for burning a young man to death. As Leibnitz says, 'The punishment should be in proportion to the crime.' You Christians on the other side of the British Channel, especially toward the South, make no more of roasting each other, be it the Counsellor Dubourg, M. Servetus, or those who were burned in the reign of Philippe II., surnamed El Discreto, than we do of roasting a joint of beef in London. But bring Miss Boca Vermeja before me, that I may learn the truth from her own mouth."

Boca Vermeja appeared weeping, looking the handsomer for her tears, as women generally do.

"Is it true, Miss, that you are devotedly attached to M. Caracucarador, and that my son has abducted you?"

"Abducted me? The English gentleman! I never met with any one so amiable and good-looking as your son. You are very fortunate in being his father. I could follow him to the world's end. I always hated that ugly inquisitor, who whipped me and Mademoiselle Las Nalgas till he nearly brought blood. If you wish to make me happy, you will cause the old fellow to be hanged at my bedroom window."

Just as Boca Vermeja was thus speaking, the Earl of Peterborough sent for the inquisitor Caracucarador, to have him hanged. You will not be surprised to hear that Mr. Freind firmly opposed this measure.

"Let your just displeasure," said he, "give way to generous feelings. A man should never be put to death but when it is absolutely necessary for the safety of others. The Spaniards say the English are barbarians, who kill all the priests that come in their way. This might have injured the cause of the archduke, for whom you have taken Barcelona. I have sufficient satisfaction in rescuing my son, and putting it out of the power of this rascally monk to exercise his inquisitorial functions."

In a word, the wise and charitable Freind was contented with getting Caracucarador flogged, as he had whipped Miss Boca Vermeja and Miss Las Nalgas.

Such clemency affected the Catalonians. The persons rescued from the inquisition felt that our religion was better than theirs. Nearly all requested to be admitted members of the established church; even some bachelors of the University of Salamanca, who chanced to be at Barcelona, requested instruction. The greater part soon became enlightened, with the exception of a certain Don Inigo-y-Medroso, y-Comodios, y-Papalamiendos, who obstinately adhered to his opinions.

CHAPTER III.

SUMMARY OF THE CONTROVERSY OF THE "BUTS," BETWEEN MR. FREIND AND DON INIGO-Y-MEDROSO, Y-COMODIOS, Y-PAPALAMIENDOS, BACHELOR OF SALAMANCA.

The following is a summary of the pleasant disputation, which our dear friend Freind and the Bachelor Don Papalamiendos held, in the presence of the Earl of Peterborough. This familiar conversation was called the dialogue of the "Buts." As you read it you will discover why.

THE BACHELOR.—But, sir, notwithstanding all the fine things you have said, you must admit that your respectable established church did not exist before the time of Don Luther and Don Ecolampade; consequently, it is quite new, and can hardly be said to belong to the family.

FREIND.—You might as well say I am not a descendant of my grandfather, because another branch of the family, living in Italy, seized on his will, and my claims. I have fortunately found them again; and it is now quite clear that I am my grandfather's grandson. You and I are, as it were, of the same family; but with this difference. We read our grandfather's testament in our mother tongue, while you are forbidden to read it in yours. You are the slaves of a foreigner; we listen to the dictates of reason.

THE BACHELOR.—But suppose your reason should lead you astray? For, in a word, you have no faith in our University of Salamanca, which has declared the infallibility of the pope, and his indisputable control of the past, the present, the future, and the paulo-post-future.

FREIND.—Neither did the apostles. It is written that Peter, who denied his master Jesus, was severely rebuked by Paul. I have not examined the case to see which was in the wrong; perhaps, as is the case in most disputes, neither was right; but I do not find one passage in the Acts of the Apostles to prove that Peter was considered the master of his companions, and of the paulo-post-future.

THE BACHELOR.—But St. Peter was certainly archbishop of Rome; for Sanchez tells us that this great man came there in the reign of Nero, and filled the archbishop's throne twenty-five years under the same Nero, who only reigned thirteen. Besides, it is a matter of faith, and Don Gullandus, the prototype of the inquisition, affirms it (for we never read the Holy Bible), that St. Peter was at Rome during a certain year, for he dates one of his letters from Babylon. Now, since Babylon is visibly the anagram of Rome, it is clear that the pope by divine right is lord of the world; moreover, all the licentiates of Salamanca have shown that Simon Grace-of-God, first sorcerer and counsellor of state at the court of Nero, sent his compliments by his dog to Simon Barjona, otherwise called St. Peter, as soon as he came to Rome; that St. Peter, who was scarcely less polite, sent also his dog to compliment Simon Grace-of-God; and then they diverted themselves by trying which could soonest raise from the dead a cousin german of Nero's; that Grace-of-God only succeeded in effecting a partial restoration, while Barjona won the game by wholly restoring the dead man to life; that Grace-of-God sought to have his revenge by flying through the air like Saint Dædalus; and that Barjona broke his legs, by making him fall. On this account St. Peter received the Martyr's crown, being crucified with his heels upward. Therefore we have proved that his holiness the pope ought to reign over all who wear crowns; that he is lord of the past, the present, and of all the futures in the world.

FREIND.—It is clear these things happened in the days when Hercules separated at a stroke the two mountains Calpe and Abyla, and crossed the straits of Gibraltar in his goblet. But it is not on such histories, however authentic they may be, that we base our religion. We found it on the gospel.

THE BACHELOR.—But, sir, on what passages of the gospel? I have read a portion of the gospel in our theological tracts. Do you base it on the descent of the angel to announce to the Virgin Mary that she had conceived by the Holy Ghost? On the journey of the three kings after the star? On the massacre of all the children of the country? On the trouble the devil took to carry God into the wilderness, to place him on a pinnacle of the temple, and on the summit of a mountain from whence he beheld all the kingdoms of the world? On the miracle of water changed into wine at a village wedding? On the miracle of two thousand pigs drowned by the devil in a lake at the command of Jesus? On—?

FREIND.—Sir, we respect these things because they are in the gospel; but we never speak of them, because they are too far above our weak human reason.

THE BACHELOR.—But they say you never call the Holy Virgin, Mother of God?

FREIND.—We revere and cherish her. But we think she cares very little for the titles given her in this world. She is never styled the Mother of God in the gospel. In the year 431, there was a great dispute at the council of Ephesus to ascertain if Mary was Theotocos; and if Jesus Christ, being at the same time God and the son of Mary, Mary could be at the same time mother of God the Father and God the Son. We do not enter into these disputes of Ephesus. The Royal Society at London does not concern itself with such controversies.

THE BACHELOR.—But, sir, you talk of Theotocos. What may Theotocos mean, if you please?

FREIND.—It means Mother of God. What, are you a Bachelor of Salamanca, and don't understand Greek?

THE BACHELOR.—But Greek! Of what use can Greek be to a Spaniard? But, sir, do you believe that Jesus Christ has one nature, one person, and one will; or two natures, two persons, and two wills; or, one will, one nature, and two persons; or, two wills, two persons and one nature; or,—?

FREIND.—This, also, belongs to the Ephesian controversy and does not concern us.

THE BACHELOR.—But what does concern you, then? Do you suppose there are only three persons in God, or that there are three Gods in one person? Does the second person proceed from the first person, and the third from the two others, or from the second *intrinsecus*, or only from the first? Has the father all the attributes of the son except paternity? And does the third person proceed by infusion, by identification, or by spiration?

FREIND.—This question is not mooted in the gospel. St. Paul never wrote the name of the Trinity.

THE BACHELOR.—But, you always refer to the gospel, and never make mention of St. Bonaventura, of Albert the Great, of Tambourini, of Gullandus, of Escobar.

FREIND.—Because I do not call myself a Dominican, a Franciscan, or a Jesuit. I am satisfied with being a Christian.

THE BACHELOR.—But if you are a Christian, tell me if you conscientiously think the rest of mankind will be damned?

FREIND.—It does not become me to limit the compassion or the justice of God.

THE BACHELOR.—But to come to the point, if you are a Christian, what do you believe?

FREIND.—I believe with Jesus Christ that we ought to love God and our neighbor, forgive our enemies, and do good for evil. These are the maxims of Jesus. So true are they, that no legislator, no philosopher, ever had other principles before him, and it is impossible that there can be any other. These truths never have and never can meet with contradiction, save from our passions.

THE BACHELOR.—But, in regard to the passions, is it true that your bishops, priests, and deacons are all married?

FREIND.—Quite true. St. Joseph, who passed for the father of Jesus, was married. James the Less, surnamed Oblia, brother of our Lord, was his son, who, after the death of Jesus, spent his life in the temple. St. Paul—the great St. Paul—was a married man.

THE BACHELOR.—But Grillandus and Molina assert the contrary.

FREIND.—Let them say what they please, I prefer believing St. Paul himself on the subject. In *I. Corinthians, ix: 4-7.* he says: "Have we not power to eat and to drink? Have we not power to lead about a sister, a wife, as well as other apostles, and as the brethren of the lord, and Cephas. Or I only and Barnabas, have we not power to forbear working? Who goeth a warfare at any time at his own charges? Who planteth a vineyard and eateth not of the fruit thereof?"

THE BACHELOR.—But, sir, did St. Paul really say that?

FREIND.—Yes, he said that and very much more.

THE BACHELOR.—But, really, that prodigy of the efficacy of grace?—

FREIND.—It is true, sir, that his conversion was a great miracle. I admit, from the *Acts of the Apostles*, that he was the most cruel satellite of the enemies of Jesus. The *Acts* say that he assisted at the stoning of Stephen. He admits himself, that when the Jews condemned to death a follower of Christ, he would see to the execution of the sentence, "detuli sententiam", I admit that Abdia, his disciple, and the translator Julius, the African, accused him of putting to death James Oblia, the brother of our Lord; but his persecutions increase the wonder of his conversion, and by no means prevented his having a wife. I assure you he was married. St. Clement of Alexandria expressly declares it.

THE BACHELOR.—But St. Paul, then, was a worthy man of God! Really, I am grieved to think he assassinated St. Stephen, and St. James, and am surprised to find he traveled to the third heaven. But pray continue.

FREIND.—We gather from St. Clement of Alexandria that St. Peter had children; one St. Petronilla is mentioned among them. Eusebius, in his *History of the Church* says that St. Nicolas, one of the first disciples, had a very handsome wife; and that the disciples blamed him for being over-fond and jealous. "Sirs," said he, "let any one take her who likes; I give her to you."

In the Jewish economy, which should have lasted for ever, but to which nevertheless the Christian dispensation succeeded, marriage was not only permitted, but expressly enjoined on priests, since they were always of the same race. Celibacy was considered infamous.

It is certain that celibacy could not have been considered a very pure and honorable state by the first Christians, since we find among the bishops excommunicated by the first councils, chiefly those who oppose the marriage of priests; such as Saturnians, Basilidians, Montanists, Encrasists, and other ans and ists. This accounts for the wife of Gregory of Nazianze bearing another Gregory of Nazianze, and enjoying the inestimable felicity of being at one and the same time the wife and mother of a canonized saint,—a privilege which even St. Monica, the mother of St. Augustin, did not enjoy.

By the same reason I might name as many and even more of the ancient bishops who were married, and account for your not having had in the earlier ages of the church bishops and popes who indulged in fornication, adultery, and even worse crimes. Things are not so now. This is also the reason why the Greek church, the mother of the Latin church, allows priests to marry. In a word, the reason why I myself am married, and have a son, as fine a fellow as you can wish to see.

Besides, my dear bachelor, have you not in your church seven sacraments which are outward signs of things invisible? Does not a bachelor of Salamanca enjoy the advantage of baptism as soon as he comes into the world; of confirmation as soon as he has committed a few follies or understands those of others; of communion, though a little different from ours, when he is fourteen years of age; of holy orders, when they shave the crown of his head and give him a living of twenty, thirty, or forty thousand piastres; and lastly of extreme unction, when he is ill? Must he then be deprived of the sacrament of marriage, when he is in health? Especially when God united Adam and Eve in marriage: Adam, the first bachelor in the world, since, according to your schools, he had knowledge by infusion; Eve, the first *female* bachelor, since she tasted the tree of knowledge before her husband.

THE BACHELOR.—But, if things are so, I may cease my "Buts." This is certain, I adopt your religion; I will belong to the established church of England; will marry an honest woman, who at least will pretend to love me while I am young, take care of me when I grow old, and whom I will bury decently, should I survive her. I think this is better than roasting men and enticing girls after the fashion of my cousin Don Caracucarador, the inquisitor of the faith.

This is a faithful summary of the conversation between Mr. Freind and the Bachelor Don Papalamiendos, since called by us Papa Dexando. This curious dialogue was drawn up by Jacob Hull, one of my lord's secretaries.

After this conversation the Bachelor took me aside and said:

"This Englishman, whom I took at first for an anthropagus, must be a very good man; for he is a theologian and can keep his temper."

I informed him that Mr. Freind was tolerant, or a quaker, and a descendant of the daughter of William Penn, who founded Philadelphia. "Quaker, Philadelphia," he cried, "I never heard of those sects."

I gave him some information on the subject. He could scarcely believe me. It seemed to him like another universe. And, indeed, he was in the right.

CHAPTER IV.

JOHN RETURNS TO LONDON, AND IS LED INTO BAD COMPANY.

While our worthy philosopher Freind was enlightening the priests of Barcelona, and his son John delighting the ladies, Lord Peterborough lost all favor with the queen and arch-duke for seizing Barcelona for them. The courtiers censured him for taking the city contrary to all rule, with an army less strong by half than the garrison. At first the arch-duke was highly incensed; and our friend was obliged to print an apology for the general. Yet this arch-duke, who had come to conquer Spain, had not the worth of his chocolate. All Queen Anne had given him was squandered.

Montecuculi, in his *Memoirs*, says three things are necessary to maintain a war; 1st, money, 2nd, money, and 3rd, money. The arch-duke wrote from Guadalaxara, where he was on the 11th of August, 1706, to Lord Peterborough, a long letter signed "Yo el Rey," in which he begged him to hasten to Genoa and raise on credit £100,000. So our Sartorius, from general of an army, thus became a Genoese banker. He communicated his distress to our friend Freind. They started for Genoa. I went with them, for you know my heart leads me thither. I admired the skill and spirit of conciliation my friend displayed in this delicate business. I saw at once that intelligence may meet every exigency. Our great Locke was a physician; he became the first metaphysician in Europe, and restored the value of the British coinage. In three days Freind raised the £100,000; but the court of Charles the VI. contrived to squander it in three weeks. After this, the general, accompanied by his theologian, was obliged to repair to London to justify himself before the parliament for conquering Catalonia against all rule, and for ruining himself in the common cause. The affair was protracted and vexatious, as are all party disputes.

You know that Mr. Freind was a member of parliament before he became a priest; and he is the only person who has been allowed to combine functions so opposed. One day, when Freind was thinking over a speech he intended to deliver in the house (of which he was a most respectable member), a Spanish lady was announced as desirous of seeing him on particular business. It was Donna Boca Vermeja herself, and in tears. Our good friend ordered a luncheon. She took some refreshment, dried her eyes, and thus began:

"You will remember, sir, when you went to Genoa, you ordered your son John to leave Barcelona for London, and to commence his duties as a clerk in the exchequer, a post which your influence had obtained for him. He embarked in the Triton with a young bachelor of arts, Don Papa Dexando, and others whom you had converted. You may well suppose that I, with my dear friend Las Nalgas, accompanied them."

Boca Vermeja then told him, again shedding tears, how John was jealous, or affected to be jealous, of the bachelor,—how a certain Madame Clive-Hart, a very bold, spiteful, masculine, young married lady, had enslaved his mind,—how he lived with libertines who had no fear of God,—how, in a word, he neglected Boca Vermeja for the artful Clive-Hart; and all because Clive-Hart had a little more red and white in her complexion than poor Boca Vermeja.

"I will look into the matter at leisure," said the worthy Mr. Freind. "I must now attend parliament, to look after Lord Peterborough's business."

Accordingly, to parliament he went; where I heard him deliver a firm and concise discourse, free from commonplace epithets, and circumlocutions. He never *invoked* a law or a testimony. He quoted, enforced, and applied them. He did not say they had taken the religion of the court by surprise, by accusing lord Peterborough of exposing Queen Anne's troops to risk; because it had nothing to do with religion. He did not call a conjecture a demonstration, nor forget his respect to an august parliament, by using common jokes. He did not call Lord Peterborough his client, because client signifies a plebian protected by a senator. Freind spoke with confidence and modesty; he was listened to in silence, only disturbed by cries of "Hear him, hear him."

The House of Commons passed a vote of thanks to Earl Peterborough, instead of condemning him. His lordship obtained the same justice from the House of Peers, and prepared to set out with his dear Freind to deliver the kingdom of Spain to the arch-duke. This did not take place, solely because things do not always turn out as we wish them to.

On leaving the house, our first care was to enquire after the health of John. We learnt that he was leading a dissipated and debauched life with Mrs. Clive-Hart, and a party of young men,—intelligent,—but atheists, who believed:

"That man is in no respect superior to the brutes;—that he lives and dies as they do;—that both spring from and both return to the earth;—that wisdom and virtue consist in enjoyment and in living with those we love, as Solomon says at the end of the 'Coheleth,' which we call 'Ecclesiastes.'"

These sentiments were chiefly advanced among them by one Warburton,[1] a very forward licentious fellow. I have glanced at some of the poor author's MSS., which heaven grant may not one day be printed. Warburton pretends that Moses did not believe in the immortality of the soul, because he never speaks of it, and considers that to be the only proof of his divine mission. This absurd conclusion leads to the supposition that the religion of the Jews is false. Infidels thence argue that ours, being founded thereon, is false also; and *ours*, which is the best of all, being false, all others are, if possible, still more false: therefore there is no religion. Hence some conclude that there is no God. Let us add to these conclusions, that this little Warburton is an intriguing, slandering fellow. See what peril!

But worse than all, John was head over ears in debt, and had a strange way of paying. One of his creditors came to him with a claim for a hundred guineas, while we were in the house. John, who always appeared polite and gentle, fought his creditor, and paid him with a sword-wound. It was apprehended the wounded man would die; and John, notwithstanding lord Peterborough's protection, ran the risk of imprisonment and hanging.

[1] In 1737 Bishop Warburton published his famous work, *The Divine Legation of Moses*, in which he asserted, "that the doctrine of a future state of reward and punishment was omitted in the books of Moses," and then proceeded to demonstrate "from that very omission, that a system which could dispense with a doctrine, the very bond and cement of human society, must have come from God, and that the people to whom it was given must have been placed under His immediate superintendence." In other words, the divine origin of the Mosaic "system" is demonstrated, because Moses did not teach to the chosen people the doctrine of a future life beyond the grave. Voltaire clearly saw the fallacy of this fantastic argument, and has not failed to severely satirize the right reverend author.

Robert Carruthers, Esq., in his *Life of Alexander Pope* styles Bishop Warburton "a learned, turbulent, ambitious adventurer"—"an indefatigable and unscrupulous divine," and says of *The Divine Legation of Moses*, that it was "so learned, so novel, so paradoxical, so arrogant and absurd, that it took the world as it were by storm, and challenged universal attention."

Dr. Johnson says that Warburton's "diction is coarse and impure, and his sentences are unmeasured;" and a writer in the seventh volume of the *Quarterly Review* (as quoted by George Godfrey Cuningham, Esq., in his *Lives of Eminent and illustrious Englishmen*) says: "the rudeness and vulgarity of his manners as a controvertist, removed all restraints of decency or decorum in scattering his jests about him. His taste seems to have been neither just nor delicate." He combined "the powers of a giant with the temper of a ruffian."

Gibbon, in his *History of Christianity*, pointedly alludes to the author of *The Divine Legation of Moses*, and satirically styles the omission of the doctrine of immortality from the law of Moses, as "a mysterious dispensation of providence." "The real merit of Warburton," he says, "was degraded by the pride and presumption with which he pronounced his infallible decrees."—E.

CHAPTER V.

THEY WANT TO GET JOHN MARRIED.

You remember the anguish of the venerable Freind when he learned that John was in the prison of the inquisition at Barcelona. Imagine his rage when he learned of the debauchery and dissipation of the unfortunate lad, his way of paying debts, and his danger of getting hanged! Yet Freind restrained himself. This excellent man's self-command is really astonishing. His reason regulates his heart, as a good master rules his servants. He does every thing reasonably, and judges wisely with as much celerity as hasty people act rashly.

"This is no time to lecture John," said he. "We must snatch him from the precipice."

You must know that the day previously, our friend had come into a handsome sum, left him by George Hubert, his uncle. He went himself in search of our great surgeon, Cheselden. We found him at home, and then proceeded together to the wounded creditor. The wound was inspected. It was not dangerous. Freind gave the sufferer a hundred guineas as a first step, and fifty others by way of reparation, and then asked forgiveness for his son. Indeed, he expressed his regret so touchingly, that the poor man embraced him, and, weeping, wished to return the money.

This sight moved and surprised young Mr. Cheselden, whose reputation is becoming very great, and whose heart is as kind as his hand is skillful.

I was carried beyond myself; never had I admired and loved our friend so much.

On returning home, I asked him if he did not intend to send for his son, and to admonish him.

"No," said he. "Let him feel his faults before I speak of them. Let us sup together to-night. We will see what in honesty I ought to do. Examples correct better than reprimands."

While waiting for supper, I called on John. I found him in the state which all men experience after their first crime,—that is, pale, with sunken eyes and hoarse voice,—absent, and answering at random when spoken to.

I told him what his father had just done.

He looked at me steadily, then turned away to dash a tear from his eye. I argued well from this, and began to hope that John would yet prove a worthy man. I felt ready to clasp him in my arms, when Madame Clive-Hart came in, accompanied by a wild fellow, called Birton.

"Well," said the lady, laughing, "have you really killed a man to-day? Some tiresome fellow. 'Tis well to rid the world of such people. When you are next in the killing mood, pray think of my husband. He plagues me to death."

I surveyed this woman from head to foot. She was handsome, but there was something sinister in her countenance. John dared not reply, and, confused by my presence, looked downward.

"What's the matter?" said Birton. "You look as if you had done something wrong. I come to give you absolution. Here is a little book I have just bought at Lintot's. It proves as clearly as two and two make four, that there is neither God, nor vice, nor virtue,—a very consoling fact! So, let us drink together."

On hearing this singular discourse, I withdrew quickly, and represented to Mr. Freind how much his son required his advice.

"I see it as clearly as you do," said this kind father; "but let us begin by paying his debts."

They were all discharged the next day. John came and threw himself at his father's feet. Will you believe it? The father made no reproaches. He left him to conscience; only observing, "Remember, my son, there is no happiness apart from virtue."

Mr. Freind then saw that the bachelor married Boca Vermeja, who really loved him, notwithstanding her tears for John. Women know how to confuse such feelings wonderfully. One would almost say that their hearts are a bundle of contradictions, perhaps because they were originally formed from one of our ribs.

Our generous Freind gave her also a dowry, and took care to secure places for his converts. It is not enough to take care of people's souls, if we neglect to provide for their present wants.

After performing these good actions, with his astonishing *sang froid*, he concluded he had nothing more to do to restore his son to virtue, than to marry him to a young person of beauty, virtue, talents, and some wealth. This, indeed, was the only way to wean him from the detestable Clive-Hart, and others, whom he frequented.

I had heard speak of a Miss Primerose, a young heiress, brought up by her relative, Lady Hervey. The Earl of Peterborough introduced me to Lady Hervey. I saw Miss Primerose, and considered her a proper person to fulfill the wishes of my friend. John, in the midst of his dissipation, had great reverence and even affection for his father. He was chiefly affected that his father had never blamed him for his follies. Debts paid without informing him; wise counsels seasonably given, and without reprimand; proofs of friendship given from time to time, yet free from the familiarity which might depreciate them. All this went to John's heart, for he was both intelligent and sensitive.

Lord Peterborough introduced the father and son to Lady Hervey. I perceived that the extreme beauty of John soon made a favorable impression on Miss Primerose; for I saw her look stealthily at him and blush. John seemed only polite; and Primerose admitted to Lady Hervey that she wished his politeness might become love.

The young man soon discovered the worth of this charming girl, though he was the complete slave of Clive-Hart. He was like the Indian invited to gather celestial fruit, but restrained by the claws of a dragon.

But here the recollection of what I witnessed overwhelms me. Tears moisten my paper. When I recover, I will resume my tale.

CHAPTER VI.

A TERRIBLE ADVENTURE.

The marriage of John and the lovely Primerose was about to be celebrated. Freind never felt more joy. I shared it. But the occasion was changed into one of deep sorrow and suffering.

Clive-Hart loved John, though constantly faithless. They say this is the lot of those women who, violating modesty, renounce their honor. Especially she deceived John for her dear Birton and for another of the same school. They lived together in debauch; and, what is perhaps peculiar to our nation, they had all of them sense and worth. Unfortunately, they employed their sense against God. Madame Clive-Hart's house was a rendezvous for atheists. Well for them had they been such atheists as Epicurus, Leontium, Lucretius, Memmius, and Spinoza,—the most upright man of Holland,—or Hobbes, so faithful to his unfortunate king, Charles I.

But however it may be, Clive-Hart, jealous of the pure and gentle Primerose, could not endure the marriage. She devised a vengeance, which I conceive to be unsurpassed even in London, where I believe our fathers have witnessed crimes of every kind. She learned that Miss Primerose, returning from shopping, would pass by her door. She took advantage of the opportunity, and had a sewer opened, communicating with her premises.

Miss Primerose's carriage, on its return, was obliged to draw up at this obstruction. Clive-Hart goes out, and entreats her to alight and take some refreshment, while the passage is being cleared. This invitation made Miss Primerose hesitate; but she perceived John standing in the hall, and, yielding to an impulse stronger than her discretion, she got out. John offered her his hand. She enters. Clive-Hart's husband was a silly drunkard, as hateful to his wife as he was submissive and troublesome by his civility. He presents refreshments to the young lady, and drinks after her. Mrs. Clive-Hart takes them away instantly and brings others. By this time the street is cleared. Miss Primerose enters her carriage, and drives to her mother's.

She soon falls sick, and complains of giddiness. They suppose it is occasioned by the motion of the carriage. But the illness increased, and the next day she was dying.

Mr. Freind and I hastened to the house. We found the lovely creature pale and livid, a prey to convulsions,—her lips open, her eyes glazed, and always staring. Black spots disfigured her face and throat. Her mother had fainted on her bed. Cheselden employed in vain all the resources of his art. I will not attempt to describe Freind's anguish. It was intense. I hurried to Clive-Hart's house, and found that the husband was just dead, and that the wife had fled.

I sought John. He could not be found. A servant told me that his mistress had besought him not to leave her in her misfortune, and that they had gone off together, accompanied by Birton, no one knew whither.

Overcome by these rapid and numerous shocks, terrified at the frightful suspicions which haunted me, I hastened to the dying lady.

"Yet," said I to myself, "if this abominable woman threw herself on John's generosity, it does not follow that he is an accomplice. John is incapable of so horrible and cowardly a crime, which he had no interest in committing, which deprives him of a charming wife, and renders him odious to the human race. Weak, he has allowed himself to be drawn away by a wretch, of whose crime he was ignorant. He did not see, as I have done, Primerose dying; he never would have deserted her pillow to accompany the poisoner of his bride. Oppressed by these thoughts, I entered, shuddering, the room which I expected contained a corpse."

She was still living. Old Clive-Hart died soon, because his constitution was worn out by debauchery; but young Primerose was sustained by a temperament as robust as her blood was pure. She saw me, and enquired, in a tender tone, after John. A flood of tears gushed from my eyes. I could not reply. I was unable to speak to the father. I was obliged to leave her to the faithful hands that served her.

We went to inform his lordship of this disaster. He is as kind to his friends as terrible to his foes. Never was there a more compassionate man with so stern a countenance. He took as much pains to assist the dying lady, and to overtake the abandoned woman, and discover John, as he had done to give Spain to the arch-duke. But all our search proved in vain. I thought it would kill Freind. Now we flew to the residence of Miss Primerose, whose dying was protracted, now to Rochester, Dover, Portsmouth. Couriers were dispatched every where. We wandered about at random, like dogs that have lost the scent;—while the unfortunate mother expected hourly the death of her child.

At length we learned that a handsome lady, accompanied by three young men and some servants, had embarked at Newport, in Monmouthshire, in a little smuggling vessel that was in the roads, and had sailed for North America.

Freind sighed deeply at this intelligence, then suddenly recovering himself, and pressing my hand, he said:

"I must go to America."

I replied, weeping with admiration: "I will not leave you. But what can you do?"

"Restore my only son," said he, "to virtue and his country, or bury myself with him."

Indeed, from our information, we could not doubt but he had fled thither with that horrible woman, Birton, and the other villains of the party.

The good father took leave of Lord Peterborough, who returned soon after to Catalonia; and we went to Bristol and freighted a ship for the Delaware and the bay of Maryland.

Freind, knowing these coasts to be in the heart of the English possessions, thought it right to go thither, whether his son had sought concealment in the North or South.

He supplied himself with money, letters of credit, and provisions, and left a confidential servant in London, to write to him by ships that were leaving every week for Maryland or Pennsylvania.

We started. The crew, judging from the placid countenance of my friend, thought we were on an excursion of pleasure. But when he was alone with me, his sighs expressed the depth of his anguish. At times I congratulated myself on the happiness of consoling such a noble mind.

A west wind kept us a long time about the Sorlingues. We were obliged to steer for New England. What enquiries we made on every coast! What time and toil were thrown away! At length a northeast wind arising, we steered for Maryland. There, it was said, John and his companions had taken refuge.

The fugitives had sojourned on the coast more than a month, and had astonished the whole colony by indulgences in luxury and debauch, till then unknown in that part of the world. Then they disappeared; no one knew whither.

We advanced into the bay, intending to go to Baltimore for fresh information.

CHAPTER VII.

WHAT HAPPENED IN AMERICA.

On the way we found, to the right, a very handsome house. It was low, but convenient and neat, placed between a spacious barn and a large stable; the whole enclosed by a garden, well stocked with fruits of the country. It belonged to an old man, who invited us to alight at his retreat. He did not look like an Englishman; his accent showed us he was a foreigner. We anchored and went on shore. The old man welcomed us cordially, and gave us the best cheer to be had in the New World.

We discreetly insinuated our wish to know to whom we were indebted for so kind a reception.

"I am," said he, "of the race you call savages. I was born on the Blue Mountains, which bound this country in the west. In my childhood I was bitten by a rattlesnake, and abandoned. I was on the point of death. The father of the present Lord Baltimore, falling in with me, confided me to his physician; and to him I owe my life. I soon discharged the debt; for I have saved his in a skirmish with the neighboring tribes. He gave me, in return, this habitation."

Mr. Freind enquired if he was of Lord Baltimore's religion?

"How," said he, "would you have me profess another man's religion? I have my own."

This short and energetic answer made us reflect a little.

"You have, then," said I, "your own law and your own God?"

"Yes," he replied, with an assurance wholly free from pride. "My God is there," and he pointed to heaven. "My law is here," and he put his hand on his breast.

My friend was struck with admiration, and, pressing my hand, he said:

"This simple nature reasons more wisely than all the bachelors with whom we conversed at Barcelona."

He was anxious to know if he could gain any information respecting his son John. It was a weight that oppressed him. He enquired if his host had heard speak of some young people, who had made a great noise in the neighborhood.

"Indeed I have," said he, "I received them in my house; and they were so satisfied with the reception I gave them, that they have carried away one of my daughters."

Judge of my friend's distress at this intelligence. In his emotion, he could not avoid exclaiming:

"What! Has my son run away with your daughter?"

"Good Englishman," said the host, "do not let that grieve you. I am glad to find he is your son. He is handsome, well made, and seems courageous. He did not run away with my dear Parouba; for you must know that Parouba is her name, because it is mine. Had he taken off Parouba, it would have been a robbery; and my five sons, who are now hunting some forty or fifty miles from here, would not have endured such an affront. It is a great sin to thieve. My daughter went of her own accord with these young people. She has gone to see the country, a pleasure one cannot deny to one of her age. These travelers will bring her back to me before a month is passed. I am sure of it. They promised to do so."

These words would have made me laugh, had not the evident distress of my friend severely afflicted me.

In the evening, just as we were about to start to take advantage of the wind, one of Parouba's sons arrived out of breath, his face expressing horror and despair.

"What is the matter, my son? I thought you were hunting far away. Are you wounded by some savage beast?"

"No, father,—not wounded, yet in pain."

"But whence do you come, son?"

"From a distance of forty miles, without stopping; and I am almost dead."

The aged father makes him sit down. They give him restoratives. Mr. Freind and I, his little brothers and sisters, with the servants, crowd around him. When he recovered his breath, he exclaimed:

"Alas, my sister Parouba is a prisoner of war, and will no doubt be killed."

The worthy Parouba was grieved at this recital. Mr. Freind, feeling for him as a father, was struck to the very heart. At last, the son informed us that a party of silly young Englishmen had attacked, for diversion, the people of the mountains. He said, they had with them a very beautiful lady and her maid; and he knew not how his sister came to be with them. The handsome English lady had been scalped and killed; and his sister captured.

"I come here for aid against the people of the Blue Mountains. I will kill them too, and will retake my dear sister, or perish."

Mr. Friend's habits of self-command supported him in this trying moment.

"God has given me a son," said he. "Let him take both father and son, when the eternal decree shall go forth. My friend, I am tempted to think God sometimes acts by a special providence, since he avenges in America crimes committed in Europe, and since this wicked Clive-Hart died as she deserved. Perhaps the Sovereign of the universe does in his government punish even in this world crimes committed here. I dare not assert; I wish to think so; indeed I should believe it, were not such an opinion opposed to all metaphysical laws."

After these sad reflections on an event common in America, Freind resumed his usual demeanor.

"I have a good ship," said he to his host, "with abundant stores. Let us go up the gulf as near as we may to the Blue Mountains. My most anxious business now is to save your daughter. Let us go to your countrymen, say I bear the pipe of peace—that I am the grandson of Penn. That name alone will suffice."

At the name of Penn, so much revered throughout North America, the worthy Parouba and his son felt the greatest respect and the greatest hope. We embarked, and in thirty-six hours reached Baltimore.

We were scarcely in sight of this almost desert place, when we saw in the distance a numerous band of mountaineers descending to the plain, armed with axes, tomahawks, and those muskets which Europeans so foolishly sold to them, to procure skins. Already you might hear their frightful howlings. From another side we saw four persons approaching on horseback, accompanied by others on foot. We were taken for people of Baltimore, come there for the purpose of fighting. The horsemen galloped toward us, sword in hand. Our companions prepared to receive them. Mr. Freind, observing them steadily, shuddered for a moment; but soon resuming his sang-froid.

"Do not stir, my friends," said he. "Leave all to me."

He advanced alone and unarmed toward the party. In a moment, we saw the chief let fall the bridle from his horse, spring to the ground, and fall prostrate. We uttered a cry of surprise, and advanced. It was John himself, who, bathed in tears, had fallen at the feet of his father. Neither of them was able to speak. Birton, and the two horsemen with him, alighted. But Birton, in his characteristic way, said:

"My dear Freind, I did not expect to see you here. You and I seem born for adventures. I am glad to see you."

Freind, without deigning to reply, looked toward the army of mountaineers, now approaching us. He walked toward them, accompanied by Parouba, who acted as interpreter.

"Fellow countrymen," said Parouba, "behold a descendant of Penn, who brings you the pipe of peace."

At these words, the eldest of the tribe raising his hands and eyes to heaven, exclaimed:

"A son of Penn! He is welcome! May the Penns live for ever! The great Penn is our Manitou, our god. He and his were the only Europeans who did not deceive us, and seize on our land. He bought the territory we gave up to him; he paid for it liberally; he maintained peace among us; he brought us remedies for the few diseases we had caught from the Europeans. He taught us new arts. We never dug up against him and against his children the hatchet of war. For the Penns we always entertain respect."

Freind immediately sent for thirty hams, as many pies and fowls, with two hundred bottles of Pontac, from the ship. He seated himself close to the chief of the Blue Mountains. John and his companions assisted at the festival. John would rather have been a hundred feet under the earth. His father said nothing to him; and this silence increased his confusion.

Birton, who cared for nothing, seemed very jovial. Freind, before he began to eat, said to Parouba:

"One person, very dear to you, is waiting here. I mean your daughter."

The chief of the Blue Mountains ordered her to be brought. She had suffered no injury; she smiled to her brother and father, as if she had only returned from a walk.

I took advantage of the freedom of the meal, to enquire why the warriors of the Blue Mountains had put to death Madame Clive-Hart, and had done nothing to Parouba's daughter.

"Because we are just," returned the chief. "That proud English woman belonged to the party that attacked us. She killed one of our men by firing a pistol behind him. We did nothing to Parouba, as soon as we ascertained that she was a daughter of our tribes, and only came here for diversion. Every one should be treated according to his desert."

Freind was affected by this maxim, but he represented to them that the custom of burning captives at the stake, was degrading to worthy people; and that, with so much virtue, they should be less ferocious.

The chief then asked us what we did with those whom we killed in battle.

"We bury them."

"I understand. You leave them for worms to eat. Cannibals think proper to give themselves the preference. Their stomachs are a more honorable grave."

Birton supported with pleasure the opinions of the mountaineer. He said, the custom of boiling and roasting a neighbor must be both ancient and natural, since it prevailed in both hemispheres; and therefore it must be an innate idea;—that men were hunted before beasts, because it was easier to kill men than wolves;—that if the Jews, in their books, so long unknown, imagined that a certain Cain killed a certain Abel, it could only be with a view to eat him—that the same Jews admit they had often fed on human flesh;—that the best historians describe the Jews as eating the bleeding flesh of Romans, whom they massacred in Egypt, Cyprus, and Asia, in their revolts against the emperors Trajan and Adrian.

We allowed him to indulge in these coarse jokes, which, though unfortunately true at the bottom, had neither Grecian wit nor Roman urbanity.

Freind, without answering him, addressed the natives. Parouba translated, phrase by phrase. Tillotson himself never spoke with more force. The insinuating Smaldridge never displayed more touching graces. The great secret of eloquence is to convince. He proved to them, accordingly, that the execrable custom of burning captives, inspired a ferocity destructive to the human race; for this reason, they were strangers to the comforts of society and the tillage of the ground.

At last, they all swore by their great Manitou, that they would not burn men and women again.

Thus, from a single conversation, Freind became their legislator, like an Orpheus taming tigers. In vain may the Jesuits describe their miracles in letters which are rarely curious or edifying; they can never equal our good friend.

After loading the chiefs of the Blue Mountains with presents, he conducted the worthy Parouba back to his residence. Young Parouba, with his sister, accompanied us. The others went hunting in the distant forest.

John, Birton, and his companions, also embarked in the ship.

Freind persisted in his plan of not reproaching his son, whenever the young scamp did wrong. He left him to self-examination, and to consume his heart, as Pythagoras has it. Nevertheless, he took up the letter thrice, which had been received from England, and looked at his son as he read it. The young man would then cast his eyes on the ground; and respect and repentance might be read on his face.

Birton continued as gay and noisy as if he had just returned from the play. He was in character like the late Duke of Rochester, extreme in debauchery, bravery, sentiments, language, and, in his Epicurean philosophy, attaching himself only to the extraordinary and soon disgusted even then; having the turn of mind that mistakes probabilities for demonstrations; more wise and eloquent than any young man of his age; but too indolent to be profound in any thing.

While dining with us on board, Mr. Freind said to me:

"Indeed, my dear friend, I hope God will inspire these young people with purer morals, and that Clive-Hart's terrible example will be a lesson to them."

Birton, hearing these words, said, in a disdainful tone:

"For a long time I had been dissatisfied with that wicked Clive-Hart. Indeed, I scarcely care more for her than I do for a trussed fowl. But do you believe there exists (I don't know where) a being perpetually occupied in punishing the wicked men and women who people and depopulate the four quarters of our little world? Do you forget that the terrible Mary, daughter of Henry VIII., was happy till her death? and yet she had caused the execution of eight hundred citizens, of both sexes, on the pretext that they did not believe in transubstantiation and the pope. Her father, nearly as cruel, and her husband, more profoundly wicked, spent their lives in enjoyment. Pope Alexander IV., worse than these, was still more fortunate. All his crimes succeeded. He died at the age of seventy-two, rich and powerful, courted by the kings of the age. Where, then, is this just and avenging God?"

Mr. Freind, with austerity and calmness, replied:

"It seems to me, sir, you ought not to say 'there is no God.' Remember, Locke and Newton never pronounced that word but in a tone of reverence, that every one remarked."

"What care I" returned Birton, "for two men's grimaces? How did Newton look, when he wrote his *Commentary on the Apocalypse*? Or Locke, when he wrote the *Dialogue between a Parrot and the Prince Maurice*?"

Then Freind repeated the golden words which should be graven on every heart:

"Let us forget the dreams of great men; and remember the truths they have taught us."

This reply gave way to a well-sustained conversation, more interesting than that of the bachelor of Salamanca. I sat in a corner and took notes. The company drew round the disputants. The worthy Parouba, his son, and daughter, John's debauched companions, and John himself, with his head resting on his hands,—all listened with eager attention.

CHAPTER VIII.

DIALOGUE BETWEEN FREIND AND BIRTON ON ATHEISM.

FREIND.—I will not repeat to you, sir, the metaphysical arguments of our celebrated Clarke; I only exhort you to read them again. They are rather intended to convince than affect you. I shall confine myself to arguments calculated to touch your heart.

BIRTON.—You will gratify me very much. I like to be amused and interested. I hate sophisms. Metaphysical arguments seem to me like balloons filled with air used between the disputants. The bladders burst; and nothing remains.

FREIND.—It is possible there may be some obscurity—some bladders—in the deep things of Clarke, the respectable Arian. Perhaps he was deceived on the subject of actual infinity. Perhaps, when he took upon himself to comment on God, he follows too closely a commentator of Homer, who attributes ideas to his author which he never entertained.

At the words "infinity," "Homer," "commentators," the worthy Parouba and his daughter, and even a few of the English, seemed disposed to go and take an airing on the deck. But Freind promising to be intelligible, they consented to remain. I explained in a whisper to Parouba scientific expressions, which a native of the Blue Mountains was not likely to understand so well as a doctor of Oxford or Cambridge.

FREIND.—It would be sad, indeed, if we could not be sure of the existence of God without being metaphysicians. In all England, scarcely a hundred minds would be found capable of fathoming the mysteries of the *for* and *against*; and the rest of the world would be enveloped in ignorance,—a prey to brutal passions,—swayed by instinct alone,—and only capable of reasoning on the vulgar notions of their carnal interests. To find out God, I only require you to make one effort,—to open your eyes.

BIRTON.—I see your aim. You are returning to the worn-out arguments that the sun turns on its axis in twenty-five days and a half, in spite of the absurd inquisition of Rome;—that the light comes to us reflected from Saturn in fifteen minutes, in spite of the absurd supposition of Descartes;—that every fixed star is a sun, like ours, surrounded by planets; that the countless stars, scattered through space, obey mathematical laws, discovered and proved by the great Newton;—that a catechist announces God to children, and that Newton reveals him to the sage, as a philosophical Frenchman said, who was persecuted in his own country for asserting as much. Do not trouble yourself to bring before me the ceaseless order which prevails in all parts of the universe. All that exists must have order of some sort. Rarefied matter must take a higher place than denser substances. The strongest press upon the weakest. Bodies moved with a greater impulse, progress more rapidly than those moved with less. Things arrange themselves in this way of their own accord. In vain, after drinking a pint of wine, like Esdras, would you talk to me for a hundred and sixty hours together without shutting the mouth, I should not be convinced. Do you wish me to adopt an eternal being, infinite and immutable, who saw fit, (I do not know when,) to create from nothing, things which change every moment, and spiders to disembowel flies? Would you have me suppose, with the gossip Niewentyt, that God gave us ears that we might have faith? since faith cometh by hearing. No! No! I will not believe these quacks who have sold their drugs at a good price to fools. I keep to the little book of a Frenchman, who maintains that nothing exists nor can exist but nature; that nature does all, and is *all*; that it is impossible and contradictory that any thing can exist beyond ALL. In a word, I only believe in nature.

FREIND.—What if I tell you there is no such thing as nature; and that in us, around us, a thousand millions of leagues from us, all is art, without any exception.

BIRTON.—What? All art! That's something new.

FREIND.—Few observe that. Nothing, however, is more true. I shall always say, make use of your eyes, and you will recognize and adore God. Think how those vast globes, which you see revolve in their immense orbits, observe deep mathematical laws. There is then a great calculator whom Plato called the eternal geometrician. You admire those newly invented machines, called orreries, because Lord Orrery invented them by imitating the maker. It is a feeble copy of our planetary system and its revolutions; also the periods of the changes of the solstice and equinox which bring us from day to day a new polar planet. This period, this slow course of about twenty-six thousand years, could not be effected in our feeble hands by human orreries. The machine is very imperfect; it must be turned by a handle; yet it is a *chef-d'œuvre* of the skill of our artisans. Conceive, then, the power and patience, the genius, of the eternal architect, if we may apply such terms to the supreme being.

When I described an orrery to Parouba, he said:

"If the copy indicates genius, how much more must there be in the original?"

All present, English and American, felt the force of these words, and raised their hands to heaven.

Birton remained thoughtful. Then he cried:

"What, all art? Nature the result of art? Can it be possible?"

FREIND.—Now, consider yourself; examine with what art, never sufficiently explored, all is constructed within and without for all your wishes and actions. I do not pretend now to lecture on anatomy. You know well enough there is not one superfluous vessel, nor one that does not, in the exercise of its functions, depend on neighboring vessels. So artificial is the arrangement throughout the body, that there is not a single vein without valves and sluices, making a passage for the blood. From the roots of the hair to the toes, all is art, design, cause, and effect. Indeed, we cannot suppress feelings of indignation toward those who presume to deny final causes, and have the rashness to say that the mouth was not made to eat and speak with—that the eyes are not admirably contrived for seeing, the ears for hearing, the nerves for feeling. Such audacity is madness. I cannot conceive it.

Let us admit that every animal renders testimony to the supreme fabricator.

The smallest herb perplexes human intellect. So true is this that the aggregate toil of all men could not create a straw unless the seed be sown in the earth. Let it not be said that the seed must rot in the earth to produce. Such nonsense should not be listened to now.

The company felt the force of these proofs more forcibly than the others, because they were more palpable. Birton murmured: "Must I then acknowledge God? We shall see. It is not yet proved."

John remained thoughtful, and seemed affected.

FREIND.—No, my friends. We make nothing, we can do nothing. It is in our power to arrange, unite, calculate, weigh, measure, but, *to make*! What a word! The essential Being, existing by Himself, alone can make. This is why quacks, who labor at the philosopher's stone, prove themselves such fools. They boast that they create gold, and they cannot even create clay. Let us then confess, my friends, that there is a necessary and incomprehensible Being who made us.

BIRTON.—If he exist, where is he? Why is he concealed? Has any one ever seen him? Should the creator of good hide himself?

FREIND.—Did you ever see Sir Christopher Wren, the architect of Saint Paul's, when you were in London? Yet it is clear that church is the work of a great architect.

BIRTON.—Every one knows that Wren erected, at a great expense, the vast edifice in which Burgess, when he preaches, sends us to sleep. We know very well why and how our fathers built it. But why and how did God make the universe from nothing? You know well the ancient maxim: "Nothing can create nothing; nothing returns to nothing." No one ever doubted that truth. Your Bible itself says that your God made heaven and earth, though the heaven, that is, the assemblage of stars, is as superior to the earth, as the earth itself is to one blade of grass. But your Bible does not tell us that God made heaven and earth from nothing. It does not pretend that the Lord made woman from nothing. She was kneaded in a very singular way, from a rib taken from her husband's side. According to the Bible, chaos existed before the world; therefore matter must be as eternal as your God.

A slight murmur then went round the company; "Birton might be right," they said.

FREIND.—I think I have proved to you that there is a supreme intelligence; an eternal power to whom we owe our passing existence. I have not engaged to tell you the how and the why. God has given me sufficient reason to know that he exists, but not enough to discover whether matter has been subject to him from eternity, or whether he created it in time. What have you to do with the creation of matter, provided you acknowledge a God the ruler of matter and of yourself? You ask me where God is? I do not know. I ought not to know. I know that he is; I know that he is my maker; that he makes all, and that we ought to depend on his goodness.

BIRTON.—His goodness! Are you jesting with me? Did you not tell me to make use of my eyes? Make use of yours. Glance at the world, and then talk of the goodness of God.

Mr. Freind saw that he had now reached the most difficult part of the dispute, and that Birton was preparing a rude assault. He saw that the hearers, especially the Americans, together with himself, required a little respite. Recommending himself therefore to God, they went on deck for exercise. When tea was served, the disputation was renewed.

CHAPTER IX.

ON ATHEISM.

BIRTON.—You must not expect such success, sir, on the subject of goodness, as you have had on ingenuity and power. First, I shall touch on the misconstructions of our globe, in many instances opposed to the cleverness so much boasted of; then I intend to dwell on the perpetual crimes and misfortunes of the inhabitants; and you will judge of the great ruler's paternal affection for them.

I shall begin by telling you that in Gloucestershire, my county, when we breed horses, we rear them with care, in fine pasturage and good stables, with hay and oats. Pray, what shelter and food had these poor Americans, when we discovered their continent? They were obliged to scour over thirty or forty miles for food. All the northern coast of the old world is exposed to the same cruel necessity; and from Swedish Laponia to the Sea of Japan, a hundred tribes spend a life as short as it is wretched, in the most complete want, amidst eternal snows.

Fine climates are continually exposed to destructive scourges. There we walk over burning precipices, covered by fertile plains, which prove but deadly snares. There is no hell but this, doubtless; and it opens a hundred times beneath our feet.

They tell us of an universal deluge, an event physically impossible, and at which all sensible people laugh. But they console us by saying it only lasted ten months. I wonder it did not put out the fires which have since destroyed so many flourishing towns. Your St. Augustin tells us of a hundred cities burnt or swallowed up in Lydia, by an earthquake. Volcanoes have several times devastated lovely Italy. As a crowning misfortune, the inhabitants of the Arctic Circle are not exempt from these subterranean fires. The Icelander, always in alarm, has hunger staring him in the face, and a hundred feet of flame or ice to the right or left, under their Mount Hecla; for the great volcanoes are always found among terrible mountains.

It is in vain to say that mountains of two thousand toises in elevation are nothing on a globe nine thousand miles in diameter, or like the irregularities of an orange compared with the bulk of that fruit—that it is scarcely one foot to every three thousand feet. Alas! What then are we, if high mountains are but as figures one foot high for every three thousand feet, or four inches for every nine thousand inches? We are then animals absolutely imperceptible; yet we are liable to be crushed by all that surrounds us, though our infinite littleness, so closely bordering on nothing, might seem to secure us from all accidents. Besides the countless cities, destroyed and re-destroyed like as many ant-hills, what shall we say to the seas of sand that cross the centre of Africa, and whose burning waves, raised by the wind, have buried entire armies? What is the use of the vast deserts on the borders of Syria,—deserts so horrible that the ferocious animals, called Jews, imagined they had reached Paradise when they passed from these scenes of horror into a little corner of land where they could cultivate a few acres? It is not enough that man (the noble creature) should be so ill lodged, clothed, and fed, for so many ages. He comes into the world to live for a few days, perplexed by deceitful hopes and real vexations. His body, contrived with useless art, is a prey to all the ills resulting from that very art. He lives between the dangers of poison and plague. No one can remember the list of ills we are subject to; and the modest doctors of Switzerland pretend they can cure them all.

While Birton said this, the company listened with attention and even emotion. Parouba said "Let us see how the doctor will get over this."

Even John said in a low tone: "On my word, he is right. I was a fool to be so soon touched by my father's conversation."

Mr. Freind waited till their imaginations were a little recovered from the assault, and then resumed the discussion.

FREIND.—A young theologian would answer these sad truths by sophisms, backed with quotations from St. Basil and St. Cyril. For my part, I shall admit that there are many physical evils in the world. I will not even lessen the number, though Mr. Birton has seen fit to exaggerate. I ask you, my dear Parouba, is not your climate made for you? It cannot be injurious, since neither you nor your companions wish to leave it. Esquimaux, Icelanders, Laplanders, Asiatics, and Indians, never think of leaving theirs. The reindeer, which God has sent to clothe and feed them, die when transported to another zone. Laplanders themselves die in southern climates. The south of Siberia is too warm for them; here they would be burnt. It is evident that God made every kind of animal and vegetable for the clime in which it thrives. Negroes, a race of men so different to ours, are so thoroughly formed for their country, that thousands of them have preferred death to slavery elsewhere. The camel and ostrich are quite at home in the sands of Africa. The bull abounds in fertile countries, where the grass is ever fresh for his nourishment. Cinnamon and spice only grow in India. Barley is only useful in those countries where God has appointed it to grow. From one end of America to the other, you have different kinds of food. The vine cannot be brought to perfection in England, nor in Sweden and Canada. This is the reason that in some countries the elements of religious rites consist in bread and wine; and they do well to thank God for the food and beverage his goodness has provided; and Americans would do well to thank him for their Indian corn and arrow-root. Throughout the world God has suited all animals, from the snail to man, to the countries in which he has placed them. Let us not reproach Providence when we owe him praises.

But to consider scourges, such as inundations, volcanoes, earthquakes. If you confine your attention to the accidents which sometimes happen to the wheels of the eternal machine, you may well consider God as a tyrant; but observe his ceaseless benefits, and he becomes a compassionate father. You have quoted Augustin and his account of the destruction of a hundred cities; but remember the African rhetorician often contradicts himself and was prodigal of exaggerations in his writings. He wrote of earthquakes as he did of the efficacy of grace, and the damnation of children dying without baptism. Has he not said in his thirty-seventh sermon, that he had seen people at Ethiopia with one eye in the middle of the forehead like the Cyclops, and a whole race without heads?

We, who are not fathers of the church, ought not to go beyond nor to stop short of truth; and the truth is, that of the houses destroyed, we cannot reckon that more than one out of every hundred thousand, is destroyed by the fires necessary to the due performance of the operations of the world.

So essential to the nature of the universe is fire, that but for it there would be no sun nor stars, no animals, vegetables, or minerals. The fire, placed under the earth, is subject to fixed natural laws. Some disasters may nevertheless occur. You cannot say a man is a poor artisan when an immense machine, formed by him, lasts unimpaired for years. If a man invented a hydraulic engine to water a province, would you disparage his work because it destroys some insects?

I have shown you that the machine of the world is the work of an intelligent and powerful being; you, who are intelligent, ought to admire him,—you, who are laden with his gifts, ought to adore him.

But how, you inquire, can the wretches who are condemned to languish under incurable evils—how can they admire and love? I must tell you, that such ills are generally brought on ourselves, or come to us from our fathers, who abused their bodies, and not from the great fabricator. No disease but decrepitude was known in America till we introduced strong liquors, the source of all evils.

Let us remember that in Milton's Poem, the simple Adam is made to inquire if he will live long. Yes, is the reply, if you take nothing to excess. Observe this rule, my friends. Can you require that God should let you live for ages, as the reward of your gluttony, your drunkenness, your incontinence, and your indulgence in infamous passions, which corrupt the blood and necessarily shorten life?

I approved of this reply. Parouba liked it; but Birton was not moved. I read in John's eyes that he was still doubtful. Birton rejoined in these terms:

BIRTON.—Since you have made use of common arguments, with a few novel remarks, I may be allowed to follow your plan. If so good and powerful a God existed, surely he would not have suffered evil to enter the world, nor have devoted his creatures to grief and crime. If he cannot prevent evil, he is not almighty; if he will not, he is cruel.

The annals of the Brahmins only extend back 8,000 years; those of the Chinese only 5,000. Our knowledge is but of yesterday; but, in that brief space, all is horror. Murder has been the practice from one end of the earth to the other; and men have been weak enough to give to those men who slew the greatest number of their fellow creatures, the titles of heroes, demi-gods, and even gods.

In America there were left two great nations, beginning to enjoy the sweets of peace and civilization, when the Spaniards came there to slay eleven millions. They hunted men down with dogs; and King Ferdinand of Castile gave those dogs pensions for their services.

The heroes who subdued the New World, massacred innocent and helpless babes, murdered peaceable and defenceless Indians, and committed the most inhuman barbarities! They roasted King Guatimozin, in Mexico, on a gridiron. They hastened to Peru to convert the Inca, Atahualpa. A priest, named Almagro, son of a priest condemned to be hanged in Spain for highway robbery, went there with one Pizarro, to inform the Emperor of the Peruvians, by the voice of another priest, that a third priest, named Alexander IV., polluted by incest, assassination, and homicide, had given, with his full consent (*proprio motu*) and with full power, not only Peru, but one half of the New World, to the King of Spain; and that Atahualpa ought instantly to submit, under pain of suffering the indignation of the apostles Peter and Paul. But as this king knew as little of Latin as the priest who read the papal bull, he was instantly declared heretical and incredulous.

They burned Atahualpa, as they had burned Guatimozin. They slew his people; and all to gain that hard and yellow earth which has only served to depopulate and impoverish Spain; for it has made her neglect the cultivation of the earth, which really nourishes man.

Now, my dear Mr. Freind, if the fantastic and ridiculous being men call the devil, had wished to make men in his image, would he have made them otherwise? Do not, then, attribute such an abominable work to God.

This speech brought the party round again to Birton's views. I saw John rejoice in himself; even young Parouba heard with horror of the priest Almagro—of the priest who read the Latin bull—of the priest Alexander IV.—of all Christians who committed, under pretence of devotion, such crimes to obtain gold. I confess, I trembled for Freind. I despaired of his cause. He replied, however, without embarrassment.

FREIND.—Remember, my friends, there is a God. This I proved to you, you agreed to it, and after being driven to admit that he exists, you strive to find out his imperfections, vices, and wickedness.

I am far from asserting, with some reasoners, that private ills form the general good. This is too ridiculous a sentiment. I admit, with grief, that the world contains much moral and physical evil: but, since it is certain that God exists, it is also certain that all these evils cannot prevent God's existence. He cannot be cruel. What interest could make him so? There are horrible evils in the world, my friends. Let us not swell their number. It is impossible that God can be other than good; but men are perverse, and make a detestable use of the liberty that God has given and ought to have given,—that is, the power of exercising their wills, without which they would be simple machines, formed by a wicked being, to be broken at his caprice.

All enlightened Spaniards agree that a small number of their ancestors abused this liberty so far as to commit crimes that make human nature shudder. The second Don Carlos did what he could to repair the atrocities committed by the Spaniards under Ferdinand and Charles V.

If there be crime in the world, my friends, there is virtue as well.

BIRTON.—Ah! ha! virtue! A good joke! I should like to see this virtue. Where is she to be found?

At these words I could not contain myself.

"You may find her," said I, "in the worthy Mr. Freind, in Parouba, even in yourself when your heart is cleansed of its vices."

He blushed; and John also. The latter looked down and seemed to feel remorse. His father surveyed him with compassion and resumed.

FREIND.—Yes, dear friends. If there have always been crimes; there have always been virtues too. Athens had such men as Socrates, as well as such as Anitus. Rome had Catos, as well as Syllas. Nero frightened the world by his atrocities, but Titus, Trajan, and the Antonines, consoled it by their benevolence, My friend will explain to Parouba who these great men were. Fortunately, I have Epictetus in my pocket. Epictetus was a slave, but the equal of Marcus Aurelius in mind. Listen; and may all who pretend to teach men hear what Epictetus says to himself,—"God made me; I feel this; and shall I dare to dishonor him by infamous thoughts, criminal actions, and base desires?" His mind agreed with his conversation. Marcus Aurelius, on the throne of Europe and two parts of our hemisphere, did not think otherwise than the slave Epictetus. The one was never humiliated by meanness, nor the other dazzled by greatness; and when they wrote their thoughts it was for the use of their disciples, and not to be extolled in the papers. Pray, in your opinion, were not Locke, Newton, Tillotson, Penn, Clarke, the good man called "The Man of Ross," and many others, in and beyond your island, models of virtue?

You have alluded to the cruel and unjust wars of which so many nations have been guilty. You have described the abominations of Christians in Mexico and Peru; you might add the St. Bartholomew of France and the Irish massacre. But are there not people who have always held in abhorrence the shedding of blood? Have not the Brahmins in all ages given this example to the world? and, even in this country, have we not near us, in Pennsylvania, our Philadelphians, whom they attempt in vain to ridicule by the name of Quakers, and who have always hated war?

Have we not the Carolinas, where the great Locke dictated laws? In these two lands of virtue, all citizens are equal; all consciences are free; all religions good; provided they worship God. There all men are brethren. You have seen, Mr. Birton, the inhabitants of the Blue Mountains lay down their arms before a descendant of Penn. They felt the force of virtue. You persist in disavowing it. Because the earth produces poisons as well as wholesome plants, will you prefer the poisons?

BIRTON.—Oh, sir, your poisons are not to the point. If God made them, they are his work. He is master, and does all. His hand directs Cromwell's, when he signs the death warrant of Charles I. His arm conducts the headsman's, who severs his head from the body. No, I cannot admit that God is a homicide.

FREIND.—Nor I. Pray, hear me. You will admit that God governs by general laws. According to these laws, Cromwell, a monster of fanaticism and envy, determines to sacrifice Charles I. to his own interest, which, no doubt, all men seek to promote, though they do not understand it alike. According to the laws of motion established by God, the executioner cuts off his head. But assuredly it is not God who commits the assassination by a particular act of his will. God was not Cromwell, nor Ravaillac, nor Balthazar Gerard, nor the preaching friar, James Clement. God does not permit, nor command, nor authorize crime. But he has made man; he has established laws of motion; and these eternal laws are equally executed by the good man who stretches out his hand to the poor, and by the hand of a villain who assassinates his brother. In the same way that God did not extinguish the sun, or swallow up Spain, to punish Cortez, Almagro, and Pizarro, so, also, he does not send a company of angels to London, nor make a hundred thousand pipes of Burgundy to descend from heaven to delight the hearts of his dear Englishmen, when they do good. His general providence would become ridiculous, if thus made manifest to every individual; and this is so striking, that God never punishes a criminal immediately, by a decided stroke of his power. He lets the sun shine on the evil and the good. If some wretches expire in their crimes, it is by the general laws that govern the world. I have read in a great book, by a Frenchman called Mézeray, that God caused our Henry V. to suffer a painful death, because he dared to sit on the throne of a Christian king.

The physical part of a bad action is the effect of the primary laws given to matter by the hand of God. All moral evil is the effect of the liberty which man abuses.

In a word, without plunging into the fogs of metaphysics, let us remember that the existence of God is proved. We have no longer to argue on that point. Take God from the world, and does the assassination of Charles I. become more lawful? Do you feel less aversion toward his executioner? God exists. Enough. If he exists, he is just. Be, then, just also.

BIRTON.—Your argument has strength and force, though it does not altogether exonerate God from being the author of physical and moral evil. I see your way of justifying him makes an impression on the assembly; but might it not be contrived that these laws should not involve such particular misfortunes? You have proved to me a powerful and eternal God, and I was almost on the point of believing. But I have some terrible objections to make. Come, John, courage; let us not be cast down.

CHAPTER X.

ON ATHEISM.

Night closed in beautifully. The atmosphere presented a vault of transparent azure, spangled with golden stars. Such a spectacle always affects man, and inspires him with pleasant reveries. The worthy Parouba admired the heavens, like a German when he beholds St. Peter's at Rome, or the Opera at Naples, for the first time.

"What a boldly arched vault," said he to Freind.

"It is no arch at all," replied Freind. "The blue dome you behold is nothing more than a collection of vapors, which God has so disposed and combined with the mechanism of your eyes, that, wherever you may be, you are still in the centre of your promenade, and perceive what is called heaven, arched above your head."

"And those stars, Mr. Freind?"

"As I have already said, they are so many suns, round which other worlds revolve. Far from being attached to that blue vault, remember that they are at various and prodigious distances from us. That star is twelve hundred millions of miles from our sun."

Then, showing him the telescope he had brought, he pointed out to him the planets;—Jupiter, with his four moons; Saturn, with his five moons and mysterious ring.

"It is the same light," said he, "which proceeds from all these luminaries, and comes to us from this planet, in a quarter of an hour, and from that star, in six months."

Parouba was deeply impressed, and said: "The heavens proclaim a God." All the crew looked on with admiration. But the pertinacious Birton, unmoved, continued as follows:

BIRTON.—Be it so! There is a God, I grant it. But what is that to you and me? What connection is there between the superior Being and worms of the earth? What relation is there between his essence and ours? Epicurus, when he supposed a God in the planets, did well to conclude that he took no part in our horrors and follies; that we could neither please nor offend him; that he had no need of us; nor we of him. You admit a God, more worthy of the human mind than the God of Epicurus, or the gods of the east and west: but if you assert, with so many others, that God made the world and man for his own glory; that he formerly required sacrifices of oxen for his glory; that he appeared for his glory in our biped form, you would, I think, be asserting an absurdity. The love of glory is nothing but pride. A proud man is a conceited fellow, such as Shakespeare would introduce in his plays. This epithet cannot suit God—it does not agree with the divine nature—any more than injustice, cruelty or inconstancy. If God condescended to regulate the universe, it could only be to make others happy. Has he done so?

FREIND.—He has doubtless succeeded with all just spirits. They will be happy one day; if they are not so now.

BIRTON.—Happy! How? When? Who told you so?

FREIND.—His justice.

BIRTON.—Will you tell me that we shall live eternally—that we have immortal souls, after admitting that the Jews, whom you boast of having succeeded, did not entertain this notion of immortality up to the time of Herod? This idea of an immortal soul was invented by the Brahmins, adopted by the Persians, Chaldeans, and Greeks, and was for a long time unknown to the insignificant and superstitious Jewish tribes. Alas! sir, how do we know that we have souls? or how do we know but other animals, who have similar passions, wills, appetites, and memories, so incomprehensible to us, have not souls as well?

Hitherto I have thought that there is in nature a power by which we have the faculty of life in all our body,—walking with our feet,—taking with our hands,—seeing with our eyes, feeling with our nerves, thinking with our brain,—and that all this is called the soul, which is merely a vague word, signifying the unknown principle of our faculties. With you, I will call God the intelligent principle animating nature; but has he condescended to reveal himself to us?

FREIND. Yes, by his works.

BIRTON.—Has he revealed his laws, or spoken to us?

FREIND.—Yes, by the voice of conscience. Is it true, that, if you killed your Father and mother, your conscience would be a prey to a remorse as terrible as it would be involuntary? Is not this truth avowed and felt throughout the world? To come down to lesser crimes,—do they not all revolt us at the first glance,—make us turn pale when we commit them for the first time,—and leave in our hearts the stings of repentance?

BIRTON.—I must confess it.

FREIND.—God, in thus speaking to your heart, has commanded you to abstain from crime. As for equivocal actions, which some condemn and others approve, what can we do better than follow the grand rule of Zoroaster,—"When you are not sure whether the action you are about to commit is good or bad, abstain from it."

BIRTON.—An admirable maxim, and doubtless the most beautiful ever advanced in morals. I admit that, from time to time, God has raised up men to teach virtue to their degraded fellows. I apologize to you for speaking lightly of virtue.

FREIND.—Rather apologize to the Supreme Being, who can reward and punish eternally.

BIRTON.—What! will God punish me for yielding to passions he has given me?

FREIND.—He has given you passions, with which you can do both good and evil. I do not tell you he will punish eternally; nor how he will punish; for no one can know that. The Brahmins were the first to conceive a place of imprisonment for those who had revolted from God; they were shut up in a description of hell, called Onderah, but were gradually liberated at various periods. Hence we have our mixture of virtues, vices, pleasures, and calamities. This conceit is ingenious;—and that of Pandora and Prometheus more so. Less polished nations have vulgarly imitated the same fable. These inventions are the fancies of Eastern philosophy. All I can say is, that if by abusing your liberty you have done evil, you cannot say God will not punish you.

BIRTON.—I have tried to convince myself that he could not; but in vain. I confess I have abused my liberty, and that God may well punish me. But I cannot be punished when I have ceased to exist.

FREIND.—The best course is to do well, while you exist.

BIRTON.—To do well! Well, I confess I think you are right. It is the best course.

I wish, my dear friend, you had witnessed the effect of Freind's discourse on both the English and Americans. The light saucy Birton became thoughtful and modest. John fell at his father's feet, with tears in his eyes, and his father embraced him. I shall now proceed to relate the last scene of this interesting disputation.

BIRTON.—I conceive that the great master of the universe is eternal; but we, who are but of yesterday, may we presume to expect immortality? All beings around us perish, from the insect devoured by the swallow, to the elephant, eaten by worms.

FREIND.—Nothing perishes; but all things change. The genus of animals and vegetables subsist, develop, and multiply. Why can you not allow that

God might preserve the principle which makes us act and think, of whatever nature it may be? God preserve me from making a system; but certainly there is in us something that wills and thinks. This something, formerly called a monad, is imperceptible. God has given it us, or, rather, God has given us to it. Are you sure he cannot preserve it in being? Can you give me any proof?

BIRTON.—No! I have sought for a proof in all the atheistical books within my reach; and especially in the third *Book of Lucrece*; but I never found any thing but conjectures.

FREIND.—And shall we on simple conjecture give ourselves up to fatal passions, and live like brutes, with no other restraint upon us than the fear of men, rendered eternally cruel to each other by their mutual dread? For we always wish to destroy what we fear. Think, sir! think seriously, my son John. To expect neither reward nor punishment is the true spirit of atheism. What is the use of a God who has no power over you? As though one should say, "There is a very powerful king in China," I reply, "Success to him, let him keep in his territory,—I, in mine. I care no more for him than he cares for me. He has no more control over me than a canon of Windsor over a member of parliament." Then should I be a God to myself,—Sacrificing the whole world to my caprice? And, recognizing no law, I should only consider myself? If others are sheep, I should become the wolf. If they choose to play the chicken, I should play the fox.

I will presume, (God forbid it), that all Englishmen are atheists. I will allow that there may be some peaceable citizens, quiet by nature, rich enough to be honest, regulated by honor, and so attentive to demeanor, that they contrive to live together in society. They cultivate the arts which improve morals; they live at peace in the innocent gaiety of honest people. But the poor and needy atheist, sure of impunity, would be a fool if he did not assassinate or steal to get money. Then would all the bonds of society be sundered. All secret crimes would inundate the world, and, like locusts, though at first imperceptible, would overspread the earth. The common people would become hordes of thieves, like those of our day, of whom not a tenth part are hung at our sessions. They would pass their wretched lives in taverns, with bad women. They would fight together, and fall down drunk amidst the pewter pots with which they break each other's heads. Nor would they rise but to steal and murder again,—to recommence the same round of hideous brutality. Who, then, would restrain great kings in their fury? An atheist king is more dangerous than a fanatical Ravaillac.

Atheism abounded in Italy during the fifteenth century. What was the consequence? It was as common a matter to poison another, as to invite him to supper. The stroke of the stiletto was as frequent as an embrace. There were then professors of crime; as we now have professors of music and mathematics. Churches, even, were the favorite scenes of murder, and princes were slain at the altar. In this way, Pope Sextus IV. and archbishop of Pisa put to death two of the most accomplished princes of Europe. Explain, my dear friend, to Parouba and his children, what I mean by a pope and an archbishop; but tell them we have no such monsters now. But to resume: A Duke of Milan was also slain in a church. Every one knows the astonishing horrors of Alexander VI. Had such morals continued, Italy would have been more desolate than Peru after the invasion.

Faith, then, in a God who rewards good actions, punishes the bad, and forgives lesser faults, is most useful to mankind. It is the only restraint on powerful men, who insolently commit crimes on the public, and on others who skillfully perpetrate offences. I do not tell you to mingle, with this necessary faith, superstitious notions that disgrace it. Atheism is a monster that would prey on mankind only to satisfy its voracity. Superstition is another phantom, preying upon men as a deity. I have often observed that an atheist may be cured; but we rarely cure superstition radically. The atheist is generally an inquiring man, who is deceived; the superstitious man is a brutal fool, having no ideas of his own. An atheist might assault Ephigenia when on the point of marrying Achilles; but a fanatic would piously sacrifice her on the altar, and think he did service to Jupiter. An atheist would steal a golden vessel from the altar to feast his favorites, but the fanatic would celebrate an *auto-da-fe* in the same church, and sing hymns while he was causing Jews to be burned alive. Yes, my friends, superstition and atheism are the two poles of a universe in confusion. Tread these paths with a firm step; believe in a good God, and *be* good. This is all that the great philosophers, Penn and Locke, require of their people.

Answer me, Mr. Birton,—and you, my friends,—what harm can the worship of God, joined to the happiness of a virtuous life, do you? We might be seized with mortal sickness, even now while I am speaking; who, then, would not wish to have lived innocently? Read, in Shakespeare, the death of our wicked Richard III., and see how the ghosts of those he had murdered haunted his imagination. Witness the death of Charles IX. after the horrors of St. Bartholomew. In vain his chaplain assured him he had done well. His blood started from every pore; all the blood he had shed cried out against him! Believe me, all these monsters were tortured by remorse, and died in despair.

Birton and his friends could contain themselves no longer. They fell at Freind's feet, "Yes," said Birton, "I believe in God, and I believe you."

CHAPTER XI.

RETURN TO ENGLAND—JOHN'S MARRIAGE.

We were already near Parouba's house; and we supped there. John could eat nothing. He sat apart in tears. His father went to console him.

"Ah!" said John, "I do not deserve such a father. I shall die of shame for yielding to the fascination of that wicked Clive-Hart. I am the cause of Miss Primerose's death; just now, when you talked of poison, I shuddered; for I thought I saw Clive-Hart presenting the horrible draught to Primerose. How could I have so far lost myself as to accompany so vile a creature? I was blind. I did not discover my error till she was taken by the savages. In a fit of rage she almost admitted her guilt. From that moment, I have loathed her; and, for a punishment, the form of Primerose is ever before me, and seems to say, 'I died because I loved you.'" His father said a blameless life could alone repair his past errors.

The next day we sailed for England, after giving presents to the Paroubas. Tears mingled with our adieus; and Birton, who had been only giddy, already seemed a reasonable person.

When we were out at sea, Freind said to John, in my presence: "Do you still cherish the memory of the amiable Primerose?" These words so wrung the heart of the young man, that I feared he would throw himself into the sea.

"Console yourself, then," said Freind. "Miss Primerose is alive, and loves you still."

Freind had received certain information on this subject from his servant, who had written to him punctually by every ship. Mr. Mead, who has since acquired so great a reputation by his skill in the counteraction of poisons, had saved the young lady's life. In a moment, John passed from despair to extreme joy. I will not attempt to describe the change. It was the happiest moment of his life. Birton and his friends shared his joy. What more shall I say? The worthy Freind was as a father to all. The wedding was celebrated at Dr. Mead's. Birton, now another man, also married; and he and John are now among the best people in England.

Admit, that a wise man can instruct fools.

Epictetus, the slave. From a painting by Giuseppe Rossi.—Marcus Aurelius, on the throne of Europe and two parts of our hemisphere, did not think otherwise than the slave Epictetus.

Grand entrance to palace. (From Layard's Discoveries among the ruins of Nineveh and Babylon.)

PRINCESS OF BABYLON

The Phœnix

I.

ROYAL CONTEST FOR THE HAND OF FORMOSANTA.

The aged Belus, king of Babylon, thought himself the first man upon earth; for all his courtiers told him so, and his historians proved it. We know that his palace and his park, situated at a few parafangs from Babylon, extended between the Euphrates and the Tigris, which washed those enchanted banks. His vast house, three thousand feet in front, almost reached the clouds. The platform was surrounded with a balustrade of white marble, fifty feet high, which supported colossal statues of all the kings and great men of the empire. This platform, composed of two rows of bricks, covered with a thick surface of lead from one extremity to the other, bore twelve feet of earth; and upon the earth were raised groves of olive, orange, citron, palm, cocoa, and cinnamon trees, and stock gillyflowers, which formed alleys that the rays of the sun could not penetrate.

The waters of the Euphrates running, by the assistance of pumps, in a hundred canals, formed cascades of six thousand feet in length in the park, and a hundred thousand *jets d'eau*, whose height was scarce perceptible. They afterward flowed into the Euphrates, from whence they came. The gardens of Semiramis, which astonished Asia several ages after, were only a feeble imitation of these ancient prodigies, for in the time of Semiramis, every thing began to degenerate amongst men and women.

But what was more admirable in Babylon, and eclipsed every thing else, was the only daughter of the king, named Formosanta. It was from her pictures and statues, that in succeeding times Praxiteles sculptured his Aphrodita, and the Venus of Medicis. Heavens! what a difference between the original and the copies! so that king Belus was prouder of his daughter than of his kingdom. She was eighteen years old. It was necessary she should have a husband worthy of her; but where was he to be found? An ancient oracle had ordained, that Formosanta could not belong to any but him who could bend the bow of Nimrod.

This Nimrod, "a mighty hunter before the Lord," (*Gen. x:9*), had left a bow seventeen Babylonian feet in length, made of ebony, harder than the iron of mount Caucasus, which is wrought in the forges of Derbent; and no mortal since Nimrod could bend this astonishing bow.

It was again said, "that the arm which should bend this bow would kill the most terrible and ferocious lion that should be let loose in the Circus of Babylon." This was not all. The bender of the bow, and the conquerer of the lion, should overthrow all his rivals; but he was above all things to be very sagacious, the most magnificent and most virtuous of men, and possess the greatest curiosity in the whole universe.

Three kings appeared, who were bold enough to claim Formosanta. Pharaoh of Egypt, the Shah of India, and the great Khan of the Scythians. Belus appointed the day and place of combat, which was to be at the extremity of his park, in the vast expanse surrounded by the joint waters of the Euphrates and the Tigris. Round the lists a marble amphitheatre was erected, which might contain five hundred thousand spectators. Opposite the amphitheatre was placed the king's throne. He was to appear with Formosanta, accompanied by the whole court; and on the right and left between the throne and the amphitheatre, there were other thrones and seats for the three kings, and for all the other sovereigns who were desirous to be present at this august ceremony.

The king of Egypt arrived the first, mounted upon the bull Apis, and holding in his hand the cithern of Isis. He was followed by two thousand priests, clad in linen vestments whiter than snow, two thousand eunuchs, two thousand magicians, and two thousand warriors.

The king of India came soon after in a car drawn by twelve elephants. He had a train still more numerous and more brilliant than Pharaoh of Egypt.

The last who appeared was the king of the Scythians. He had none with him but chosen warriors, armed with bows and arrows. He was mounted upon a superb tiger, which he had tamed, and which was as tall as any of the finest Persian horses. The majestic and important mien of this king effaced the appearance of his rivals; his naked arms, as nervous as they were white, seemed already to bend the bow of Nimrod.

These three lovers immediately prostrated themselves before Belus and Formosanta. The king of Egypt presented the princess with two of the finest crocodiles of the Nile, two sea horses, two zebras, two Egyptian rats, and two mummies, with the books of the great Hermes, which he judged to be the scarcest things upon earth.

The king of India offered her a hundred elephants, each bearing a wooden gilt tower, and laid at her feet the *vedam*, written by the hand of Xaca himself.

The king of the Scythians, who could neither write nor read, presented a hundred warlike horses with black fox skin housings.

The princess appeared with a downcast look before her lovers, and reclined herself with such a grace as was at once modest and noble.

Belus ordered the kings to be conducted to the thrones that were prepared for them. "Would I had three daughters," said he to them, "I should make six people this day happy!" He then made the competitors cast lots which should try Nimrod's bow first. Their names inscribed were put into a golden casque. That of the Egyptian king came out first, then the name of the King of India appeared. The king of Scythia, viewing the bow and his rivals, did not complain at being the third.

Whilst these brilliant trials were preparing, twenty thousand pages and twenty thousand youthful maidens distributed, without any disorder, refreshments to the spectators between the rows of seats. Every one acknowledged that the gods had instituted kings for no other cause than every day to give festivals, upon condition they should be diversified—that life is too short for any other purpose—that lawsuits, intrigues, wars, the altercations of theologians, which consume human life, are horrible and absurd—that man is born only for happiness that he would not passionately and incessantly pursue pleasure, were he not designed for it—that the essence of human nature is to enjoy ourselves, and all the rest is folly. This excellent moral was never controverted but by facts.

Whilst preparations were making for determining the fate of Formosanta, a young stranger, mounted upon an unicorn, accompanied by his valet, mounted on a like animal, and bearing upon his hand a large bird, appeared at the barrier. The guards were surprised to observe in this equipage, a figure that had an air of divinity. He had, as hath been since related, the face of Adonis upon the body of Hercules; it was majesty accompanied by the graces. His black eye-brows and flowing fair tresses, wore a mixture of beauty unknown at Babylon, and charmed all observers. The whole amphitheatre rose up, the better to view the stranger. All the ladies of the court viewed him with looks of astonishment. Formosanta herself, who had hitherto kept her eyes fixed upon the ground, raised them and blushed. The three kings turned pale. The spectators, in comparing Formosanta with the stranger, cried out, "There is no other in the world, but this young man, who can be so handsome as the princess."

The ushers, struck with astonishment, asked him if he was a king? The stranger replied, that he had not that honor, but that he had come from a distant country, excited by curiosity, to see if there were any king worthy of Formosanta. He was introduced into the first row of the amphitheatre, with his valet, his two unicorns, and his bird. He saluted, with great respect, Belus, his daughter, the three kings, and all the assembly. He then took his seat, not without blushing. His two unicorns lay down at his feet; his bird perched upon his shoulder; and his valet, who carried a little bag, placed himself by his side.

The trials began. The bow of Nimrod was taken out of its golden case. The first master of the ceremonies, followed by fifty pages, and preceded by twenty trumpets, presented it to the king of Egypt, who made his priests bless it; and supporting it upon the head of the bull Apis, he did not question his gaining this first victory. He dismounted, and came into the middle of the circus. He tries, exerts all his strength, and makes such ridiculous contortions, that the whole amphitheatre re-echoes with laughter, and Formosanta herself could not help smiling.

His high almoner approached him:

"Let your majesty give up this idle honor, which depends entirely upon the nerves and muscles. You will triumph in every thing else. You will conquer the lion, as you are possessed of the favor of Osiris. The Princess of Babylon is to belong to the prince who is most sagacious, and you have solved enigmas. She is to wed the most virtuous: you are such, as you have been educated by the priests of Egypt. The most generous is to marry her, and you have presented her with two of the handsomest crocodiles, and two of the finest rats in all the Delta. You are possessed of the bull Apis, and the books of Hermes, which are the scarcest things in the universe. No one can hope to dispute Formosanta with you."

"You are in the right," said the King of Egypt, and resumed his throne.

The bow was then put in the hands of the king of India. It blistered his hands for a fortnight; but he consoled himself in presuming that the Scythian King would not be more fortunate than himself.

The Scythian handled the bow in his turn. He united skill with strength. The bow seemed to have some elasticity in his hands. He bent it a little, but he could not bring it near a curve. The spectators, who had been prejudiced in his favor by his agreeable aspect, lamented his ill success, and concluded that the beautiful princess would never be married.

The unknown youth leaped into the arena and addressing himself to the king of Scythia said:

"Your majesty need not be surprised at not having entirely succeeded. These ebony bows are made in my country. There is a peculiar method in using them. Your merit is greater in having bent it, than if I were to curve it."

He then took an arrow and placing it upon the string, bent the bow of Nimrod, and shot the arrow beyond the gates. A million hands at once applauded the prodigy. Babylon re-echoed with acclamations; and all the ladies agreed it was fortunate for so handsome a youth to be so strong.

He then took out of his pocket a small ivory tablet, wrote upon it with a golden pencil, fixed the tablet to the bow, and then presented it to the princess with such a grace as charmed every spectator. He then modestly returned to his place between his bird and his valet. All Babylon was in astonishment; the three kings were confounded, whilst the stranger did not seem to pay the least attention to what had happened.

Formosanta was still more surprised to read upon the ivory tablet, tied to the bow, these lines, written in the best Chaldean:

L'arc de Nembrod est celui de la guerre;
L'arc de l'amour est celui du bonheur;
Vous le portez. Par vous ce Dieu vainqueur
Est devenu le maitre de la terre.
Trois Rois puissants, trois rivaux aujourd'hui,
Osent pretendre a l'honneur de vous plaire.
Je ne sais pas qui votre cœur prefere,
Mais l'univers sera jaloux de lui.

[The bow of Nimrod is that of war;
The bow of love is that of happiness
Which you possess. Through you this conquering God
Has become master of the earth.
Three powerful kings,—three rivals now,
Dare aspire to the honor of pleasing you.
I know not whom your heart may prefer,
But the universe will be jealous of him.]

This little madrigal did not displease the princess; but it was criticised by some of the lords of the ancient court, who said that, in former times, Belus would have been compared to the sun, and Formosanta to the moon; his neck to a tower, and her breast to a bushel of wheat. They said the stranger had no sort of imagination, and that he had lost sight of the rules of true poetry, but all the ladies thought the verses very gallant. They were astonished that a man who handled a bow so well should have so much wit. The lady of honor to the princess said to her:

"Madam, what great talents are here entirely lost? What benefit will this young man derive from his wit, and his skill with Nimrod's bow?"

"Being admired!" said Formosanta.

"Ah!" said the lady, "one more madrigal, and he might well be beloved."

The king of Babylon, having consulted his sages, declared that though none of these kings could bend the bow of Nimrod, yet, nevertheless, his daughter was to be married, and that she should belong to him who could conquer the great lion, which was purposely kept in training in his great menagerie.

The king of Egypt, upon whose education all the wisdom of Egypt had been exhausted, judged it very ridiculous to expose a king to the ferocity of wild beasts in order to be married. He acknowledged that he considered the possession of Formosanta of inestimable value; but he believed that if the lion should strangle him, he could never wed this fair Babylonian. The king of India held similar views to the king of Egypt. They both concluded that the king of Babylon was laughing at them, and that they should send for armies to punish him—that they had many subjects who would think themselves highly honored to die in the service of their masters, without it costing them a single hair of their sacred heads,—that they could easily dethrone the king of Babylon, and then they would draw lots for the fair Formosanta.

This agreement being made, the two kings sent each an express into his respective country, with orders to assemble three hundred thousand men to carry off Formosanta.

However, the king of Scythia descended alone into the arena, scimitar in hand. He was not distractedly enamored with Formosanta's charms. Glory till then had been his only passion, and it had led him to Babylon. He was willing to show that if the kings of India and Egypt were so prudent as not to tilt with lions, he was courageous enough not to decline the combat, and he would repair the honor of diadems. His uncommon valor would not even allow him to avail himself of the assistance of his tiger. He advanced singly, slightly armed with a shell casque ornamented with gold, and shaded with three horses' tails as white as snow.

One of the most enormous and ferocious lions that fed upon the Antilibanian mountains was let loose upon him. His tremendous paws appeared capable of tearing the three kings to pieces at once, and his gullet to devour them. The two proud champions fled with the utmost precipitancy and in the most rapid manner to each other. The courageous Scythian plunged his sword into the lion's mouth; but the point meeting with one of those thick teeth that nothing can penetrate, was broken; and the monster of the woods, more furious from his wound, had already impressed his fearful claws into the monarch's sides.

The unknown youth, touched with the peril of so brave a prince, leaped into the arena swift as lightning, and cut off the lion's head with as much dexterity as we have lately seen, in our carousals, youthful knights knock off the heads of black images.

Then drawing out a small box, he presented it to the Scythian king, saying to him.

"Your majesty will here find the genuine dittany, which grows in my country. Your glorious wounds will be healed in a moment. Accident alone prevented your triumph over the lion. Your valor is not the less to be admired."

The Scythian king, animated more with gratitude than jealousy, thanked his benefactor; and, after having tenderly embraced him, returned to his seat to apply the dittany to his wounds.

The stranger gave the lion's head to his valet, who, having washed it at the great fountain which was beneath the amphitheatre, and drained all the blood, took an iron instrument out of his little bag, with which having drawn the lion's forty teeth, he supplied their place with forty diamonds of equal size.

His master, with his usual modesty, returned to his place; he gave the lion's head to his bird:—"Beauteous bird," said he, "carry this small homage, and lay it at the feet of Formosanta."

"The unknown youth, touched with the peril of so brave a prince, leaped into the arena swift as lightning, and cut off the lion's head."

The bird winged its way with the dreadful triumph in one of its talons, and presented it to the princess; bending with humility his neck, and crouching before her. The sparkling diamonds dazzled the eyes of every beholder. Such magnificence was unknown even in superb Babylon. The emerald, the topaz, the sapphire, and the pyrope, were as yet considered as the most precious ornaments. Belus and the whole court were struck with admiration. The bird which presented this present surprised them still more. It was of the size of an eagle, but its eyes were as soft and tender as those of the eagle are fierce and threatening. Its bill was rose color, and seemed somewhat to resemble Formosanta's handsome mouth. Its neck represented all the colors of Iris, but still more striking and brilliant. Gold, in a thousand shades, glittered upon its plumage. Its feet resembled a mixture of silver and purple. And the tails of those beautiful birds, which have since drawn Juno's car, did not equal the splendor of this incomparable bird.

The attention, curiosity, astonishment, and ecstasy of the whole court were divided between the jewels and the bird. It had perched upon the balustrade between Belus and his daughter Formosanta. She petted it, caressed it, and kissed it. It seemed to receive her attentions with a mixture of pleasure and respect. When the princess gave the bird a kiss, it returned the embrace, and then looked upon her with languishing eyes. She gave it biscuits and pistachios, which it received in its purple-silvered claw, and carried to its bill with inexpressible grace.

Belus, who had attentively considered the diamonds, concluded that scarce any one of his provinces could repay so valuable a present. He ordered that more magnificent gifts should be prepared for the stranger than those destined for the three monarchs, "This young man," said he, "is doubtless son to the emperor of China; or of that part of the world called Europe, which I have heard spoken of; or of Africa, which is said to be in the vicinity of the kingdom of Egypt."

He immediately sent his first equerry to compliment the stranger, and ask him whether he was himself the sovereign, or son to the sovereign of one of those empires; and why, being possessed of such surprising treasures, he had come with nothing but his valet and a little bag?

Whilst the equerry advanced toward the amphitheatre to execute his commission, another valet arrived upon an unicorn. This valet, addressing himself to the young man, said. "Ormar, your father is approaching the end of his life: I am come to acquaint you with it."

The stranger raised his eyes to heaven, whilst tears streamed from them, and answered only by saying, "*Let us depart.*"

The equerry, after having paid Belus's compliments to the conqueror of the lion, to the giver of the forty diamonds, and to the master of the beautiful bird, asked the valet, "Of what kingdom was the father of this young hero sovereign?"

The valet replied:

"His father is an old shepherd, who is much beloved in his district."

During this conversation, the stranger had already mounted his unicorn. He said to the equerry:

"My lord, vouchsafe to prostrate me at the feet of King Belus and his daughter. I must entreat her to take particular care of the bird I leave with her, as it is a nonpareil like herself."

In uttering these last words he set off, and flew like lightning. The two valets followed him, and in an instant he was out of sight.

Formosanta could not refrain from shrieking. The bird, turning toward the amphitheatre where his master had been seated, seemed greatly afflicted to find him gone; then viewing steadfastly the princess, and gently rubbing her beautiful hand with his bill, he seemed to devote himself to her service.

Belus, more astonished than ever, hearing that this very extraordinary young man was the son of a shepherd, could not believe it. He dispatched messengers after him; but they soon returned with the information, that the three unicorns, upon which these men were mounted, could not be overtaken; and that, according to the rate they went, they must go a hundred leagues a day.

Every one reasoned upon this strange adventure, and wearied themselves with conjectures. How can the son of a shepherd make a present of forty large diamonds? How comes it that he is mounted upon an unicorn? This bewildered them, and Formosanta, whilst she caressed her bird, was sunk into a profound reverie.

[1] The phœnix—born of myth and fable—was supposed to have originated in Arabia. In size it resembled an eagle, and was said to exist singly. At the end of six hundred years, it built for itself a nest filled with myrrh and the choicest spices. This was ignited by the ardent rays of the sun, and in it the phœnix was consumed in flames of fragrance. It was believed, however, that it soon rose again, from its own ashes, in renewed youth, strength, and beauty; and therefore it was considered by the ancients as symbolical of "the resurrection" and also of immortality.—E.

II.

THE KING OF BABYLON CONVENES HIS COUNCIL, AND CONSULTS THE ORACLE.

Princess Aldea, Formosanta's cousin-german, who was very well shaped, and almost as handsome as the King's daughter, said to her:

"Cousin, I know not whether this demi-god be the son of a shepherd, but methinks he has fulfilled all the conditions stipulated for your marriage. He has bent Nimrod's bow; he has conquered the lion; he has a good share of sense, having written for you extempore a very pretty madrigal. After having presented you with forty large diamonds, you cannot deny that he is the most generous of men. In his bird he possessed the most curious thing upon earth. His virtue cannot be equaled, since he departed without hesitation as soon as he learned his father was ill, though he might have remained and enjoyed the pleasure of your society. The oracle is fulfilled in every particular, except that wherein he is to overcome his rivals. But he has done more; he has saved the life of the only competitor he had to fear; and when the object is to surpass the other two, I believe you cannot doubt but that he will easily succeed."

"All that you say is very true," replied Formosanta: "but is it possible that the greatest of men, and perhaps the most amiable too, should be the son of a shepherd?"

The lady of honor, joining in the conversation, said that the title of shepherd was frequently given to kings—that they were called shepherds because they attended very closely to their flocks—that this was doubtless a piece of ill-timed pleasantry in his valet—that this young hero had not come so badly equipped, but to show how much his personal merit alone was above the fastidious parade of kings. The princess made no answer, but in giving her bird a thousand tender kisses.

A great festival was nevertheless prepared for the three kings, and for all the princes who had come to the feast. The king's daughter and niece were to do the honors. The king distributed presents worthy the magnificence of Babylon. Belus, during the time the repast was being served, assembled his council to discuss the marriage of the beautiful Formosanta, and this is the way he delivered himself as a great politician:

"I am old: I know not what is best to do with my daughter, or upon whom to bestow her. He who deserves her is nothing but a mean shepherd. The kings of India and Egypt are cowards. The king of the Scythians would be very agreeable to me, but he has not performed any one of the conditions imposed. I will again consult the oracle. In the meantime, deliberate among you, and we will conclude agreeably to what the oracle says; for a king should follow nothing but the dictates of the immortal gods."

He then repaired to the temple: the oracle answered in few words according to custom: *Thy daughter shall not be married until she hath traversed the globe.* In astonishment, Belus returned to the council, and related this answer.

All the ministers had a profound respect for oracles. They therefore all agreed, or at least appeared to agree, that they were the foundation of religion—that reason should be mute before them—that it was by their means that kings reigned over their people—that without oracles there would be neither virtue nor repose upon earth.

At length, after having testified the most profound veneration for them, they almost all concluded that this oracle was impertinent, and should not be obeyed—that nothing could be more indecent for a young woman, and particularly the daughter of the great king of Babylon, than to run about, without any particular destination—that this was the most certain method to prevent her being married, or else engage her in a clandestine, shameful, and ridiculous union that,—in a word, this oracle had not common sense.

The youngest of the ministers, named Onadase, who had more sense than the rest, said that the oracle doubtless meant some pilgrimage of devotion, and offered to be the princess's guide. The council approved of his opinion, but every one was for being her equerry. The king determined that the princess might go three hundred parasangs upon the road to Arabia, to the temple whose saint had the reputation of procuring young women happy marriages, and that the dean of the council should accompany her. After this determination they went to supper.

The shrine at Bassora.—A devotee at the shrine imploring the felicity of a happy marriage.

III.

ROYAL FESTIVAL GIVEN IN HONOR OF THE KINGLY VISITORS. THE BIRD CONVERSES ELOQUENTLY WITH FORMOSANTA.

In the centre of the gardens, between two cascades, an oval saloon, three hundred feet in diameter was erected, whose azure roof, intersected with golden stars, represented all the constellations and planets, each in its proper station; and this ceiling turned about, as well as the canopy, by machines as invisible as those which direct the celestial spheres. A hundred thousand flambeaux, inclosed in rich crystal cylinders, illuminated the gardens and the dining-hall. A buffet, with steps, contained twenty thousand vases and golden dishes; and opposite the buffet, upon other steps, were seated a great number of musicians. Two other amphitheatres were decked out; the one with the fruits of each season, the other with crystal decanters, that sparkled with the choicest wines.

The guests took their seats round a table divided into compartments that resembled flowers and fruits, all in precious stones. The beautiful Formosanta was placed between the kings of India and Egypt—the amiable Aldea next the king of Scythia. There were about thirty princes, and each was seated next one of the handsomest ladies of the court. The king of Babylon, who was in the middle, opposite his daughter, seemed divided between the chagrin of being yet unable to effect her marriage, and the pleasure of still beholding her. Formosanta asked leave to place her bird upon the table next her; the king approved of it.

The music, which continued during the repast, furnished every prince with an opportunity of conversing with his female neighbor. The festival was as agreeable as it was magnificent. A ragout was served before Formosanta, which her father was very fond of. The princess said it should be carried to his majesty. The bird immediately took hold of it, and carried it in a miraculous manner to the king. Never was any thing more astonishing witnessed. Belus caressed it as much as his daughter had done. The bird afterward took its flight to return to her. It displayed, in flying, so fine a tail, and its extended wings set forth such a variety of brilliant colors—the gold of its plumage made such a dazzling eclat, that all eyes were fixed upon it. All the musicians were struck motionless, and their instruments afforded harmony no longer. None ate, no one spoke, nothing but a buzzing of admiration was to be heard. The Princess of Babylon kissed it during the whole supper, without considering whether there were any kings in the world. Those of India and Egypt felt their spite and indignation rekindle with double force, and they resolved speedily to set their three hundred thousand men in motion to obtain revenge.

As for the king of Scythia, he was engaged in entertaining the beautiful Aldea. His haughty soul despising, without malice, Formosanta's inattention, had conceived for her more indifference than resentment. "She is handsome," said he, "I acknowledge: but she appears to me one of those women who are entirely taken up with their own beauty, and who fancy that mankind are greatly obliged to them when they deign to appear in public. I should prefer an ugly complaisant woman, that exhibited some amiability, to that beautiful statue. You have, madam, as many charms as she possesses, and you, at least, condescend to converse with strangers. I acknowledge to you with the sincerity of a Scythian, that I prefer you to your cousin."

He was, however, mistaken in regard to the character of Formosanta. She was not so disdainful as she appeared. But his compliments were very well received by the princess Aldea. Their conversation became very interesting. They were well contented, and already certain of one another before they left the table. After supper the guests walked in the groves. The king of Scythia and Aldea did not fail to seek for a place of retreat. Aldea, who was sincerity itself, thus declared herself to the prince:

"I do not hate my cousin, though she be handsomer than myself, and is destined for the throne of Babylon. The honor of pleasing you may very well stand in the stead of charms. I prefer Scythia with you, to the crown of Babylon without you. But this crown belongs to me by right, if there be any right in the world; for I am of the elder branch of the Nimrod family, and Formosanta is only of the younger. Her grandfather dethroned mine, and put him to death."

"Such, then, are the rights of inheritance in the royal house of Babylon!" said the Scythian. "What was your grandfather's name?"

"He was called Aldea, like me. My father bore the same name. He was banished to the extremity of the empire with my mother; and Belus, after their death, having nothing to fear from me, was willing to bring me up with his daughter. But he has resolved that I shall never marry."

"I will avenge the cause of your grandfather—of your father and also your own cause," said the king of Scythia. "I am responsible for your being married. I will carry you off the day after to-morrow by day-break—for we must dine to-morrow with the king of Babylon—and I will return and support your rights with three hundred thousand men."

"I agree to it," said the beauteous Aldea: and, after having mutually pledged their words of honor, they separated.

The incomparable Formosanta, before retiring to rest, had ordered a small orange tree, in a silver case, to be placed by the side of her bed, that her bird might perch upon it. Her curtains had long been drawn, but she was not in the least disposed to sleep. Her heart was agitated, and her imagination excited. The charming stranger was ever in her thoughts. She fancied she saw him shooting an arrow with Nimrod's bow. She contemplated him in the act of cutting off the lion's head. She repeated his madrigal. At length, she saw him retiring from the crowd upon his unicorn. Tears, sighs, and lamentations overwhelmed her at this reflection. At intervals, she cried out: "Shall I then never see him more? Will he never return?"

"He will surely return," replied the bird from the top of the orange tree. "Can one have seen you once, and not desire to see you again?"

"Heavens! eternal powers! my bird speaks the purest Chaldean." In uttering these words she drew back the curtain, put out her hand to him, and knelt upon her bed, saying:

"Art thou a god descended upon earth? Art thou the great Oromasdes concealed under this beautiful plumage? If thou art, restore me this charming young man."

"I am nothing but a winged animal," replied the bird; "but I was born at the time when all animals still spoke; when birds, serpents, asses, horses, and griffins, conversed familiarly with man. I would not speak before company, lest your ladies of honor should have taken me for a sorcerer. I would not discover myself to any but you."

Formosanta was speechless, bewildered, and intoxicated with so many wonders. Desirous of putting a hundred questions to him at once, she at length asked him how old he was.

"Only twenty-seven thousand nine hundred years and six months. I date my age from the little revolution of the equinoxes, and which is accomplished in about twenty-eight thousand of your years. There are revolutions of a much greater extent, so are there beings much older than me. It is twenty-two thousand years since I learnt Chaldean in one of my travels. I have always had a very great taste for the Chaldean language, but my brethren, the other animals, have renounced speaking in your climate."

"And why so, my divine bird?"

"Alas! because men have accustomed themselves to eat us, instead of conversing and instructing themselves with us. Barbarians! should they not have been convinced, that having the same organs with them, the same sentiments, the same wants, the same desires, we have also what is called a soul, the same as themselves;—that we are their brothers, and that none should be dressed and eaten but the wicked? We are so far your brothers, that the Supreme Being, the Omnipotent and Eternal Being, having made a compact with men, expressly comprehended us in the treaty. He forbade you to nourish yourselves with our blood, and we to suck yours.

"The fables of your ancient Locman, translated into so many languages, will be a testimony eternally subsisting of the happy commerce you formerly carried on with us. They all begin with these words: 'In the time when beasts spoke.' It is true, there are many families among you who keep up an incessant conversation with their dogs; but the dogs have resolved not to answer, since they have been compelled by whipping to go a hunting, and become accomplices in the murder of our ancient and common friends, stags, deers, hares, and partridges.

"You have still some ancient poems in which horses speak, and your coachmen daily address them in words; but in so barbarous a manner, and in uttering such infamous expressions, that horses, though formerly entertaining so great a kindness for you, now detest you.

"The country which is the residence of your charming stranger, the most perfect of men, is the only one in which your species has continued to love ours, and to converse with us; and this is the only country in the world where men are just."

"And where is the country of my dear incognito? What is the name of his empire? For I will no more believe he is a shepherd than that you are a bat."

"His country, is that of the Gangarids, a wise, virtuous, and invincible people, who inhabit the eastern shore of the Ganges. The name of my friend is Amazan. He is no king; and I know not whether he would so humble himself as to be one. He has too great a love for his fellow countrymen. He is a shepherd like them. But do not imagine that those shepherds resemble yours; who, covered with rags and tatters, watch their sheep, who are better clad than themselves; who groan under the burden of poverty, and who pay to an extortioner half the miserable stipend of wages which they receive from their masters. The Gangaridian shepherds are all born equal, and own the innumerable herds which cover their vast fields and subsist on the abundant verdure. These flocks are never killed. It is a horrid crime, in that favored country, to kill and eat a fellow creature. Their wool is finer and more brilliant than the finest silk, and constitutes the greatest traffic of the East. Besides, the land of the Gangarids produces all that can flatter the desires of man. Those large diamonds that Amazan had the honor of presenting you with, are from a mine that belongs to him. An unicorn, on which you saw him mounted, is the usual animal the Gangarids ride upon. It is the finest, the proudest, most terrible, and at the same time most gentle animal that ornaments the earth. A hundred Gangarids, with as many unicorns,[1] would be sufficient to disperse innumerable armies. Two centuries ago, a king of India was mad enough to attempt to conquer this nation. He appeared, followed by ten thousand elephants and a million of warriors. The unicorns pierced the elephants, just as I have seen upon your table beads pierced in golden brochets. The warriors fell under the sabres of the Gangarids like crops of rice mowed by the people of the East. The king was taken prisoner, with upwards of six thousand men. He was bathed in the salutary water of the Ganges, and followed the regimen of the country, which consists only of vegetables, of which nature hath there been amazingly liberal to nourish every breathing creature. Men who are fed with carnivorous aliments, and drenched with spirituous liquors, have a sharp adust blood, which turns their brains a hundred different ways. Their chief rage is a fury to spill their brother's blood, and, laying waste fertile plains, to reign over church-yards. Six full months were taken up in curing the king of India of his disorder. When the physicians judged that his pulse had become natural, they certified this to the council of the Gangarids. The council then followed the advice of the unicorns and humanely sent back the king of India, his silly court, and impotent warriors, to their own country. This lesson made them wise, and from that time the Indians respected the Gangarids, as ignorant men, willing to be instructed, revere the philosophers they cannot equal.

"Apropos, my dear bird," said the princess to him, "do the Gangarids profess any religion? have they one?"

"Yes, we meet to return thanks to God on the days of the full moon; the men in a great temple made of cedar, and the women in another, to prevent their devotion being diverted. All the birds assemble in a grove, and the quadrupeds on a fine down. We thank God for all the benefits he has bestowed upon us. We have in particular some parrots *that preach wonderfully well.*

"Such is the country of my dear Amazan; there I reside. My friendship for him is as great as the love with which he has inspired you. If you will credit me, we will set out together, and you shall pay him a visit."

"Really, my dear bird, this is a very pretty invitation of yours," replied the princess smiling, and who flamed with desire to undertake the journey, but did not dare say so.

"I serve my friend," said the bird; "and, after the happiness of loving you, the greatest pleasure is to assist you."

Formosanta was quite fascinated. She fancied herself transported from earth. All she had seen that day, all she then saw, all she heard, and particularly what she felt in her heart, so ravished her as far to surpass what those fortunate Mussulmen now feel, who, disencumbered from their terrestrial ties, find themselves in the ninth heaven in the arms of their Houris, surrounded and penetrated with glory and celestial felicity.

[1] Pliny, the Roman naturalist, describes the unicorn as "a very ferocious beast, similar in the rest of its body to a horse, with the head of a deer, the feet of an elephant, the tail of a boar, a deep bellowing voice, and a single black horn, two cubits in length, standing out in the middle of its forehead." A familiar representation of this "ferocious beast" may be seen on the English coat of arms.—E.

IV.

THE BEAUTIFUL BIRD IS KILLED BY THE KING OF EGYPT. FORMOSANTA BEGINS A JOURNEY. ALDEA ELOPES WITH THE KING OF SCYTHIA.

Formosanta passed the whole night in speaking of Amazan. She no longer called him any thing but her shepherd; and from this time it was that the names of shepherd and lover were indiscriminately used throughout every nation.

Sometimes she asked the bird whether Amazan had had any other mistresses. It answered, "No," and she was at the summit of felicity. Sometimes she asked how he passed his life; and she, with transport, learned, that it was employed in doing good; in cultivating arts, in penetrating into the secrets of nature, and improving himself. She at times wanted to know if the soul of her lover was of the same nature as that of her bird; how it happened that it had lived twenty thousand years, when her lover was not above eighteen or nineteen. She put a hundred such questions, to which the bird replied with such discretion as excited her curiosity. At length sleep closed their eyes, and yielded up Formosanta to the sweet delusion of dreams sent by the gods, which sometimes surpass reality itself, and which all the philosophy of the Chaldeans can scarce explain.

Formosanta did not awaken till very late. The day was far advanced when the king, her father, entered her chamber. The bird received his majesty with respectful politeness, went before him, fluttered his wings, stretched his neck, and then replaced himself upon his orange tree. The king seated himself upon his daughter's bed, whose dreams had made her still more beautiful. His large beard approached her lovely face, and after having embraced her, he spoke to her in these words:

"My dear daughter, you could not yesterday find a husband agreeable to my wishes; you nevertheless must marry; the prosperity of my empire requires it. I have consulted the oracle, which you know never errs, and which directs all my conduct. His commands are, that you should traverse the globe. You must therefore begin your journey."

"Ah! doubtless to the Gangarids," said the princess; and in uttering these words, which escaped her, she was sensible of her indiscretion. The king, who was utterly ignorant of geography, asked her what she meant by the Gangarids? She easily diverted the question. The king told her she must go on a pilgrimage, that he had appointed the persons who were to attend her— the dean of the counsellors of state, the high almoner, a lady of honor, a physician, an apothecary, her bird, and all necessary domestics.

Formosanta, who had never been out of her father's palace, and who, till the arrival of the three kings and Amazan, had led a very insipid life, according to the *etiquette* of rank and the parade of pleasure, was charmed at setting out upon a pilgrimage. "Who knows," said she, whispering to her heart, "if the gods may not inspire Amazan with the like desire of going to the same chapel, and I may have the happiness of again seeing the pilgrim?" She affectionately thanked her father, saying she had always entertained a secret devotion for the saint she was going to visit.

Belus gave an excellent dinner to his guests, who were all men. They formed a very ill assorted company—kings, ministers, princes, pontiffs—all jealous of each other; all weighing their words, and equally embarassed with their neighbors and themselves. The repast was very gloomy, though they drank pretty freely. The princesses remained in their apartments, each meditating upon her respective journey. They dined at their little cover. Formosanta afterward walked in the gardens with her dear bird, which, to amuse her, flew from tree to tree, displaying his superb tail and divine plumage.

The king of Egypt, who was heated with wine, not to say drunk, asked one of his pages for a bow and arrow. This prince was, in truth, the most unskillful archer in his whole kingdom. When he shot at a mark, the place of the greatest safety was generally the spot he aimed at. But the beautiful bird, flying as swiftly as the arrow, seemed to court it, and fell bleeding in the arms of Formosanta. The Egyptian, bursting into a foolish laugh, retired to his place. The princess rent the skies with her moans, melted into tears, tore her hair, and beat her breast. The dying bird said to her, in a low voice:

"Burn me, and fail not to carry my ashes to the east of the ancient city of Aden or Eden, and expose them to the sun upon a little pile of cloves and cinnamon." After having uttered these words it expired. Formosanta was for a long time in a swoon, and revived again only to burst into sighs and groans. Her father, partaking of her grief, and imprecating the king of Egypt, did not doubt but this accident foretold some fatal event. He immediately went to consult the oracle, which replied: *A mixture of everything—life and death, infidelity and constancy, loss and gain, calamities and good fortune.* Neither he nor his council could comprehend any meaning in this reply; but, at length, he was satisfied with having fulfilled the duties of devotion.

His daughter was bathed in tears, whilst he consulted the oracle. She paid the funeral obsequies to the bird, which it had directed, and resolved to carry its remains into Arabia at the risk of her life. It was burned in incombustible flax, with the orange-tree on which it used to perch. She gathered up the ashes in a little golden vase, set with rubies, and the diamonds taken from the lion's mouth. Oh! that she could, instead of fulfilling this melancholy duty, have burned alive the detestable king of Egypt! This was her sole wish.

She, in spite, put to death the two crocodiles, his two sea horses, his two zebras, his two rats, and had his two mummies thrown into the Euphrates. Had she possessed his bull Apis, she would not have spared him.

The king of Egypt, enraged at this affront, set out immediately to forward his three hundred thousand men. The king of India, seeing his ally depart, set off also on the same day, with a firm intention of joining his three hundred thousand Indians to the Egyptian army, the king of Scythia decamped in the night with the princess Aldea, fully resolved to fight for her at the head of three hundred thousand Scythians, and to restore to her the inheritance of Babylon, which was her right, as she had descended from the elder branch of the Nimrod family.

As for the beautiful Formosanta, she set out at three in the morning with her caravan of pilgrims, flattering herself that she might go into Arabia, and execute the last will of her bird; and that the justice of the gods would restore her the dear Amazan, without whom life had become insupportable.

When the king of Babylon awoke, he found all the company gone.

"How mighty festivals terminate," said he; "and what a surprising vacuum they leave when the hurry is over."

But he was transported with a rage truly royal, when he found that the princess Aldea had been carried off. He ordered all his ministers to be called up, and the council to be convened. Whilst they were dressing, he failed not to consult the oracle; but the only answer he could obtain was in these words, so celebrated since throughout the universe: *When girls are not provided for in marriage by their relatives, they marry themselves.*

Orders were immediately issued to march three hundred thousand men against the king of Scythia. Thus was the torch of a most dreadful war lighted up, which was caused by the amusements of the finest festival ever given upon earth. Asia was upon the point of being over-run by four armies of three hundred thousand men each. It is plain that the war of Troy, which astonished the world some ages after, was mere child's play in comparison to this; but it should also be considered, that in the Trojans quarrel, the object was nothing more than a very immoral old woman, who had contrived to be twice run away with; whereas, in this case, the cause was tripartite—two girls and a bird.

The king of India went to meet his army upon the large fine road which then led straight to Babylon, at Cachemir. The king of Scythia flew with Aldea by the fine road which led to Mount Imaus. Owing to bad government, all these fine roads have disappeared in the lapse of time. The king of Egypt had marched to the west, along the coast of the little Mediterranean sea, which the ignorant Hebrews have since called the Great Sea.

Consulting the oracle.

As to the charming Formosanta, she pursued the road to Bassora, planted with lofty palm trees, which furnished a perpetual shade, and fruit at all seasons. The temple in which she was to perform her devotions, was in Bassora itself. The saint to whom this temple had been dedicated, was somewhat in the style of him who was afterward adored at Lampsacus, and was generally successful in procuring husbands for young ladies. Indeed, he was the holiest saint in all Asia.

Formosanta had no sort of inclination for the saint of Bassora. She only invoked her dear Gangaridian shepherd, her charming Amazan. She proposed embarking at Bassora, and landing in Arabia Felix, to perform what her deceased bird had commanded.

At the third stage, scarce had she entered into a fine inn, where her harbingers had made all the necessary preparations for her, when she learned that the king of Egypt had arrived there also. Informed by his emissaries of the princess's route, he immediately altered his course, followed by a numerous escort. Having alighted, he placed sentinels at all the doors; then repaired to the beautiful Formosanta's apartment, when he addressed her by saying:

"Miss, you are the lady I was in quest of. You paid me very little attention when I was at Babylon. It is just to punish scornful capricious women. You will, if you please, be kind enough to sup with me to-night; and I shall behave to you according as I am satisfied with you."

Formosanta saw very well that she was not the strongest. She judged that good sense consisted in knowing how to conform to one's situation. She resolved to get rid of the king of Egypt by an innocent stratagem. She looked at him through the corners of her eyes, (which in after ages has been called ogling,) and then she spoke to him, with a modesty, grace, and sweetness, a confusion, and a thousand other charms, which would have made the wisest man a fool, and deceived the most discerning:

"I acknowledge, sir, I always appeared with a downcast look, when you did the king, my father, the honor of visiting him. I had some apprehensions for my heart. I dreaded my too great simplicity. I trembled lest my father and your rivals should observe the preference I gave you, and which you so highly deserved. I can now declare my sentiments. I swear by the bull Apis, which after you is the thing I respect the most in the world, that your proposals have enchanted me. I have already supped with you at my father's, and I will sup with you again, without his being of the party. All that I request of you is, that your high almoner should drink with us. He appeared to me at Babylon to be an excellent guest. I have some Chiras wine remarkably good. I will make you both taste it. I consider you as the greatest of kings, and the most amiable of men."

This discourse turned the king of Egypt's head. He agreed to have the almoner's company.

"I have another favor to ask of you," said the princess, "which is to allow me to speak to my apothecary. Women have always some little ails that require attention, such as vapors in the head, palpitations of the heart, colics, and the like, which often require some assistance. In a word, I at present stand in need of my apothecary, and I hope you will not refuse me this slight testimony of confidence."

"Miss," replied the king of Egypt, "I know life too well to refuse you so just a demand. I will order the apothecary to attend you whilst supper is preparing. I imagine you must be somewhat fatigued by the journey; you will also have occasion for a chambermaid; you may order her you like best to attend you. I will afterward wait your commands and convenience."

He then retired, and the apothecary and the chambermaid, named Irla, entered. The princess had an entire confidence in her. She ordered her to bring six bottles of Chiras wine for supper, and to make all the sentinels, who had her officers under arrest, drink the same. Then she recommended her apothecary to infuse in all the bottles certain pharmaceutic drugs, which make those who take them sleep twenty-four hours, and with which he was always provided. She was implicitly obeyed. The king returned with his high almoner in about half an hour's time. The conversation at supper was very gay. The king and the priest emptied the six bottles, and acknowledged there was not such good wine in Egypt. The chambermaid was attentive to make the servants in waiting drink. As for the princess, she took great care not to drink any herself, saying that she was ordered by her physician a particular regimen. They were all presently asleep.

The king of Egypt's almoner had one of the finest beards that a man of his rank could wear. Formosanta lopped it off very skillfully; then sewing it to a ribbon, she put it on her own chin. She then dressed herself in the priest's robes, and decked herself in all the marks of his dignity, and her waiting maid clad herself like the sacristan of the goddess Isis. At length, having furnished herself with his urn and jewels, she set out from the inn amidst the sentinels, who were asleep like their master. Her attendant had taken care to have two horses ready at the door. The princess could not take with her any of the officers of her train. They would have been stopped by the great guard.

Formosanta and Irla passed through several ranks of soldiers, who, taking the princess for the high priest, called her, "My most Reverend Father in God," and asked his blessing. The two fugitives arrived in twenty-four hours at Bassora, before the king awoke. They then threw off their disguise, which might have created some suspicion. They fitted out with all possible expedition a ship, which carried them, by the Straits of Ormus, to the beautiful banks of Eden in Arabia Felix. This was that Eden, whose gardens were so famous, that they have since been the residence of the best of mankind. They were the model of the Elysian fields, the gardens of the Hesperides, and also those of the Fortunate Islands. In those warm climates men imagined there could be no greater felicity than shades and murmuring brooks. To live eternally in heaven with the Supreme Being, or to walk in the garden of paradise, was the same thing to those who incessantly spoke without understanding one another, and who could scarce have any distinct ideas or just expressions.

As soon as the princess found herself in this land, her first care was to pay her dear bird the funeral obsequies he had required of her. Her beautiful hands prepared a small quantity of cloves and cinnamon. What was her surprise, when, having spread the ashes of the bird upon this funeral pyre, she saw it blaze of itself! All was presently consumed. In the place of the ashes there appeared nothing but a large egg, from whence she saw her bird issue more brilliant than ever. This was one of the most happy moments the princess had ever experienced in her whole life. There was but another that could ever be dearer to her; it was the object of her wishes, but almost beyond her hopes.

"I plainly see," said she, to the bird, "you are the phœnix which I have heard so much spoken of. I am almost ready to expire with joy and astonishment. I did not believe in your resurrection; but it is my good fortune to be convinced of it."

"Resurrection, in fact," said the phœnix to her, "is one of the most simple things in the world. There is nothing more in being born twice than once. Every thing in this world is the effect of resurrection. Caterpillars are regenerated into butterflies; a kernel put into the earth is regenerated into a tree. All animals buried in the earth regenerate into vegetation, herbs, and plants, and nourish other animals, of which they speedily compose part of the substance. All particles which compose bodies are transformed into different beings. It is true, that I am the only one to whom Oromasdes[1] has granted the favor of regenerating in my own form."

Formosanta, who from the moment she first saw Amazan and the phœnix, had passed all her time in a round of astonishment, said to him:

"I can easily conceive that the Supreme Being may form out of your ashes a phœnix nearly resembling yourself; but that you should be precisely the same person, that you should have the same soul, is a thing, I acknowledge, I cannot very clearly comprehend. What became of your soul when I carried you in my pocket after your death?"

"Reflect one moment! Is it not as easy for the great Oromasdes to continue action upon a single atom of my being, as to begin afresh this action? He had before granted me sensation, memory, and thought. He grants them to me again. Whether he united this favor to an atom of elementary fire, latent within me, or to the assemblage of my organs, is, in reality, of no consequence. Men, as well as phœnixes, are entirely ignorant how things come to pass, but the greatest favor the Supreme Being has bestowed upon me, is to regenerate me for you. Oh! that I may pass the twenty-eight thousand years which I have still to live before my next resurrection, with you and my dear Amazan."

"My dear phœnix, remember what you first told me at Babylon, which I shall never forget, and which flattered me with the hope of again seeing my dear shepherd, whom I idolize; 'we must absolutely pay the Gangarids a visit together,' and I must carry Amazan back with me to Babylon."

"This is precisely my design," said the phœnix. "There is not a moment to lose. We must go in search of Amazan by the shortest road, that is, through the air. There are in Arabia Felix two griffins,[2] who are my particular friends, and who live only a hundred and fifty thousand leagues from here. I am going to write to them by the pigeon post, and they will be here before night. We shall have time to make you a convenient palankeen, with drawers, in which you may place your provisions. You will be quite at your ease in this vehicle, with your maid. These two griffins are the most vigorous of their kind. Each of them will support one of the poles of the canopy between their claws. But, once for all, time is very precious."

He instantly went with Formosanta to order the carriage at an upholsterer's of his acquaintance. It was made complete in four hours. In the drawers were placed small fine loaves, biscuits superior to those of Babylon, large lemons, pine-apples, cocoa, and pistachio nuts, Eden wine, which is as superior to that of Chiras, as Chiras is to that of Surinam.

The two griffins arrived at Eden at the appointed time. The vehicle was as light as it was commodious and solid, and Formosanta and Irla placed themselves in it. The two griffins carried it off like a feather. The phœnix sometimes flew after it, and sometimes perched upon its roof. The two griffins winged their way toward the Ganges with the velocity of an arrow which rends the air. They never stopped but a moment at night for the travelers to take some refreshment, and the carriers to take a draught of water.

They at length reached the country of the Gangarids. The princess's heart palpitated with hope, love, and joy. The phœnix stopped the vehicle before Amazan's house; but Amazan had been absent from home three hours, without any one knowing whither he had gone.

There are no words, even in the Gangaridian language, that could express Formosanta's extreme despair.

"Alas! this is what I dreaded," said the phœnix: "the three hours which you passed at the inn, upon the road to Bassora, with that wretched king of Egypt, have perhaps been at the price of the happiness of your whole life. I very much fear we have lost Amazan, without the possibility of recovering him."

He then asked the servants if he could salute the mother of Amazan? They answered, that her husband had died only two days before, and she could speak to no one. The phœnix, who was not without influence in the house, introduced the princess of Babylon into a saloon, the walls of which were covered with orange-tree wood inlaid with ivory. The inferior shepherds and shepherdesses, who were dressed in long white garments, with gold colored trimmings, served up, in a hundred plain porcelain baskets, a hundred various delicacies, amongst which no disguised carcasses were to be seen. They consisted of rice, sago, vermicelli, macaroni, omelets, milk, eggs, cream, cheese, pastry of every kind, vegetables, fruits, peculiarly fragrant and grateful to the taste, of which no idea can be formed in other climates; and they were accompanied with a profusion of refreshing liquors superior to the finest wine.

Whilst the princess regaled herself, seated upon a bed of roses, four peacocks, who were luckily mute, fanned her with their brilliant wings; two hundred birds, one hundred shepherds and shepherdesses, warbled a concert in two different choirs; the nightingales, thistlefinches, linnets, chaffinches, sung the higher notes with the shepherdesses, and the shepherds sung the tenor and bass. The princess acknowledged, that if there was more magnificence at Babylon, nature was infinitely more agreeable among the Gangarids; but whilst this consolatory and voluptuous music was playing, tears flowed from her eyes, whilst she said to the damsel Irla:

"These shepherds and shepherdesses, these nightingales, these linnets, are making love; and for my part, I am deprived of the company of the Gangaridian hero, the worthy object of my most tender thoughts."

Whilst she was taking this collation, her tears and admiration kept pace with each other, and the phœnix addressed himself to Amazan's mother, saying:

"Madam, you cannot avoid seeing the princess of Babylon; you know—"

"I know every thing," said she, "even her adventure at the inn, upon the road to Bassora. A blackbird related the whole to me this morning; and this cruel blackbird is the cause of my son's going mad, and leaving his paternal abode."

"You have not been informed, then, that the princess regenerated me?"

"No, my dear child, the blackbird told me you were dead, and this made me inconsolable. I was so afflicted at this loss, the death of my husband, and the precipitate flight of my son, that I ordered my door to be shut to every one. But since the princess of Babylon has done me the honor of paying me a visit, I beg she may be immediately introduced. I have matters of great importance to acquaint her with, and I choose you should be present."

She then went to meet the princess in another saloon. She could not walk very well. This lady was about three hundred years old; but she had still some agreeable vestiges of beauty. It might be conjectured, that about her two hundred and fortieth, or two hundred and fiftieth year, she must have been a most charming woman. She received Formosanta with a respectful nobleness, blended with an air of interest and sorrow, which made a very lively impression upon the princess.

Formosanta immediately paid her the compliments of condolence upon her husband's death.

"Alas!" said the widow, "you have more reason to lament his death than you imagine."

"I am, doubtless, greatly afflicted," said Formosanta; "he was father to—." Here a flood of tears prevented her from going on. "For his sake only I undertook this journey, in which I have so narrowly escaped many dangers. For him I left my father, and the most splendid court in the universe. I was detained by a King of Egypt, whom I detest. Having escaped from this tyrant,

I have traversed the air in search of the only man I love. When I arrive, he flies from me!" Here sighs and tears stopped her impassioned harangue.

His mother then said to her:

"When the king of Egypt made you his prisoner,—when you supped with him at an inn upon the road to Bassora,—when your beautiful hands filled him bumpers of Chiras wine, did you observe a blackbird that flew about the room?"

"Yes, really," said the princess, "I now recollect there was such a bird, though at that time I did not pay it the least attention. But in collecting my ideas, I now remember well, that at the instant when the king of Egypt rose from the table to give me a kiss, the blackbird flew out at the window giving a loud cry, and never appeared after."

"Alas! madam," resumed Amazan's mother, "this is precisely the cause of all our misfortunes; my son had dispatched this blackbird to gain intelligence of your health, and all that passed at Babylon. He proposed speedily to return, throw himself at your feet, and consecrate to you the remainder of his life. You know not to what a pitch he adores you. All the Gangarids are both loving and faithful; but my son is the most passionate and constant of them all. The blackbird found you at an inn, drinking very cheerfully with the king of Egypt and a vile priest; he afterward saw you give this monarch who had killed the phœnix,—the man my son holds in utter detestation,—a fond embrace. The blackbird, at the sight of this, was seized with a just indignation. He flew away imprecating your fatal error. He returned this day, and has related every thing. But, just heaven, at what a juncture! At the very time that my son was deploring with me the loss of his father and that of the wise phœnix, the very instant I had informed him that he was your cousin german—"

"Oh heavens! my cousin, madam, is it possible? How can this be? And am I so happy as to be thus allied to him, and yet so miserable as to have offended him?"

"My son is, I tell you," said the Gangaridian lady, "your cousin, and I shall presently convince you of it; but in becoming my relation, you rob me of my son. He cannot survive the grief that the embrace you gave to the king of Egypt has occasioned him."

"Ah! my dear aunt," cried the beautiful Formosanta, "I swear by him and the all-powerful Oromasdes, that this embrace, so far from being criminal, was the strongest proof of love your son could receive from me. I disobeyed my father for his sake. For him I went from the Euphrates to the Ganges. Having fallen into the hands of the worthless Pharaoh of Egypt, I could not escape his clutches but by artifice. I call the ashes and soul of the phœnix, which were then in my pocket, to witness. He can do me justice. But how can your son, born upon the banks of the Ganges, be my cousin? I, whose family have reigned upon the banks of the Euphrates for so many centuries?"

"You know," said the venerable Gangaridian lady to her, "that your grand uncle, Aldea, was king of Babylon, and that he was dethroned by Belus's father?"

"Yes, madam."

"You know that this Aldea had in marriage a daughter named Aldea, brought up in your court? It was this prince, who, being persecuted by your father, took refuge under another name in our happy country. He married me, and is the father of the young prince Aldea Amazan, the most beautiful, the most courageous, the strongest, and most virtuous of mortals; and at this hour the most unhappy. He went to the Babylonian festival upon the credit of your beauty; since that time he idolizes you, and now grieves because he believes that you have proved unfaithful to him. Perhaps I shall never again set eyes upon my dear son."

She then displayed to the princess all the titles of the house of Aldea. Formosanta scarce deigned to look at them.

"Ah! madam, do we examine what is the object of our desire? My heart sufficiently believes you. But where is Aldea Amazan? Where is my kinsman, my lover, my king? Where is my life? What road has he taken? I will seek for him in every sphere the Eternal Being hath framed, and of which he is the greatest ornament. I will go into the star Canope, into Sheath, into Aldebaran; I will go and tell him of my love and convince him of my innocence."

The phœnix justified the princess with regard to the crime that was imputed to her by the blackbird, of fondly embracing the king of Egypt; but it was necessary to undeceive Amazan and recall him. Birds were dispatched on every side. Unicorns sent forward in every direction. News at length arrived that Amazan had taken the road toward China.

"Well, then," said the princess, "let us set out for China. I will seek him in defiance of both difficulty and danger. The journey is not long, and I hope I shall bring you back your son in a fortnight at farthest."

At these words tears of affection streamed from his mother's eyes and also from those of the princess. They most tenderly embraced, in the great sensibility of their hearts.

The phœnix immediately ordered a coach with six unicorns. Amazan's mother furnished two thousand horsemen, and made the princess, her niece, a present of some thousands of the finest diamonds of her country. The phœnix, afflicted at the evil occasioned by the blackbird's indiscretion, ordered all the blackbirds to quit the country; and from that time none have been met with upon the banks of the Ganges.

[1] The god Ormuzd, (called Oromasdes by the Greeks), was regarded by the Magi as the source of all good. His followers were in reality worshipers of nature, and used neither temples, altars, nor statues, but performed their simple rites on mountain tops. They adored Oromasdes as the source of all light and purity, and regarded the sun and fire as symbols of the divinity. They were, in the language of Wadsworth:

"—zealous to reject
Altar and Image, and the inclusive walls
And roofs of temples built by human hands,—
The loftiest heights ascending,
Presented sacrifice to Moon and Stars
And to the Winds and mother Elements,
And the whole circle of the Heavens, for him
A sensitive existence and a God."

Byron, in Childe Harold, contrasts the "unwalled temples," of the worshipers of Nature, with the "idol-dwellings," where images are adored:

"Not vainly did the early Persian make
His altar the high places and the peak
Of earth-o'er-gazing mountains, and thus take
A fit and unwalled temple, there to seek
The Spirit, in whose honor shrines are weak,
Upreared of human hands. Come and compare
Columns and idol-dwellings, Goth or Greek,
With Nature's realms of worship, earth and air,
Nor fix on fond abodes to circumscribe thy prayer."

In Moore's *Lalla Rookh* will be found an exquisite sketch of the Magi, or ancient Fire Worshipers,—

"Those slaves of Fire, that morn and even
Hal their creator's dwelling-place
Among the living lights of heaven."—E.

[2] On ancient coins and armorial bearings, the Griffin is represented as having the head and wings of an eagle, joined to the body and paws of a lion, thus representing strength and swiftness combined. It was supposed to watch over mines of gold, and also whatever was secretly hidden. It built its nest like a bird, using gold as the material, and hence it was necessary to vigilantly guard its treasures from the rapacity of mankind—who, says Milton, in *Paradise Lost*, "by stealth purloined its guarded gold." The poets

intimate that the chariot of Apollo, the god of the sun, was drawn by griffins.—E.

V.

FORMOSANTA VISITS CHINA AND SCYTHIA IN SEARCH OF AMAZAN.

The unicorns, in less than eight days, carried Formosanta, Irla, and the phœnix, to Cambalu, the capital of China. This city was larger than that of Babylon, and in appearance quite different. These fresh objects, these strange manners, would have amused Formosanta could any thing but Amazan have engaged her attention.

As soon as the emperor of China learned that the princess of Babylon was at the city gates, he dispatched four thousand Mandarins in ceremonial robes to receive her. They all prostrated themselves before her, and presented her with an address written in golden letters upon a sheet of purple silk. Formosanta told them, that if she were possessed of four thousand tongues, she would not omit replying immediately to every Mandarin; but that having only one, she hoped they would be satisfied with her general thanks. They conducted her, in a respectful manner, to the emperor.

He was the wisest, most just and benevolent monarch upon earth. It was he who first tilled a small field with his own imperial hands, to make agriculture respectable to his people. Laws in all other countries were shamefully confined to the punishment of crimes: he first allotted premiums to virtue. This emperor had just banished from his dominions a gang of foreign Bonzes, who had come from the extremities of the West, with the frantic hope of compelling all China *to think like themselves*; and who, under pretence of teaching truths, had already acquired honors and riches. In expelling them, he delivered himself in these words, which are recorded in the annals of the empire:

"You may here do us much harm as you have elsewhere. You have come to preach dogmas of intolerance, to the most tolerant nation upon earth. I send you back, that I may never be compelled to punish you. You will be honorably conducted to my frontiers. You will be furnished with every thing necessary to return to the confines of the hemisphere from whence you came. Depart in peace, if you can be at peace, and never return."

The princess of Babylon heard with pleasure of this speech and determination. She was the more certain of being well received at court, as she was very far from entertaining any dogmas of intolerance. The emperor of China, in dining with her *tête-à-tête*, had the politeness to banish all disagreeable *etiquette*. She presented the phœnix to him, who was gently caressed by the emperor, and who perched upon his chair. Formosanta, toward the end of the repast, ingenuously acquainted him with the cause of her journey, and entreated him to search for the beautiful Amazan in the city of Cambalu; and in the meanwhile she acquainted the emperor with her adventures, without concealing the fatal passion with which her heart burned for this youthful hero.

"He did me the honor of coming to my court," said the emperor of China. "I was enchanted with this amiable Amazan. It is true that he is deeply afflicted; but his graces are thereby the more affecting. Not one of my favorites has more wit. There is not a gown Mandarin who has more knowledge,—not a military one who has a more martial or heroic air. His extreme youth adds an additional value to all his talents. If I were so unfortunate, so abandoned by the Tien and Changti, as to desire to be a conqueror, I would wish Amazan to put himself at the head of my armies, and I should be sure of conquering the whole universe. It is a great pity that his melancholy sometimes disconcerts him."

"Ah! sir," said Formosanta, with much agitation and grief, blended with an air of reproach, "why did you not request me to dine with him? This is a cruel stroke you have given me. Send for him immediately, I entreat you."

"He set out this very morning," replied the emperor, "without acquainting me with his destination."

Formosanta, turning toward the phœnix, said to him:

"Did you ever know so unfortunate a damsel as myself?" Then resuming the conversation, she said:

"Sir, how came he to quit in so abrupt a manner, so polite a court, in which, methinks, one might pass one's life?"

"The case was as follows," said he. "One of the most amiable of the princesses of the blood, falling desperately in love with him, desired to meet him at noon. He set out at day-break, leaving this billet for my kinswoman, whom it hath cost a deluge of tears:

> "Beautiful princess of the mongolian race. You are deserving of a heart that was never offered up at any other altar. I have sworn to the immortal gods never to love any other than Formosanta, princess of Babylon, and to teach her how to conquer one's desires in traveling. She has had the misfortune to yield to a worthless king of Egypt. I am the most unfortunate of men; having lost my father, the phœnix, and the hope of being loved by Formosanta. I left my mother in affliction, forsook my home and country, being unable to live a moment in the place where I learned that Formosanta loved another than me. I swore to traverse the earth, and be faithful. You would despise me, and the

gods punish me, if I violated my oath. Choose another lover, madam, and be as faithful as I am."

"Ah! give me that miraculous letter," said the beautiful Formosanta; "it will afford me some consolation. I am happy in the midst of my misfortunes. Amazan loves me! Amazan, for me, renounces the society of the princesses of China. There is no one upon earth but himself endowed with so much fortitude. He sets me a most brilliant example. The phœnix knows I did not stand in need of it. How cruel it is to be deprived of one's lover for the most innocent embrace given through pure fidelity. But, tell me, whither has he gone? What road has he taken? Deign to inform me, and I will immediately set out."

The emperor of China told her, that, according to the reports he had received, her lover had taken the road toward Scythia. The unicorns were immediately harnessed, and the princess, after the most tender compliments, took leave of the emperor, and resumed her journey with the phœnix, her chambermaid Irla, and all her train.

As soon as she arrived in Scythia, she was more convinced than ever how much men and governments differed, and would continue to differ, until noble and enlightened minds should by degrees remove that cloud of darkness which has covered the earth for so many ages; and until there should be found in barbarous climes, heroic souls, who would have strength and perseverance enough to transform brutes into men. There are no cities in Scythia, consequently no agreeable arts. Nothing was to be seen but extensive fields, and whole tribes whose sole habitations were tents and chars. Such an appearance struck her with terror. Formosanta enquired in what tent or char the king was lodged? She was informed that he had set out eight days before with three hundred thousand cavalry to attack the king of Babylon, whose niece, the beautiful princess Aldea, he had carried off.

"What! did he run away with my cousin?" cried Formosanta. "I could not have imagined such an incident. What! has my cousin, who was too happy in paying her court to me, become a queen, and I am not yet married?" She was immediately conducted, by her desire, to the queen's tent.

Their unexpected meeting in such distant climes—the uncommon occurrences they mutually had to impart to each other, gave such charms to this interview, as made them forget they never loved one another. They saw each other with transport; and a soft illusion supplied the place of real tenderness. They embraced with tears, and there was a cordiality and frankness on each side that could not have taken place in a palace.

Aldea remembered the phœnix and the waiting maid Irla. She presented her cousin with zibelin skins, who in return gave her diamonds. The war between the two kings was spoken of. They deplored the fate of soldiers who were forced into battle, the victims of the caprice of princes, when two honest men might, perhaps, settle the dispute in less than an hour, without a single throat being cut. But the principal topic was the handsome stranger, who had conquered lions, given the largest diamonds in the universe, written madrigals, and had now become the most miserable of men from believing the statements of a blackbird.

"He is my dear brother," said Aldea. "He is my lover," cried Formosanta. "You have, doubtless, seen him. Is he still here? for, cousin, as he knows he is your brother, he cannot have left you so abruptly as he did the king of China.

"Have I seen him? good heavens! yes. He passed four whole days with me. Ah! cousin, how much my brother is to blame. A false report has absolutely turned his brain. He roams about the world, without knowing whither he is destined. Imagine to yourself his distraction of mind, which is so great, that he has refused to meet the handsomest lady in all Scythia. He set out yesterday, after writing her a letter which has thrown her into despair. As for him, he has gone to visit the Cimmerians."

"God be thanked!" cried Formosanta, "another refusal in my favor. My good fortune is beyond my hopes, as my misfortunes surpass my greatest apprehensions. Procure me this charming letter, that I may set out and follow him, loaded with his sacrifices. Farewell, cousin. Amazan is among the Cimmerians, and I fly to meet him."

Aldea judged that the princess, her cousin, was still more frantic than her brother Amazan. Hut as she had herself been sensible of the effects of this epidemic contagion, having given up the delights and magnificence of Babylon for a king of Scythia; and as the women always excuse those follies that are the effects of love, she felt for Formosanta's affliction, wished her a happy journey, and promised to be her advocate with her brother, if ever she was so fortunate as to see him again.

VI.

THE PRINCESS CONTINUES HER JOURNEY.

From Scythia the princess of Babylon, with her phœnix, soon arrived at the empire of the Cimmerians, now called Russia; a country indeed much less populous than Scythia, but of far greater extent.

After a few days' journey, she entered a very large city, which has of late been greatly improved by the reigning sovereign. The empress, however, was not there at that time, but was making a journey through her dominions, on the frontiers of Europe and Asia, in order to judge of their state and condition with her own eyes,—to enquire into their grievances, and to provide the proper remedies for them.

The principal magistrate of that ancient capital, as soon as he was informed of the arrival of the Babylonian lady and the phœnix, lost no time in paying her all the honors of his country; being certain that his mistress, the most polite and generous empress in the world, would be extremely well pleased to find that he had received so illustrious a lady with all that respect which she herself, if on the spot, would have shown her.

The princess was lodged in the palace, and entertained with great splendor and elegance. The Cimmerian lord, who was an excellent natural philosopher, diverted himself in conversing with the phœnix, at such times as the princess chose to retire to her own apartment. The phœnix told him, that he had formerly traveled among the Cimmerians, but that he should not have known the country again.

"How comes it," said he, "that such prodigious changes have been brought about in so short a time? Formerly, when I was here, about three hundred years ago, I saw nothing but savage nature in all her horrors. At present, I perceive industry, arts, splendor, and politeness."

"This mighty revolution," replied the Cimmerian, "was begun by one man, and is now carried to perfection by one woman;—a woman who is a greater legislator than the Isis of the Egyptians, or the Ceres of the Greeks. Most law-givers have been, unhappily, of a narrow genius and an arbitrary disposition, which conned their views to the countries they governed. Each of them looked upon his own race as the only people existing upon the earth, or as if they ought to be at enmity with all the rest. They formed institutions, introduced customs, and established religions exclusively for themselves. Thus the Egyptians, so famous for those heaps of stones called pyramids, have dishonored themselves with their barbarous superstitions. They despise all other nations as profane; refuse all manner of intercourse with them; and, excepting those conversant in the court, who now and then rise above the prejudices of the vulgar, there is not an Egyptian who will eat off a plate that has ever been used by a stranger. Their priests are equally cruel and absurd. It were better to have no laws at all, and to follow those notions of right and wrong engraven on our hearts by nature, than to subject society to institutions so inhospitable.

"Our empress has adopted quite a different system. She considers her vast dominions, under which all the meridians on the globe are united, as under an obligation of correspondence with all the nations dwelling under those meridians. The first and most fundamental of her laws, is an universal toleration of all religions, and an unbounded compassion for every error. Her penetrating genius perceives, that though the modes of religious worship differ, yet morality is every where the same. By this principle, she has united her people to all the nations on earth, and the Cimmerians will soon consider the Scandinavians and the Chinese as their brethren. Not satisfied with this, she has resolved to establish this invaluable toleration, the strongest link of society, among her neighbors. By these means, she obtained the title of the parent of her country; and, if she persevere, will acquire that of the benefactress of mankind.

"Before her time, the men, who were unhappily possessed of power, sent out legions of murderers to ravage unknown countries, and to water with the blood of the children the inheritance of their fathers. Those assassins were called heroes, and their robberies accounted glorious achievements. But our sovereign courts another sort of glory. She has sent forth her armies to be the messengers of peace; not only to prevent men from being the destroyers, but to oblige them to be the benefactors of one another. Her standards are the ensigns of public tranquillity."

The phœnix was quite charmed with what he heard from this nobleman. He told him, that though he had lived twenty-seven thousand nine hundred years and seven months in this world, he had never seen any thing like it. He then enquired after his friend Amazan. The Cimmerian gave the same account of him that the princess had already heard from the Chinese and the Scythians. It was Amazan's constant practice to run away from all the courts he visited, the instant any lady noticed him in particular and seemed anxious to make his acquaintance. The phœnix soon acquainted Formosanta with this fresh instance of Amazan's fidelity—a fidelity so much the more surprising, since he could not imagine his princess would ever hear of it.

Amazan had set out for Scandinavia, where he was entertained with sights still more surprising. In this place, he beheld monarchy and liberty subsisting together in a manner thought incompatible in other states; the laborers of the ground shared in the legislature with the grandees of the realm. In another place he saw what was still more extraordinary; a prince equally remarkable for his extreme youth and uprightness, who possessed a sovereign authority over his country, acquired by a solemn contract with his people.

Amazan beheld a philosopher on the throne of Sarmatia, who might be called a king of anarchy; for he was the chief of a hundred thousand petty kings, one of whom with his single voice could render ineffectual the resolution of all the rest. Eolus had not more difficulty to keep the warring winds within their proper bounds, than this monarch to reconcile the tumultuous discordant spirits of his subjects. He was the master of a ship surrounded with eternal storms. But the vessel did not founder, for he was an excellent pilot.

In traversing those various countries, so different from his own, Amazan persevered in rejecting all the advances made to him by the ladies, though incessantly distracted with the embrace given by Formosanta to the king of Egypt, being resolved to set Formosanta an amazing example of an unshaken and unparalleled fidelity.

The princess of Babylon was constantly close at his heels, and scarcely ever missed of him but by a day or two; without the one being tired of roaming, or the other losing a moment in pursuing him.

Thus he traversed the immense continent of Germany, where he beheld with wonder the progress which reason and philosophy had made in the north. Even their princes were enlightened, and had become the patrons of freedom of thought. Their education had not been trusted to men who had an interest in deceiving them, or who were themselves deceived. They were brought up in the knowledge of universal morality, and in the contempt of superstition.

They had banished from all their estates a senseless custom which had enervated and depopulated the southern countries. This was to bury alive in immense dungeons, infinite numbers of both sexes who were eternally separated from one another, and sworn to have no communication together. This madness had contributed more than the most cruel wars to lay waste and depopulate the earth.

In opposing these barbarous institutions, so inimical to the laws of nature and the best interests of society, the princes of the north had become the benefactors of their race. They had likewise exploded other errors equally absurd and pernicious. In short, men had at last ventured to make use of their reason in those immense regions; whereas it was still believed almost every where else, that they could not be governed but in proportion to their ignorance.

VII.

AMAZAN VISITS ALBION.

From Germany, Amazan arrived at Batavia; where his perpetual chagrin was in a good measure alleviated, by perceiving among the inhabitants a faint resemblance to his happy countrymen, the Gangarids. There he saw liberty, security, and equality,—with toleration in religion; but the ladies were so indifferent, that none made him any advances; an experience he had not met with before. It is true, however, that had he been inclined to address them, they would not have been offended; though, at the same time, not one would have been the least in love; but he was far from any thoughts of making conquests.

Formosanta had nearly caught him in this insipid nation. He had set out but a moment before her arrival.

Amazan had heard so much among the Batavians in praise of a certain island called Albion, that he was led by curiosity to embark with his unicorns on board a ship, which, with a favorable easterly wind, carried him in a few hours to that celebrated country, more famous than Tyre, or Atlantis.

The beautiful Formosanta, who had followed him, as it were on the scent, to the banks of the Volga, the Vistula, the Elbe, and the Weser, and had never been above a day or two behind him, arrived soon after at the mouth of the Rhine, where it disembogues its waters into the German Ocean.

Here she learned that her beloved Amazan had just set sail for Albion. She thought she saw the vessel on board of which he was, and could not help crying out for joy; at which the Batavian ladies were greatly surprised, not imagining that a young man could possibly occasion so violent a transport. They took, indeed, but little notice of the phœnix, as they reckoned his feathers would not fetch near so good a price as those of their own ducks, and other water fowl. The princess of Babylon hired two vessels to carry herself and her retinue to that happy island, which was soon to possess the only object of her desires, the soul of her life, and the god of her idolatry.

An unpropitious wind from the west suddenly arose, just as the faithful and unhappy Amazan landed on Albion's sea-girt shore, and detained the ships of the Babylonian princess just as they were on the point of sailing. Seized with a deep melancholy, she went to her room, determined to remain there till the wind should change; but it blew for the space of eight days, with an unremitting violence. The princess, during this tedious period, employed her maid of honor, Irla, in reading romances; which were not indeed written by the Batavians; but as they are the factors of the universe, they traffic in the wit as well as commodities of other nations. The princess purchased of Mark

Michael Rey, the bookseller, all the novels which had been written by the Ausonians and the Welch, the sale of which had been wisely prohibited among those nations to enrich their neighbors, the Batavians. She expected to find in those histories some adventure similar to her own, which might alleviate her grief. The maid of honor read, the phœnix made comments, and the princess, finding nothing in the *Fortunate Country Maid*, in *Tansai*, or in the *Sopha*, that had the least resemblance to her own affairs, interrupted the reader every moment, by asking how the wind stood.

VIII.

AMAZAN LEAVES ALBION TO VISIT THE LAND OF SATURN.

In the mean time Amazan was on the road to the capital of Albion, in his coach and six unicorns, all his thoughts employed on his dear princess. At a small distance he perceived a carriage overturned in a ditch. The servants had gone in different directions in quest of assistance, but the owner kept his seat, smoking his pipe with great tranquillity, without manifesting the smallest impatience. His name was my lord What-then, in the language from which I translate these memoirs.

Amazan made all the haste possible to help him, and without assistance set the carriage to rights, so much was his strength superior to that of other men. My lord What-then took no other notice of him, than saying, "a stout fellow, by Jove!" In the meantime the neighboring people, having arrived, flew into a great passion at being called out to no purpose, and fell upon the stranger. They abused him, called him an outlandish dog, and challenged him to strip and box.

Amazan seized a brace of them in each hand, and threw them twenty paces from him; the rest seeing this, pulled off their hats, and bowing with great respect, asked his honor for something to drink. His honor gave them more money than they had ever seen in their lives before. My lord What-then now expressed great esteem for him, and asked him to dinner at his country house, about three miles off. His invitation being accepted, he went into Amazan's coach, his own being out of order from the accident.

After a quarter of an hour's silence, my lord What-then, looking upon Amazan for a moment, said. "How d'ye do?" which, by the way, is a phrase without any meaning, adding, "You have got six fine unicorns there." After which he continued smoking as usual.

The traveler told him his unicorns were at his service, and that he had brought them from the country of the Gangarids. From thence he took occasion to inform him of his affair with the princess of Babylon, and the unlucky kiss she had given the king of Egypt; to which the other made no reply, being very indifferent whether there were any such people in the world, as a king of Egypt, or a princess of Babylon.

He remained dumb for another quarter of an hour; after which he asked his companion a second time how he did, and whether they had any good roast beef among the Gangarids.

Amazan answered with his wonted politeness, "that they did not eat their brethren on the banks of the Ganges." He then explained to him that system which many ages afterward was surnamed the Pythagorean philosophy. But my lord fell asleep in the meantime, and made but one nap of it till he came to his own house.

He was married to a young and charming woman, on whom nature had bestowed a soul as lively and sensible as that of her husband was dull and stupid. A few gentlemen of Albion had that day come to dine with her; among whom there were characters of all sorts; for that country having been almost always under the government of foreigners, the families that had come over with these princes had imported their different manners. There were in this company some persons of an amiable disposition, others of superior genius, and a few of profound learning.

The mistress of the house had none of that awkward stiffness, that false modesty, with which the young ladies of Albion were then reproached. She did not conceal by a scornful look and an affected taciturnity, her deficiency of ideas: and the embarrassing humility of having nothing to say. Never was a woman more engaging. She received Amazan with a grace and politeness that were quite natural to her. The extreme beauty of this young stranger, and the involuntary comparison she could not help making between him and her prosaic husband, did not increase her happiness or content.

Dinner being served, she placed Amazan at her side, and helped him to a variety of puddings, he having informed her that the Gangarids never dined upon any thing which had received from the gods the celestial gift of life. The events of his early life, the manners of the Gangarids, the progress of arts, religion, and government, were the subjects of a conversation equally agreeable and instructive all the time of the entertainment, which lasted till night: during which my lord What-then did nothing but push the bottle about, and call for the toast.

After dinner, while my lady was pouring out the tea, still feeding her eyes on the young stranger, he entered into a long conversation with a member of parliament; for every one knows that there was, even then, a parliament called Wittenagemot, or the assembly of wise men. Amazan enquired into the constitution, laws, manners, customs, forces, and arts, which made this country so respectable; and the member answered him in the following manner.

"For a long time we went stark naked, though our climate is none of the hottest. We were likewise for a long time enslaved by a people who came from the ancient country of Saturn, watered by the Tiber. But the mischief we have done one another has greatly exceeded all that we ever suffered from our first conquerors. One of our princes carried his superstition to such a pitch, as to declare himself the subject of a priest, who dwells also on the banks of the Tiber, and is called the Old Man of the Seven Mountains. It has been the fate of the seven mountains to domineer over the greatest part of Europe, then inhabited by brutes in human shape.

Religious wars in Albion.

"To those times of infamy and debasement, succeeded the ages of barbarity and confusion. Our country, more tempestuous than the surrounding ocean, has been ravaged and drenched in blood by our civil discords. Many of our crowned heads have perished by a violent death. Above a hundred princes of the royal blood have ended their days on the scaffold, whilst the hearts of their adherents have been torn from their breasts, and thrown in their faces. In short, it is the province of the hangman to write the history of our island, seeing that this personage has finally determined all our affairs of moment.

"But to crown these horrors, it is not very long since some fellows wearing black mantles, and others who cast white shirts over their jackets, having become aggressive and intolerant, succeeded in communicating their madness to the whole nation. Our country was then divided into two parties, the murderers and the murdered, the executioners and the sufferers, plunderers and slaves; and all in the name of God, and whilst they were seeking the Lord.

"Who would have imagined, that from this horrible abyss, this chaos of dissension, cruelty, ignorance, and fanaticism, a government should at last spring up, the most perfect, it may be said, now in the world; yet such has been the event. A prince, honored and wealthy, all-powerful to do good, but without power to do evil, is at the head of a free, warlike, commercial, and enlightened nation. The nobles on one hand, and the representatives of the people on the other, share the legislature with the monarch.

"We have seen, by a singular fatality of events, disorder, civil wars, anarchy and wretchedness, lay waste the country, when our kings aimed at arbitrary power: whereas tranquillity, riches, and universal happiness, have only reigned among us, when the prince has remained satisfied with a limited authority. All order had been subverted whilst we were disputing about mysteries, but was re-established the moment we grew wise enough to despise them. Our victorious fleets carry our flag on every ocean; our laws place our lives and fortunes in security; no judge can explain them in an arbitrary manner, and no decision is ever given without the reasons assigned for it. We should punish a judge as an assassin, who should condemn a citizen to death without declaring the evidence which accused him, and the law upon which he was convicted.

"It is true, there are always two parties among us, who are continually writing and intriguing against each other, but they constantly re-unite, whenever it is needful to arm in defence of liberty and our country. These two parties watch over one another, and mutually prevent the violation of the sacred *deposit* of the laws. They hate one another, but they love the state. They are like those jealous lovers, who pay court to the same mistress, with a spirit of emulation.

"From the same fund of genius by which we discovered and supported the natural rights of mankind, we have carried the sciences to the highest pitch to which they can attain among men. Your Egyptians, who pass for such great mechanics—your Indians, who are believed to be such great philosophers—your Babylonians, who boast of having observed the stars for the course of four hundred and thirty thousand years—the Greeks, who have written so much, and said so little, know in reality nothing in comparison to our inferior scholars, who have studied the discoveries of Our great masters. We have ravished more secrets from nature in the space of an hundred years, that the human species had been able to discover in as many ages.

"This is a true account of our present state. I have concealed from you neither the good nor the bad; neither our shame nor our glory; and I have exaggerated nothing."

At this discourse Amazan felt a strong desire to be instructed in those sublime sciences his friend had spoken of; and if his passion for the princess of Babylon, his filial duty to his mother whom he had quitted, and his love for his native country, had not made strong remonstrances to his distempered heart, he would willingly have spent the remainder of his life in

Albion. But that unfortunate kiss his princess had given the king of Egypt, did not leave his mind at sufficient ease to study the abstruse sciences.

"I confess," said he, "having made a solemn vow to roam about the world, and to escape from myself. I have a curiosity to see that ancient land of Saturn—that people of the Tiber and of the Seven Mountains, who have been heretofore your masters. They must undoubtedly be the first people on earth."

"I advise you by all means," answered the member, "to take that journey, if you have the smallest taste for music or painting. Even we ourselves frequently carry our spleen and melancholy to the Seven Mountains. But you will be greatly surprised when you see the descendants of our conquerors."

This was a long conversation, and Amazan had spoken in so agreeable a manner; his voice was so charming; his whole behavior so noble and engaging, that the mistress of the house could not resist the pleasure of having a little private chat with him in her turn. She accordingly sent him a little billet-doux intimating her wishes in the most agreeable language. Amazan had once more the courage to resist the fascination of female society, and, according to custom, wrote the lady an answer full of respect,— representing to her the sacredness of his oath, and the strict obligation he was under to teach the princess of Babylon to conquer her passions by his example; after which he harnessed his unicorns and departed for Batavia, leaving all the company in deep admiration of him, and the lady in profound astonishment. In her confusion she dropped Amazan's letter. My lord What-then read it next morning:

"D—n it," said he, shrugging up his shoulders, "what stuff and nonsense have we got here?" and then rode out a fox hunting with some of his drunken neighbors.

Amazan was already sailing upon the sea, possessed of a geographical chart, with which he had been presented by the learned Albion he had conversed with at lord What-then's. He was extremely astonished to find the greatest part of the earth upon a single sheet of paper.

His eyes and imagination wandered over this little space; he observed the Rhine, the Danube, the Alps of Tyrol, there specified under their different names, and all the countries through which he was to pass before he arrived at the city of the Seven Mountains. But he more particularly fixed his eyes upon the country of the Gangarids, upon Babylon, where he had seen his dear princess, and upon the country of Bassora, where she had given a fatal kiss to the king of Egypt. He sighed, and tears streamed from his eyes at the unhappy remembrance. He agreed with the Albion who had presented him with the universe in epitome, when he averred that the inhabitants of the banks of the Thames were a thousand times better instructed than those upon the banks of the Nile, the Euphrates, and the Ganges.

As he returned into Batavia, Formosanta proceeded toward Albion with her two ships at full sail. Amazan's ship and the princess's crossed one another and almost touched; the two lovers were close to each other, without being conscious of the fact. Ah! had they but known it! But this great consolation tyrannic destiny would not allow.

IX.

AMAZAN VISITS ROME.

No sooner had Amazan landed on the flat muddy shore of Batavia, than he immediately set out toward the city of the Seven Mountains. He was obliged to traverse the southern part of Germany. At every four miles he met with a prince and princess, maids of honor, and beggars. He was greatly astonished every where at the coquetries of these ladies and maids of honor, in which they indulged with German good faith. After having cleared the Alps he embarked upon the sea of Dalmatia, and landed in a city that had no resemblance to any thing he had heretofore seen. The sea formed the streets, and the houses were erected in the water. The few public places, with which this city was ornamented, were filled with men and women with double faces—that which nature had bestowed on them, and a pasteboard one, ill painted, with which they covered their natural visage; so that this people seemed composed of spectres. Upon the arrival of strangers in this country, they immediately purchase these visages, in the same manner as people elsewhere furnish themselves with hats and shoes. Amazan despised a fashion so contrary to nature. He appeared just as he was.

Many ladies were introduced, and interested themselves in the handsome Amazan. But he fled with the utmost precipitancy, uttering the name of the incomparable princess of Babylon, and swearing by the immortal gods, that she was far handsomer than the Venetian girls.

"Sublime traitoress," he cried, in his transports, "I will teach you to be faithful!"

Now the yellow surges of the Tiber, pestiferous fens, a few pale emaciated inhabitants clothed in tatters which displayed their dry tanned hides, appeared to his sight, and bespoke his arrival at the gate of the city of the Seven Mountains,—that city of heroes and legislators who conquered and polished a great part of the globe.

He expected to have seen at the triumphal gate, five hundred battalions commanded by heroes, and in the senate an assembly of demi-gods giving laws to the earth. But the only army he found consisted of about thirty tatterdemalions, mounting guard with umbrellas for fear of the sun. Having arrived at a temple which appeared to him very fine, but not so magnificent as that of Babylon, he was greatly astonished to hear a concert performed by men with female voices.

"This," said he, "is a mighty pleasant country, which was formerly the land of Saturn. I have been in a city where no one showed his own face; here is another where men have neither their own voices nor beards."

He was told that these eunuchs had been trained from childhood, that they might sing the more agreeably the praises of a great number of persons of merit. Amazan could not comprehend the meaning of this.

They then explained to him very pleasantly, and with many gesticulations, according to the custom of their country, the point in question. Amazan was quite confounded.

"I have traveled a great way," said he, "but I never before heard such a whim."

After they had sung a good while, the Old Man of the Seven Mountains went with great ceremony to the gate of the temple. He cut the air in four parts with his thumb raised, two fingers extended and two bent, in uttering these words in a language no longer spoken: "*To the city and to the universe.*" Amazan could not see how two fingers could extend so far.

He presently saw the whole court of the master of the world file off. This court consisted of grave personages, some in scarlet, and others in violet robes. They almost all eyed the handsome Amazan with a tender look; and bowed to him, while commenting upon his personal appearance.

The zealots whose vocation was to show the curiosities of the city to strangers, very eagerly offered to conduct him to several ruins, in which a muleteer would not choose to pass a night, but which were formerly worthy monuments of the grandeur of a royal people. He moreover saw pictures of two hundred years standing, and statues that had remained twenty ages, which appeared to him masterpieces of their kind.

"Can you still produce such work?" said Amazan.

"No, your excellency," replied one of the zealots; "but we despise the rest of the earth, because we preserve these rarities. We are a kind of old clothes men, who derive our glory from the cast-off garbs in our warehouses."

Amazan was willing to see the prince's palace, and he was accordingly conducted thither. He saw men dressed in violet colored robes, who were reckoning the money of the revenues of the domains of lands, some situated upon the Danube, some upon the Loire, others upon the Guadalquivir, or the Vistula.

"Oh! Oh!" said Amazan, having consulted his geographical map, "your master, then, possesses all Europe, like those ancient heroes of the Seven Mountains?"

"He should possess the whole universe by divine right," replied a violet-livery man; "and there was even a time when his predecessors nearly compassed universal monarchy, but their successors are so good as to content themselves at present with some monies which the kings, their subjects, pay to them in the form of a tribute."

"Your master is then, in fact, the king of kings. Is that his title?" said Amazan.

The Old Man of the Seven Mountains.—"The Old Man of the Seven Mountains went with great ceremony to the gate of the temple. He cut the air in four parts with his thumb raised, two fingers extended and two bent, in uttering these words in a language no longer spoken: '*To the city and to the universe.*'"

"Your excellency, his title is *the servant of servants*! He was originally a fisherman and porter, wherefore the emblems of his dignity consist of keys and nets; but he at present issues orders to every king in Christendom. It is not a long while since he sent one hundred and one mandates to a king of the Celts, and the king obeyed."

THE SERVANT OF SERVANTS.

The personal service of Pius IX. as it existed in 1873, without counting Swiss gensdarmes, palatine guards, &c., is thus described by the author of *The Religion of Rome*, page 21.

"The pope for his own exclusive personal service has four palatine cardinals, three prelates and a master, ten prelates of the private chamber, amongst whom are a cup-bearer, and a keeper of the wardrobe; then two hundred and fifteen domestic prelates. Then follow two hundred and forty-nine supernumerary prelates of the private chamber, four private chamberlains of the sword and cloak, Roman patricians, one of whom is a master of Santo Ospizto.

"What things are these? what service do these private chamberlains render? what is the use of this cloak and sword? We will undertake to say that they do not know themselves. Let us proceed. Then come next a quartermaster major, a correspondent general of the post, and one hundred and thirty fresh private chamberlains of the sword and cloak! Oh! it is a labor to count them! Next come two hundred and sixty-five honorary monsignori *extra urbem*, six honorary chamberlains of the sword and cloak, then eight private chaplains. What a number of *private* affairs must the pope have? Then eighty-one honorary chaplains *extra urbem*; then—but enough, enough, enough!

"No! not enough for the pope. Then come two private monsignori of the tonsure—still private!—then eighteen supernumeraries: two adjutants of the chamber, a private steward—again private!—then nineteen ushers, participants, and twenty-four supernumeraries. Then—ah! there are no more. Let us cast up those we have named; they amount only to a bagatelle of one thousand and twenty-five persons! And take note, that there are not included in this list the palatine administration, and the tribunal of the majordomo, the Swiss guards, the gensdarmes, etc., etc.

"If it be difficult for a rich man to enter into the kingdom of heaven, how shall he who inhabits the Vatican enter there?—who has treasures of all sorts, money, precious gems, precious and countless works of art, vessels of silver and gold, and who has on his head not one crown but three? who causes himself to be borne on the shoulders of men; who causes them to kiss his feet; who has millions of income, and a thousand persons to attend upon him?

"There is, in fact, nothing to be compared with the effrontery with which the Vatican enacts the comedy of poverty. Yes, it has reason to believe still in miracles; it is an actual miracle which the Roman court works, in drawing from the pockets of the poor the obolus necessary to buy them bread, to spend it before their faces in Sybaritic luxury, in a palace of *The Thousand and One Nights*. On the day of

Epiphany, the Jesuits sent to the Vatican some hundreds of women and children of the Trastevere, to carry to the pope a gift of money. The children to succor the poverty of the pope, who consumes on himself and household enough to maintain a whole city, gave him the money which they had received in gifts from their parents, and the women of the Trastevere, the few pence that they had laid aside for the needs of their families.

"But what is most extraordinary is, that these women and children who bestowed their charity on the pope, went to do it into halls full of gold, marble, precious stones, velvet, silk, embroidery, paintings, and statues, into the Vatican, that gigantic palace, which occupies a space of fifteen hundred feet in length, and eight hundred in breadth, with twenty courts, two hundred staircases, eleven thousand rooms, galleries and halls full of treasures, and the construction of which has cost hundreds of millions. These children and these women passing through so much wealth never were struck with the idea that Pius IX. ought to be something more than a beggar; that there is no monarch in the world who has an abode like the popes of Rome—the very sight of the gifts sent by all the world to Pius IX. being enough to strike them dumb with astonishment.

"Now these women and these children don't comprehend this, and here is the miracle. This Pius IX. ought to go into the cottages of these poor women and take them money, instead of their going to carry it into the luxurious palace of the pope.

"The miracle becomes still greater every time that the Pope, replying to those who bring money, talks of Jesus; for Jesus was in a stable, not in a palace of eleven thousand rooms. Jesus would at once have sent away the Swiss, the gensdarmes, the palatine guards, the chamberlains private and not private, etc., and would have said to the people of the Trastevere, and of the quarters of the poor: 'Come here into the Vatican, poor people, leave those wretched cabins where you suffer so much; come to me; I have eleven thousand rooms to offer you, one of which is quite enough for me, and so I will divide these amongst those who have none.' This would have been said by Christ, whom Pius IX. invokes so often, calling himself His vicar or steward. But try, ye poor, to enter into the Vatican, and you will find at once at the door a Swiss, who will chase you away by blows of his halberd. He will let in anyone who comes to bring money, but not a soul who comes to ask for it."—E.

"Your fisherman must then have sent five or six hundred thousand men to put these orders in execution?"

"Not at all, your excellency. Our holy master is not rich enough to keep ten thousand soldiers on foot: but he has five or six hundred thousand divine prophets dispersed in other countries. These prophets of various colors are, as they ought to be, supported at the expense of the people where they reside. They proclaim, from heaven, that my master may, with his keys, open and shut all locks, and particularly those of strong boxes. A Norman priest, who held the post of confident of this king's thoughts, convinced him he ought to obey, without questioning, the one hundred and one thoughts of my master; for you must know that one of the prerogatives of the Old Man of the Seven Mountains is never to err, whether he deigns to speak or deigns to write."

"In faith," said Amazan, "this is a very singular man; I should be pleased to dine with him."

"Were your excellency even a king, you could not eat at his table. All that he could do for you, would be to allow you to have one served by the side of his, but smaller and lower. But if you are inclined to have the honor of speaking to him, I will ask an audience for you on condition of the *buona mancia*, which you will be kind enough to give me." "Very readily," said the Gangarid. The violet-livery man bowed: "I will introduce you to-morrow," said he. "You must make three very low bows, and you must kiss the feet of the Old Man of the Seven Mountains." At this information Amazan burst into so violent a fit of laughing that he was almost choked; which, however, he surmounted, holding his sides, whilst the violent emotions of the risible muscles forced the tears down his cheeks, till he reached the inn, where the fit still continued upon him.

At dinner, twenty beardless men and twenty violins produced a concert. He received the compliments of the greatest lords of the city during the remainder of the day; but from their extravagant actions, he was strongly tempted to throw two or three of these violet-colored gentry out of the window. He left with the greatest precipitation this city of the masters of the world, where young men were treated so whimsically, and where he found himself necessitated to kiss an old man's toe, as if his cheek were at the end of his foot.

X.

AN UNFORTUNATE ADVENTURE IN GAUL.

In all the provinces through which Amazan passed, he remained ever faithful to the princess of Babylon, though incessantly enraged at the king of Egypt. This model of constancy at length arrived at the new capital of the Gauls. This city, like many others, had alternately submitted to barbarity, ignorance, folly, and misery. The first name it bore was Dirt and Mire; it then took that of Isis, from the worship of Isis, which had reached even here. Its first senate consisted of a company of watermen. It had long been in bondage, and submitted to the ravages of the heroes of the Seven Mountains; and some ages after, some other heroic thieves who came from the farther banks of the Rhine, had seized upon its little lands.

Time, which changes all things, had formed it into a city, half of which was very noble and very agreeable, the other half somewhat barbarous and ridiculous. This was the emblem of its inhabitants. There were within its walls at least a hundred thousand people, who had no other employment than play and diversion. These idlers were the judges of those arts which the others cultivated. They were ignorant of all that passed at court; though they were only four short miles distant from it: but it seemed to them at least six hundred thousand miles off. Agreeableness in company, gaiety and frivolty, formed the important and sole considerations of their lives. They were governed like children, who are extravagantly supplied with gewgaws, to prevent their crying. If the horrors were discussed, which two centuries before had laid waste their country, or if those dreadful periods were recalled, when one half of the nation massacred the other for sophisms, they, indeed, said, "this was not well done;" then, presently, they fell to laughing again, or singing of catches.

Kissing an old man's toe.

KISSING THE POPE'S FOOT.

On page 181 of *The Religion of Rome*, the author asks the questions: "Why does the pope cause his foot, or rather his slipper, to be kissed? And when did this custom begin?" His explanation is as follows:

"Theophilus Rainaldo and the Bollandist fathers, as well as other Roman Catholic authors, tell us a gallant story of Pope St. Leo I., called the Great, which, if it were true, might show the origin of the practice. They say that a young and very handsome devotee was admitted on Easter day, to kiss the hand of Pope St. Leo after the mass. The pope felt himself very much excited by this kiss, and remembering the words of the Savior, 'If thy hand offend thee, cut it off, and cast it from thee' (Matt. v. 30), he at once cut off his hand. But as he was unable to perform mass with only one hand, the people were in a great rage. The pope therefore prayed to God to restore his hand, and God complied: his hand was again united to the stump. And to avoid such dilemmas in future, Leo ordered that thereafter no one should kiss his hand, but only his foot. A very little common sense is sufficient to make us understand that such was not the origin of this custom.

"The first who invented this degrading act of kissing feet was the Emperor Caligula. He, in his quality of Pontifex Maximus, ordered the people to kiss his foot. Succeeding emperors refused such an act of base slavery. But Heliogabalus, as emperor, and Pontifex Maximus, again introduced it. After him, the custom fell into disuse; but the Christian emperors retaining some of the wicked fables given to the pagan emperors, permitted the kissing of the foot as a compliment on the presentation of petitions. We may cite a few instances. The acts of the Council of Chalcedon say that Fazius, Bishop of Tyre, in his petition to the emperor, said, 'I supplicate, prostrate, at your immaculate and divine feet.' Bassianus, Bishop of Ephesus, says, 'I prostrate myself at your feet.' Eunomius, Bishop of Nicomedia, says, 'I prostrate myself before the footsteps of your power.' The Abbot Saba says, 'I am come to adore the footsteps of your piety. Procogius, in his *History of Mysteries*, says that the Emperor Justinian, at the instigation of the proud Theodora, his wife, was the first amongst the Christian emperors who ordered prostrations before himself and his wife, and the kissing of their feet.

"The ecclesiastics, the bishops, and, finally, the popes, were not exempt from paying this homage to the emperors. The prelates of Syria held this language to the Emperor Justinian. 'The pope of holy memory, and the archbishop of ancient Rome, has come to your pious conversation, and has been honored by your holy feet.' Pope Gregory I., writing to Theodorus, the physician of the Emperor Mauritius, in the year A.D. 593, said: 'My tongue cannot sufficiently express the great benefits that I have received from God Almighty and from our great emperor, for which I can only love him and kiss his feet.' In the year A.D. 681 Pope Agathon, sending his legates to the sixth council, writes to the Emperor Constantine Pogonatus: 'As prostrate in your presence, and embracing your feet, I implore you,' etc. In the seventh century, therefore, not only did the popes not have their feet kissed, but they themselves were obliged to kiss those of the emperor. Becoming sovereigns of Rome, they soon began to adopt the same custom. Pope Eugenius II., who died in 827, was the first who made it the law to kiss the papal foot. From that time it was necessary to kneel before the popes. Gregory VII. ordered all princes to submit to this practice.

"From what we have said it is clear that the origin of feet-kissing was entirely pagan and idolatrous. That this custom is in total contradiction to the precepts of the Gospel would be a waste of words to assert. Jesus Christ was so far from desiring people to kiss his feet, that he set himself on one occasion to wash the feet of his disciples. These are the words of the Gospel: 'He riseth from supper, and laid aside his garments; and took a towel and girded himself. After that he poured water into a basin, and began to wash the disciples' feet, and to wipe them with the towel wherewith he was girded.'

"This act of Jesus Christ is in perfect keeping (John xiii. 4.5) with all his precepts, with his inculcations of modesty, equality, humility, and with his condemnation of those who set themselves above others. Who would have said that a day would come in which those claiming to be his vicars should cause people to kiss their feet? How thoroughly has Catholicism borrowed from paganism its idolatries? And notwithstanding this flagrant violation of the religion of Christ, what a herd of people go and press their lips on the slipper of the pope, as was done formerly to the Roman emperors, the pontifices maximi, that is to say, the priests of Jove."—E.

In proportion as the idlers were polished, agreeable, and amiable, it was observed that there was a greater and more shocking contrast between them and those who were engaged in business.

Among the latter, or such as pretended so to be, there was a gang of melancholy fanatics, whose absurdity and knavery divided their character,—whose appearance alone diffused misery,—and who would have overturned the world, had they been able to gain a little credit. But the nation of idlers, by dancing and singing, forced them into obscurity in their caverns, as the warbling birds drive the croaking bats back to their holes and ruins.

A smaller number of those who were occupied, were the preservers of ancient barbarous customs, against which nature, terrified, loudly exclaimed. They consulted nothing but their worm-eaten registers. If they there discovered a foolish or horrid custom, they considered it as a sacred law. It was from this vile practice of not daring to think for themselves, but extracting their ideas from the ruins of those times when no one thought at all, that in the metropolis of pleasure there still remained some shocking manners. Hence it was that there was no proportion between crimes and punishments. A thousand deaths were sometimes inflicted upon an innocent victim, to make him acknowledge a crime he had not committed.

The extravagancies of youth were punished with the same severity as murder or parricide. The idlers screamed loudly at these exhibitions, and the next day thought no more about them, but were buried in the contemplation of some new fashion.

This people saw a whole age elapse, in which the fine arts attained a degree of perfection that far surpassed the most sanguine hopes. Foreigners then repaired thither, as they did to Babylon, to admire the great monuments of architecture, the wonders of gardening, the sublime efforts of sculpture and painting. They were charmed with a species of music that reached the heart without astonishing the ears.

True poetry, that is to say, such as is natural and harmonious, that which addresses the heart as well as the mind, was unknown to this nation before this happy period. New kinds of eloquence displayed sublime beauties. The theatres in particular reëchoed with masterpieces that no other nation ever approached. In a word, good taste prevailed in every profession to that degree, that there were even good writers among the Druids.

So many laurels that had branched even to the skies, soon withered in an exhausted soil. There remained but a very small number, whose leaves were of a pale dying verdure. This decay was occasioned by the facility of producing; laziness preventing good productions, and by a satiety of the brilliant, and a taste for the whimsical. Vanity protected arts that brought back times of barbarity; and this same vanity, in persecuting persons of real merit, forced them to quit their country. The hornets banished the bees.

There were scarce any real arts, scarce any real genius, talent now consisted in reasoning right or wrong upon the merit of the last age. The dauber of a sign-post criticised with an air of sagacity the works of the greatest painters; and the blotters of paper disfigured the works of the greatest writers. Ignorance and bad taste had other daubers in their pay. The same things were repeated in a hundred volumes under different titles. Every work was either a dictionary or a pamphlet. A Druid gazetteer wrote twice a week the obscure annals of an unknown people possessed with the devil, and of celestial prodigies operated in garrets by little beggars of both sexes. Other Ex-Druids, dressed in black, ready to die with rage and hunger, set forth their complaints in a hundred different writings, that they were no longer allowed to cheat mankind—this privilege being conferred on some goats clad in grey; and some Arch-Druids were employed in printing defamatory libels.

Amazan was quite ignorant of all this, and even if he had been acquainted with it, he would have given himself very little concern about it, having his head filled with nothing but the princess of Babylon, the king of Egypt, and the inviolable vow he had made to despise all female coquetry in whatever country his despair should drive him.

The gaping ignorant mob, whose curiosity exceeds all the bounds of nature and reason, for a long time thronged about his unicorns. The more sensible women forced open the doors of his *hotel* to contemplate his person.

Gaiety and frivolity.—"There are within its walls at least a hundred thousand people, who had no other employment than play and diversion."

He at first testified some desire of visiting the court; but some of the idlers, who constituted good company and casually went thither, informed him that it was quite out of fashion, that times were greatly changed, and that all amusements were confined to the city. He was invited that very night to sup with a lady whose sense and talents had reached foreign climes, and who had traveled in some countries through which Amazan had passed. This lady gave him great pleasure, as well as the society he met at her house. Here reigned a decent liberty, gaiety without tumult, silence without pedantry, and wit without asperity. He found that *good company* was not quite ideal, though the title was frequently usurped by pretenders. The next day he dined in a society far less amiable, but much more voluptuous. The more he was satisfied with the guests, the more they were pleased with him. He found his soul soften and dissolve, like the aromatics of his country, which gradually melt in a moderate heat, and exhale in delicious perfumes.

After dinner he was conducted to a place of public entertainment which was enchanting; but condemned, however, by the Druids, because it deprived them of their auditors, which, therefore, excited their jealousy. The representation here consisted of agreeable verses, delightful songs, dances which expressed the movements of the soul, and perspectives that charmed the eye in deceiving it. This kind of pastime, which included so many kinds, was known only under a foreign name. It was called an *Opera*, which formerly signified, in the language of the Seven Mountains, work, care, occupation, industry, enterprise, business. This exhibition enchanted him. A female singer, in particular, charmed him by her melodious voice, and the graces that accompanied her. This child of genius, after the performance, was introduced to him by his new friends. He presented her with a handful of diamonds; for which she was so grateful, that she could not leave him all the rest of the day. He supped with her and her companions, and during the delightful repast he forgot his sobriety, and became heated and oblivious with wine. What an instance of human frailty!

The beautiful princess of Babylon arrived at this juncture, with her phœnix, her chambermaid Irla, and her two hundred Gangaridian cavaliers mounted on their unicorns. It was a long while before the gates were opened. She immediately asked, if the handsomest, the most courageous, the most sensible, and the most faithful of men was still in that city? The magistrates readily concluded that she meant Amazan. She was conducted to his *hotel*. How great was the palpitation of her heart!—the powerful operation of the tender passion. Her whole soul was penetrated with inexpressible joy, to see once more in her lover the model of constancy. Nothing could prevent her entering his chamber; the curtains were open; and she saw the beautiful Amazan asleep and stupefied with drink.

Formosanta expressed her grief with such screams as made the house echo. She swooned into the arms of Irla. As soon as she had recovered her senses, she retired from this fatal chamber with grief blended with rage.

"Oh! just heaven; oh, powerful Oromasdes!" cried the beautiful princess of Babylon, bathed in tears. "By whom, and for whom am I thus betrayed? He that could reject for my sake so many princesses, to abandon me for the company of a strolling Gaul! No! I can never survive this affront."

"This is the disposition of all young people," said Irla to her, "from one end of the world to the other. Were they enamoured with a beauty descended from heaven, they would at certain moments forget her entirely."

"It is done," said the princess, "I will never see him again whilst I live. Let us depart this instant, and let the unicorns be harnessed."

The phœnix conjured her to stay at least till Amazan awoke, that he might speak with him.

"He does not deserve it," said the princess. "You would cruelly offend me. He would think that I had desired you to reproach him, and that I am willing to be reconciled to him. If you love me, do not add this injury to the insult he has offered me."

The phœnix, who after all owed his life to the daughter of the king of Babylon, could not disobey her. She set out with all her attendants.

"Whither are you going?" said Irla to her.

"I do not know," replied the princess; "we will take the first road we find. Provided I fly from Amazan for ever, I am satisfied."

Ancient barbarous customs.

ANCIENT BARBAROUS CUSTOMS.

William Howitt, in a note to his translation of *The Religion of Rome*, (page 19), points out very clearly the evils which have resulted to man from the sinister teaching of the upholders of ancient barbarous customs:—

"If anyone would satisfy himself of what Popery is at its centre; what it does where it has had its fullest sway, let him make a tour into the mountains in the vicinity of Rome, and see in a country exceedingly beautiful by nature, what is the condition of an extremely industrious population. In the rock towns of the Alban, Sabine, and Volscian hills, you find a swarming throng of men, women, and children, asses, pigs, and hens, all groveling in inconceivable filth, squalor, and poverty. Filth in the streets, in the houses, everywhere; fleas, fever, and small-pox, and the densest ignorance darkening minds of singular natural cleverness. A people brilliant in intellect, totally uneducated, and steeped in the grossest superstition.

"These dens of dirt, disease and, till lately, or brigandage, are the evidences of a thousand years of priestly government! They, and the country around them, are chiefly the property of the great princely and ducal families which sprung out of the papal neposm of Rome, and have by successive popes, their founders, been loaded with the wealth of the nation. These families live in Rome, in their great palaces, amidst every luxury and splendor, surrounded by the finest works of art, and leave their tenants and dependents without any attention from them. Some steward or middleman screws the last soldo from them for rent; and when crops fail, lifts not a finger to alleviate their misery.

"And the Papal Government, too—a government pretendedly based on the direct ordination of Him who went about doing good—what has it done for them? Nothing but debauch their minds with idle ceremonies and unscriptural dogmas,—legends, priests, monks and beggary! The whole land is a land of beggars, made so by inculcated notions of a spurious charity. Every countrywoman, many men, and every child, boy or girl, are literally beggars—beggars importunate, unappeasable, irrepressible! What a condition of mind for a naturally noble and capable people to be reduced to by—a religion!"

The phœnix, who was wiser than Formosanta, because he was divested of passion, consoled her upon the road. He gently insinuated to her that it was shocking to punish one's self for the faults of another; that Amazan had given her proofs sufficiently striking and numerous of his fidelity, so that she should forgive him for having forgotten himself for one moment in social company; that this was the only time in which he had been wanting of the grace of Oromasdes; that it would render him only the more constant in love and virtue for the future; that the desire of expiating his fault would raise him beyond himself; that it would be the means of increasing her happiness; that many great princesses before her had forgiven such slips, and had had no reason to be sorry afterward; and he was so thoroughly possessed of the art of persuasion, that Formosanta's mind grew more calm and peaceable. She was now sorry she had set out so soon. She thought her unicorns went too fast, but she did not dare return. Great was the conflict between her desire of forgiving and that of showing her rage—between her love and vanity. However, her unicorns pursued their pace; and she traversed the world, according to the prediction of her father's oracle.

When Amazan awoke, he was informed of the arrival and departure of Formosanta and the phœnix. He was also told of the rage and distraction of the princess, and that she had sworn never to forgive him.

"Then," said he, "there is nothing left for me to do, but follow her, and kill myself at her feet."

The report of this adventure drew together his festive companions, who all remonstrated with him. They said that he had much better stay with them; that nothing could equal the pleasant life they led in the centre of arts and refined delicate pleasures; that many strangers, and even kings, preferred such an agreeable enchanting repose to their country and their thrones. Moreover, his vehicle was broken, and another was being made for him according to the newest fashion; that the best tailor of the whole city had already cut out for him a dozen suits in the latest style; that the most vivacious, amiable, and fashionable ladies, at whose houses dramatic performances were represented, had each appointed a day to give him a regale. The girl from the opera was in the meanwhile drinking her chocolate, laughing, singing, and ogling the beautiful Amazan—who by this time clearly perceived she had no more sense than a goose.

A sincerity, cordiality, and frankness, as well as magnanimity and courage, constituted the character of this great prince, he related his travels and misfortunes to his friends. They knew that he was cousin-german to the princess. They were informed of the fatal kiss she had given the king of Egypt. "Such little tricks," said they, "are often forgiven between relatives, otherwise one's whole life would pass in perpetual uneasiness."

Nothing could shake his design of pursuing Formosanta; but his carriage not being ready, he was compelled to remain three days longer among the idlers, who were still feasting and merry-making. He at length took his leave of them, by embracing them and making them accept some of his diamonds that were the best mounted, and recommending to them a constant pursuit of frivolity and pleasure, since they were thereby made more agreeable and happy.

"The Germans," said he, "are the greyheads of Europe; the people of Albion are men formed; the inhabitants of Gaul are the children,—and I love to play with children."

XI.

AMAZAN AND FORMOSANTA BECOME RECONCILED.

The guides had no difficulty in following the route the princess had taken. There was nothing else talked of but her and her large bird. All the inhabitants were still in a state of fascination. The banks of the Loire, of the Dordogue—the Garonne, and the Gironde, still echoed with acclamation.

When Amazan reached the foot of the Pyrenees, the magistrates and Druids of the country made him dance, whether he would or not, a *Tambourin*; but as soon as he cleared the Pyrenees, nothing presented itself that was either gay or joyous. If he here and there heard a peasant sing, it was a doleful ditty. The inhabitants stalked with much gravity, having a few strung beads and a girted poniard. The nation dressed in black, and appeared to be in mourning.

Dancing a tambourin.—"When Amazan reached the foot of the Pyrenees, the magistrates and druids of the country made him dance, whether he would or not, a Tambourin; but as soon as he cleared the Pyrenees, nothing presented itself that was either gay or joyous."

If Amazan's servants asked passengers any questions, they were answered by signs; if they went into an inn, the host acquainted his guests in three words, that there was nothing in the house, but that the things they so pressingly wanted might be found a few miles off.

When these votaries to taciturnity were asked if they had seen the beautiful princess of Babylon pass, they answered with less brevity than usual: "We have seen her—she is not so handsome—there are no beauties that are not tawny—she displays a bosom of alabaster, which is the most disgusting thing in the world, and which is scarce known in our climate."

Amazan advanced toward the province watered by the Betis. The Tyrians discovered this country about twelve thousand years ago, about the time they discovered the great Atlantic Isle, inundated so many centuries after. The Tyrians cultivated Betica, which the natives of the country had never done, being of opinion that it was not their place to meddle with anything, and that their neighbors, the Gauls, should come and reap their harvests. The Tyrians had brought with them some Palestines, or Jews, who, from that time, have wandered through every clime where money was to be gained. The Palestines, by extraordinary usury, at fifty per cent., had possessed themselves of almost all the riches of the country. This made the people of Betica imagine the Palestines were sorcerers; and all those who were accused of witchcraft were burnt, without mercy, by a company of Druids, who were called the Inquisitors, or the *Anthropokaies*. These priests immediately put their victims in a masquerade habit, seized upon their effects, and devoutly repeated the Palestines' own prayers, whilst burning them by a slow fire, *por l'amor de Dios*.

The princess of Babylon alighted in that city which has since been called Sevilla. Her design was to embark upon the Betis to return by Tyre to Babylon, and see again king Belus, her father; and forget, if possible, her perdious lover—or, at least, to ask him in marriage. She sent for two Palestines, who transacted all the business of the court. They were to furnish her with three ships. The phœnix made all the necessary contracts with them, and settled the price after some little dispute.

The hostess was a great devotee, and her husband, who was no less religious, was a Familiar: that is to say, a spy of the Druid Inquisitors or *Anthropokaies*.

He failed not to inform them, that in his house was a sorceress and two Palestines, who were entering into a compact with the devil, disguised like a large gilt bird.

The Inquisitors having learned that the lady possessed a large quantity of diamonds, swore point blank that she was a sorceress. They waited till night to imprison the two hundred cavaliers and the unicorns, (which slept in very extensive stables), for the Inquisitors are cowards.

Having strongly barricaded the gates, they seized the princess and Irla; but they could not catch the phœnix, who flew away with great swiftness. He did not doubt of meeting with Amazan upon the road from Gaul to Sevilla.

He met him upon the frontiers of Betica, and acquainted him with the disaster that had befallen the princess.

Amazan was struck speechless with rage. He armed himself with a steel cuirass damasquined with gold, a lance twelve feet long, two javelins, and an edged sword called the Thunderer, which at one single stroke would rend trees, rocks, and Druids. He covered his beautiful head with a golden casque, shaded with heron and ostrich feathers. This was the ancient armor of Magog, which his sister Aldea gave him when upon his journey in Scythia. The few attendants he had with him all mounted their unicorns.

Amazan, in embracing his dear phœnix, uttered only these melancholy expressions: "I am guilty! Had I not dined with the child of genius from the opera, in the city of the idlers, the princess of Babylon would not have been in this alarming situation. Let us fly to the *Anthropokaies*." He presently entered Sevilla. Fifteen hundred Alguazils guarded the gates of the inclosure in which the two hundred Gangarids and their unicorns were shut up, without being allowed anything to eat. Preparations were already made for sacrificing the princess of Babylon, her chambermaid Irla, and the two rich Palestines.

The high *Anthropokaie*, surrounded by his subaltern *Anthropokaies*, was already seated upon his sacred tribunal. A crowd of Sevillians, wearing strung beads at their girdles, joined their two hands, without uttering a syllable, when the beautiful Princess, the maid Irla, and the two Palestines were brought forth, with their hands tied behind their backs and dressed in masquerade habits.

The phœnix entered the prison by a dormer window, whilst the Gangarids began to break open the doors. The invincible Amazan shattered them without. They all sallied forth armed, upon their unicorns, and Amazan put himself at their head. He had no difficulty in overthrowing the Alguazils, the Familiars, or the priests called *Anthropokaies*. Each unicorn pierced dozens at a time. The thundering Amazan cut to pieces all he met. The people in black cloaks and dirty frize ran away, always keeping fast hold of their blest beads, *por l'amor de Dios*.

Amazan collared the high Inquisitor upon his tribunal, and threw him upon the pile, which was prepared about forty paces distant; and he also cast upon it the other Inquisitors, one after the other. He then prostrated himself at Formosanta's feet. "Ah! how amiable you are," said she; "and how I should adore you, if you had not forsaken me for the company of an opera singer."

Whilst Amazan was making his peace with the princess, whilst his Gangarids cast upon the pile the bodies of all the *Anthropokaies*, and the flames ascended to the clouds, Amazan saw an army that approached him at a distance. An aged monarch, with a crown upon his head, advanced upon a car drawn by eight mules harnessed with ropes. An hundred other cars followed. They were accompanied by grave looking men in black cloaks or frize, mounted upon very fine horses. A multitude of people, with greasy hair, followed silently on foot.

Amazan immediately drew up his Gangarids about him, and advanced with his lance couched. As soon as the king perceived him, he took off his crown, alighted from his car, and embraced Amazan's stirrup, saying to him: "Man sent by the gods, you are the avenger of human kind, the deliverer of my country. These sacred monsters, of which you have purged the earth, were my masters, in the name of the Old Man of the Seven Mountains. I was forced to submit to their criminal power. My people would have deserted me, if I had only been inclined to moderate their abominable crimes. From this moment I breathe, I reign, and am indebted to you for it."

He afterward respectfully kissed Formosanta's hand, and entreated her to get into his coach (drawn by eight mules) with Amazan, Irla, and the phœnix.

The two Palestine bankers, who still remained prostrate on the ground through fear and terror, now raised their heads. The troop of unicorns followed the king of Betica into his palace.

As the dignity of a king who reigned over a people of characteristic brevity, required that his mules should go at a very slow pace, Amazan and Formosanta had time to relate to him their adventures. He also conversed with the phœnix, admiring and frequently embracing him. He easily comprehended how brutal and barbarous the people of the west should be considered, who ate animals, and did not understand their language; that the Gangarids alone had preserved the nature and dignity of primitive man; but he particularly agreed, that the most barbarous of mortals were the *Anthropokaies*, of whom Amazan had just purged the earth. He incessantly blessed and thanked him. The beautiful Formosanta had already forgotten the affair in Gaul, and had her soul filled with nothing but the valor of the hero who had preserved her life. Amazan being made acquainted with the innocence of the embrace she had given to the king of Egypt, and being told of the resurrection of the phœnix, tasted the purest joy, and was intoxicated with the most violent love.

They dined at the palace, but had a very indifferent repast. The cooks of Betica were the worst in Europe. Amazan advised the king to send for some from Gaul. The king's musicians performed, during the repast, that celebrated air which has since been called *the Follies of Spain*. After dinner, matters of business came upon the carpet.

The king enquired of the handsome Amazan, the beautiful Formosanta, and the charming phœnix, what they proposed doing. "For my part," said

Amazan, "my intention is to return to Babylon, of which I am the presumptive heir, and to ask of my uncle Belus the hand of my cousin-german, the incomparable Formosanta."

"My design certainly is," said the princess, "never to separate from my cousin-germain. But I imagine he will agree with me, that I should return first to my father, because he only gave me leave to go upon a pilgrimage to Bassora, and I have wandered all over the world."

"For my part," said the phœnix, "I will follow every where these two tender, generous lovers."

"You are in the right," said the king of Betica; "but your return to Babylon is not so easy as you imagine. I receive daily intelligence from that country by Tyrian ships, and my Palestine bankers, who correspond with all the nations of the earth. The people are all in arms toward the Euphrates and the Nile. The king of Scythia claims the inheritance of his wife, at the head of three hundred thousand warriors on horseback. The kings of Egypt and India are also laying waste the banks of the Tygris and the Euphrates, each at the head of three hundred thousand men, to revenge themselves for being laughed at. The king of Ethiopia is ravaging Egypt with three hundred thousand men, whilst the king of Egypt is absent from his country. And the king of Babylon has as yet only six hundred thousand men to defend himself.

"I acknowledge to you," continued the king, "when I hear of those prodigious armies which are disembogued from the east, and their astonishing magnificence—when I compare them to my trifling bodies of twenty or thirty thousand soldiers, which it is so difficult to clothe and feed; I am inclined to think the eastern subsisted long before the western hemisphere. It seems as if we sprung only yesterday from chaos and barbarity."

"Sire," said Amazan, "the last comers frequently outstrip those who first began the career. It is thought in my country that man was first created in India; but this I am not certain of."

"And," said the king of Betica to the phœnix, "what do you think?"

"Sire," replied the phœnix, "I am as yet too young to have any knowledge concerning antiquity. I have lived only about twenty-seven thousand years; but my father, who had lived five times that age, told me he had learned from his father, that the eastern country had always been more populous and rich than the others. It had been transmitted to him from his ancestors, that the generation of all animals had begun upon the banks of the Ganges. For my part, said he, I have not the vanity to be of this opinion. I cannot believe that the foxes of Albion, the marmots of the Alps, and the wolves of Gaul, are descended from my country. In the like manner, I do not believe that the firs and oaks of your country descended from the palm and cocoa trees of India."

"But from whence are we descended, then?" said the king.

"I do not know," said the phœnix; "all I want to know is, whither the beautiful princess of Babylon and my dear Amazan may repair."

"I very much question," said the king, "whether with his two hundred unicorns he will be able to destroy so many armies of three hundred thousand men each."

"Why not?" said Amazan. The king of Betica felt the force of this sublime question, "Why not?" but he imagined sublimity alone was not sufficient against innumerable armies.

"I advise you," said he, "to seek the king of Ethiopia. I am related to that black prince through my Palestines. I will give you recommendatory letters to him. As he is at enmity with the king of Egypt, he will be but too happy to be strengthened by your alliance. I can assist you with two thousand sober, brave men; and it will depend upon yourself to engage as many more of the people who reside, or rather skip, about the foot of the Pyrenees, and who are called Vasques or Vascons. Send one of your warriors upon an unicorn, with a few diamonds. There is not a Vascon that will not quit the castle, that is, the thatched cottage of his father, to serve you. They are indefatigable, courageous, and agreeable; and whilst you wait their arrival, we will give you festivals, and prepare your ships. I cannot too much acknowledge the service you have done me."

Amazan realized the happiness of having recovered Formosanta, and enjoyed in tranquillity her conversation, and all the charms of reconciled love,—which are almost equal to a growing passion.

A troop of proud, joyous Vascons soon arrived, dancing a *tambourin*. The haughty and grave Betican troops were now ready. The old sun-burnt king tenderly embraced the two lovers. He sent great quantities of arms, beds, chests, boards, black clothes, onions, sheep, fowls, flour, and particularly garlic, on board the ships, and wished them a happy voyage, invariable love, and many victories.

Proud Carthage was not then a sea-port. There were at that time only a few Numidians there, who dried fish in the sun. They coasted along Bizacenes, the Syrthes, the fertile banks where since arose Cyrene and the great Chersonese.

They at length arrived toward the first mouth of the sacred Nile. It was at the extremity of this fertile land that the ships of all commercial nations were already received in the port of Canope, without knowing whether the god

Canope had founded this port, or whether the inhabitants had manufactured the god—whether the star Canope had given its name to the city, or whether the city had bestowed it upon the star. All that was known of this matter was, that the city and the star were both very ancient; and this is all that can be known of the origin of things, of what nature soever they may be.

It was here that the king of Ethiopia, having ravaged all Egypt, saw the invincible Amazan and the adorable Formosanta come on shore. He took one for the god of war, and the other for the goddess of beauty. Amazan presented to him the letter of recommendation from the king of Spain. The king of Ethiopia immediately entertained them with some admirable festivals, according to the indispensable custom of heroic times. They then conferred about their expedition to exterminate the three hundred thousand men of the king of Egypt, the three hundred thousand of the emperor of the Indies, and the three hundred thousand of the great Khan of the Scythians, who laid siege to the immense, proud, voluptuous city of Babylon.

The two hundred Spaniards, whom Amazan had brought with him, said that they had nothing to do with the king of Ethiopia's succoring Babylon; that it was sufficient their king had ordered them to go and deliver it; and that they were formidable enough for this expedition.

The Vascons said they had performed many other exploits; that they would alone defeat the Egyptians, the Indians, and the Scythians; and that they would not march unless the Spaniards were placed in the rear-guard.

The two hundred Gangarids could not refrain from laughing at the pretensions of their allies, and they maintained that with only one hundred unicorns, they could put to flight all the kings of the earth. The beautiful Formosanta appeased them by her prudence, and by her enchanting discourse. Amazan introduced to the black monarch his Gangarids, his unicorns, his Spaniards, his Vascons, and his beautiful bird.

Every thing was soon ready to march by Memphis, Heliopolis, Arsinoe, Petra, Artemitis, Sora, and Apamens, to attack the three kings, and to prosecute this memorable war, before which all the wars ever waged by man sink into insignificance.

Fame with her hundred tongues has proclaimed the victories Amazan gained over the three kings, with his Spaniards, his Vascons, and his unicorns. He restored the beautiful Formosanta to her father. He set at liberty all his mistress's train, whom the king of Egypt had reduced to slavery. The great Khan of the Scythians declared himself his vassal; and his marriage was confirmed with princess Aldea. The invincible and generous Amazan, was acknowledged the heir to the kingdom of Babylon, and entered the city in triumph with the phœnix, in the presence of a hundred tributary kings. The festival of his marriage far surpassed that which king Belus had given. The bull Apis was served up roasted at table. The kings of Egypt and India were cup-bearers to the married pair; and these nuptials were celebrated by five hundred illustrious poets of Babylon.

Oh, Muses! daughters of heaven, who are constantly invoked at the beginning of a work, I only implore you at the end. It is needless to reproach me with saying grace, without having said *benedicite*. But, Muses! you will not be less my patronesses. Inspire, I pray you, the *Ecclesiastical Gazetteer*, the illustrious orator of the *Convulsionnaires*, to say every thing possible against *The Princess of Babylon*, in order that the work may be condemned by the Sorbonne, and, therefore, be universally read. And prevent, I beseech you, O chaste and noble Muses, any supplemental scribblers spoiling, by their fables, the truths I have taught mortals in this faithful narrative.

Clio, the muse of history. From a painting by Antonio Canova.—"Prevent, I beseech you, O chaste and noble Muses, any supplemental scribblers spoiling, by their fables, the truths I have taught mortals in this faithful narrative."

THE MAN OF FORTY CROWNS.

The Tax Collector.

I.

NATIONAL POVERTY.

An old man, who is forever *pitying the present times, and extolling the past*, was saying to me: "Friend, France is not so rich as it was under Henry the IVth."

"And why?"

"Because the lands are not so well cultivated; because hands are wanting for the cultivation; and because the day-laborer having raised the price of his work, many land owners let their inheritances he fallow."

"Whence comes this scarcity of hands?"

"From this, that whoever finds in himself anything of a spirit of industry, takes up the trades of embroiderer, chaser, watchmaker, silk weaver, attorney, or divine. It is also because the revocation of the Edict of Nantes has left a great void in the kingdom; because nuns and beggars of all kinds have greatly multiplied; because the people in general avoid as much as possible the hard labor of cultivation, for which we are born by God's destination, and which we have rendered ignominious by our own opinions; so very wise are we!

"Another cause of our poverty lies in our new wants. We pay our neighbors four millions of livres on one article, and five or six upon another, such, for example, as a stinking powder for stuffing up our noses brought from America. Our coffee, tea, chocolate, cochineal, indigo, spices, cost us above sixty millions a year. All these were unknown to us in the reign of Henry the IVth, except the spices, of which, however, the consumption was not so great as it is now. We burn a hundred times more wax-lights than were burnt then; and get more than the half of the wax from foreign countries, because we neglect our own hives. We see a hundred times more diamonds in the ears, round the necks, and on the hands of our city ladies of Paris, and other great towns, than were worn by all the ladies of Henry the IVth's court, the Queen included. Almost all the superfluities are necessarily paid for with ready specie.

"Observe especially that we pay to foreigners above fifteen millions of annuities on the *Hôtel-de-Ville*; and that Henry the IVth, on his accession, having found two millions of debt in all on this imaginary *Hôtel*, very wisely paid off a part, to ease the state of this burden.

"Consider that our civil wars were the occasion of the treasures of Mexico being poured into the kingdom, when Don Philip *el Discreto* took it into his head to buy France, and that since that time, our foreign wars have eased us of a good half of our money.

"These are partly the causes of our poverty; a poverty which we hide under varnished ceilings, or with the help of our dealers in fashion. We are poor with taste. There are some officers of revenue, there are contractors or jobbers, there are merchants, very rich; their children, their sons-in-law, are also very rich, but the nation in general is unfortunately not so."

This old man's discourse, well or ill grounded, made a deep impression on me; for the curate of my parish, who had always had a friendship for me, had taught me a little of geometry and of history: and I begin to reflect a little, which is very rare in my province. I do not know whether he was right or not in every thing, but being very poor, I could very easily believe that I had a great many companions of my misery.

II.

DISASTER OF THE MAN OF FORTY CROWNS.

I very readily make known to the *universe* that I have a landed estate which would yield me forty crowns a year, were it not for the tax laid on it.

There came forth several edicts from certain persons, who, having nothing better to do, govern the state at their fire-side, the preamble of these edicts was, "that the legislative and executive was born, *jure divino*, the co-proprietor of my land;" and that I owe it at least the half of what I possess. The enormity of this legislative and executive power made me bless myself. What would it be if that power which presides over "the essential order of society," were to take the whole of my little estate? The one is still more divine than the other.

The comptroller general knows that I used to pay, in all, but twelve livres; that even this was a heavy burden on me, and that I should have sunk under it, if God had not given me the talent of making wicker baskets, which helped to carry me through my trials. But how should I, on a sudden, be able to give the king twenty crowns?

The new ministers also said in their preamble, that it was not fit to tax anything but the land, because every thing arises from the land, even rain itself, and consequently that nothing was properly liable to taxation, but the fruits of the land.

During the last war, one of their collectors came to my house, and demanded of me, for my quota, three measures of corn, and a sack of beans, the whole worth twenty crowns, to maintain the war—of which I never knew the reason, having only heard it said, that there was nothing to be got by it for our country, and a great deal to lose. As I had not at that time either corn, or beans, or money, the legislative and executive power had me dragged to prison; and the war went on as well as it could.

On my release from the dungeon, being nothing but skin and bone, whom should I meet but a jolly fresh colored man in a coach and six? He had six footmen, to each of whom he gave for his wages more than the double of my revenue. His head-steward, who, by the way, looked in as good plight as himself, had of him a salary of two thousand livres, and robbed him every year of twenty thousand more. His mistress had in six months stood him in forty thousand crowns. I had formerly known him when he was less well to pass than myself. He owned, by way of comfort to me, that he enjoyed four hundred thousand livres a year.

"I suppose, then," said I, "that you pay out of this income two hundred thousand to the state, to help to support that advantageous war we are carrying on; since I, who have but just a hundred and twenty livres a year, am obliged to pay half of them."

"I," said he, "I contribute to the wants of the state? You are surely jesting, my friend. I have inherited from an uncle his fortune of eight millions, which he got at Cadiz and at Surat; I have not a foot of land; my estate lies in government contracts, and in the funds. I owe the state nothing. It is for you to give half of your substance,—you who are a proprietor of land. Do you not see, that if the minister of the revenue were to require anything of me in aid of our country, he would be a blockhead, that could not calculate? for every thing is the produce of the land. Money and the paper currency are nothing but pledges of exchange. If, after having laid the sole tax, the tax that is to supply the place of all others, on those commodities, the government were to ask money of me; do you not see, that this would be a double load? that it would be asking the same thing twice over? My uncle sold at Cadiz to the amount of two millions of your corn, and of two millions of stuffs made of your wool; upon these two articles he gained cent. per cent. You must easily think that this profit came out of lands already taxed. What my uncle bought for tenpence of you, he sold again for above fifty livres at Mexico; and thus he made a shift to return to his own country with eight millions clear.

"You must be sensible, then, that it would be a horrid injustice to re-demand of him a few farthings on the tenpence he paid you. If twenty nephews like me, whose uncles had gained each eight millions at Buenos Ayres, at Lima, at Surat, or at Pondicherry, were, in the urgent necessities of the state, each to lend to it only two hundred thousand livres, that would produce four millions. But what horror would that be! Pay then thou, my friend, who enjoyest quietly the neat and clear revenue of forty crowns; serve thy country well, and come now and then to dine with my servants in livery."

This plausible discourse made me reflect a good deal, but I cannot say it much comforted me.

III.

CONVERSATION WITH A GEOMETRICIAN.

It sometimes happens that a man has no answer to make, and yet is not persuaded. He is overthrown without the feeling of being convinced. He feels at the bottom of his heart a scruple, a repugnance, which hinders him from believing what has been proved to him. A geometrician demonstrates to you, that between a circle and a tangent, you may thread a number of curves, and yet cannot get one straight line to pass. Your eyes, your reason, tell you the contrary. The geometrician gravely answers you, that it is an infinitesimal of the second order. You stare in stupid silence, and quit the field all astonished, without having any clear idea, without comprehending anything, and without having any reply to make.

Consult but a geometrician of more candor, and he explains the mystery to you.

"We suppose," says he, "what cannot be in nature, lines which have length without breadth. Naturally and philosophically speaking, it is impossible for one real line to penetrate another. No curve, nor no right line can pass between two real lines that touch one another. These theorems that puzzle you are but sports of the imagination, ideal chimeras. Whereas true geometry is the art of measuring things actually existent."

I was perfectly well satisfied with the confession of the sensible mathematician, and, with all my misfortune, could not help laughing on learning that there was a quackery even in that science, which is called the sublime science. My geometrician was a kind of philosophical patriot, who had deigned to chat with me sometimes in my cottage. I said to him:

"Sir, you have tried to enlighten the cockneys of Paris, on a point of the greatest concern to mankind, that of the duration of human life. It is to you alone that the ministry owes its knowledge of the due rate of annuities for lives, according to different ages. You have proposed to furnish the houses in town with what water they may want, and to deliver us at length from the shame and ridicule of hearing water cried about the streets, and of seeing women inclosed within an oblong hoop, carrying two pails of water, both together of about thirty pounds weight, up to a fourth story. Be so good, in the name of friendship, to tell me, how many two-handed bipeds there may be in France?"

THE GEOMETRICIAN.—It is assumed, that there may be about twenty millions, and I am willing to adopt this calculation as the most probable, till it can be verified, which it would be very easy to do, and which, however, has not hitherto been done, because *one does not always think of every thing.*

THE MAN OF FORTY CROWNS.—How many acres, think you, the whole territory of France contains?

THE GEOMETRICIAN.—One hundred and thirty millions, of which almost the half is in roads, in towns, villages, moors, heaths, marshes, sands, barren lands, useless convents, gardens of more pleasure than profit, uncultivated grounds, and bad grounds ill cultivated. We might reduce all the land which yields good returns to seventy-five millions of square acres; but let us state them at fourscore millions. One cannot do too much for one's country.

THE MAN OF FORTY CROWNS.—How much may you think each acre brings in yearly, one year with another, in corn, seeds of all kinds, wine, fish-ponds, wood, metals, cattle, fruit, wool, silk, oil, milk, clear of all charges, without reckoning the tax?

THE GEOMETRICIAN.—Why, if they produce each twenty-five livres, (about twenty English shillings), it is a great deal; but not to discourage our countrymen, let us put them at thirty livres. There are acres which produce constantly regenerating value, and which are estimated at three hundred livres: there are others which only produce three livres. The mean proportion between three and three hundred is thirty; for you must allow that three is to thirty as thirty is to three hundred. If, indeed, there were comparatively many acres at thirty livres, and very few at three hundred, our account would not hold good; but, once more, I would not be over punctilious.

THE MAN OF FORTY CROWNS.—Well, sir; how much will these fourscore millions of acres yield of revenue, estimated in money?

THE GEOMETRICIAN.—The account is ready made; they will produce two thousand four hundred millions of livres of the present currency.

THE MAN OF FORTY CROWNS.—I have read that Solomon possessed, of his own property, twenty-five thousand millions of livres, in ready money; and certainly there are not two thousand four hundred millions of specie circulating in France, which, I am told, is much greater and much richer than Solomon's country.

THE GEOMETRICIAN.—There lies the mystery. There may be about nine hundred millions circulating throughout the kingdom; and this money, passing from hand to hand, is sufficient to pay for all the produce of the land, and of industry. The same crown may pass ten times from the pocket of the cultivator, into that of the ale-housekeeper, and of the tax-gatherer.

THE MAN OF FORTY CROWNS.—I apprehend you. But you told me that we are, in all, about twenty millions of inhabitants, men, women, old and young. How much, pray, do you allow for each?

THE GEOMETRICIAN.—One hundred and twenty livres, or forty crowns.

THE MAN OF FORTY CROWNS.—You have just guessed my revenue. I have four acres, which, reckoning the fallow years with those of produce, bring me in one hundred and twenty livres; which is little enough, God knows.

But if every individual were to have his contingent, would that be no more than five louis d'ors a year?

THE GEOMETRICIAN.—Certainly not, according to our calculation, which I have a little amplified. Such is the state of human nature. Our life and our fortune have narrow limits. In Paris, they do not, one with another, live above twenty-two or twenty-three years, and, one with another, have not, at the most, above a hundred and twenty livres a year to spend. So that your food, your raiment, your lodging, your movables, are all represented by the sum of one hundred and twenty livres.

THE MAN OF FORTY CROWNS.—Alas! What have I done to you, that you thus abridge me of my fortune and life? Can it then be true, that I have but three and twenty years to live, unless I rob my fellow-creatures of their share?

THE GEOMETRICIAN.—This is incontestable in the good city of Paris. But from these twenty-three years you must deduct ten, at the least, for your childhood, as childhood is not an enjoyment of life; it is a preparation; it is the porch of the edifice; it is the tree that has not yet given fruits; it is the dawn of a day. Then again, from the thirteen years which remain to you, deduct the time of sleep, and that of tiresomeness of life, and that will be at least a moiety. You will then have six years and a half left to pass in vexation, in pain, in some pleasures, and in hopes.

THE MAN OF FORTY CROWNS.—Merciful heaven! At this rate, your account does not allow us above three years of tolerable existence.

THE GEOMETRICIAN.——That is no fault of mine. Nature cares very little for individuals. There are insects which do not live above one day, but of which the species is perpetual. Nature resembles those great princes, who reckon as nothing the loss of four hundred thousand men, so they but accomplish their august designs.

THE MAN OF FORTY CROWNS.—Forty Crowns and three years of life! What resource can you imagine against two such curses?

THE GEOMETRICIAN.—As to life, it would be requisite to render the air of Paris more pure—that men should eat less and take more exercise—that mothers should suckle their own children—that people should be no longer so ill-advised as to dread inoculation. This is what I have already said; and as to fortune, why, even marry and rear a family.

THE MAN OF FORTY CROWNS.—How! Can the way to live more at ease be to associate to my own bad circumstances those of others?

THE GEOMETRICIAN.—Five or six bad circumstances put together form a tolerable establishment. Get a good wife, and we will say only two sons and two daughters; this will make seven hundred and twenty livres for your little family, that is to say, if distributive justice were to take place, and that each individual had an hundred and twenty livres a year. Your children, in their infancy, stand you in almost nothing; when grown up they will ease and help you. Their mutual aid will save you a good part of your expenses, and you may live very happy, like a philosopher. Always provided, however, that those worthy gentlemen who govern the state have not the barbarity to extort from each of you twenty crowns a year. But the misfortune is, we are no longer in the golden age, where the men, born all equals, had an equal part in the nutritive productions of uncultivated land. The case is now far from being so good a one, as that every two-handed biped possesses land to the value of an hundred and twenty livres a year.

THE MAN OF FORTY CROWNS.—'Sdeath! You ruin us. You said but just now, that in a country of fourscore millions of inhabitants, each of them ought to enjoy an hundred and twenty livres a year, and now you take them away from us again!

THE GEOMETRICIAN.—I was computing according to the registers of the golden age, but we must reckon according to that of iron. There are many inhabitants who have but the value of ten crowns a year, others no more than four or five, and above six millions of men who have absolutely nothing.

THE MAN OF FORTY CROWNS.—Nothing? Why they would perish of hunger in three days' time.

THE GEOMETRICIAN.—Not in the least. The others, who possess their portions, set them to work, and share with them. It is from this arrangement that the pay comes for the divine, the confectioner, the apothecary, the preacher, the actor, the attorney, and the hackney-coachman. You thought yourself very ill off, to have no more than a hundred and twenty livres a year, reduced to a hundred and eight by your tax of twelve livres. But consider the soldiers who devote their blood to their country at the rate of fourpence a day. They have not above sixty-three livres a year for their livelihood, and yet they make a comfortable shift, by a number of them joining their little stock and living in common.

THE MAN OF FORTY CROWNS.—So then an ex-Jesuit has more than five times the pay of a soldier. And yet the soldiers have done more service to the state under the eyes of the king at Fontenoy, at Laufelt, at the siege of Fribourg, than the reverend Father Le Valette ever did in his life.

THE GEOMETRICIAN.—Nothing can be truer: nay, every one of these turned-adrift Jesuits, having now become free, has more to spend than what he cost his convent. There are even some among them who have gained a good deal of money by scribbling pamphlets against the parliaments, as for example, the reverend father Patouillet, and the reverend father Monote. In short, in this world every one sets his wits to work for a livelihood. One is at the head of a manufactory of stuffs; another of porcelain; another undertakes the opera; another the *Ecclesiastical Gazette*; another a tragedy in familiar life, or a novel or romance in the English style; this maintains the stationer, the ink-maker, the bookseller, the hawker, who might else be reduced to beggary. There is nothing, then, but the restitution of the hundred and twenty livres to those who have nothing, that makes the state flourish.

THE MAN OF FORTY CROWNS.—A pretty way of flourishing, truly!

THE GEOMETRICIAN.—And yet there is no other. In every country it is the rich that enable the poor to live. This is the sole source of the industry of commerce. The more industrious a nation itself is, the more it gains from foreign countries. Could we, on our foreign trade, get ten millions a year by the balance in our favor, there would, in twenty years, be two hundred millions more in the nation. This would afford ten livres a head more, on the supposition of an equitable distribution; that is to say, that the dealers would make each poor person earn ten livres the more, once paid, in the hopes of making still more considerable gains. But commerce, like the fertility of the earth, has its bounds, otherwise its progression would be *ad infinitum*. Nor, besides, is it clear, that the balance of our trade is constantly favorable to us; there are times in which we lose.

THE MAN OF FORTY CROWNS.—I have heard much talk of population. If our inhabitants were doubled, so that we numbered forty millions of people instead of twenty, what would be the consequence?

THE GEOMETRICIAN.—It would be this: that, one with another, each would have, instead of forty, but twenty crowns to live upon; or that the land should produce double the crops it now does; or that there should be double the national industry, or of gain from foreign countries; or that half of the people should be sent to America; or that one half of the nation should eat the other.

THE MAN OF FORTY CROWNS.—Let us then remain satisfied with our twenty millions of inhabitants, and with our hundred and twenty livres a head, distributed as it shall please the Lord. Yet this situation is a sad one, and your iron age is hard indeed.

THE GEOMETRICIAN.—There is no nation that is better off; and there are many that are worse. Do you believe that there is in the North wherewithal to afford to each inhabitant the value of an hundred and twenty of our livres a year? If they had had the equivalent of this, the Huns, the Vandals, and the Franks would not have deserted their country, in quest of establishments elsewhere, which they conquered, fire and sword in hand.

THE MAN OF FORTY CROWNS.—If I were to listen to you, you would persuade me presently that I am happy with my hundred and twenty livres.

THE GEOMETRICIAN.—If you would but think yourself happy, you would then be so.

THE MAN OF FORTY CROWNS.—A man cannot imagine what actually is not, unless he be mad.

THE GEOMETRICIAN.—I have already told you, that in order to be more at your ease, and more happy than you are, you should take a wife; to which I tack, however, this clause, that she has, as well as you, one hundred and twenty livres a year; that is to say, four acres at ten crowns an acre. The ancient Romans had each but one. If your children are industrious, they can each earn as much by their working for others.

THE MAN OF FORTY CROWNS.—So that they may get money, without others losing it.

THE GEOMETRICIAN.—Such is the law of all nations: there is no living but on these terms.

THE MAN OF FORTY CROWNS.—And must my wife and I give each of us the half of our produce to the legislative and executive power, and the new ministers of state rob us of the price of our hard labor, and of the substance of our poor children, before they are able to get their livelihood? Pray, tell me, how much money will these new ministers of ours bring into the king's coffers, by this *jure divino* system?

THE GEOMETRICIAN.—You pay twenty crowns on four acres, which bring you in forty. A rich man, who possesses four hundred acres will, by the new tariff, pay two thousand crowns; and the whole fourscore millions of acres will yield to the king, twelve hundred millions of livres a year, or four hundred millions of crowns.

THE MAN OF FORTY CROWNS.—That appears to me impracticable and impossible.

THE GEOMETRICIAN.—And very much you are in the right to think so: and this impossibility is a geometrical demonstration that there is a fundamental defect in the calculation of our new ministers.

THE MAN OF FORTY CROWNS.—Is not there also demonstrably a prodigious injustice in taking from me the half of my corn, of my hemp, of the wool of my sheep, etc., and, at the same time, to require no aid from those who shall have gained ten, twenty, or thirty thousand livres a year, by my hemp, of which they will have made linen,—by my wool, of which they will have made cloth,—by my corn, which they will have sold at so much more than it cost them?

THE GEOMETRICIAN.—The injustice of this administration is as evident as its calculation is erroneous. It is right to favor industry; but opulent industry ought to contribute to support the state. This industry will have certainly taken from you a part of your one hundred and twenty livres, and appropriated that part to itself, in selling you your shirts and your coat twenty times dearer than they would have cost you, if you had made them yourself. The manufacturer who shall have enriched himself, at your expense, will, I allow, have also paid wages to his workmen, who had nothing of themselves, but he will, every year, have sunk, and put by a sum that will, at length, have produced to him thirty thousand livres a year. This fortune then he will have acquired at your expense. Nor can you ever sell him the produce of your land dear enough to reimburse you for what he will have got by you; for were you to attempt such an advance of your price, he would procure what he wanted cheaper from other countries. A proof of which is, that he remains constantly possessor of his thirty thousand livres a year, and you of your one hundred and twenty livres, that often diminish, instead of increasing.

It is then necessary and equitable, that the refined industry of the trader should pay more than the gross industry of the farmer. The same is to be said of the collectors of the revenue. Your tax had previously been but twelve livres, before our great ministers were pleased to take from you twenty crowns. On these twelve livres, the collector retained tenpence, or ten *sols* for himself. If in your province there were five hundred thousand souls, he will have gained two hundred and fifty thousand livres a year. Suppose he spends fifty thousand, it is clear, that at the end of ten years he will be two millions in pocket. It is then but just that he should contribute his proportion, otherwise, every thing would be perverted, and go to ruin.

THE MAN OF FORTY CROWNS.—I am very glad you have taxed the officer of the revenue. It is some relief to my imagination. But since he has so well increased his superfluity, what shall I do to augment my small modicum?

THE GEOMETRICIAN.—I have already told you, by marrying, by laboring, by trying to procure from your land some sheaves of corn in addition to what it previously produced.

THE MAN OF FORTY CROWNS.—Well! granted then that I shall have been duly industrious; that all my countrymen will have been so too; and that the legislative and executive power shall have received a good round tax; how much will the nation have gained at the end of the year?

THE GEOMETRICIAN.—Nothing at all; unless it shall have carried on a profitable foreign trade. But life will have been more agreeable in it. Every one will, respectively, in proportion, have had more clothes, more linen, more movables than he had before. There will have been in the nation a more abundant circulation. The wages would have been, in process of time, augmented, nearly in proportion to the number of the sheaves of corn, of the tods of wool, of the ox-hides, of the sheep and goats, that will have been added, of the clusters of grapes that will have been squeezed in the wine-press. More of the value of commodities will have been paid to the king in money, and the king will have returned more value to those he will have employed under his orders; but there will not be half a crown the more in the kingdom.

THE MAN OF FORTY CROWNS.—-What will then remain to the government at the end of the year?

THE GEOMETRICIAN.—Once more, nothing. This is the case of government in general. It never lays by anything. It will have got its living, that is to say, its food, raiment, lodging, movables. The subject will have done so too. Where a government amasses treasure, it will have squeezed from the circulation so much money as it will have amassed. It will have made so many wretched, as it will have put by forty crowns in its coffers.

THE MAN OF FORTY CROWNS.—At this rate, then, Henry IV. was but a mean-spirited wretch, a miser, a plunderer, for I have been told that he had chested up in the Bastile, above fifty millions of livres according to our present currency.

THE GEOMETRICIAN.—He was a man as good, and as prudent, as he was brave. He was preparing to make a just war, and by amassing in his coffers twenty-two millions of the currency of that time, besides which he had twenty more to receive, which he left in circulation, he spared the people above a hundred millions that it would have cost, if he had not taken those useful measures. He made himself morally sure of success against an enemy who had not taken the like precaution. The probabilities were prodigiously in his favor. His twenty-two millions, in bank, proved that there was then in this kingdom, twenty-two millions of surplusage of the territorial produce, so that no one was a sufferer.

THE MAN OF FORTY CROWNS.—My father then told me the truth, when he said that the subject was in proportion more rich under the administration of the Duke of Sully than under that of our new ministers, who had laid on the *single* tax, the *sole* tax, and who, out of my forty crowns, have taken away twenty. Pray, tell me, is there another nation in the world that enjoys this precious advantage of the *sole tax*?

THE GEOMETRICIAN.—Not one opulent nation. The English, who are not much giving to laughing, could not, however, help bursting out, when they heard that men of intelligence, among us, had proposed this kind of administration. The Chinese exact a tax from all the foreign trading ships that resort to Canton. The Dutch pay, at Nangazaqui, when they are received in Japan, under pretext that they are not Christians. The Laplanders, and the Samoieds, are indeed subjected to a sole tax in sables or marten-skins. The republic of St. Marino pays nothing more than tithes for the maintenance of that state in its splendor.

There is, in Europe, a nation celebrated for its equity and its valor, that pays no tax. This is Switzerland. But thus it has happened. The people have put themselves in the place of the Dukes of Austria and of Zeringue. The small cantons are democratical, and very poor. Each inhabitant pays but a trifling sum toward the support of this little republic. In the rich cantons, the people are charged, for the state, with those duties which the Archdukes of Austria and the lords of the land used to exact. The protestant cantons are, in proportion, twice as rich as the catholic, because the state, in the first, possesses the lands of the monks. Those who were formerly subjects to the Archdukes of Austria, to the Duke of Zeringue, and to the monks, are now the subjects of their own country. They pay to that country the same tithes, the same fines of alienation, that they paid to their former masters; and as the subjects, in general, have very little trade, their merchandise is liable to no charges, except some small staple duties. The men make a trade of their courage, in their dealings with foreign powers, and sell themselves for a certain term of years, which brings some money into their country at our expense: and this example is as singular a one in the civilized world, as is the sole tax now laid on by our new legislators.

THE MAN OF FORTY CROWNS.—So, sir, the Swiss are not plundered, *jure divino*, of one-half of their goods; and he that has four cows in Switzerland is not obliged to give two of them to the state?

THE GEOMETRICIAN.—Undoubtedly, not. In one canton, upon thirteen tons of wine, they pay one, and drink the other twelve. In another canton, they pay the twelfth, and drink the remaining eleven.

THE MAN OF FORTY CROWNS.—Why am not I a Swiss? That cursed tax, that single and singularly iniquitous tax, that has reduced me to beggary! But then again, three or four hundred taxes, of which it is impossible for me to retain or pronounce the bare names, are they more just and more tolerable? Was there ever a legislator, who, in founding a state, wished to create counselors to the king, inspectors of coal-meters, gaugers of wine, measurers of wood, searchers of hog-tongues, comptrollers of salt butter? or to maintain an army of rascals, twice as numerous as that of Alexander, commanded by sixty generals, who lay the country under contribution, who gain, every day, signal victories, who take prisoners, and who sometimes sacrifice them in the air, or on a boarded stage, as the ancient Scythians did, according to what my vicar told me?

Now, was such a legislation, against which so many outcries were raised, and which caused the shedding of so many tears, much better than the newly imposed one, which at one stroke, cleanly and quietly takes away half of my subsistence? I am afraid, that on a fair liquidation, it will be found that under the ancient system of the revenue, they used to take, at times and in detail, three-quarters of it.

THE GEOMETRICIAN.—*Iliacos intra muros peccatur et extra. Est modus in retus. Caveas fine quidnimie.*

THE MAN OF FORTY CROWNS.—I have learned a little of history, and something of geometry; but I do not understand a word of Latin.

THE GEOMETRICIAN.—The sense is, pretty nearly, as follows. *There is wrong on both sides. Keep to a medium in every thing. Nothing too much.*

THE MAN OF FORTY CROWNS.—I say, nothing too much; that is really my situation; but the worst of it is, I have not enough.

THE GEOMETRICIAN.—I allow that you must perish of want, and I too, and the state too, if the new administration should continue only two years longer; but it is to be hoped heaven will have mercy on us.

THE MAN OF FORTY CROWNS.—We pass our lives in hope, and die hoping to the last. Adieu, sir, you have enlightened me, but my heart is grieved.

THE GEOMETRICIAN.—This is, indeed, often the fruit of knowledge.

Palace of the barefooted Carmelites.—"*What would you please to have, my son?*"—"*A morsel of bread, my reverend father. The new edicts have stripped me of everything.*"—"*Son, know that we ourselves beg charity; we do not bestow it.*"

IV.

AN ADVENTURE WITH A CARMELITE.

When I had thanked the academician of the Academy of Sciences, for having set me right, I went away quite out of heart, praising providence, but muttering between my teeth these doleful words: "*What! to have no more than forty crowns a year to live on, nor more than twenty-two years to live!* Alas! may our life be yet shorter, since it is to be so miserable!"

As I was saying this, I found myself just opposite a very superb house. Already was I feeling myself pressed by hunger. I had not so much as the hundred and twentieth part of the sum that by right belongs to each individual. But as soon as I was told that this was the palace of my reverend fathers, the bare-footed Carmelites, I conceived great hopes, and said to myself, since these saints are humble enough to go bare-footed, they will be charitable enough to give me a dinner.

I rang. A Carmelite came to the door.

"What would you please to have, my son?"

"A morsel of bread, my reverend father. The new edicts have stripped me of every thing."

Son, know that we ourselves beg charity; we do not bestow it."[1]

"What! while your holy institute forbids you to wear shoes, you have the house of a prince, and can you refuse to me a meal?"

"My son, it is true, we go without stockings and shoes; that is an expense the less; we feel no more cold in our feet than in our hands. As to our fine house, we built it very easily, as we have a hundred thousand livres a year of income from houses in the same street."

"So, then! you suffer me to die of hunger, while you have an income of a hundred thousand livres! I suppose you pay fifty thousand of these to the new government?"

"Heaven preserve us from paying a single farthing! It is only the produce of the land cultivated by laborious hands, callous with work, and moistened with tears, that owes taxes to the legislative and executive power. The alms which have been bestowed upon us, have enabled us to build those houses, by the rent of which we get a hundred thousand livres a year. But these alms, coming from the fruits of the earth, and having, consequently, already paid the tax, ought not to pay twice. They have sanctified the faithful believers, who have impoverished themselves to enrich us, and we continue to beg charity, and to lay under contribution the Fauxbourg of St. Germain, in order to sanctify a still greater number of the faithful believers."[2]

Having thus spoken, the Carmelite politely shut the door in my face.

I then passed along and stopped before the *Hôtel* of the *Mousquetaires gris*, and related to those gentlemen what had just happened to me. They gave me a good dinner and half a crown, (*un ecu*). One of them proposed to go directly and set fire to the convent; but a musqueteer, more discreet than he, remonstrated with him, insisting that the time for action had not yet arrived, and implored him to wait patiently a little longer.[3]

[1] Victor Hugo in his poem, *Christ at the Vatican*, (translated by G.B. Burleigh,) rebukes this inhuman spirit of monkish greed and avarice, which always receives but neves gives in return. In the poem, Christ is represented as saying:

"———I have said,
'I will have mercy and not sacrifice;'—
Have said, 'Give freely what, without a price,
Was given to you.' To my redeemed, instead,
You sell baptism upon their natal bed;
Sell to the sinner void indulgences;
To lovers sell the natural right to wed;
Sell to the dying the privilege of decease,
And sell your funeral masses to the dead!
Your prayers and masses and communions sell;
Beads, benedictions, crosses; in your eyes
Nothing is sacred,—all is merchandise."—E.

[2] In a recent number of *The Nineteenth Century*, Mr. Alex. A. Knox, in an able criticism on the writings of Voltaire, says very truly:

"It should not be forgotten that in his day a very large portion of the soil of France was in the hands of the clergy, free from all burdens, save in so far as the clergy chose to execute them by the way of 'gratuitous gifts.' The condition of the French peasant was frightful. Arthur Young, Dr. Moore, and others have described it at a somewhat later date, but it was even so in Voltaire's time. Of course the 'clerical immunities' were far from being the only cause of all this misery; but they were a frightful addition to it."

[3] The degradation of labor, and the corruption and injustice of the papal priesthood, were the inciting causes of the great revolution in France, which at length overturned the monarchy, and convulsed, for so long a period, every nation in Europe. In reading this romance of the hardships of the laborer, we may learn to comprehend the true principles of Voltaire, and recognize his great benevolence and sympathy with suffering and distress.

We may also listen to the first faint mutterings of the terrible storm of blood and retribution, that was so soon to burst over unhappy France, and overwhelm in its lurid course all ranks and conditions of mankind—the innocent and the guilty, the oppressed and the oppressor, the peasant and the priest.—E.

V.

AUDIENCE OF THE COMPTROLLER GENERAL.

I went, with my half-crown, to present a petition to the comptroller general, who was that day giving audience.

His anti-chamber was filled with people of all kinds. There were there especially some with more bluff faces, more prominent bellies, and more arrogant looks than my man of eight millions. I durst not draw near to them; I saw them, but they did not observe me.

A monk, a great man for tithes, had begun a suit at law against certain subjects of the state, whom he called his tenants. He had already a larger income than the half of his parishioners put together, and was moreover lord of the manor. His claim was, that whereas his vassals had, with infinite pains, converted their heaths into vineyards, they owed him a tithe of the wine, which, taking into the account the price of labor, of the vine-props, of the casks and cellarage, would carry off above a quarter of the produce.

"But," said he, "as the tithes are due, *jure divino*, I demand the quarter of the substance of my tenants, in the name of God."

The minister of the revenue said to him, "I see how charitable you are."

A farmer-general, extremely well-skilled in assessments, interposed, saying:

"Sir, that village can afford nothing to this monk; as I have, but the last year, made the parishioners pay thirty-two taxes on their wine, besides their overconsumption of the allowance for their own drinking. They are entirely ruined. I have seized and sold their cattle and movables, and yet they are still my debtors. I protest, then, against the claim of the reverend father."

"You are in the right," answered the minister of the revenue, "to be his rival; you both equally love your neighbor, and you both edify me."

A third, a monk and lord of the manor, whose tenants were in mortmain, was waiting for a decree of the council that should put him in possession of all the estate of a Paris cockney, who having, inadvertently, lived a year and a day in a house subject to this servitude, and inclosed within the hands of this priest, had died at the year's end. The monk was claiming all the estate of this cockney, and claiming it *jure divino*.

The minister found by this, that the heart of this monk was as just and as tender as those of the others.

A fourth, who was comptroller of the royal domains, presented a specious memorial, in which he justified himself for his having reduced twenty families to beggary. They had inherited from their uncles, their aunts, their brothers, or cousins; and were liable to pay the duties. The officers of the domain had generously proved to them, that they had not set the full value on their inheritances,—that they were much richer than they believed, and, consequently, having condemned them to a triple fine, ruined them in charges, and threw the heads of the families into jail, he had bought their best possessions without untying his purse-strings.

The comptroller general said to him, in a tone indeed rather bitter:

"Euge, controlleur bone et fidelis, quia supra pauca fuisti fidelis, fermier-general te constituam."

But to a master of the requests, who was standing at his side, he said in a low voice:

"We must make these blood-suckers, sacred and profane, disgorge. It is time to give some relief to the people, who, without our care, and our equity, would have nothing to live upon in this world at least, however they might fare in the other."

Some, of profound genius, presented projects to him. One of them had imagined a scheme to lay a tax on wit. "All the world," said he, "will be eager to pay, as no one cares to pass for a fool."

The minister declared to him, "I exempt you from the tax."

Another proposed to lay the *only* tax upon songs and laughing, in consideration that we were the merriest nation under the sun, and that a song was a relief and comfort for every thing. But the minister observed, that of late there were hardly any songs of pleasantry made; and he was afraid that, to escape the tax, we would become too serious.

The next that presented himself, was a trusty and loyal subject, who offered to raise for the king three times as much, by making the nation pay three times less. The minister advised him to learn arithmetic.

A fourth proved to the king in the way of *friendship*, that he could not raise above seventy-five millions, but that he was going to procure him two hundred and twenty-five. "You will oblige me in this," said the minister, "as soon as we shall have paid the public debts."

At length, who should appear but a deputy of the new author, who makes the legislative power co-proprietor of all our lands, *jure divino*, and who was giving the king twelve hundred millions of revenue. I knew the man again who had flung me into prison for not having paid my twenty crowns, and throwing myself at the feet of the comptroller general, I implored his justice; upon which, he burst out a laughing, and telling me, it was a trick that had been played me, he ordered the doers of this mischief in jest to pay me a hundred crowns damages, and exempted me from the land-tax for the rest of my life. I said to him, "God bless your honor!"

VI.

THE MAN OF FORTY CROWNS MARRIES, BECOMES A FATHER, AND DESCANTS UPON THE MONKS.

The Man of Forty Crowns having improved his understanding, and having accumulated a moderate fortune, married a very pretty girl, who had an hundred crowns a year of her own. As soon as his son was born, he felt himself a man of some consequence in the state. He was famous for making the best baskets in the world, and his wife was an excellent seamstress. She was born in the neighborhood of a rich abbey of a hundred thousand livres a year. Her husband asked me one day, why those gentlemen, who were so few in number, had swallowed so many of the forty crown lots? "Are they more useful to their country than I am?" "No, dear neighbor." "Do they, like me, contribute at least to the population of it?" "No." "Do they cultivate the land? Do they defend the state when it is attacked?" "No, they pray to God for us." "Well, then, I will pray to God for us." "Well, then, I will pray to God for them, in return."

QUESTION.—How many of these useful gentry, men and women, may the convents in this kingdom contain?

ANSWER.—By the lists of the superintendents, taken toward the end of the last century, there were about ninety thousand.

QUESTION.—According to our ancient account, they ought not, at forty crowns a head, to possess above ten millions eight hundred thousand livres. Pray, how much have they actually?

ANSWER.—They have to the amount of fifty millions, including the masses, and alms to the mendicant monks, who really lay a considerable tax on the people. A begging friar of a convent in Paris, publicly bragged that his wallet was worth fourscore thousand livres a year.

QUESTION.—Let us now consider how much the repartition of fifty millions among ninety thousand shaven crowns gives to each? Let us see, is it not five hundred and fifty-five livres?

ANSWER.—Yes, and a considerable sum it is in a numerous society, where the expenses even diminish by the quantity of consumers; for ten persons may live together much cheaper than if each had his separate lodging and table.

QUESTION.—So that the ex-Jesuits, to whom there is now assigned a pension of four hundred livres, are then really losers by the bargain.

ANSWER.—I do not think so; for they are almost all of them retired among their friends, who assist them. Several of them say masses for money, which they did not do before; others get to be preceptors; some are maintained by female bigots; each has made a shift for himself: and, perhaps, at this time, there are few of them, who have tasted of the world, and of liberty, that would resume their former chains. The monkish life, whatever they may say, is not at all to be envied. It is a maxim well known, that the monks are a kind of people who assemble without knowing, live without loving, and die without regretting each other.

QUESTION.—You think, then, that it would be doing them a great service, to strip them of all their monks' habits?

ANSWER.—They would undoubtedly gain much by it, and the state still more. It would restore to the country a number of subjects, men and women, who have rashly sacrificed their liberty, at an age to which the laws do not allow a capacity of disposing of tenpence a year income. It would be taking these corpses out of their tombs, and afford a true resurrection. Their houses might become hospitals, or be turned into places for manufactures. Population would be increased. All the arts would be better cultivated. One might at least diminish the number of these voluntary victims by fixing the number of novices. The country would have subjects more useful, and less unhappy. Such is the opinion of all the magistrates, such the unanimous wish of the public, since its understanding is enlightened. The example of England, and other states, is an evident proof of the necessity of this reformation. What would England do at this time, if, instead of forty thousand seamen, it had forty thousand monks? The more they are multiplied, the greater need there is of a number of industrious subjects. There are undoubtedly buried in the cloisters many talents, which are lost to the state. To make a kingdom nourish, there should be the fewest priests and the most artisans possible. So far ought the ignorance and barbarism of our forefathers to be from being any rule for us, that they ought rather to be an admonition to us, to do what they would do, if they were in our place, with our improvements in knowledge.

QUESTION.—It is not then out of hatred to monks that you wish to abolish them, but out of love to your country? I think as you do. I would not have my son a monk. And if I thought I was to rear children for nothing better than a cloister, I would not wish to become a father.

ANSWER.—Where in fact, is that good father of a family that would not groan to see his son and daughter lost to society? This is seeking the safety of the soul. It may be so, but a soldier that seeks the safety of his body, when his duty is to fight, is punished. We are all soldiers of the state; we are in the pay of society; we become deserters when we quit it.

Why, then, has monkishness prevailed? Because, since the days of Constantine, the government has been everywhere absurd and detestable;

because the Roman empire came to have more monks than soldiers; because there were a hundred thousand of them in Egypt alone; because they were exempt from labor and taxes; because the chiefs of those barbarous nations which destroyed the empire, having turned Christians, in order to govern Christians, exercised the most horrid tyranny; because, to avoid the fury of these tyrants, people threw themselves in crowds into cloisters, and so, to escape one servitude, put themselves into another; because the popes, by instituting so many different orders of sacred drones, contrived to have so many subjects to themselves in other states; because a peasant likes better to be called reverend father, and to give his benedictions, than to follow a plough's tail; because he does not know that the plough is nobler than a monk's habit; because he had rather live at the expense of fools than by a laborious occupation; in short, because he does not know that, in making a monk of himself, he is preparing for himself unhappy days, of which the sad groundwork will be nothing but a *tedium vitæ* and repentance.

QUESTION.—I am satisfied. Let us have no monks, for the sake of their own happiness, as well as ours. But I am sorry to hear it said by the landlord of our village, who is father to four boys and three girls, that he does not know how to dispose of his daughters, unless he makes nuns of them.

ANSWER.—This too often repeated plea is at once inhuman, detrimental to the country, and destructive to society. Every time that it can be said of any condition of life whatever, that if all the world were to embrace it mankind would perish, it is proved that that condition is a worthless one, and that whoever embraces it does all the mischief to mankind that in him lies.

Now, it being a clear consequence that if all the youth of both sexes were to shut themselves up in cloisters the world would perish, monkery is, if it were but in that light alone, the enemy to human nature, independently of the horrid evils it has formerly caused.

QUESTION.—Might not as much be said of soldiers?

Entering the convent.—"There is a necessity for houses of retreat for old age, for infirmity, for deformity. But by the most detestable of all abuses, these foundations are for well-made persons. Let a hump-backed woman present herself to enter into a cloister, and she will be rejected with contempt, unless she will give an immense portion to the house."

ANSWER. Certainly not; for if every subject carried arms in his turn, as formerly was the practice in all republics, and especially in that of Rome, the soldier is but the better farmer for it. The soldier, as a good subject ought to do, marries, and fights for his wife and children. Would it were the will of heaven that every laborer was a soldier and a married man! They would make excellent subjects. But a monk, merely in his quality of a monk, is good for nothing but to devour the substance of his countryman. There is no truth more generally acknowledged.

QUESTION.—But, sir, the daughters of poor gentlemen, who cannot portion them off in marriage, what are they to do?

ANSWER.—Do! They should do, as has a thousand times been said, like the daughters in England, in Scotland, Ireland, Switzerland, Holland, half Germany, Sweden, Norway, Denmark, Tartary, Turkey, Africa, and in almost all the rest of the globe. They will prove much better wives, much better mothers, when it shall have been the custom, as in Germany, to marry women without fortune. A woman, industrious and a good economist, will do more good in a house, than a daughter of a farmer of the revenue, who spends more in superfluities than she will have brought of income to her husband.

There is a necessity for houses of retreat for old age, for infirmity, for deformity. But by the most detestable of all abuses, these foundations are for well-made persons. Let a hump-backed old woman present herself to enter into a cloister, and she will be rejected with contempt, unless she will give an immense portion to the house. But what do I say? Every nun must bring her dower with her; she is else the refuse of the convent. Never was there a more intolerable abuse.

QUESTION.—Thank you, sir. I swear to you that no daughter of mine shall be a nun. They shall learn to spin, to sew, to make lace, to embroider, to render themselves useful. I look on the vows of convents to be crimes against one's country and one's self. Now, sir, I beg you will explain to me, how comes it that a certain writer, in contradiction to human kind, pretends that monks are useful to the population of a state, because their buildings are kept in better repair than those of the nobility, and their lands better cultivated?

ANSWER.—He has a mind to divert himself; he knows but too well, that ten families who have each five thousand livres a year in land, are a hundred, nay, a thousand times more useful than a convent that enjoys fifty thousand livres a year, and which has always a secret hoard. He cries up the fine houses built by the monks, and it is precisely those fine houses that provoke the rest of the subjects; it is the very cause of complaint to all Europe. The vow of poverty condemns those palaces, as the vow of humility protests against pride, and as the vow of extinguishing one's race is in opposition to nature.

QUESTION.—Bless me! Who can this be that advances so strange a proposition?

ANSWER. It is the *friend of mankind*, [Monsieur le M. de Mirabeau, in his book entitled *L'Ami des Hommes*. It is against this marquis that the jest on the *only tax* is leveled; a tax proposed by him], or rather the friend of the monks.

QUESTION.—I begin to think it advisable to be very distrustful of books.

ANSWER.—The best way is to make use, with regard to them, of the same caution, as with men. Choose the most reasonable, examine them, and never yield unless to evidence.

VII.

ON TAXES PAID TO A FOREIGN POWER.

About a month ago, the Man of Forty Crowns came to me, holding both his sides, which seemed ready to burst with laughing. In short, he laughed so heartily that I could not help laughing also, without knowing at what. So true it is, that man is born an imitative animal, that instinct rules us, and that the great emotions of the soul are catching. *Ut ridentibus arrident, ita flentibus adflent, Humani vultus.*

When he had had his laugh out, he told me that he had just come from meeting with a man who called himself the prothonotary of the Holy See, and that this personage was sending away a great sum of money to an Italian, three hundred leagues off, in the name and behalf of a Frenchman, on whom the king had bestowed a small fief or fee; because the said Frenchman could never enjoy this benefit of the king's conferring, if he did not give to this Italian the first year's income.

"The thing," said I, "is very true; but it is not quite such a laughing matter either. It costs France about four hundred thousand livres a year, in petty duties of this kind; and in the course of two centuries and a half, that this custom has lasted, we have already sent to Italy fourscore millions."

"Heavenly Father!" he exclaimed, "how many forty crowns would that make? Some Italian, then, subdued us, I suppose, two centuries and a half ago, and laid that tribute upon us!"

"In good faith," answered I, "he used to impose on us in former times, in a much more burthensome way. That is but a trifle in comparison to what, for a long time, he levied on our poor nations of Europe."

Then I related to him how those holy usurpations had taken place, and came to be established. He knows a little of history, and does not want for sense. He easily conceived that we had been slaves, and that we were still dragging a little bit of our chain that we could not get rid of. He spoke much and with energy, against this abuse; but with what respect for religion in general. With what reverence did he express himself for the bishops! How heartily did he wish them many forty crowns a year, that they might spend them in their dioceses in good works.

He also wished that all the country vicars might have a number of forty crowns, that they might live with decency.

"It is a sad thing," said he, "that a vicar should be obliged to dispute with his flock for two or three sheaves of corn, and that he should not be amply paid by the country. These eternal contests for imaginary rights, for the tithes, destroy the respect that is owing to them. The unhappy cultivator who shall have already paid to the collectors his tenth penny, and the twopence a livre, and the tax, and the capitation, and the purchase of his exemption from lodging soldiers,—after he shall have lodged soldiers,—for this unfortunate man, I say, to see the vicar take away in addition the tithe of his produce, he can no longer look on him as his pastor, but as one that flays him alive,—that tears from him the little skin that is left him. He feels but too sensible, that while they are, *jure divino*, robbing him of his tenth sheaf, they have the diabolical cruelty not to give him credit for all that it will have cost him to make that sheaf grow. What then remains to him for himself and family? Tears, want, discouragement, despair, and thus he dies of fatigue and misery. If the vicar were paid by the country, he would be a comfort to his parishioners, instead of being looked on by them as their enemy."

The worthy man melted as he uttered these words; he loved his country, and the public good was his idol. He would sometimes emphatically say, "What a nation would the French be if it pleased!" We went to see his son, whom the mother, a very neat and clean woman, was nursing. "Alas!" said the father, "here thou art, poor child, and hast nothing to pretend to but twenty-three years of life, and forty crowns a year."

VIII.

ON PROPORTIONS.

The produce of the extremes is equal to the produce of the means: but two sacks of corn stolen, are not, to those who stole them, as the loss of their lives is to the interest of the person from whom they were stolen.

The prior of ——, from whom two of his domestic servants in the country had stolen two measures of corn, has just had the two delinquents hanged. This execution has cost him more than all his harvest has been worth to him; and since that time he has not been able to get a servant.

If the laws had ordained that such as stole their master's corn should work in his grounds, during their lives in fetters, and with a bell at their neck fixed to a collar, the prior would have been a considerable gainer by it.

"Terror should be preventively employed against crimes;" very true: but work, on compulsion, and lasting shame, strike more terror than the gallows.

The rack.—"I was summoned to give evidence against a miller, who has been put to the torture, ordinary and extraordinary, and who has been found innocent. I saw him faint away under redoubled tortures. I heard the crash of his bones. His outcries and screams of agony are not yet out of my ears; they haunt me. I shed tears for pity, and shudder with horror."

There was, some months ago at London, a malefactor who had been condemned to be transported to America to work there at the sugar works with the negroes. In England, any criminal, as in many other countries, may get a petition presented to the king, either to obtain a free pardon, or a mitigation of the sentence. This one presented a petition to be hanged, alleging that he mortally hated work, and that he had rather suffer strangling for a minute, than to make sugar all his lifetime.

Others may think otherwise, every one to his taste. But it has been already said, and cannot be too often repeated, that a man hanged is good for nothing, and that punishments ought to be useful.

Some years ago, in Turkey, two young men were condemned to be impaled, for having, (without taking off their caps,) stood to see the procession of the Lama pass by. The Emperor of China, who is a man of very good sense, said, that for his part, he should have condemned them to walk bareheaded, in every public procession, for three months afterwards.

"Proportion punishments to crimes," says the Marquis Beccaria; but those who made the laws were not geometricians.

I hate the laws of Draco, which punish equally crimes and faults, wickedness and folly. Let us,—especially in all litigations,—in all dissensions, in all quarrels,—distinguish the aggressor from the party offended, the oppressor from the oppressed. An offensive war is the procedure of a tyrant; he who defends himself is in the character of a just man.

As I was absorbed in these reflections, the Man of Forty Crowns came to me all in tears. I asked, with emotion, if his son, who was by right to live twenty-three years, was dead?

"No," said he, "the little one is very well, and so is my wife; but I was summoned to give evidence against a miller, who has been put to the torture, ordinary and extraordinary, and who has been found innocent. I saw him faint away under redoubled tortures. I heard the crash of his bones. His outcries and screams of agony are not yet out of my ears; they haunt me. I shed tears for pity, and shudder with horror."

His tears drew mine. I trembled, too, like him; for I have naturally an extreme sensibility.

My memory then represented to me the dreadful fate of the Calas family! A virtuous mother in irons,—her children in tears, and forced to fly, her house given up to pillage,—a respectable father of a family broken with torture, agonizing on a wheel, and expiring in the flames; a son loaded with chains, and dragged before the judges, one of whom said to him:

"We have just now broken your father on the wheel; we will break you alive too."

I remembered the family of Sirven, who one of my friends met with among the mountains covered with ice, as they were flying from the persecution of a judge as ignorant as he was unjust. This judge (he told me) had condemned an innocent family to death on a supposition, without the least shadow of proof, that the father and mother, assisted by two of their daughters, had cut the throat of the third, and drowned her besides, for going to mass. I saw in judgments of this kind, at once an excess of stupidity, of injustice, and of barbarity.

The Man of Forty Crowns joined with me in pitying human nature. I had in my pocket the discourse of an attorney-general of Dauphiny, which turned upon very important matters. I read to him the following passages:

"Certainly those must have been truly great men, who, at first, dared to take upon themselves the office of governing their fellow creatures, and to set their shoulders to the burthen of the public welfare; who, for the sake of the good they meant to do to men, exposed themselves to their ingratitude, and for the public repose renounced their own; who made themselves, as one may say, middle-men between their fellow-creatures and Providence, to compose for them, by artifice, a happiness which Providence seems otherwise to have refused to them by any other means.

"What magistrate, was ever so careless of his responsibilities and duties to humanity as to entertain such ideas? Could he, in the solitude of his closet, without shuddering with horror and pity, cast his eyes on those papers, the unfortunate monuments of gilt or of innocence? Should he not think he hears a plaintive voice and groans issue from those fatal writings, and press him to decide the destiny of a subject, of a husband, of a father, or of a whole family? What judge can be so unmerciful (if he is charged with but one single process) as to pass in cold blood before the door of a prison? Is it I (must he say to himself) who detain in that execrable place my fellow-creature, perhaps my countryman, one of humankind, in short? Is it I that confine him every day,—that shut those execrable doors upon him? Perhaps despair will have seized him. He sends up to heaven my name loaded with his curses; and doubtless calls to witness against me that great Judge of the world, who observes us, and will judge us both."

"Here a dreadful sight presents itself on a sudden to my eyes: The judge, tired with interrogating bywords, has recourse to interrogation by tortures. Impatient in his inquiries and researches, and perhaps irritated at their inutility, he has brought to him torches, chains, levers, and all those instruments invented for producing pain. An executioner comes to interpose in the functions of the magistracy, and terminates by violence a judicial interrogation.

"Gentle philosophy! Thou who never seekest truth but with attention and patience, couldst thou expect, in an age that takes thy name, that such instruments would be employed to discover that truth?

"Can it be really true, that our laws approve this inconceivable method, and that custom consecrates it?

"Their laws imitate their prejudices; their public punishments are as cruel as their private vengeance; and the acts of their reason are scarce less unmerciful than those of their passions. What can be the cause of this strange contrariety? It is because our prejudices are ancient, and our morality new; it is because we are as penetrated with our opinions as we are inattentive to our ideas; it is because our passion for pleasures hinders us from reflecting on our wants, and that we are more eager to live than to direct ourselves right; it is, in a word, because our morals are gentle without being good; it is because we are polite, and are not so much as humane."

These fragments, which eloquence had dictated to humanity, filled the heart of my friend with a sweet consolation. He admired with tenderness.

"What!" said he, "are such masterpieces as these produced in a province? I had been told that Paris was all the world, or the only place in it."

"It is," said I, "the only place for producing comic operas; but there are at this time, in the provinces, magistrates who think, with the same virtue and express themselves with the same force. Formerly, the oracles of justice, like those of morality, were nothing but matter of mere ridicule. Dr. Balordo declaimed at the bar, and Harlequin in the pulpit. Philosophy has at length come, and has said, 'Do not speak in public, unless to set forth new and useful truths, with the eloquence of sentiment and of reason.'"

But, say the praters, if we have nothing new to say, what then? Why, hold your tongues, replies philosophy. All those vain discourses for parade, that contain nothing but phrases, are like the fire on the eve of St. John's, kindled on that day of the year in which there is the least want of it to heat one's self—it causes no pleasure, and not so much as the ashes of it remain.

Let all France read good books. But notwithstanding all the progress of the human understanding, there are few that read; and among those who sometimes seek instruction, the reading for the most part is very ill chosen. My neighbors, men and women, pass their time, after dinner, at playing an English game, which I have much difficulty to pronounce, since they call it whist. Many good citizens, many thick heads, who take themselves for good heads, tell you, with an air of importance, that books are good for nothing. But, Messieurs, the critics, do not you know that you are governed only by books? Do not you know that the statutes, the military code, and the gospel, are books on which you continually depend? Read; improve yourselves. It is reading alone that invigorates the understanding; conversation dissipates it; play contracts it.

Thus it was that the Man of Forty Crowns proceeded to form, as one may say, his head and his heart. He not only succeeded to the inheritance of his two fair cousins, but he came also to a fortune left by a very distant relation, who had been a sub-farmer of the military hospitals, where he had fattened himself on the strict abstinence to which he had put the wounded soldiers. This man never would marry, he never would own any of his relations. He lived in the height of debauchery, and died at Paris of a surfeit. He was, as any one may see, a very useful member of the state.

Our new philosopher was obliged to go to Paris to get possession of the inheritance of this relative. At first, the farmers of the domain disputed it with him. He had the good luck, however, to gain his cause, and the generosity to give to the poor of his neighborhood, who had not their contingent of forty crowns a year, a part of the spoils of the deceased son of fortune. After which he set himself about satisfying his passion for having a library.

He read every morning and made extracts. In the evening, he consulted the learned to know in what language the serpent had talked to our good mother; whether the soul is in the callous body, or in the pineal gland; whether St. Peter lived five and twenty years at Rome; what specific difference there is between a throne and a dominion; and why the negroes have a flat nose. He proposed to himself, besides, never to govern the state, nor to write any pamphlets against new dramatic pieces. He was called Mr. Andrew, which was his Christian name. Those who have known him, do justice to his modesty and to his qualities, both natural and acquired.

IX.

A GREAT QUARREL.

During the stay of Mr. Andrew at Paris, there happened a very important quarrel. The point was, to decide whether Marcus Antoninus was an honest man, and whether he was in hell, or in purgatory, or in limbo, waiting till the day of resurrection. All the men of sense took the part of Marcus Antoninus. They said: Antoninus has been always just, temperate, chaste, and beneficent. It is true, he has not so good a place in paradise as St. Anthony; for proportions ought to be observed, as has been before recommended. But certainly the soul of Antoninus is not roasting on a spit in hell. If he is in purgatory, he ought to be delivered out of it; there need only be masses said for him. Let the Jesuits, who have no longer anything to do, say three thousand masses for the repose of the soul of Marcus Antoninus. Putting each mass at fifteen pence, they will get two thousand two hundred and fifty livres by it. Besides, some respect is owing to a crowned head. He should not be lightly damned.

The party opposed to these good people pretended, on the contrary, that no compounding for salvation ought to be allowed to Marcus Antoninus; that he was a heretic; that the Carpocratians and the Alcgi were not so bad as he; that he had died without confession; that it was necessary to make an example; that it was right to damn him, if but to teach better manners to the emperors of China and Japan,—to those of Persia, Turkey, and Morocco,—to the kings of England, Sweden, Denmark, and Prussia, to the stadtholder of Holland,—to the avoyers of the Canton of Berne, who no more go to confession than did the Emperor Marcus Antoninus; that, in short, there is an unspeakable pleasure in passing sentence against a dead sovereign, which one could not fulminate against him in his lifetime, for fear of losing one's ears.

This quarrel became as furious as was formerly that of the Ursulines and the Annonciades. In short, it was feared that it would come to a schism, as in the time of the hundred and one Mother Goose's tales, and of certain bills payable to the bearer in the other world. To be sure, a schism is something very terrible. The meaning of the word is a division in opinion, and till this fatal moment all men had been agreed to think the same thing.

Mr. Andrew, who was an excellent member of society, invited the chiefs of the two parties to sup with him. He is one of the best companions that we have. His humor is gentle and lively; his gaiety is not noisy; he is open, frank, and easy. He has not that sort of wit which seems to aim at stifling that of others. The authority which he conciliates to himself is due to nothing but his graceful manner, to his moderation, and to a round good-natured face, which is quite persuasive. He could have brought to sup cheerfully together a Corsican and a Genoese,—a representative of Geneva and a negative man, the mufti and an archbishop. He managed so dextrously, as to make the first stroke that the disputants of both parties aimed at each other fall to the ground, by turning off the discourse, and by telling a very diverting tale, which pleased equally the damning and the damned. In short, when they had got a little good-humored and elevated with wine, he made them sign an agreement, that the soul of Marcus Antoninus should remain in *status quo*— that is to say, nobody knows where,—till the day of final judgment.

The souls of the doctors of divinity returned quietly to their limbos after supper, and all was calm. This adjustment of the quarrel did great honor to the Man of Forty Crowns; and, since then, whenever any very peevish virulent dispute arose among men of letters, or among men not of letters, the advice given was, "*Gentlemen, go and sup at Master Andrew's!*"

X.

A RASCAL REPULSED.

The reputation which Mr. Andrew had acquired for pacifying quarrels,—by giving good suppers,—drew upon him last week a singular visit. A dark complexioned man, shabbily enough dressed, rather crook-backed, with his head leaning toward one shoulder, a haggard eye, and dirty hands, asked to be invited to a supper with his enemies.

"Who are your enemies?" said Mr. Andrew, "and who are you?"

"Alas, sir," said he, "I am forced to confess that I am taken for one of those wretches that compose libels to get bread, and who are forever crying out,—'Religion,—Religion,—Religion,' in order to come at some little benefice. I am accused of having caluminated some of the most truly religious subjects, the most sincere adorers of divinity, and the most honest men of the kingdom. It is true, sir, that in the heat of composition, there often fall from the pen of those of my trade, certain little inadvertencies or slips, which are taken for gross errors; and some liberties taken with the truth, which are termed impudent lies. Our zeal is looked upon in the light of a horrid mixture of villainy and fanaticism. It has been alleged, that while we are insnaring the easy faith of some silly old women, we are the scorn and execration of all the men of worth who can read.

"My enemies are the principal members of the most illustrious academies of Europe, writers much esteemed, and beneficent members of society. I have but just published a book under the title of *Anti-philosophical*. I had nothing but the best intentions, and yet no one would buy my book. Those to whom I made presents of it, threw it into the fire, telling me it was not only anti-reasonable, but anti-christian, and extremely anti-decent."

"Well, then!" said Mr. Andrew to him, "follow the example of those to whom you presented your libel, throw it into the fire, and let no more be said of it. It is unnecessary to ask you to sup with men of wit, who can never be your enemies, since they will never read you."

"Could not you, sir, at least," said the hypocrite to him, "reconcile me with the relations of the deceased Monsieur de Montesquieu, to whose memory I offered an indignity, that I might give honor and glory to the reverend father Rout."

"Zounds!" said Mr. Andrew, "the reverend father Rout has been dead this long time; go and sup with him."

XI.

THE GOOD SENSE OF MR. ANDREW.

But how greatly did the sense of Mr. Andrew improve in vigor from the time he procured a library! He lives with books as with men, and is careful in his choice of them. What a pleasure it is to gain instruction, to enlarge one's mind by studying the best works of the greatest authors.

He congratulates himself on being born at a time when human reason is tending toward perfection. "How unhappy should I have been," he used to say, "if the age I live in had been that in which they used to condemn to the galleys those who wrote against the categories of Aristotle."

Distress had weakened the springs of Mr. Andrew's soul; but good fortune restored their elasticity. There are many Andrews in the world to whom nothing is wanting but a turn of the wheel of fortune to make of them men of true merit. He is now well acquainted with all the affairs of Europe, and especially with the progress of the human understanding.

He recently remarked to me, that Reason travels by slow journeys from north to south, in company with her two intimate friends, Experience and Toleration. Agriculture and Commerce attend them. When Reason presented herself in Italy, the congregation of the Index sternly repulsed her. All she could do, was to secretly send some of her agents, who, in spite of her enemies, do some good. Let but some years more pass, and it is to be hoped that the country of the Scipios will no longer be that of harlequins in monks' habits.

She has sometimes met with cruel foes in France; but she has now so many friends in that kingdom, that she stands a good chance of at length becoming first minister there.

When she presented herself in Bavaria and Austria, she found two or three great wig-blocks that stared at her with stupid and astonished eyes. Their greeting was: "Madam, we never heard of you; we do not know you." Her answer to which was: "Gentlemen, in time you will come to know me, and to love me. I have been well received at Berlin, at Moscow, at Copenhagen, at Stockholm. It is long ago that I have been naturalized by Act of Parliament in England, through the labors of Locke, Gordon, Trenchard, Lord Shaftsbury, and a number of others of the same nation. You will, some day or other, confer on me the like grant. I am the daughter of Time. I expect every thing from my father."

When she passed over the frontiers of Spain and Portugal, she blessed God on observing that the fires of the Inquisition were less frequently kindled. She rejoiced on seeing the Jesuits expelled; but was afraid that, while the country had been cleared of the foxes, it was still left exposed to the ravages of wolves.

If she makes any fresh attempts to gain entrance into Italy it is thought she will begin by establishing herself at Venice; and that she will take up her abode in the kingdom of Naples, in spite of the liquefaction of the saint's blood in that country, which awakens in her mind mournful reflections on human credulity. It is pretended, that she has an infallible secret for untying the strings of a crown, which are entangled, nobody knows how, in those of a mitre.

XII.

The GOOD SUPPER AT MR. ANDREW'S.

We supped at Mr. Andrew's yesterday, together with a Doctor Sorbonne, with Monsieur Pinto, the celebrated Jew, with the Chaplain of the Protestant chapel of the Dutch Embassador, the secretary of the Prince Galitzin of the Greek church, a Calvinist Swiss Captain, two philosophers, and three Ladies of great wit.

The supper was a very long one; and yet, so polite it must be owned we are grown—so much is one afraid at supper to give any cause of offence to one's brethren, that there was no more disputing upon religion than as if not one of those at table had ever had any. It is not so with the Regent Coge, and the ex-Jesuit Patouillet, and with all the animals of that kind. Those pitiful creatures will say more stupidly abusive things in one pamphlet of two pages, than the best company in Paris can say agreeable and instructive ones in a supper of four hours. And what is stranger yet, they dare not tell a man to his face, what they have the impudence to print.

The conversation turned at first on a piece of pleasantry in the Persian Letters, in which it is repeated, after a number of grave personages, that the world is not only growing worse, but that it is becoming depopulated, so that if the proverb should have any truth in it, that "the more fools there are," "the more laughter," laughing is likely to be soon banished from the face of the earth.

The Doctor of Sorbonne assured us that, in fact, the world was almost reduced to nothing. He quoted the Father Petavius, who demonstrates that in less than three hundred years, the descendants of one of the sons of Noah (I forget whether it was Shem or Japhet), amounted to six hundred and twelve millions three hundred and fifty-eight thousand true believers within two hundred and eighty-five years after the universal deluge.

Mr. Andrew asked, why in the time of Philip de Bel, that is to say, about three hundred years after Hugh Capet, there were not six hundred and twenty-three thousand millions of princes of the royal family?

"It is," said the Doctor of Sorbonne, "because the stock of faith has greatly decreased."

A great deal was said about Thebes and its hundred gates, and of the million of soldiers that issued out of those gates with the twenty thousand chariots of war.

"Shut the book there," said Mr. Andrew. "Since I have taken to reading, I beg to suspect that the same genius that wrote Garagantua, used of yore to write all the histories."

"But, in short," said one of the company, "Thebes, Memphis, Babylon, Nineveh, Troy, Seleucia, were great cities once, and now no longer exist."

"Granted," answered the secretary of the Prince Galitzin; "but Moscow, Constantinople, London, Paris, Amsterdam, Lyons, (which is better than ever Troy was,) and all the towns of France, Germany, Spain, and the North, were then deserts."

The Swiss captain, a gentleman of great knowledge, owned to us, that when his ancestors took it into their heads to quit their mountains and their precipices, to go and take forcible possession, as was but reasonable, of a finer country, Cæsar, who saw with his own eyes the list of those emigrants, found that their number amounted to three hundred and sixty-eight thousand, inclusive of the old, the children, and the women. At this time, the single canton of Berne possesses as many inhabitants, which is not quite the half of Switzerland, and I can assure you, that the thirteen cantons have above seven hundred and twenty thousand souls, including the natives who are serving or carrying on business in other countries. From such data, gentlemen of learning make absurd calculations, and they base fallacious systems on no better footing.

The question next agitated was, whether the citizens of Rome, in the time of the Cæsars, were richer than the citizens of Paris, in the time of Monsieur Silhouette?

"Oh," says Mr. Andrew, "this is a point on which I have some call to speak. I was a long time the Man of Forty Crowns; but I conceive that the citizens of Rome had more. Those illustrious robbers on the highway pillaged the finest countries of Asia, of Africa, and of Europe. They lived splendidly on the produce of their rapines; but yet there were doubtless some beggars at Rome. I am persuaded that, among those conquerors of the world, there were some reduced to an income of forty Crowns a year, as I formerly was."

"Do you know," said a learned member of the Academy of Inscriptions and Belles Lettres, "that it cost Lucullus for every supper he gave in the saloon of Apollo, thirty-nine thousand three hundred and twelve livres of our money; but that the celebrated epicurean Atticus did not expend above two hundred and thirty livres a month for his table."

"If that be true," said I, "he deserved to be president of the Miser-society, lately established in Italy. I have read, as you have done, in Florus, that incredible anecdote; but, perhaps Florus had never supped with Atticus, or else his text, like so many others, has been corrupted by copyists. No Florus shall ever make me believe that the friend of Cæsar and of Pompey, of Cicero and of Antony, all of whom were often entertained at his house, got off for something less than ten Louis d'ors a month. *But thus exactly 'tis that history is written.*"

Madam Andrew, for her part, told the learned member of the Academy, that if he would keep her table for ten times as much, she would be greatly obliged to him.

I am persuaded, that this evening at Mr. Andrew's cost him as much as the monthly expense of Atticus. As for the ladies, they expressed a doubt whether the suppers of Rome were more agreeable than those of Paris. The conversation was very gay, though leaning a little to the learned. There was no talk of new fashions, nor of the ridiculous part of any one's character or conduct, nor of the scandalous history of the day.

The question upon luxury was discussed and searched to the bottom. It was mooted whether or not luxury had been the ruin of the Roman empire; and it was proved that the two empires of the east and west owed their destruction to nothing but to religious controversies, and to the monks; and, in fact, when Alaric took Rome, its whole attention was engrossed by theological disputes; when Mahomet took Constantinople, the monks defended much better the eternity of the light of Mount Thabor, which they saw on their navel,[1] than they defended the town against the Turks.

One of our men of learning made a very significant remark. It was that those two great empires were annihilated, but that the works of Virgil, Horace, and Ovid still exist.

From the age of Augustus, they made but one skip to the age of Louis the XIVth. A lady put the question, why it was that with a great deal of wit there was no longer produced scarcely any work of genius?

Mr. Andrew answered, that it was because such works had been produced in the last age. This idea was fine spun, and yet solidly true. It bore a thorough handling. After that, they fell with some harshness upon a Scotchman, who had taken it into his head to give rules to taste, and to criticise the most admirable passages of Racine, without understanding French. But there was one Denina still more severely treated. He had abused Montesquieu's *Spirit of Laws*, without comprehending him, and had especially censured what is the most liked and approved in that work.

This recalled to my mind Boileau's making a parade of his affected contempt of Tasso. One of the company advanced that Tasso, with all his faults, was as superior to Homer, as Montesquieu, with his still greater imperfections, was above the farrago of Grotius. But there was presently a strong opposition made to these false criticisms, dictated by national hatred and prejudice. The

Seignior Denina was treated as he deserved, and as pedants ought to be by men of wit.

It was especially remarked, with much sagacity, that the greatest part of the literary works of this age, as well as of the conversations, turned on the examination of the masterpieces of the last century; in which we are like disinherited children, who are taking an estimate of their father's estate. It was confessed that philosophy had made great progress, but that the language and style was somewhat corrupted.

It is the nature of all these conversations, to make transitions from one subject to another. All these objects of curiosity, of science, and of taste, soon vanished, to give way to the great scene which the Empress of Russia, and the King of Poland, were giving to the world. They had been just raising up and restoring the rights of oppressed humanity, and establishing liberty of conscience in a part of the globe of a much greater extent than the old Roman Empire. This service done to human kind, this example given to so many courts, was mentioned with the applause it deserved. Healths were drank to the philosophical empress, to the royal philosopher, and to the philosophical primate, with the wish of their having many imitators. Even the doctors of Sorbonne admired them; for there are some persons of good sense in that body, as there were formerly some men of wit among the Bœotians.

The Russian secretary astonished us with a recital of the great establishments they were forming in Russia. It was asked, why people were in general more fond of reading the history of Charles the XIIth, who passed his life in destroying, than that of Peter the Great, who consumed his in creating? On this we concluded, that weakness and a frivolous turn of mind are the causes of this preference; that Charles the XIIth was the Don Quixote, and Peter the Solon of the North; that superficial understandings prefer a wild extravagant heroism, to the great views of a legislator: that the particulars of the foundation of a town are less pleasing to them, than the rashness of a man, who, at the head of only his domestics, braves an army of ten thousand Turks; and that, in short, most readers love amusement better than instruction. Thence it is, that a hundred women read *The Thousand and One Arabian Nights*, for one that reads two chapters of Locke.

What was not talked of at this supper? of which I shall long retain the remembrance. It was also in course to say a word of the actors and actresses, that eternal subject of the table-talk of Versailles and of Paris. It was agreed, that a good declaimer was as rare as a good poet. For my part, I must own that Plato's banquet could not have given me more pleasure than that of Monsieur and Madame Andrew.

Our very pretty gentlemen, and our very fine ladies, would, doubtless, have found it dull, and been tired with it. They pretend to be the only good company: but neither Mr. Andrew nor I ever willingly sup with that kind of good company.

[1] See Gibbon's *History of Christianity*, page 777, for an account of the monks of Mount Athos, who adored the divine light, as above stated.—E.

The Priory entrance.

THE HURON; OR, PUPIL OF NATURE.[1]

I.

THE HURON ARRIVES IN FRANCE.

One day, Saint Dunstan, an Irishman by nation, and a saint by trade, left Ireland on a small mountain, which took its route toward the coast of France, and set his saintship down in the bay of St. Malo. When he had dismounted, he gave his blessing to the mountain, which, after some profound bows, took its leave, and returned to its former place.

Here St. Dunstan laid the foundation of a small priory, and gave it the name of the Priory Mountain, which it still keeps, as every body knows.

In the year 1689, the fifteenth day of July, in the evening, the abbot Kerkabon, prior of our Lady of the Mountain, happened to take the air along the shore with Miss Kerkabon, his sister. The prior, who was becoming aged, was a very good clergyman, beloved by his neighbors. What added most to the respect that was paid him, was, that among all his clerical neighbors, he was the only one that could walk to his bed after supper. He was tolerably read in theology; and when he was tired of reading St. Augustin, he refreshed himself with Rabelais. All the world spoke well of him.

Miss Kerkabon, who had never been married, notwithstanding her hearty wishes so to be, had preserved a freshness of complexion in her forty-fifth year. Her character was that of a good and sensible woman. She was fond of pleasure, and was a devotee.

As they were walking, the prior, looking on the sea, said to his sister:

"It was here, alas! that our poor brother embarked with our dear sister-in-law, Madam Kerkabon, his wife, on board the frigate 'Swallow,' in 1669, to serve the king in Canada. Had he not been killed, probably he would have written to us."

"Do you believe," says Miss Kerkabon, "that our sister-in-law has been eaten by the Cherokees, as we have been told?"

"Certain it is, had she not been killed, she would have come back. I shall weep for her all my lifetime. She was a charming woman; and our brother, who had a great deal of wit, would no doubt have made a fortune."

Thus were they going on with mutual tenderness, when they beheld a small vessel enter the bay of Rence with the tide. It was from England, and came to sell provisions. The crew leaped on shore without looking at the prior or Miss, his sister, who were shocked at the little attention shown them.

That was not the behavior of a well-made youth, who, darting himself over the heads of his companions, stood on a sudden before Miss Kerkabon.

Being unaccustomed to bowing, he made her a sign with his head. His figure and his dress attracted the notice of brother and sister. His head was uncovered, and his legs bare. Instead of shoes, he wore a kind of sandals. From his head his long hair flowed in tresses, A small close doublet displayed the beauty of his shape. He had a sweet and martial air.[2] In one hand he held a small bottle of Barbadoes water, and in the other a bag, in which he had a goblet, and some sea biscuit. He spoke French very intelligibly. He offered some of his Barbadoes to Miss Kerkabon and her brother. He drank with them, he made them drink a second time, and all this with an air of such native simplicity, that quite charmed brother and sister. They offered him their service, and asked him who he was, and whither going? The young man answered: That he knew not where he should go; that he had some curiosity; that he had a desire to see the coast of France; that he had seen it, and should return.

The prior, judging by his accent that he was not an Englishman, took the liberty of asking of what country he was.

"I am a Huron," answered the youth.

Miss Kerkabon, amazed and enchanted to see a Huron who had behaved so politely to her, begged the young man's company to supper. He complied immediately, and all three went together to the priory of our Lady of the Mountain. This short and round Miss devoured him with her little eyes, and said from time to time to her brother:

"This tall lad has a complexion of lilies and roses. What a fine skin he has for a Huron!"

"Very true, sister," says the prior.

She put a hundred questions, one after another, and the traveler answered always pertinently.

The report was soon spread that there was a Huron at the priory. All the genteel company of the country came to supper. The abbot of St. Yves came with Miss, his sister, a fine, handsome, well-educated girl. The bailiff, the tax-gatherer, and their wives, came all together. The foreigner was seated between Miss Kerkabon and Miss St. Yves. The company eyed him with admiration. They all questioned him together. This did not confound the Huron. He seemed to have taken Lord Bolingbroke's motto, *Nil admirari*. But at last, tired out with so much noise, he told them in a sweet, but serious tone:

"Gentlemen, in my country one talks after another. How can I answer you, if you will not allow me to hear you?"

Reasoning always brings people to a momentary reflection. They were all silent.

Mr. Bailiff, who always made a property of a foreigner wherever he found him, and who was the first man for asking questions in the province, opening a mouth of large size, began:

"Sir, what is your name?"

"I have always been called the *Ingenu*," answered the Huron; "and the English have confirmed that name, because I always speak as I think, and act as I like."

"But, being born a Huron, how could you come to England?"

"I have been carried thither. I was made prisoner by the English after some resistance, and the English, who love brave people, because they are as brave and honest as we, proposed to me, either to return to my family, or go with them to England. I accepted the latter, having naturally a relish for traveling."

"But, sir," says the bailiff, with his usual gravity, "how could you think of abandoning father and mother?"

"Because I never knew either father or mother," says the foreigner.

This moved the company; they all repeated:

"Neither father nor mother!"

"We will be in their stead," says the mistress of the house, to her brother, the prior: "How interesting this Huron gentleman is!"

The *Ingenu* thanked her with a noble and proud cordiality, and gave her to understand, that he wanted the assistance of nobody.

"I perceive, Mr. Huron," said the huge bailiff, "that you talk better French than can be expected from an Indian."

"A Frenchman," answered he, "whom they had made prisoner when I was a boy, and with whom I contracted a great friendship, taught it me. I rapidly learn what I like to learn. When I came to Plymouth, I met with one of your French refugees, whom you, I know not why, call Huguenots. He improved my knowledge of your language; and as soon as I could express myself intelligibly, I came to see your country, because I like the French well enough, if they do not put too many questions."

Notwithstanding this candid remark, the abbé of St. Yves asked him, which of the three languages pleased him best, the Huron, English, or French?

"The Huron, to be sure," answered the *Ingenu*.

"Is it possible?" cried Miss Kerkabon. "I always thought the French was the first of all languages, after that of Low Britany."

Then all were eager to know how, in Huron, they asked for snuff? He replied:

"*Taya.*"

"What signifies to eat?"

"*Essenten.*"

Miss Kerkabon was impatient to know how they called, to make love?

He informed her, *Trovander*; and insisted on it, not without reason, that these words were well worth their synonyms in French and English. *Trovander*, especially, seemed very pretty to all the company. The prior, who had in his library a Huron grammar, which had been given him by the Rev. Father Sagar Theodat, a Recollet and famous missionary, rose from the table to consult it. He returned quite panting with tenderness and joy. He acknowledged the foreigner for a true Huron. The company speculated a little on the multiplicity of languages; and all agreed, that had it not been for the unfortunate affair of the Tower of Babel, all the world would have spoken French.

The inquisitive bailiff, who till then had some suspicions of the foreigner, conceived the deepest respect for him. He spoke to him with more civility than before, and the Huron took no notice of it.

Miss St. Yves was very curious to know how people made love among the Hurons.

"In performing great actions to please such as resemble you." All the company admired and applauded. Miss St. Yves blushed, and was extremely well pleased. Miss Kerkabon blushed likewise, but was not so well pleased. She was a little piqued that this gallantry was not addressed to her; but she was so good-natured, that her affection for the Huron was not diminished at all. She asked him, with great complacency, how many mistresses he had at home.

"Only one," answered the foreigner; "Miss Abacaba, the good friend of my dear nurse. The reed is not straighter, nor is ermine whiter,—no lamb meeker, no eagle fiercer, nor a stag swifter, than was my Abacaba. One day she pursued a hare not above fifty leagues from my habitation: a base Algonquin, who dwells an hundred leagues further, took her hare from her. I was told of it; I ran thither, and with one stroke of my club leveled him with the ground. I brought him to the feet of my mistress, bound hand and foot. Abacaba's parents were for burning him, but I always had a disrelish for such scenes. I set him at liberty. I made him my friend. Abacaba was so pleased with my conduct, that she preferred me to all her lovers. And she would have continued to love me, had she not been devoured by a bear! I slew the bear, and wore his skin a long while; but that has not comforted me."

Miss St. Yves felt a secret pleasure at hearing that Abacaba had been his only mistress, and that she was no more; yet she understood not the cause of her own pleasure. All eyes were riveted on the Huron, and he was much applauded for delivering an Algonquin from the cruelty of his countrymen.

The merciless bailiff had now grown so furious, that he even asked the Huron what religion he was of; whether he had chosen the English, the French, or that of the Huguenots?

"I am of my own religion," said he, "just as you are of yours."

"Lord!" cried Miss Kerkabon, "I see already that those wretched English have not once thought of baptizing him!"

"Good heavens," said Miss St. Yves, "how is it possible? How is it possible the Hurons should not be Roman Catholics? Have not those reverend fathers, the Jesuits, converted all the world?"

The Huron assured her, that no true American had ever changed his opinion, and that there was not in their language a word to express inconstancy.

These last words extremely pleased Miss St. Yves.

"Oh! we'll baptize him, we'll baptize him," said Miss Kerkabon to the prior. "You shall have that honor, my dear brother, and I will be his god-mother. The Abbot St. Yves shall present him to the font. It will make a fine appearance: it will be talked of all over Britany, and do us the greatest honor."

The company were all of the same mind with the mistress of the house; they all cried:

"We'll baptize him."

The Huron interrupted them by saying, that in England every one was allowed to live as he pleased. He rather showed some aversion to the proposal which was made, and could not help telling them, that the laws of the Hurons were to the full as good as those of Low Britany. He finished with saying, that he should return the next day. The bottles grew empty, and the company went to bed.

After the Huron had been conducted to his room, they saw that he spread the blankets on the floor, and laid himself down upon them in the finest attitude in the world.

[1] *Le Huron* was dramatized, under the name of *Civilization*, by Mr. John H. Wilkins, and successfully produced at the City of London Theatre, on

Wednesday, November 10, 1852. Mr. James Anderson enacted the part of *Hercule, the Huron*, and added to his well-earned reputation by his correct conception and representation of the Indian character.

Mr. James Wallack, Jr., afterward introduced the play to a New York audience at Burton's old Chambers Street Theatre, where it was also received with great favor. Unfortunately for dramatic literature, the promising young author of *Civilisation* did not long survive his success, but soon filled an early grave.—E.

[2] In Mr. Wilkins's dramatic version of this romance, the Huron is described as

"A modell'd Hercules! Mien, stature, glance,
That are the blazons of the inner man,
And voice it to the stars! A hero born,
Whose air commands respect above a king's;
Bearing the stamp from the great mint of heaven,
And current to the world!"—E.

II.

THE HURON, CALLED THE INGENU, ACKNOWLEDGED BY HIS RELATIONS.

The *Ingenu*, according to custom, awoke with the sun, at the crowing of the cock, which is called in England and Huronia, "the trumpet of the day." He did not imitate what is styled good company, who languish in the bed of indolence till the sun has performed half its daily journey, unable to sleep, but not disposed to rise, and lose so many precious hours in that doubtful state between life and death, and who nevertheless complain that life is too short.

He had already traversed two or three leagues, and killed fifteen brace of game with his rifle, when, upon his return, he found the prior of the Lady of the Mountain, with his discreet sister, walking in their nightcaps in their little garden. He presented them with the spoils of his morning labor, and taking from his bosom a kind of little talisman, which he constantly wore about his neck, he entreated them to accept of it as an acknowledgment for the kind reception they had given him.

"It is," said he, "the most valuable thing I am possessed of. I have been assured that I shall always be happy whilst I carry this little toy about me; and I give it you that you may be always happy."

The prior and Miss smiled with pity at the frankness of the *Ingenu*. This present consisted of two little portraits, poorly executed, and tied together with a greasy string.

Miss Kerkabon asked him, if there were any painters in Huronia?

"No," replied the *Ingenu*, "I had this curiosity from my nurse. Her husband had obtained it by conquest, in stripping some of the French of Canada, who had made war upon us. This is all I know of the matter."

The prior looked attentively upon these pictures, whilst he changed color; his hands trembled, and he seemed much affected.

"By our Lady of the Mountain," he cried out, "I believe these to be the faces of my brother, the captain, and his lady."

Miss, after having consulted them with the like emotion, thought the same. They were both struck with astonishment and joy blended with grief. They both melted, they both wept, their hearts throbbed, and during their disorder, the pictures were interchanged between them at least twenty times in a second. They seemed to devour the Huron's pictures with their eyes. They asked one after another, and even both at once, at what time, in what place, and how these miniatures fell into the hands of the nurse? They reckoned and computed the time from the captain's departure; they recollected having received notice that he had penetrated as far as the country of the Hurons; and from that time they had never heard anything more of him.

The Huron had told them, that he had never known either father or mother. The prior, who was a man of sense, observed that he had a little beard, and he knew very well that the Hurons never had any. His chin was somewhat hairy; he was therefore the son of an European. My brother and sister-in-law were never seen after the expedition against the Hurons, in 1669. My nephew must then have been nursing at the breast. The Huron nurse has preserved his life, and been a mother to him. At length, after an hundred questions and answers, the prior and his sister concluded that the Huron was their own nephew. They embraced him, whilst tears streamed from their eyes: and the Huron laughed to think that an Indian should be nephew to a prior of Lower Britany.

The Huron identified.—"*By our Lady of the Mountain*," he cried out, "*I believe these to be the faces of my brother, the captain, and his lady.*"

All the company went down stairs. Mr. de St. Yves, who was a great physiognomist, compared the two pictures with the Huron's countenance. They observed, very skillfully, that he had the mother's eyes, the forehead and nose of the late Captain Kerkabon, and the cheeks common to both.

Miss St. Yves, who had never seen either father or mother, was strenuously of opinion, that the young man had a perfect resemblance of them. They all admired Providence, and wondered at the strange events of this world. In a word, they were so persuaded, so convinced of the birth of the Huron, that he himself consented to be the prior's nephew, saying, that he would as soon have him for his uncle as another.

The prior went to return thanks in the church of our Lady of the Mountain; whilst the Huron, with an air of indifference, amused himself with drinking in the house.

The English who had brought him over, and who were ready to set sail, came to tell him that it was time to depart.

"Probably," said he to them, "you have not met with any of your uncles and aunts. I shall stay here. Go you back to Plymouth. I give you all my clothes, as I have no longer occasion for anything in this world, since I am the nephew of a prior."

The English set sail, without being at all concerned whether the Huron had any relations or not in Lower Britany.

After the uncle, the aunt, and the company had sung *Te Deum*; after the bailiff had once more overwhelmed the Huron with questions, after they had exhausted all their astonishment, joy, and tenderness, the prior of the Mountain and the Abbé of St. Yves concluded that the Huron should be baptized with all possible expedition. But the case was very different with a tall robust Indian of twenty-two, and an infant who is regenerated without his knowing anything of the matter. It was necessary to instruct him, and this appeared difficult; for the Abbé of St. Yves supposed that a man who was not born in France, could not be endowed with common sense.

The prior, indeed, observed to the company, that though, in fact, the ingenious gentleman, his nephew, was not so fortunate as to be born in Lower Britany, he was not, upon that account, any way deficient in sense; which might be concluded from all his answers; and that, doubtless, nature had greatly favored him, as well on his father's as on his mother's side?

He then was asked if he had ever read any books? He said, he had read Rabelais translated into English, and some passages in Shakespeare, which he knew by heart; that these books belonged to the captain, on board of whose ship he came from America to Plymouth; and that he was very well pleased with them. The bailiff failed not to put many questions to him concerning these books.

"I acknowledge," said the Huron, "I thought, in reading them, I understood some things, but not the whole."

The Abbé of St. Yves reflected upon this discourse, that it was in this manner he had always read, and that most men read no other way.

"You have," said he, to the Huron, "doubtless read the bible?"

"Never, Mr. Abbé: it was not among the captain's books. I never heard it mentioned."

"This is the way with those cursed English," said Miss Kerkabon; "they think more of a play of Shakespeare's, a plum pudding, or a bottle of rum, than they do of the Pentateuch. For this reason they have never converted any Indians in America. They are certainly cursed by God; and we shall conquer Jamaica and Virginia from them in a very short time."

Be this as it may, the most skillful tailor in all St. Malo was sent for to dress the Huron from head to foot. The company separated, and the bailiff went elsewhere to display his inquisitiveness. Miss St. Yves, in parting, returned several times to observe the young stranger, and made him lower courtesies than ever she did any one in her life.

The bailiff, before he took his leave, presented to Miss St. Yves a stupid dolt of a son, just come from college; but she scarce looked at him, so much was she taken up with the politeness of the Huron.

III.

THE HURON CONVERTED.

The prior finding that he was somewhat advanced in years, and that God had sent him a nephew for his consolation, took it into his head that he would resign his benefice in his favor, if he succeeded in baptizing him and of making him enter into orders.

The Huron had an excellent memory. A good constitution, inherited from his ancestors of Lower Britany, strengthened by the climate of Canada, had made his head so vigorous that when he was struck upon it he scarce felt it; and when any thing was graven in it, nothing could efface it. Nothing had ever escaped his memory. His conception was the more sure and lively, because his infancy had not been loaded with useless fooleries, which overwhelm ours. Things entered into his head without being clouded. The prior at length resolved to make him read the New Testament. The Huron devoured it with great pleasure; but not knowing at what time, or in what country all the adventures related in this book had happened, he did not in the least doubt that the scene of action had been in Lower Britany; and he swore, that he would cut off Caiphas and Pontius Pilate's ears, if ever he met those scoundrels.

His uncle, charmed with this good disposition, soon brought him to the point. He applauded his zeal, but at the same time acquainted him that it was needless, as these people had been dead upwards of 1690 years. The Huron soon got the whole book by heart. He sometimes proposed difficulties that greatly embarrassed the prior. He was often obliged to consult the Abbé St. Yves, who, not knowing what to answer, brought a Jesuit of Lower Britany to perfect the conversion of the Huron.

Grace, at length, operated; and the Huron promised to become a Christian. He did not doubt but that the first step toward it was circumcision.

"For," said he, "I do not find in the book that was put into my hands a single person who was not circumcised. It is therefore evident, that I must make a sacrifice to the Hebrew custom, and the sooner the better."

He sent for the surgeon of the village, and desired him to perform the operation. The surgeon, who had never performed such an operation, acquainted the family, who screamed out. The good Miss Kerkabon trembled lest her nephew, whom she knew to be resolute and expeditious, should perform the operation unskillfully himself; and that fatal consequences might ensue.

The prior rectified the Huron's mistake, representing to him, that circumcision was no longer in fashion; that baptism was much more gentle and salutary; that the law of grace was not like the law of rigor. The Huron, who had much good sense, and was well disposed, disputed, but soon acknowledged his error, which seldom happens in Europe among disputants. In a word, he promised to let himself be baptized whenever they pleased.

But before baptism it was necessary that he should go to confession, and this was the greatest difficulty to surmount. The Huron had still in his pocket the book his uncle gave him. He did not there find that a single apostle had ever been confessed, and this made him very restive. The prior silenced him, by showing him, in the epistle of St. James the Minor, these words: "Confess your sins to one another." The Huron was mute, and confessed his sins to a Recollet. When he had done, he dragged the Recollet from the confessional chair, and seizing him with a vigorous arm, placed himself in his seat, making the Recollet kneel before him:

"Come, my friend, it is said, 'we must confess our sins to one another;' I have related to you my sins, and you shall not stir till you recount yours."

Whilst he said this, he fixed his great knee against his adversary's stomach. The Recollet roared and groaned, till he made the church re-echo. The noise brought people to his assistance, who found the catechumen cuffing the monk in the name of St. James the Minor. The joy diffused at the baptizing at once a Low-Breton, a Huron, and an Englishman, surmounted all these singularities. There were even some theologians of opinion that confession was not necessary, as baptism supplied the place of every thing.

The Bishop of St. Malo was chosen for the ceremony, who flattered, as may be believed, at baptizing a Huron, arrived in a pompous equipage, followed by his clergy. Miss St. Yves put on her best gown to bless God, and sent for a hair dresser from St. Malo's, to shine at the ceremony. The inquisitive bailiff brought the whole country with him. The church was magnificently ornamented. But when the Huron was summoned to attend the baptismal font, he was not to be found.

His uncle and aunt sought for him every where. It was imagined that he had gone a hunting, according to his usual custom. Every one present at the festival, searched the neighboring woods and villages; but no intelligence could be obtained of the Huron. They began to fear he had returned to England. Some remembered that he had said he was very fond of that country. The prior and his sister were persuaded that nobody was baptized there, and were troubled for their nephew's soul. The bishop was confounded, and ready to return home. The prior and the Abbé St. Yves were in despair. The bailiff interrogated all passengers with his usual gravity. Miss Kerkabon melted into tears. Miss St. Yves did not weep, but she vented such deep sighs, as seemed to testify her sacramental disposition. They were walking in this melancholy mood, among the willows and reeds upon the banks of the little river Rence, when they perceived, in the middle of the stream, a large figure, tolerably white, with its two arms across its breast. They screamed out, and ran away. But, curiosity being stronger than any other consideration, they advanced softly amongst the reeds; and when they were pretty certain they could not be seen, they were willing to descry what it was.

IV.

THE HURON BAPTIZED.

The prior and the abbé having run to the river side, they asked the Huron what he was doing?

"In faith," said he, "gentlemen, I am waiting to be baptized. I have been an hour in the water, up to my neck, and I do not think it is civil to let me be quite exhausted."

"My dear nephew," said the prior to him, tenderly, "this is not the way of being baptized in Lower Britany. Put on your clothes, and come with us."

Miss St. Yves, listening to the discourse, said in a whisper to her companion:

"Miss, do you think he will put his clothes on in such a hurry?"

The Huron, however, replied to the prior:

"You will not make me believe now as you did before. I have studied very well since, and I am very certain there is no other kind of baptism. The eunuch of Queen Candace was baptized in a rivulet. I defy you to show me, in the book you gave me, that people were ever baptized in any other way. I either will not be baptized at all, or the ceremony shall be performed in the river."

It was in vain to remonstrate to him that customs were altered. He always recurred to the eunuch of Queen Candace. And though Miss and his aunt, who had observed him through the willows, were authorized to tell him, that he had no right to quote such a man, they, nevertheless, said nothing;—so great was their discretion. The bishop came himself to speak to him, which was a great thing; but he could not prevail. The Huron disputed with the bishop.

"Show me," said he, "in the book my uncle gave me, one single man that was not baptized in a river, and I will do whatever you please."

His aunt, in despair, had observed, that the first time her nephew bowed, he made a much lower bow to Miss St. Yves, than to any one in the company—that he had not even saluted the bishop with so much respect, blended with cordiality, as he did that agreeable young lady. She thought it advisable to apply to her in this great embarrassment. She earnestly entreated her to use her influence to engage the Huron to be baptized according to the custom of Britany, thinking that her nephew could never be a Christian if he persisted in being christened in the stream.

The Huron baptized.—"*I have been an hour in the water, up to my neck, and I do not think it is civil to let me be quite exhausted.*"

Miss St. Yves blushed at the secret joy she felt in being appointed to execute so important a commission. She modestly approached the Huron, and squeezing his hand in quite a noble manner, she said to him.

"What, will you do nothing to please me?"

And in uttering these words, she raised her eyes from a downcast look, into a graceful tenderness.

"Oh! yes, Miss, every thing you require, all that you command, whether it is to be baptized in water, fire, or blood;—there is nothing I can refuse you."

Miss St. Yves had the glory of effecting, in two words, what neither the importunities of the prior, the repeated interrogations of the bailiff, nor the reasoning of the bishop, could effect. She was sensible of her triumph; but she was not yet sensible of its utmost latitude.

Baptism was administered, and received with all the decency, magnificence, and propriety possible. His uncle and aunt yielded to the Abbé St. Yves and his sister the favor of supporting the Huron upon the font. Miss St. Yves's eyes sparkled with joy at being a god-mother. She was ignorant how much this high title compromised her. She accepted the honor, without being acquainted with its fatal consequences.

As there never was any ceremony that was not followed by a good dinner, the company took their seats at table after the christening. The humorists of Lower Britany said, "they did not choose to have their wine baptized." The prior said, "that wine, according to Solomon, cherished the heart of man." The bishop added, "that the Patriarch Judah ought to have tied his ass-colt to the vine, and steeped his cloak in the blood of the grape; and that he was sorry the same could not be done in Lower Britany, to which God had not allotted vines." Every one endeavored to say a good thing upon the Huron's christening, and strokes of gallantry to the god-mother. The bailiff, ever interrogating, asked the Huron, "if he was faithful in keeping his promises?"

"How," said he, "can I fail keeping them, since I have deposited them in the hands of Miss St. Yves?"

The Huron grew warm; he had drank repeatedly his god-mother's health.

"If," said he, "I had been baptized with your hand, I feel that the water which was poured on the nape of my neck would have burnt me."

The bailiff thought that this was too poetical, being ignorant that allegory is a familiar figure in Canada. But his god-mother was very well pleased.

The Huron had, at his baptism, received the name of Hercules. The bishop of St. Malo frequently enquired, who was this tutelar saint, whom he had never heard mentioned before? The Jesuit, who was very learned, told him, "that he was a saint who had wrought twelve miracles." There was a thirteenth, which was well worth the other twelve, but it was not proper for a Jesuit to mention it. This was the marriage of fifty girls at one time—the daughters of king Thespius. A wag, who was present, related this miracle very feelingly. And all judged, from the appearance of the Huron, that he was a worthy representative of the saint whose name he bore.

V.

THE HURON IN LOVE.

It must be acknowledged, that from the time of this christening and this dinner, Miss St. Yves passionately wished that the bishop would again make her an assistant with Mr. Hercules in some other fine ceremony—that is, the marriage ceremony. However, as she was well brought up, and very modest,—she did not entirely agree with herself in regard to these tender sentiments; but if a look, a word, a gesture, a thought, escaped from her, she concealed it admirably under the veil of modesty. She was tender, lively, and sagacious.

As soon as the bishop was gone, the Huron and Miss St. Yves met together, without thinking they were in search of one another. They spoke together, without premeditating what they said. The sincere youth immediately declared, "that he loved her with all his heart; and that the beauteous Abacaba, with whom he had been desperately in love in his own country, was far inferior to her." Miss replied, with her usual modesty, "that the prior, her uncle, and the lady, her aunt, should be spoken to immediately; and that, on her side, she would say a few words to her dear brother, the Abbé of St. Yves, and that she flattered herself it would meet with no opposition."

The youth replied: "that the consent of any one was entirely superfluous; that it appeared to him extremely ridiculous to go and ask others what they were to do; that when two parties were agreed, there was no occasion for a third, to accomplish their union."

"I never consult any one," said he, "when I have a mind to breakfast, to hunt, or to sleep. I am sensible, that in love it is not amiss to have the consent of the person whom we wish for; but as I am neither in love with my uncle nor my aunt, I have no occasion to address myself to them in this affair; and if you will believe me, you may equally dispense with the advice of the Abbé of St. Yves."

It may be supposed that the young lady exerted all the delicacy of her wit, to bring her Huron to the terms of good breeding. She was very angry, but soon softened. In a word, it cannot be said how this conversation would have ended, if the declining day had not brought the Abbé to conduct his sister home. The Huron left his uncle and aunt to rest, they being somewhat fatigued with the ceremony, and long dinner. He passed part of the night in writing verses in the Huron language, upon his well-beloved; for it should be known, that there is no country where love has not rendered lovers poets.[1]

The next day his uncle spoke to him in the following manner. "I am somewhat advanced in years. My brother has left only a little bit of ground, which is a very small matter. I have a good priory. If you will only make yourself a sub-deacon, as I hope you will, I will resign my priory in your favor; and you will live quite at your ease, after having been the consolation of my old age."

The Huron replied:

"Uncle, much good may it do you; live as long as you can. I do not know what it is to be a sub-deacon, or what it is to resign, but every thing will be agreeable to me, provided I have Miss St. Yves at my disposal."

"Good heavens, nephew! what is it you say? Do you love that beautiful young lady so earnestly?"

"Yes, uncle."

"Alas! nephew, it is impossible you should ever marry her."

"It is very possible, uncle; for she did not only squeeze my hand when she left me, but she promised she would ask me in marriage. I certainly shall wed her."

"It is impossible, I tell you, she is your god-mother. It is a dreadful sin for a god-mother to give her hand to her god-son. It is contrary to all laws, human and divine."

"Why the deuce, uncle, should it be forbidden to marry one's god-mother, when she is young and handsome? I did not find, in the book you gave me, that it was wrong to marry young women who assisted at christenings. I perceive, every day, that an infinite number of things are done here which are not in your book, and nothing is done that is said in it. I must acknowledge to you, that this astonishes and displeases me. If I am deprived of the charming Miss St. Yves on account of my baptism, I give you notice, that I will run away with her and unbaptize myself."

The prior was confounded; his sister wept.

"My dear brother," said she, "our nephew must not damn himself; our holy father the pope can give him a dispensation, and then he may be happy, in a christian-like manner, with the person he likes."

The ingenuous Hercules embraced his aunt:

"For goodness sake," said he, "who is this charming man, who is so gracious as to promote the amours of girls and boys? I will go and speak to him this instant."

The dignity and character of the pope was explained to him, and the Huron was still more astonished than before.

"My dear uncle," said he, "there is not a word of all this in your book; I have traveled, and am acquainted with the sea; we are now upon the coast of the ocean, and I must leave Miss St. Yves, to go and ask leave to marry her of a man who lives toward the Mediterranean, four hundred leagues from hence, and whose language I do not understand! This is most incomprehensibly ridiculous! But I will go first to the Abbé St. Yves, who lives only a league from hence; and I promise you I will wed my mistress before night."

Whilst he was yet speaking, the bailiff entered, and, according to his usual custom, asked him where he was going?

"I am going to get married," replied the ingenuous Hercules, running along; and in less than a quarter of an hour he was with his charming dear mistress, who was still asleep.

"Ah! my dear brother," said Miss Kerkabon to the prior, "you will never make a sub-deacon of our nephew."

The bailiff was very much displeased at this journey; for he laid claim to Miss St. Yves in favor of his son, who was a still greater and more insupportable fool than his father.

[1] "Love," says Robert G. Ingersoll, "writes every poem, sings every song, paints every picture, chisels every statue—makes kings and queens of common clay, and is the perfume of that wondrous flower, the human heart."—E.

VI.

THE HURON FLIES TO HIS MISTRESS, AND BECOMES QUITE FURIOUS.

No sooner had the ingenuous Hercules reached the house, than having asked the old servant, which was his mistress's apartment, he forced open the door, which was badly fastened, and flew toward the bed. Miss St. Yves, startled out of her sleep, cried.

"Ah! what, is it you! Stop, what are you about?" He answered:

"I am going to marry."

She opposed him with all the decency of a young lady so well educated; but the Huron did not understand raillery, and found all evasions extremely disagreeable.

"Miss Abacaba, my first mistress," said he, "did not behave in this manner; you have no honesty; you promised me marriage, and you will not marry; this is being deficient in the first laws of honor."

The outcries of the lady, brought the sagacious Abbé de St. Yves with his housekeeper, an old devotee servant, and the parish priest. The sight of these moderated the courage of the assailant.

"Good heavens!" cried the Abbé, "my dear neighbor, what are you about?"

"My duty," replied the young man, "I am fulfilling my promises, which are sacred."

Miss St. Yves adjusted herself, not without blushing. The lover was conducted into another apartment. The Abbé remonstrated to him on the enormity of his conduct. The Huron defended himself upon the privileges of the law of nature, which he understood perfectly well. The Abbé maintained, that the law positive should be allowed all its advantages; and that without conventions agreed on between men, the law of nature must almost constantly be nothing more than natural felony. Notaries, priests, witnesses, contracts, and dispensations, were absolutely necessary.

The ingenuous Hercules made answer with the observation constantly adopted by savages:

"You are then very great rogues, since so many precautions are necessary."

This remark somewhat disconcerted the Abbé.

"There are, I acknowledge, libertines and cheats among us, and there would be as many among the Hurons, if they were united in a great city: but, at the same time, we have direct, honest, enlightened people; and these are the men who have framed the laws. The more upright we are, the more readily we should submit to them, as we thereby set an example to the vicious, who respect those bounds which virtue has given herself."

This answer struck the Huron. It has already been observed, that his mind was well disposed. He was softened by flattering speeches, which promised him hopes; all the world is caught in these snares; and Miss St. Yves herself appeared, after having been at her toilet. Every thing was now conducted with the utmost good breeding.

The separation.

It was with much difficulty that Hercules was sent back to his relations. It was again necessary for the charming Miss St. Yves to interfere; the more she perceived the influence she had upon him, the more she loved him. She made him depart, and was much affected at it. At length, when he was gone, the Abbé, who was not only Miss St. Yves's elder brother by many years, but was also her guardian, endeavored to wean his ward from the importunities of this dreadful lover. He went to consult the bailiff, who had always intended his son for the Abbé's sister, and who advised him to place the poor girl in a convent. This was a terrible stroke. Such a measure would, to a young lady unaffected with any particular passion, have been inexpressible punishment; but to a love-sick maid, equally sagacious and tender, it was despair itself.

When the ingenuous Hercules returned to the Prior's, he related all that had happened with his usual frankness. He met with the same remonstrances, which had some effect upon his mind, though none upon his senses; but the next day, when he wanted to return to his mistress, in order to reason with her upon the law of nature and the law of convention, the bailiff acquainted him, with insulting joy, that she was in a convent.

"Very well," said he, "I'll go and reason with her in this convent."

That cannot be, said the bailiff; and then entered into a long explanation of the nature of a convent, telling him that this word was derived from *conventus*, in the Latin, which signifies "an assembly;" and the Huron could not comprehend, why he might not be admitted into this assembly. As soon as he was informed that this assembly was a kind of prison, in which girls were shut up, a shocking institution, unknown in Huronia and England; he became as furious as was his patron Hercules, when Euritus, king of Œchalia, no less cruel than the Abbé of St. Yves, refused him the beauteous Iola, his daughter, not inferior in beauty to the Abbé's sister. He was upon the point of going to set fire to the convent to carry off his mistress, or be burnt with her. Miss Kerkabon, terrified at such a declaration, gave up all hopes of ever seeing her nephew a sub-deacon; and, sadly weeping, she exclaimed: "The devil has certainly been in him since he has been christened."

VII.

THE HURON REPULSES THE ENGLISH.

The ingenuous Hercules walked toward the sea-coast wrapped in deep and gloomy melancholy, with his double charged fusee upon his shoulder, and his cutlass by his side, shooting now and then a bird, and often tempted to shoot himself; but he had still some affection for life, for the sake of his dear mistress; by turns execrating his uncle and aunt, all Lower Britany, and his christening; then blessing them, as they had introduced him to the knowledge of her he loved. He resolved upon going to burn the convent, and he stopped short for fear of burning his mistress. The waves of the Channel are not more agitated by the easterly and westerly winds, than was his heart by so many contrary emotions.

He was walking along very fast, without knowing whither he was going, when he heard the beat of a drum. He saw, at a great distance, a vast multitude, part of whom ran toward the coast, and the other part in the opposite direction.

A thousand shrieks re-echoed on every side. Curiosity and courage hurried him, that instant, toward the spot where the greatest clamor arose, which he attained in a few leaps. The commander of the militia, who had supped with him at the Prior's, knew him immediately, and he ran to the Huron with open arms:

"Ah! it is the sincere American: he will fight for us."

Upon which the militia, who were almost dead with fear, recovered themselves, crying with one voice:

"It is the Huron, the ingenuous Huron."

"Gentlemen," said he, "what is the matter? Why are you frightened? Have they shut your mistresses up in convents?"

Instantly a thousand confused voices cried out:

"Do you not see the English, who are landing?"

"Very well," replied the Huron, "they are a brave people; they never proposed making me a sub-deacon; they never carried off my mistress."

The commander made him understand, that they were coming to pillage the Abbé of the Mountain, drink his uncle's wine, and perhaps carry off Miss St. Yves; that the little vessel which set him on shore in Britany had come only to reconnoitre the coast; that they were committing acts of hostility, without having declared war against France; and that the province was entirely exposed to them.

"If this he the case," said he, "they violate the law of nature: let me alone; I lived a long time among them; I am acquainted with their language, and I will speak to them. I cannot think they can have so wicked a design."

During this conversation the English fleet approached; the Huron ran toward it, and having jumped into a little boat, soon rowed to the Admiral's ship, and having gone on board, asked "whether it was true, that they were come to ravage the coast, without having honestly declared war?"

The Admiral and all his crew burst out into laughter, made him drink some punch, and sent him back.

The ingenuous Hercules, piqued at this reception, thought of nothing else but beating his old friends for his countrymen and the Prior. The gentlemen of the neighborhood ran from all quarters, and joined them; they had some cannon, and he discharged them one after the other. The English landed, and he flew toward them, when he killed three of them with his own hand. He even wounded the Admiral, who had made a joke of him. The entire militia were animated with his prowess. The English returned to their ships, and went on board; and the whole coast re-echoed with the shouts of victory, "Live the king! live the ingenuous Hercules!"

Every one ran to embrace him; every one strove to stop the bleeding of some slight wounds he had received.

"Ah!" said he, "if Miss St. Yves were here, she would put on a plaster for me."

The bailiff, who had hid himself in his cellar during the battle, came to pay his compliments like the rest. But he was greatly surprised, when he heard the ingenuous Hercules say to a dozen young men, well disposed for his service, who surrounded him:

"My friends, having delivered the Abbé of the Mountain is nothing; we must rescue a nymph."

The warm blood of these youths was fired at the expression. He was already followed by crowds, who repaired to the convent. If the bailiff had not immediately acquainted the commandant with their design, and he had not sent a detachment after the joyous troop, the thing would have been done. The Huron was conducted back to his uncle and aunt, who overwhelmed him with tears and tenderness.

"I see very well," said his uncle, "that you will never be either a sub-deacon or a prior; you will be an officer, and one still braver than my brother the Captain, and probably as poor."

Miss Kerkabon could not stop an incessant flood of tears, whilst she embraced him, saying, "he will be killed too, like my brother; it were much better he were a sub-deacon."

The Huron had, during the battle, picked up a purse full of guineas, which the Admiral had probably lost. He did not doubt but that this purse would buy all Lower Britany, and, above all, make Miss St. Yves a great lady. Every one persuaded him to repair to Versailles, to receive the recompense due to his services. The commandant, and the principal officers, furnished him with certificates in abundance. The uncle and aunt also approved of this journey. He was to be presented to the king without any difficulty. This alone would give him great weight in the province. These two good folks added to the English purse a considerable present out of their savings. The Huron said to himself, "When I see the king, I will ask Miss St. Yves of him in marriage, and certainly he will not refuse me." He set out accordingly, amidst the acclamations of the whole district, stifled with embraces, bathed in tears by his aunt, blessed by his uncle, and recommending himself to the charming Miss St. Yves.

VIII.

THE HURON GOES TO COURT. SUPS UPON THE ROAD WITH SOME HUGUENOTS.

The ingenuous Hercules took the Saumur road in the coach, because there was at that time no other convenience. When he came to Saumur, he was astonished to find the city almost deserted, and to see several families going away. He was told, that half a dozen years before, Saumur contained upwards of fifty thousand inhabitants, and that at present there were not six thousand. He mentioned this at the inn, whilst at supper. Several Protestants were at table; some complained bitterly, others trembled with rage, others, weeping, said, *Nos dulcia linquimus arva, nos patriam fugimus*. The Huron, who did not understand Latin, had these words explained to him, which signified, "We abandon our sweet fields;—We fly from our country."

"And why do you fly from your country, gentlemen?"

"Because we must otherwise acknowledge the Pope."

"And why not acknowledge him? You have no god-mothers, then, that you want to marry; for, I am told it is he that grants this permission."

"Ah! sir, this Pope says, that he is master of the domains of kings."

"But, gentlemen, what religion are you of?"

"Why, sir, we are for the most part drapers and manufacturers."

"If the Pope, then, is not the master of your clothes and manufactures, you do very well not to acknowledge him; but as to kings, it is their business, and why do you trouble yourselves about it?"

Here a little black man took up the argument, and very learnedly set forth the grievances of the company. He talked of the revocation of the edict of Nantes with so much energy; he deplored, in so pathetic a manner, the fate of fifty thousand fugitive families, and of fifty thousand others converted by dragoons; that the ingenuous Hercules could not refrain from shedding tears.

"Whence arises it," said he, "that so great a king, whose renown expands itself even to the Hurons, should thus deprive himself of so many hearts that would have loved him, and so many arms that would have served him."

"Because he has been imposed upon, like other great kings," replied the little orator, "He has been made to believe, that as soon as he utters a word, all people think as he does; and that he can make us change our religion, just as his musician Lulli, in a moment, changes the decorations of his opera. He has not only already lost five or six hundred thousand very useful subjects, but he has turned many of them into enemies; and King William, who is at this time master of England, has formed several regiments of these identical Frenchmen, who would otherwise have fought for their monarch.

"Such a disaster is more astonishing, as the present Pope, to whom Louis XIV. sacrifices a part of his people, is his declared enemy. A violent quarrel has subsisted between them for nearly nine years. It has been carried so far, that France was in hopes of at length casting off the yoke, by which it has been kept in subjection for so many ages to this foreigner, and, more particularly, of not giving him any more money, which is the *primum mobile* of the affairs of this world. It, therefore, appears evident, that this great king has been imposed on, as well with respect to his interest, as the extent of his power, and that even the magnanimity of his heart has been struck at."

The Huron, becoming more and more interested, asked:

"Who were the Frenchmen who thus deceived a monarch so dear to the Hurons?"

"They are the Jesuits," he was answered, "and, particularly, Father la Chaise, the kings confessor. It is to be hoped that God will one day punish them for it, and that they will be driven out, as they now drive us. Can any misfortune equal ours? Mons. de Louvois besets us on all sides with Jesuits and dragoons."

"Well gentlemen," replied the Huron, "I am going to Versailles to receive the recompense due to my services; I will speak to Mons. de Louvois. I am told it is he who makes war from his closet. I shall see the king, and I will acquaint him with the truth. It is impossible not to yield to this truth, when it is felt. I shall return very soon to marry Miss St. Yves, and I beg you will be present at our nuptials."

These good people now took him for some great Lord, who traveled *incognito* in the coach. Some took him for the king's fool.

There was at table a disguised Jesuit, who acted as a spy to the Reverend Father de la Chaise. He gave him an account of everything that passed, and Father de la Chaise reported it to M. de Louvois. The spy wrote. The Huron and the letter arrived almost at the same time at Versailles.

IX.

THE ARRIVAL OF THE HURON AT VERSAILLES. HIS RECEPTION AT COURT.

The ingenuous Hercules was set down from a public carriage, in the court of the kitchens. He asks the chairmen, what hour the king can be seen? The chairmen laugh in his face, just as the English Admiral had done: and he treated them in the same manner—he beat them. They were for retaliation, and the scene had like to have proved bloody, if a soldier, who was a gentleman of Britany, had not passed by, and who dispersed the mob.

"Sir," said the traveler to him, "you appear to me to be a brave man. I am nephew to the Prior of our Lady of the Mountain. I have killed Englishmen, and I am come to speak to the king. I beg you will conduct me to his chamber."

The soldier, delighted to find a man of courage from his province, who did not seem acquainted with the customs of the court, told him it was necessary to be presented to M. de Louvois.

"Very well, then, conduct me to M. de Louvois, who will doubtless conduct me to the king."

"It is more difficult to speak to M. de Louvois than the king. But I will conduct you to Mr. Alexander, first commissioner of war, and this will be just the same as if you spoke to the minister."

They accordingly repair to Mr. Alexander's, who is first clerk, but they cannot be introduced, he being closely engaged in business with a lady of the court, and no person is allowed admittance.

"Well," said the soldier, "there is no harm done, let us go to Mr. Alexander's first clerk. This will be just the same as if you spoke to Mr. Alexander himself."

The Huron quite astonished, followed him. They remained together half an hour in a little anti-chamber.

"What is all this?" said the ingenuous Hercules. "Is all the world invisible in this country? It is much easier to fight in Lower Britany against Englishmen, than to meet with people at Versailles, with whom one hath business."

He amused himself for some time with relating his amours to his countryman; but the clock striking, recalled the soldier to his post, when a mutual promise was given of meeting on the morrow.

The Huron remained another half hour in the anti-chamber, meditating upon Miss St. Yves, and the difficulty of speaking to kings and first clerks.

At length the patron appeared.

"Sir," said the ingenuous Hercules, "If I had waited to repulse the English as long as you have made me wait for my audience, they would certainly have ravaged all Lower Britany without opposition."

These words impressed the clerk. He at length said to the inhabitant of Britany, "What is your request?"

"A recompense," said the other: "these are my titles;" showing his certificates.

The clerk read, and told him, "that probably he might obtain leave to purchase a lieutenancy."

"Me? what, must I pay money for having repulsed the English? Must I pay a tax to be killed for you, whilst you are peaceably giving your audience here? You are certainly jesting. I require a company of cavalry for nothing. I require that the king shall set Miss St. Yves at liberty from the convent, and give her to me in marriage. I want to speak to the king in favor of fifty thousand families, whom I propose restoring to him. In a word, I want to be useful. Let me be employed and advanced."

"What is your name, sir, who talk in such a high style?"

"Oh! oh!" answered the Huron; "you have not then read my certificates? This is the way they are treated. My name is *Hercules de Kerkabon*. I am christened, and I lodge at the Blue Dial." The clerk concluded, like the people at Saumur, that his head was turned, and did not pay him any further attention.

The same day, the Reverend Father de la Chaise, confessor to Louis XIV., received his spy's letter, which accused the Breton Kerkabon of favoring in his heart the Huguenots, and condemning the conduct of the Jesuits. M. de Louvois had, on his side, received a letter from the inquisitive bailiff, which depicted the Huron as a wicked, lewd fellow, inclined to burn convents, and carry off the nuns.

Hercules, after having walked in the gardens of Versailles, which had become irksome to him; after having supped like a native of Huronia and Lower Britany: had gone to rest, in the pleasant hope of seeing the king the next day; of obtaining Miss St. Yves in marriage; of having, at least, a company of cavalry; and of setting aside the persecution against the Huguenots. He was rocking himself asleep with these flattering ideas, when the *Marechaussée* entered his chamber, and seized upon his double-charged fusee and his great sabre.

They took an inventory of his ready money, and then conducted him to the castle erected by King Charles V., son to John II., near the street of St. Antoine, at the gate des Tournelles.

What was the Huron's astonishment in his way thither the reader is left to imagine. He at first fancied it was all a dream; and remained for some time in a state of stupefaction. Presently, transported with rage, that gave him more than common strength, he collared two of his conductors who were with him in the coach, flung them out of the door, cast himself after them, and then dragged the third, who wanted to hold him. He fell in the attempt, when they tied him, and replaced him in the carriage.

"This, then," said he, "is what one gets for driving the English out of Lower Britany! What wouldst thou say, charming Miss St. Yves, if thou didst see me in this situation?"

They at length arrived at the place of their destination. He was carried without any noise into the chamber in which he was to be locked up, like a dead corpse going to the grave. This room was already occupied by an old solitary student of Port Royal, named Gordon, who had been languishing here for two years.

"See," said the chief of the Marechaussée, "here is company I bring you;" and immediately the enormous bolts of this strong door, secured with large iron bars, were fastened upon them. These two captives were thus separated from all the universe besides.

X.

THE HURON IS SHUT UP IN THE BASTILE WITH A JANSENIST.

Mr. Gordon was a healthy old man, of a serene disposition, who was acquainted with two great things; the one was, to bear adversity; the other, to console the afflicted. He approached his companion with an open sympathizing air, and said to him, whilst he embraced him:

"Whoever thou art that is come to partake of my grave, be assured, that I shall constantly forget myself to soften thy torments in the infernal abyss where we are plunged. Let us adore Providence that has conducted us here. Let us suffer in peace, and trust in hope."

These words had the same effect upon the youth as cordial drops, which recall a dying person to life, and show to his astonished eyes a glimpse of light.

After the first compliments were over, Gordon, without urging him to relate the cause of his misfortune, inspired him by the sweetness of his discourse and by that interest which two unfortunate persons share with each other, with a desire of opening his heart and of disburdening himself of the weight which oppressed him; but he could not guess the cause of his misfortune, and the good man Gordon was as much astonished as himself.

"God must, doubtless," said the Jansenist to the Huron, "have great designs upon you, since he conducted you from Lake Ontario into England, from thence to France; caused you to be baptized in Lower Britany, and has now lodged you here for your salvation."

"I' faith," replied Hercules, "I believe the devil alone has interfered in my destiny.[1] My countrymen in America would never have treated me with the barbarity that I have here experienced; they have not the least idea of it. They are called savages;—they are good people, but rustic, and the men of this country are refined villains. I am indeed, greatly surprised to have come from another world, to be shut up in this, under four bolts with a priest; but I consider what an infinite number of men set out from one hemisphere to go and get killed in the other, or are cast away in the voyage, and are eaten by the fishes. I cannot discover the gracious designs of God over all these people."

Their dinner was brought them through a wicket. The conversation turned upon Providence, *lettres de cachet*, and upon the art of not sinking under disgrace, to which all men in this world are exposed.

"It is now two years since I have been here," said the old man, "without any other consolation than myself and books; and yet I have never been a single moment out of temper."

"Ah! Mr. Gordon," cried Hercules, "you are not then in love with your godmother. If you were as well acquainted with Miss St. Yves as I am, you would be in a state of desperation."

At these words he could not refrain from tears, which greatly relieved him from his oppression.

"How is it then that tears solace us?" said the Huron, "It seems to me that they should have quite an opposite effect."

"My son," said the good old man, "every thing is physical about us; all secretions are useful to the body, and all that comforts it, comforts the soul. We are the machines of Providence."

The ingenuous Huron, who, as we have already observed more than once, had a great share of understanding, entered deeply into the consideration of this idea, the seeds whereof appeared to be in himself. After which he asked his companion.

"Why his machine had for two years been confined by four bolts?"

"By effectual grace," answered Gordon; "I pass for a Jansenist; I know Arnaud and Nicole; the Jesuits have persecuted us. We believe that the Pope is nothing more than a bishop, like another, and therefore Father la Chaise has obtained from the king, his penitent, an order for robbing me without any form of justice, of the most precious inheritance of man—liberty!"

"This is very strange," said the Huron, "all the unhappy people I have met with have been made so solely by the Pope. With respect to your effectual grace, I acknowledge I do not understand what you mean. But I consider it as a very great favor, that God has let me, in my misfortunes, meet with a man, who pours into my heart such consolation as I thought myself incapable of receiving."

The conversation became each day more interesting and instructive. The souls of the two captives seemed to unite in one body. The old man had acquired knowledge, and the young man was willing to receive instruction. At the end of the first month, he eagerly applied himself to the study of geometry. Gordon made him read *Rohault's Physics*, which book was still in fashion, and he had good sense enough to find in it nothing but doubts and uncertainties.

He afterward read the first volume of the *Enquiry After Truth*. This instructive work gave him new light.

"What!" said he, "do our imagination and our senses deceive us to that degree? What, are not our ideas formed by objects, and can we not acquire them by ourselves?"

When he had gone through the second volume, he was not so well satisfied; and he concluded it was much easier to destroy than to build.

His colleague, astonished that a young ignoramus should make such a remark, conceived a very high opinion of his understanding, and was more strongly attached to him.

"Your Malebranche," said he to Gordon one day, "seems to have written half his book whilst he was in possession of his reason, and the other half with the assistance only of imagination and prejudice."

Some days after, Gordon asked him what he thought of the soul, and the manner in which we receive our ideas of volition, grace, and free agency.

"Nothing," replied the Huron. "If I think sometimes, it is that we are under the power of the Eternal Being, like the stars and the elements—that he operates everything in us—that we are small wheels of the immense machine, of which he is the soul—that he acts according to general laws, and not from particular views. This is all that appears to me intelligible; all the rest is to me a dark abyss."

"But this, my son, would be making God the author of sin!"

"But, father, your effectual grace would equally make him the author of sin; for certainly all those to whom this grace was refused, would sin; and is not an all-powerful being who permits evil, virtually the author of evil?"

This sincerity greatly embarrassed the good man; he found that all his endeavors to extricate himself from this quagmire were ineffectual; and he heaped such quantities of words upon one another, which seemed to have meaning, but which in fact had none, that the Huron could not help pitying him. This question evidently determined the origin of good and evil; and poor Gordon was reduced to the necessity of recurring to Pandora's box—Oromasdes's egg pierced by Arimanes—the enmity between Typhon and Osiris—and, at last, original sin; and these he huddled together in profound darkness, without their throwing the least glimmering light upon one another. However, this romance of the soul diverted their thoughts from the contemplation of their own misery; and, by a strange magic, the multitude of calamities dispersed throughout the world diminished the sensation of their own miseries. They did not dare complain when all mankind was in a state of sufferance.

But in the repose of night, the image of the charming Miss St. Yves effaced from the mind of her lover every metaphysical and moral idea. He awoke with his eyes bathed in tears; and the old Jansenist forgot his effectual grace, and the Abbé of St. Cyran, and even Jansenius himself, to afford consolation to a youth whom he had judged guilty of a mortal sin.

After these lectures and their reasonings were over, their adventures furnished them with subjects of conversation; after this store was exhausted, they read together, or separately. The Huron's understanding daily increased; and he would certainly have made great progress in mathematics, if the thought of Miss St. Yves had not frequently distracted him.

He read histories, which made him melancholy. The world appeared to him too wicked and too miserable. In fact, history is nothing more than a picture of crimes and misfortunes. The crowd of innocent and peaceable men are always invisible upon this vast theatre. The *dramatis personæ* are composed of ambitious, perverse men. The pleasure which history affords is derived from the same source as tragedy, which would languish and become insipid, were it not inspired with strong passions, great events, and piteous misfortunes. Clio must be armed with a poniard as well as Melpomene.

Though the history of France is not less filled with horror than those of other nations, it nevertheless appeared to him so disgusting in the beginning, so dry in the continuation, and so trifling in the end, (even in the time of Henry IV.); ever destitute of grand monuments, or foreign to those fine discoveries which have illustrated other nations; that he was obliged to resolve upon not being tired, in order to go through all the particulars of obscure calamities confined to a little corner of the world.

Gordon thought like him. They both laughed with pity when they read of the sovereigns of Fezensacs, Fesansaguet, and Astrac: such a study could be relished only by their heirs, if they had any. The brilliant ages of the Roman Republic made him sometimes quite indifferent as to any other part of the globe. The spectacle of victorious Rome, the lawgiver of nations, engrossed his whole soul. He glowed in contemplating a people who were governed for seven hundred years by the enthusiasm of liberty and glory.

Thus rolled days, weeks, and months; and he would have thought himself happy in the sanctuary of despair, if he had not loved.

The natural goodness of his heart was softened still more when he reflected upon the Prior of our Lady of the Mountain, and the sensible Kerkabon.

"What must they think," he would often repeat, "when they can get no tidings of me? They must think me an ungrateful wretch." This idea rendered him inconsolable. He pitied those who loved him much more than he pitied himself.

[1] In the play called *Civilization*, Hercules uses the following language:

"In my barbarian days, I spoke the truth:
Wrong'd not my neighbor: paid back benefits,
With benefit and gratitude to boot;
Dealt justly: held a friend to be a gift,
Precious as stars dropt down from heaven: bowed
Before the works of God: beheld in them
His presence, palpable, as at an altar:
And worshipp'd heaven at the mountain's foot.
But this
Was Barbarism, I am wiser now;
More civilized. I know the way to lie,
To cheat, deceive, and be a zealous Christian!"—E.

XI.

HOW THE HURON DISCLOSES HIS GENIUS.

Reading aggrandizes the soul, and an enlightened friend affords consolation. Our captive had these two advantages in his favor which he had never expected.

"I shall begin to believe in the Metamorphoses," said he, "for I have been transformed from a brute into a man."

He formed a chosen library with part of the money which he was allowed to dispose of. His friend encouraged him to commit to writing such observations as occurred to him. These are his notes upon ancient history:

"I imagine that nations were for a long time like myself; that they did not become enlightened till very late; that for many ages they were occupied with nothing but the present moment which elapsed: that they thought very little of what was past, and never of the future. I have traversed five or six hundred leagues in Canada, and I did not meet with a single monument: no one is the least acquainted with the actions of his predecessors. Is not this the natural state of man? The human species of this continent appears to me superior to that of the other. They have extended their being for many ages by arts and knowledge. Is this because they have beards upon their chins and God has refused this ornament to the Americans? I do not believe it; for I find the Chinese have very little beard, and that they have cultivated arts for upwards of five thousand years. In effect, if their annals go back upwards of four thousand years, the nation must necessarily have been united and in a flourishing state more than five hundred centuries.

"One thing particularly strikes me in this ancient history of China, which is, that almost every thing is probable and natural. I admire it because it is not tinctured with anything of the marvelous.

"Why have all other nations adopted fabulous origins? The ancient chronicles of the history of France, which, by the by, are not very ancient, make the French descend from one Francus, the son of Hector. The Romans said they were the issue of a Phrygian, though there was not in their whole language a single word that had the least connection with the language of Phrygia. The gods had inhabited Egypt for ten thousand years, and the devils Scythia, where they had engendered the Huns. I meet with nothing before Thucydides but romances similar to the Amadis, and far less amusing. Apparitions, oracles, prodigies, sorcery, metamorphoses, are interspersed throughout with the explanation of dreams, which are the bases of the destiny of the greatest empires and the smallest states. Here are speaking beasts, there brutes that are adored, gods transformed into men, and men into gods. If we must have fables, let us, at least, have such as appear the emblem of truth. I admire the fables of philosophers, but I laugh at those of children, and hate those of impostors."

He one day hit upon a history of the Emperor Justinian. It was there related, that some Appedeutes of Constantinople had delivered, in very bad Greek, an edict against the greatest captain of the age, because this hero had uttered the following words in the warmth of conversation: "Truth shines forth with its proper light, and people's minds are not illumined with flaming piles." The Appedeutes declared that this proposition was heretical, bordering upon heresy, and that the contrary action was catholic, universal, and Grecian: "The minds of the people are enlightened but with flaming piles, and truth cannot shine forth with its own light." These Linostolians thus condemned several discourses of the captain, and published an edict.

"What!" said the Huron, with much emotion, "shall such people publish edicts?"

"They are not edicts," replied Gordon: "they are contradictions, which all the world laughed at in Constantinople, and the Emperor the first. He was a wise prince, who knew how to reduce the Linostolian Appedeutes to a state incapable of doing anything but good. He knew that these gentlemen, and several other Pastophores, had tired the patience of the Emperors, his predecessors, with contradictions in more serious matters."

"He did quite right," said the Huron, "the Pastophores should not be supported, but constrained."

He committed several other observations to paper, which astonished old Gordon. "What," said he to himself, "have I consumed fifty years in instruction and not attained to the degree of natural good sense of this child, who is almost a savage? I tremble to think I have so arduously strengthened prejudices, and he listens to simple nature only."

The good man had some little books of criticism, some of those periodical pamphlets wherein men, incapable of producing anything themselves, blacken the productions of others; where a Vise insults a Racine, and a Faidit a Fénelon. The Huron ran over some of them. "I compare them," said he, "to certain gnats that lodge their eggs in the nostrils of the finest horses, which do not, however, retard their speed."

The two philosophers scarce deigned to cast their eyes upon these dregs of literature.

They soon after went through the elements of astronomy. The Huron sent for some globes: he was ravished at this great spectacle.

"How hard it is," said he, "that I should only begin to be acquainted with heaven, when the power of contemplating it is ravished from me! Jupiter and Saturn revolve in these immense spaces;—millions of suns illumine myriads of worlds; and, in this corner of the earth on which I am cast, there are beings that deprive me of seeing and studying those worlds to which my eye might reach, and even that in which God has placed me. The light created for the whole universe is lost to me. It was not hidden from me in the northern horizon, where I passed my infancy and youth. Without you, my dear Gordon, I should be annihilated."

XII.

THE HURON'S SENTIMENTS UPON THEATRICAL PIECES.

The young Huron resembled one of those vigorous trees, which, languishing in an ungrateful soil, extend in a little time their roots and branches when transplanted to a more favorable spot; and it was very extraordinary that this favorable spot should be a prison.

Among the books which employed the leisure of the two captives were some poems and also translations of Greek tragedies, and some dramatic pieces in French. Those passages that dwelt on love communicated at once pleasure and pain to the soul of the Huron. They were but so many images of his dear Miss St. Yves. The fable of the two pigeons rent his heart: for he was far estranged from his tender dove.

Molière enchanted him. He taught him the manners of Paris and of human nature.

"To which of his comedies do you give the preference?"

"Doubtless to his *Tartuffe*."

"I am of your opinion," said Gordon; "it was a Tartuffe that flung me into this dungeon, and perhaps they were Tartuffes who have been the cause of your misfortunes."

"What do you think of these Greek tragedies?"

"They are very good for Grecians."

But when he read the modern *Iphigenia*, *Phædrus*, *Andromache*, and *Athalia*, he was in ecstacy, he sighed, he wept,—and he learned them by heart, without having any such intention.

"Read *Rodogune*," said Gordon; "that is said to be a capital production; the other pieces which have given you so much pleasure, are trifles compared to this."

The young man had scarce got through the first page, before he said, "This is not written by the same author."

"How do you know it?"

"I know nothing yet; but these lines neither touch my ear nor my heart."

"O!" said Gordon, "the versification does not signify." The Huron asked, "What must I judge by then?"

After having read the piece very attentively without any other design than being pleased, he looked steadfastly at his friend with much astonishment, not knowing what to say. At length, being urged to give his opinion with respect to what he felt, this was the answer he made: "I understood very little of the beginning; the middle disgusted me; but the last scene greatly moved me, though there appears to me but little probability in it. I have no prejudices for or against any one, but I do not remember twenty lines, I, who recollect them all when they please me."

"This piece, nevertheless, passes for the best upon our stage."

"If that be the case," said he, "it is perhaps like many people who are not worthy of the places they hold. After all, this is a matter of taste, and mine cannot yet be formed. I may be mistaken; but you know I am accustomed to say what I think or rather what I feel. I suspect that illusion, fashion, caprice, often warp the judgments of men."

Here he repeated some lines from *Iphigenia*, which he was full of; and though he declaimed but indifferently, he uttered them with such truth and emotion that he made the old Jansenist weep. He then read *Cinna*, which did not excite his tears, but his admiration.

XIII.

THE BEAUTIFUL MISS ST. YVES GOES TO VERSAILLES.

Whilst the unfortunate Hercules was more enlightened than consoled; whilst his genius, so long stifled, unfolded itself with so much rapidity and strength; whilst nature, which was attaining a degree of perfection in him, avenged herself of the outrages of fortune; what became of the Prior, his good sister, and the beautiful recluse, Miss St. Yves? The first month they were uneasy, and the third they were immersed in sorrow. False conjectures, ill-grounded reports, alarmed them. At the end of six months, it was concluded he was dead. At length, Mr. and Miss Kerkabon learned, by a letter of ancient date, which one of the king's guards had written to Britany, that a young man resembling the Huron arrived one night at Versailles, but that since that time no one had heard him spoken of.

"Alas," said Miss Kerkabon, "our nephew has done some ridiculous thing, which has brought on some terrible consequences. He is young, a *Low Breton*, and cannot know how to behave at court. My dear brother, I never saw Versailles nor Paris; here is a fine opportunity, and we shall perhaps find our poor nephew. He is our brother's son, and it is our duty to assist him. Who knows? we may perhaps at length prevail upon him to become a sub-deacon when the fire of youth is somewhat abated. He was much inclined to the sciences. Do you recollect how he reasoned upon the Old and New Testaments? We are answerable for his soul. He was baptized at our instigation. His dear mistress Miss St. Yves does nothing but weep incessantly. Indeed, we must go to Paris. If he is concealed in any of those infamous houses of pleasure, which I have often heard of, we will get him out."

The Prior was affected at his sister's discourse. He went in search of the Bishop of St. Malo's, who had baptized the Huron, and requested his protection and advice. The Prelate approved of the journey. He gave the Prior letters of recommendation to Father la Chaise, the king's confessor, who was invested with the first dignity in the kingdom; to Harlai, the Archbishop of Paris, and to Bossuet, Bishop of Meaux.

At length, the brother and sister set out; but when they came to Paris, they found themselves bewildered in a great labyrinth without clue or end. Their fortune was but middling, and they had occasion every day for carriages to pursue their discovery, which they could not accomplish.

The Prior waited upon the Reverend Father la Chaise; he was with Mademoiselle du Tron, and could not give audience to Priors. He went to the Archbishop's door: the Prelate was shut up with the beautiful

Mademoiselle de Lesdiguières about church matters. He flew to the country house of the Bishop of Meaux: he was engaged in a close examination with Mademoiselle de Mauleon, of the mystery relating to Mademoiselle Guyon. At length, however, he gained access to these two prelates; they both declared they could not interfere with regard to his nephew, as he was not a sub-deacon.

He at length saw the Jesuit, who received him with open arms, protesting he had always entertained the greatest private esteem for him, though he had never known him. He swore that his society had always been attached to the inhabitants of Lower Britany.

"But," said he, "has not your nephew the misfortune of being a Huguenot?"

"No, certainly, Reverend Father."

"May he not be a Jansenist?"

"I can assure your Reverence, that he is scarce a Christian. It is about eleven months since he was christened."

"This is very well;—we will take care of him. Is your benefice considerable?"

"No, a very trifle, and our nephew costs us a great deal."

"Are there any Jansenists in your neighborhood? Take great care, my dear Mr. Prior, they are more dangerous than Huguenots, or even Atheists."

"My Reverend Father, we have none; it is not even known at our Lady of the Mountain what Jansenism is."

"So much the better; go, there is nothing I will not do for you."

He dismissed the Prior in this affectionate manner, but thought no more about him.

Time slipped away, and the Prior and his good sister were almost in despair.

In the meanwhile, the cursed bailiff urged very strenuously the marriage of his great booby son with the beautiful Miss St. Yves, who was taken purposely out of the convent. She always entertained a passion for her god-son in proportion as she detested the husband who was designed for her. The insult that had been offered her, by shutting her up in a convent, increased her affection; and the mandate for wedding the bailiff's son completed her antipathy for him. Chagrin, tenderness, and terror, racked her soul. Love, we know, is much more inventive and more daring in a young woman than friendship in an aged Prior and an aunt upwards of forty-five. Besides, she had received good instructions in her convent with the assistance of romances, which she read by stealth.

The beautiful Miss St. Yves remembered the letter that had been sent by one of the king's guards to Lower Britany, which had been spoken of in the province. She resolved to go herself and gain information at Versailles; to throw herself at the minister's feet, if her husband should be in prison as it was said, and obtain justice for him. I know not what secret intelligence she had gained that at court nothing is refused to a pretty woman; but she knew not the price of these boons.

Having taken this resolution, it afforded her some consolation; and she enjoyed some tranquillity without upraiding Providence with the severity of her lot. She receives her detested intended father-in-law, caresses her brother, and spreads happiness throughout the house. On the day appointed for the ceremony, she secretly departs at four o'clock in the morning, with the little nuptial presents she has received, and all she could gather. Her plan was so well laid, that she was about ten leagues upon her journey, when, about noon, her absence was discovered, and when every one's consternation and surprise was inexpressible. The inquisitive bailiff asked more questions that day than he had done for a week before; the intended bridegroom was more stupefied than ever. The Abbé St. Yves resolved in his rage to pursue his sister. The bailiff and his son were disposed to accompany him. Thus fate led almost the whole canton of Lower Britany to Paris.

The beautiful Miss St. Yves was not without apprehensions that she should be pursued. She rode on horseback, and she got all the intelligence she could from the couriers, without being suspected. She asked if they had not met a fat abbé, an enormous bailiff, and a young booby, galloping as fast as they could to Paris. Having learned, on the third day, that they were not far behind, she took quite a different road, and was skillful and lucky enough to arrive at Versailles, whilst they were in a fruitless pursuit after her, at Paris. But how was she to behave at Versailles? Young, handsome, untutored, unsupported, unknown, exposed to every danger, how could she dare go in search of one of the king's guards? She had some thoughts of applying to a Jesuit of low rank, for there were some for every station of life; as God, they say, has given different aliments to every species of animals. He had given the king his confessor, who was called, by all solicitors of benefices, the head of the Gallican Church. Then came the princes' confessors. The ministers had none, they were not such dupes. There were Jesuits for the genteel mob, and particularly those for chambermaids, by whom were known the secrets of their mistresses; and this was no small vocation, the beautiful Miss St. Yves addressed herself to one of these last, who was called *Father Tout-à-tous* (all to every one). She confessed to him, set forth her adventure, her situation, her danger, and conjured him to get her a lodging with some good devotee, who might shelter her from temptation.

The Confessional.

Father *Tout-à-tous* introduced her to the wife of the cup-bearer, one of his most trusty penitents. From the moment Miss St. Yves became her lodger, she did her utmost to obtain the confidence and friendship of this penitent. She gained intelligence of the Breton-Guard, and invited him to visit her. Having learned from him that her lover had been carried off after having had a conference with one of the clerks, she flew to this clerk. The sight of a fine woman softened him, for it must be allowed God created woman only to tame mankind.

The scribe, thus mollified, acknowledged to her every thing.

"Your lover has been in the bastile almost a year, and without your intercession he would, perhaps, have ended hid days there."

The tender Miss St. Yves swooned at this intelligence. When she had recovered herself, her informer told her:

"I have no power to do good; all my influence extends to doing harm. Take my advice, wait upon M. de St. Pouange, who has the power of doing both good and ill; he is Mons. de Louvois's cousin and favorite. This minister has two souls: the one is M. de St. Pouange, and Mademoiselle de Belle is the other, but she is at present absent from Versailles; so that you have nothing to do but captivate the protector I have pointed out to you."

The beautiful Miss St. Yves, divided between some trifling joy and excessive grief, between a glimmering of hope and dreadful apprehensions,—pursued by her brother, idolizing her lover, wiping her tears, which flowed in torrents; trembling and feeble, yet summoning all her courage;—in this situation, she flew on the wings of love to M. de St. Pouange's.

XIV.

RAPID PROGRESS OF THE HURON'S INTELLECT.

The ingenuous youth was making a rapid progress in the sciences, and particularly in the science of man. The cause of this sudden disclosure of his understanding was as much owing to his savage education as to the disposition of his soul; for, having learned nothing in his infancy, he had not imbibed any prejudices. His mind, not having been warped by error, had retained all its primitive rectitude. He saw things as they were; whereas the ideas that are communicated to us in our infancy make us see them all our life in a false light.

"Your persecutors are very abominable wretches," said he to his friend Gordon. "I pity you for being oppressed, but I condemn you for being a Jansenist. All sects appear to me to be founded in error. Tell me if there be any sectaries in geometry?"

"No, my child," said the good old Gordon, heaving a deep sigh; "all men are agreed concerning truth when demonstrated, but they are too much divided about latent truths."

"If there were but one single hidden truth in your load of arguments, which have been so often sifted for such a number of ages, it would doubtless have been discovered, and the universe would certainly have been unanimous, at least, in that respect. If this truth had been as necessary as the sun is to the earth, it would have been as brilliant as that planet. It is an absurdity, an insult to human nature—it is an attack upon the Infinite and Supreme Being to say there is a truth essential to the happiness of man which God conceals."

All that this ignorant youth, instructed only by nature, said, made a very deep impression upon the mind of the old unhappy scholiast.

"Is it really certain," he cried, "that I should have made myself truly miserable for mere chimeras? I am much more certain of my misery than of effectual grace. I have spent my time in reasoning about the liberty of God and human nature, but I have lost my own. Neither St. Augustine nor St. Prosner will extricate me from my present misfortunes."

The ingenuous Huron, who gave way to his natural instincts, at length said:

"Will you give me leave to speak to you boldly and frankly? Those who bring upon themselves persecution for such idle disputes seem to me to have very little sense; those who persecute, appear to me very monsters."

The two captives entirely coincided with respect to the injustice of their captivity.

"I am a hundred times more to be pitied than you," said the Huron; "I am born free as the air: I had two lives, liberty and the object of my love; and I am deprived of both. We are both in fetters, without knowing who put them on us, or without being able to enquire. It is said that the Hurons are barbarians, because they avenge themselves on their enemies; but they never oppress their friends. I had scarce set foot in France, before I shed my blood for this country. I have, perhaps, preserved a whole province, and my recompense is imprisonment. In this country men are condemned without being heard. This is not the case in England. Alas! it was not against the English that I should have fought."

Thus his growing philosophy could not brook nature being insulted in the first of her rights, and he gave vent to his just indignation.

His companion did not contradict him. Absence ever increases ungratified love, and philosophy does not diminish it. He as frequently spoke of his dear Miss St. Yves, as he did of morality or metaphysics. The more he purified his sentiments, the more he loved. He read some new romances; but he met with few that depicted to him the real state of his soul. He felt that his heart stretched beyond the bounds of his author.

"Alas!" said he, "almost all these writers have nothing but wit and art."

At length, the good Jansenist priest became, insensibly, the confident of his tenderness. He was already acquainted with love as a sin with which a penitent accuses himself at confession. He now learned to know it as a sentiment equally noble and tender; which can elevate the soul as well as soften it, and can at times produce virtues. In fine, for the last miracle, a Huron converted a Jansenist.

XV.

THE BEAUTIFUL MISS ST. YVES VISITS M. DE ST. POUANGE.

The charming Miss St. Yves, still more afflicted than her lover, waited accordingly upon M. de St. Pouange, accompanied by her friend with whom she lodged, each having their faces covered with their hoods. The first thing she saw at the door was the Abbé St. Yves, her brother coming out. She was terrified, but her friend supported her spirits.

"For the very reason," said she, "that people have been speaking against you, speak to him for yourself. You may he assured, that the accusers in this part of the world are always in the right, unless they are immediately detected. Besides, your presence will have greater effect, or else I am much mistaken, than the words of your brother."

Ever so little encouragement to a passionate lover makes her intrepid. Miss St. Yves appears at the audience. Her youth, her charms, her languishing eyes, moistened with some involuntary tears, attract every one's attention. Every sycophant to the deputy minister forgot for an instant the idol of power to contemplate that of beauty. St. Pouange conducted her into a closet. She spoke with an affecting grace. St. Pouange felt some emotion. She trembled, but he told her not to be afraid.

"Return to-night," said he; "your business requires some reflection, and it must be discussed at leisure. There are too many people here at present. Audiences are rapidly dispatched. I must get to the bottom of all that concerns you."

He then paid her some compliments upon her beauty and address, and advised her to come at seven in the evening.

She did not fail attending at the hour appointed, and her pious friend again accompanied her; but she remained in the hall, where she read the *Christian Pedagogue*, whilst St. Pouange and the beauteous Miss St. Yves were in the back closet. He began by saying:

"Would you believe it, Miss, that your brother has been to request me to grant him a *lettre de cachet* against you; but, indeed, I would sooner grant one to send him back to Lower Britany."

"Alas! sir," said she, "*lettres de cachet* are granted very liberally in your offices, since people come from the extremity of the kingdom to solicit them like pensions. I am very far from requesting one against my brother, yet I have much reason to complain of him. But I respect the liberty of mankind; and, therefore, supplicate for that of a man whom I want to make my husband;

of a man to whom the king is indebted for the preservation of a province; who can beneficially serve him; and who is the son of an officer killed in his service. Of what is he accused? How could he be treated so cruelly without being heard?"

The deputy minister then showed her the letter of the spy Jesuit, and that of the perfidious bailiff.

"What!" said she with astonishment, "are there such monsters upon earth? and would they force me to marry the stupid son of a ridiculous, wicked man? and is it upon such evidence that the fate of citizens is determined?"

She threw herself upon her knees, and with a flood of tears solicited the freedom of a brave man who adored her. Her charms appeared to the greatest advantage in such a situation. She was so beautiful, that St. Pouange, bereft of all shame, used words with some reserve, which brought on others less delicate, which were succeeded by those still more expressive. The revocation of the *lettre de cachet* was proposed, and he at length went so far as to state the only means of obtaining the liberty of the man whose interest she had so violently and affectionately at heart.

This uncommon conversation continued for a long time. The devotee in the anti-chamber, in reading her *Christian Pedagogue*, said to herself:

"My Lord St. Pouange never before gave so long an audience. Perhaps he has refused every thing to this poor girl, and she is still entreating him."

At length her companion came out of the closet in the greatest confusion, without being able to speak. She was lost in deep meditation upon the character of the great and the half great, who so slightly sacrifice the liberty of men and the honor of women.

She did not utter a syllable all the way back. But having returned to her friend's, she burst out, and told all that had happened. Her pious friend made frequent signs of the cross.

"My dear friend," said she, "you must consult to-morrow Father *Tout-à-tous*, our director. He has much influence over M. de St. Pouange. He is confessor of many of the female servants of the house. He is a pious accommodating man, who has also the direction of some women of fashion. Yield to him; this is my way; and I always found myself right. We weak women stand in need of a man to lead us: and so, my dear friend, I'll go to-morrow in search of Father *Tout-à-tous*."

XVI.

MISS ST. YVES CONSULTS A JESUIT.

No sooner was the beautiful and disconsolate Miss St. Yves with her holy confessor, than she told him, "that a powerful, voluptuous man, had proposed to her to set at liberty the man whom she intended making her lawful husband, and that he required a great price for his service; that she held such infidelity in the highest detestation; and that if her life only had been required, she would much sooner have sacrificed it than to have submitted."

"This is a most abominable sinner," said Father *Tout-à-tous*, "You should tell me the name of this vile man. He must certainly be some Jansenist. I will inform against him to his Reverence, Father de la Chaise, who will place him in the situation of your dear beloved intended bridegroom."

The poor girl, after much hesitation and embarrassment, at length mentioned St. Pouange.

"My Lord St. Pouange!" cried the Jesuit, "Ah! my child, the case is quite different. He is cousin to the greatest minister we have ever had; a man of worth, a protector of the good cause, a good Christian. He could not entertain such a thought. You certainly must have misunderstood him."

"Oh! Father, I did but understand him too well. I am lost on which ever side I turn. The only alternative I have to choose is misery or shame; either my lover must be buried alive, or I must make myself unworthy of living. I cannot let him perish, nor can I save him."

Father *Tout-à-tous* endeavored to console her with these gentle expressions:

"In the *first place*, my child, never use the word lover. It intimates something worldly, which may offend God. Say my husband. You consider him as such, and nothing can be more decent.

"*Secondly*: Though he be ideally your husband, and you are in hopes he will be such eventually, yet he is not so in reality, consequently, you are still free and the mistress of your own conduct.

Father Tout-à-tous.

"*Thirdly*: Actions are not maliciously culpable, when the intention is virtuous; and nothing can be more virtuous than to procure your husband his liberty.

"*Fourthly*: You have examples in holy antiquity, that miraculously serve you for a guide. St. Augustin relates, that under the proconsulate of Septimius Acyndius, in the thirty-fourth year of our salvation, a poor man could not pay unto Cæsar what belonged to Cæsar, and was justly condemned to die, notwithstanding the maxim, 'Where there is nothing, the king must lose his right.' The object in question was a pound of gold. The culprit had a wife in whom God had united beauty and prudence.

"You may assure yourself, my child, that when a Jesuit quotes St. Augustin, that saint must certainly have been in the right. I advise you to nothing. You are prudent, and it is to be presumed that you will do your husband a service. My Lord St. Pouange is an honest man. He will not deceive you. This is all I can say. I will pray to God for you, and I hope every thing will take place for his glory."

The beautiful Miss St. Yves, who was no less terrified with the Jesuit's discourse than with the proposals of the deputy minister, returned in despair to her friend. She was tempted to deliver herself by death from the horror of her situation.

XVII.

THE JESUIT TRIUMPHS.

The unfortunate Miss St. Yves entreated her friend to kill her; but this lady, who was fully as indulgent as the Jesuit, spoke to her still more clearly.

"Alas!" said she, "at this agreeable, gallant, and famous court, business is always thus transacted. The most considerable, as well as the most indifferent places are seldom given away without a consideration. The dignities of war are solicited by the queen of love, and, without regard to merit, a place is often given to him who has the handsomest advocate.

"You are in a situation that is extremely critical. The object is to restore your lover to liberty, and to marry him. It is a sacred duty that you are to fulfill. The world will applaud you. It will be said, that you only allowed yourself to be guilty of a weakness, through an excess of virtue."

"Heavens!" cried Miss St. Yves, "What kind of virtue is this? What a labyrinth of distress! What a world! What men to become acquainted with! A Father de la Chaise and a ridiculous bailiff imprison my lover; I am persecuted by my family; assistance is offered me, only that I may be dishonored! A Jesuit has ruined a brave man, another Jesuit wants to ruin me. On every side snares are laid for me, and I am upon the very brink of destruction! I must even speak to the king; I will throw myself at his feet as he goes to mass or to the theatre."

"His attendants will not let you approach," said her good friend; "and if you should be so unfortunate as to speak to him, M. de Louvois, or the Reverend Father de la Chaise, might bury you in a convent for the rest of your days."

Whilst this generous friend thus increased the perplexities of Miss St. Yves's tortured soul, and plunged the dagger deeper in her heart, a messenger arrived from M. de St. Pouange with a letter, and two fine pendant earrings. Miss St. Yves, with tears, refused to accept of any part of the contents of the packet; but her friend took the charge of them upon herself.

As soon as the messenger had gone, the *confidante* read the letter, in which a *petit-souper* (a little supper) was proposed to the two friends for that night. Miss St. Yves protested she would not go, whilst her pious friend endeavored to make her try on the diamond earrings; but Miss St. Yves could not endure them, and opposed it all the day long; being entirely wrapped up in the contemplation of her lover's imprisonment. At length, after a long resistance—after sighs, moans, and torrents of tears—driven by excitement almost to the verge of insanity—weakened with the conflict, overwhelmed and irresolute, the innocent victim, not knowing whether she was going, was dragged by this artful woman to the fatal supper of the "good Christian and protector of the good cause," M. de St. Pouange.

The meeting.

XVIII.

MISS ST. YVES DELIVERS HER LOVER AND A JANSENIST.

At day-break she fled to Paris with the minister's mandate. It would be difficult to depict the agitation of her mind in this journey. Imagine a virtuous and noble soul, humbled by its own reproaches, intoxicated with tenderness, distracted with the remorse of having betrayed her lover, and elated with the pleasure of releasing the object of her adoration. Her torments and conflicts by turns engaged her reflections. She was no longer that innocent girl whose ideas were confined to a provincial education. Love and misfortunes had united to remould her. Sentiment had made as rapid a progress in her mind, as reason had in that of her lover.

Her dress was dictated by the greatest simplicity. She viewed with horror the trappings with which she had appeared before her fatal benefactor. Her companion had taken the earrings without her having looked at them. Anxious and confused, idolizing the Huron and detesting herself, she at length arrived at the gate of that dreadful castle—the palace of vengeance—where crimes and innocence are alike immured.

When she was upon the point of getting out of the coach her strength failed her. Some people came to her assistance. She entered, whilst her heart was in the greatest palpitation, her eyes streaming, and her whole frame bespoke the greatest consternation. She was presented to the governor. He was going to speak to her, but she had lost all power of expression: she showed her order, whilst, with great difficulty, she articulated some accents. The governor entertained a great esteem for his prisoner, and he was greatly pleased at his being released. His heart was not callous, like those of most of his brethren, who think of nothing but the fees their captives are to pay them; extort their revenues from their victims; and living by the misery of others, conceive a horrid joy at the lamentations of the unfortunate.

He sent for the prisoner into his apartment. The two lovers swooned at the sight of each other. The beautiful Miss St. Yves remained for a long time motionless, without any symptoms of life; the other soon recalled his fortitude.

"This lady," said the governor, "is probably your wife. You did not tell me you were married. I am informed that it is through her generous solicitude that you have obtained your liberty."

"Alas!" said the beautiful Miss St. Yves, in a faltering voice, "I am not worthy of being his wife;" and swooned again.

When she recovered her senses, she presented, with a trembling hand and averted eyes, the grant and written promise of a company.

The Huron, equally astonished and affected, awoke from one dream to fall into another.

"Why was I shut up here? How could you deliver me? Where are the monsters that immured me? You are a divinity sent from heaven to succor me."

The beautiful Miss St. Yves, with a dejected air, looked at her lover, blushed, and instantly turned away her streaming eyes. In a word, they told him all she knew, and all she had undergone, except what she was willing to conceal forever, but which any other than the Huron, more accustomed to the world and better acquainted with the customs of courts, would easily have guessed.

"Is it possible," said he, "that a wretch like the bailiff can have deprived me of my liberty?"

"Alas! I find that men, like the vilest of animals, can all injure."

"But is it possible that a monk, a Jesuit, the king's confessor, should have contributed to my misfortunes as much as the bailiff, without my being able to imagine under what pretence this detestable knave has persecuted me? Did he make me pass for a Jansenist? In fine, how came you to remember me? I did not deserve it; I was then only a savage."

"What! could you, without advice, without assistance, undertake a journey to Versailles?"

"You there appeared, and my fetters were broken!"

"There must then be in beauty and virtue an invincible charm, that opens gates of adamant and softens hearts of steel."

At the word virtue, a flood of tears issued from the eyes of the beautiful Miss St. Yves. She did not know how far she had been virtuous in the crime with which she reproached herself.

Her lover thus continued:

"Thou angel, who hast broken my chains, if thou hast had sufficient influence (which I cannot yet comprehend) to obtain justice for me, obtain it likewise for an old man who first taught me to think, as thou didst to love. Misfortunes have united us; I love him as a father; I can neither live without thee nor him."

"I solicit?"

"The same man."

"Who!"

"Yes, I will be beholden to you for everything, and I will owe nothing to any one but yourself. Write to this man in power. Overwhelm me with kindness—complete what you have begun—perfect your miracle."

She was sensible she ought to do everything her lover desired. She wanted to write, but her hand refused its office. She began her letter three times, and tore it as often. At length she got to the end, and the two lovers left the prison, after having embraced the old martyr to efficacious grace.

The happy yet disconsolate Miss St. Yves knew where her brother lodged: thither she repaired; and her lover took an apartment at the same house.

They had scarce reached their lodging, before her protector sent the order for releasing the good old Gordon, at the same time making an appointment with her for the next day.

She gave the order of release to her lover, and refused the appointment of a benefactor whom she could no more see without expiring with shame and grief.

Her lover would not have left her upon any other errand than to release his friend. He flew to the place of his confinement and fulfilled this duty, reflecting, meanwhile, upon the strange vicissitudes of this world, and admiring the courageous virtue of a young lady, to whom two unfortunate men owed more than life.

XIX.

THE HURON, THE BEAUTIFUL MISS ST. YVES, AND THEIR RELATIONS, ARE CONVENED.

The generous and respectable, but injured girl, was with her brother the Abbé de St. Yves, the good Prior of the Mountain, and Lady de Kerkabon. They were equally astonished, but their situations and sentiments were very different. The Abbé de St. Yves was expiating the wrongs he had done his sister at her feet, and she pardoned him. The prior and his sympathizing sister likewise wept, but it was for joy. The filthy bailiff and his insupportable son did not trouble this affecting scene. They had set out upon the first report that their antagonist had been released. They flew to bury in their own province their folly and fear.

The four *dramatis personæ*, variously agitated, were waiting for the return of the young man who had gone to deliver his friend. The Abbé de St. Yves did not dare to raise his eyes to meet those of his sister. The good Kerkabon said:

"I shall then see once more my dear nephew."

"You will see him again," said the charming Miss St. Yves, "but he is no longer the same man. His behavior, his manners, his ideas, his sense, have all undergone a complete mutation. He has become as respectable, as he was before ignorant and strange to everything. He will be the honor and consolation of your family; would to heaven that I might also be the honor of mine!"

"What, are you not the same as you were?" said the prior. "What then has happened to work so great a change?"

During this conversation the Huron returned in company with the Jansenist. The scene was now changed, and became more interesting. It began by the uncle and aunt's tender embraces. The Abbé de St. Yves almost kissed the knees of the ingenuous Huron, who, by the by, was no longer ingenuous. The language of the eyes formed all the discourse of the two lovers, who, nevertheless, expressed every sentiment with which they were penetrated. Satisfaction and acknowledgment sparkled in the countenance of the one, whilst embarrassment was depicted in Miss St. Yves's melting but half averted eyes. Every one was astonished that she should mingle grief with so much joy.

The venerable Gordon soon endeared himself to the whole family. He had been unhappy with the young prisoner, and this was a sufficient title to their esteem. He owed his deliverance to the two lovers, and this alone reconciled him to love. The acrimony of his former sentiments was dismissed from his heart—he was converted by gratitude, as well as the Huron. Every one related his adventures before supper. The two Abbés and the aunt listened like children to the relation of stories of ghosts, and both were deeply interested.

"Alas!" said Gordon, "there are perhaps upwards of five hundred virtuous people in the same fetters as Miss St. Yves has broken. Their misfortunes are unheeded. Many hands are found to strike the unhappy multitude,—how seldom one to succor them."

This very just reflection increased his sensibility and gratitude. Everything heightened the triumph of the beautiful Miss St. Yves. The grandeur and intrepidity of her soul were the subject of each one's admiration. This admiration was blended with that respect which we feel in spite of ourselves for a person who we think has some influence at court. But the Abbé de St. Yves enquired:

"What could my sister do to obtain this influence so soon?"

Supper being ready, every one was already seated, when, lo! the worthy *confidante* of Versailles arrived, without being acquainted with anything that had passed. She was in a coach and six, and it was easily seen to whom the equipage belonged. She entered with that air of authority assumed by people in power who have a great deal of business—saluted the company with much indifference, and, pulling the beautiful Miss St. Yves on one side, said:

"Why do you make people wait so long? Follow me. There are the diamonds you forgot."

However softly she uttered these expressions, the Huron, nevertheless, overheard them. He saw the diamonds. The brother was speechless. The uncle and aunt exhibited the surprise of good people, who had never before beheld such magnificence. The young man, whose mind was now formed by an experience of twelve months, could not help making some reflections against his will, and was for a moment in anxiety. His mistress perceived it, and a mortal paleness spread itself over her countenance; a tremor seized her, and it was with difficulty she could support herself.

"Ah! madam," said she to her fatal friend, "you have ruined me—you have given me the mortal blow."

These words pierced the heart of the Huron: but he had already learned to possess himself. He did not dwell upon them, lest he should make his mistress uneasy before her brother, but turned pale as well as she.

Miss St. Yves, distracted with the change she perceived in her lover's countenance, pulled the woman out of the room into the passage, and there threw the jewels at her feet, saying:

"Alas! these were not my seducers, as you well know: but he that gave them shall never set eyes on me again."

Her friend took them up, whilst Miss St. Yves added:

"He may either take them again, or give them to you. Begone, and do not make me still more odious to myself."

The ambassadress at length departed, not being able to comprehend the remorse to which she had been witness.

The beautiful Miss St. Yves, greatly oppressed and feeling a revolution in her body that almost suffocated her, was compelled to go to bed; but that she might not alarm any one she kept her pains and sufferings to herself: and under pretence of only being weary, she asked leave to take a little rest. This, however, she did not do till she had reanimated the company with consolatory and flattering expressions, and cast such a kind look upon her lover as darted fire into his soul.

The supper, of which she did not partake, was in the beginning gloomy; but this gloominess was of that interesting kind which inspires reflection and useful conversation, so superior to that frivolous excitement commonly exhibited, and which is usually nothing more than a troublesome noise.

Gordon, in a few words, gave the history of Jansenism and Molinism; of those persecutions with which one party hampered the other; and of the obstinacy of both. The Huron entered into a criticism thereupon, pitying those men who, not satisfied with all the confusion occasioned by these opposite interests, create evils by imaginary interests and unintelligible absurdities. Gordon related—the other judged. The guests listened with emotion, and gained new lights. The duration of misfortunes, and the shortness of life, then became the topics. It was remarked that all professions have peculiar vices and dangers annexed to them; and that from the prince down to the lowest beggar, all seemed alike to accuse providence. How happens it that so many men, for so little, perform the office of persecutors, sergeants, and executioners, to others? With what inhuman indifference does a man in authority sign papers for the destruction of a family; and with what joy, still more barbarous, do mercenaries execute them.

"I saw in my youth," said the good old Gordon, "a relation of the Marshal de Marillic, who, being prosecuted in his own province on account of that illustrious but unfortunate man, concealed himself under a borrowed name in Paris. He was an old man near seventy-two years of age. His wife, who accompanied him, was nearly of the same age. They had a libertine son, who at fourteen years of age absconded from his father's house, turned soldier, and deserted. He had gone through every gradation of debauchery and misery; at length, having changed his name, he was in the guards of Cardinal

Richelieu, (for this priest, as well as Mazarine, had guards) and had obtained an exempt's staff in their company of sergeants.

"This adventurer was appointed to arrest the old man and his wife, and acquitted himself with all the obduracy of a man who was willing to please his master. As he was conducting them, he heard these two victims deplore the long succession of miseries which had befallen them from their cradle. This aged couple reckoned as one of their greatest misfortunes the wildness and loss of their son. He recollected them, but he nevertheless led them to prison; assuring them, that his Reverence was to be served in preference to every body else. His Eminence rewarded his zeal.

"I have seen a spy of Father de la Chaise betray his own brother, in hopes of a little benefice, which he did not obtain; and I saw him die, not of remorse, but of grief at having been cheated by the Jesuit.

"The vocation of a confessor, which I for a long while exercised, made me acquainted with the secrets of families. I have known very few, who, though immersed in the greatest distress, did not externally wear the mask of felicity and every appearance of joy; and I have always observed that great grief was the fruit of our unconstrained desires."

"For my part," said the Huron, "I imagine, that a noble, grateful, sensible man, may always be happy; and I hope to enjoy an unchecked felicity with the charming, generous Miss St. Yves. For I flatter myself," added he, in addressing himself to her brother with a friendly smile, "that you will not now refuse me as you did last year: besides, I shall pursue a more decent method."

The Abbé was confounded in apologies for the past, and in protesting an eternal attachment.

Uncle Kerkabon said this would be the most glorious day of his whole life. His good aunt Kerkabon, in ecstasies of joy, cried out:

"I always said you would never be a sub-deacon. This sacrament is preferable to the other; would to God I had been honored with it! but I will serve you for a mother."

And now all vied with each other in applauding the gentle Miss St. Yves.

Her lover's heart was too full of what she had done for him, and he loved her too much, for the affair of the jewels to make any permanent impression on him. But those words, which he too well heard, "*you have given me the mortal blow*", still secretly terrified him, and interrupted all his joy; whilst the eulogiums paid his beautiful mistress still increased his love. In a word, nothing was thought of but her,—nothing was mentioned but the happiness those two lovers deserved. A plan was agitated to live altogether at Paris, and schemes of grandeur and fortune were formed. These hopes, which the smallest ray of happiness engenders, were predominant. But the Huron felt, in the secret recesses of his heart, a sentiment that exploded the illusion. He read over the promises signed by St. Pouange, and the commission signed Louvois. These men were painted to him such as they were, or such as they were thought to be. Every one spoke of the ministers and administration with the freedom of convivial conversation, which is considered in France as the most precious liberty to be obtained on earth.

"If I were king of France," said the Huron, "this is the kind of minister that I would choose for the war department. I would have a man of the highest birth, as he is to give orders to the nobility. I would require that he should himself have been an officer, and have passed through the various gradations; or, at least, that he had attained the rank of Lieutenant General, and was worthy of being a Marshal of France. For, to be acquainted with the details of the service, is it not necessary that he himself should have served? and will not officers obey, with a hundred times more alacrity, a military man, who like themselves has been signalized by his courage, rather than a mere man of the cabinet, who, whatever natural ability he may possess, can, at most, only guess at the operations of a campaign? I should not be displeased at my minister's generosity, even though it might sometimes embarrass a little the keeper of the royal treasure. I should desire him to have a facility in business, and that he should distinguish himself by that kind of gaiety of mind, which is the lot of men superior to business, which is so agreeable to the nation, and which renders the performance of every duty less irksome."

This is the character he would have chosen for a minister, as he had constantly observed that such an amiable disposition is incompatible with cruelty.

Monsieur de Louvois would not, perhaps, have been satisfied with the Huron's wishes. His merit lay in a different walk. But whilst they were still at table, the disorder of the unhappy Miss St. Yves took a fatal turn. Her blood was on fire,—the symptoms of a malignant fever had appeared. She suffered, but did not complain, being unwilling to disturb the pleasure of the guests.

Her brother, thinking that she was not asleep, went to the foot of her bed. He was astonished at the condition he found her in. Every body flew to her. Her lover appeared next to her brother. He was certainly the most alarmed, and the most affected of any one; but he had learned to unite discretion to all the happy gifts nature had bestowed upon him, and a quick sensibility of decorum began to prevail over him.

A neighboring physician was immediately sent for. He was one of those itinerant doctors who confound the last disorder they were consulted upon with the present;—who follow a blind practice in a science from which the most mature investigations and careful observations do not preclude uncertainty and danger. He greatly increased the disorder by prescribing a fashionable nostrum. Can fashion extend to medicine? This frenzy was then too prevalent in Paris.

The grief of Miss St. Yves contributed still more than her physician to render her disorder fatal. Her body suffered martyrdom in the torments of her mind. The crowd of thoughts which agitated her breast, communicated to her veins a more dangerous poison than that of the most burning fever.

XX.

THE DEATH OF THE BEAUTIFUL MISS ST. YVES, AND ITS CONSEQUENCES.

Another physician was called in. But, instead of assisting nature and leaving it to act in a young person whose organs recalled the vital stream, he applied himself solely to counteract the effects of his brother's prescription. The disorder, in two days, became mortal. The brain, which is thought to be the seat of the mind, was as violently affected as the heart, which, we are told, is the seat of the passions. By what incomprehensible mechanism are our organs held in subjection to sentiment and thought? How is it that a single melancholy idea shall disturb the whole course of the blood; and that the blood should in turn communicate irregularities to the human understanding? What is that unknown fluid which certainly exists and which, quicker and more active than light, flies in less than the twinkling of an eye into all the channels of life,—produces sensations, memory, joy or grief, reason or frenzy,—recalls with horror what we would choose to forget; and renders a thinking animal, either a subject of admiration, or an object of pity and compassion?

These were the reflections of the good old Gordon; and these observations, so natural, which men seldom make, did not prevent his feeling upon this occasion; for he was not of the number of those gloomy philosophers who pique themselves upon being insensible.

He was affected at the fate of this young woman, like a father who sees his dear child yielding to a slow death. The Abbé de St. Yves was desperate; the prior and his sister shed floods of tears; but who could describe the situation of her lover? All expression falls far short of the intensity of his affliction.

His aunt, almost lifeless, supported the head of the departing fair in her feeble arms; her brother was upon his knees at the foot of the bed; her lover squeezed her hand, which he bathed in tears; his groans rent the air, whilst he called her his guardian angel, his life, his hope, his better half, his mistress, his wife. At the word wife, a sigh escaped her, whilst she looked upon him with inexpressible tenderness, and then abruptly gave a horrid scream. Presently in one of those intervals when grief, the oppression of the senses, and pain subside and leave the soul its liberty and powers, she cried out:

"I your wife? Ah! dear lover, this name, this happiness, this felicity, were not destined for me! I die, and I deserve it. O idol of my heart! O you, whom I sacrificed to infernal demons—it is done—I am punished—live and be happy!"

These tender but dreadful expressions were incomprehensible; yet they melted and terrified every heart. She had the courage to explain herself, and her auditors quaked with astonishment, grief, and pity. They with one voice detested the man in power, who repaired a shocking act of injustice only by his crimes, and who had forced the most amiable innocence to be his accomplice.

"Who? you guilty?" said her lover, "no, you are not. Guilt can only be in the heart;—yours is devoted solely to virtue and to me."

This opinion he corroborated by such expressions as seemed to recall the beautiful Miss St. Yves back to life. She felt some consolation from them and was astonished at being still beloved. The aged Gordon would have condemned her at the time he was only a Jansenist; but having attained wisdom, he esteemed her, and wept.

In the midst of these lamentations and fears, whilst the dangerous situation of this worthy girl engrossed every breast, and all were in the greatest consternation, a courier arrived from court.

"A courier? from whom, and upon what account?"

He was sent by the king's confessor to the Prior of the Mountain. It was not Father de la Chaise who wrote, but brother Vadbled, his valet de chambre, a man of great consequence at that time, who acquainted the archbishops with the reverend Father's pleasure, who gave audiences, promised benefices, and sometimes issued *lettres de cachet*.

He wrote to the Abbé of the Mountain, "that his reverence had been informed of his nephew's exploits: that his being sent to prison was through mistake; that such little accidents frequently happened, and should therefore not be attended to; and, in fine, it behoved him, the prior, to come and present his nephew the next day: that he was to bring with him that good man Gordon; and that he, brother Vadbled, should introduce them to his reverence and M. de Louvois, who would say a word to them in his antichamber."

To which he added, "that the history of the Huron, and his combat against the English, had been related to the king; that doubtless the king would deign to take notice of him in passing through the gallery, and perhaps he might even nod his head to him."

The letter concluded by flattering him with hopes that all the ladies of the court would show their eagerness to recognize his nephew; and that several among them would say to him, "Good day, Mr. Huron;" and that he would certainly be talked of at the king's supper.

The letter was signed, "Your affectionate brother Jesuit, Vadbled."

The prior having read the letter aloud, his furious nephew for an instant suppressed his rage, and said nothing to the bearer: but turning toward the companion of his misfortunes, asked him, what he thought of that communication? Gordon replied:

"This, then, is the way that men are treated! They are first beaten and then, like monkeys, they dance."

The Huron resuming his character, which always returned in the great emotions of his soul, tore the letter to bits, and threw them in the courier's face:

"There is my answer," said he.

Death of Miss St. Ives.—"When the fatal moment came, all around her most feelingly expressed their grief by incessant tears and lamentations. The Huron was senseless. Great souls feel more violent sensations than those of less tender dispositions."

His uncle was in terror, and fancied he saw thunderbolts, and twenty *lettres de cachet* at once fall upon him. He immediately wrote the best excuse he could for these transports of passion in a young man, which he considered as the ebullition of a great soul.

But a solicitude of a more melancholy stamp now seized every heart. The beautiful and unfortunate Miss St. Yves was already sensible of her approaching end; she was serene, but it was that kind of shocking serenity, the result of exhausted nature being no longer able to withstand the conflict.

"Oh, my dear lover!" said she, in a faltering voice, "death punishes me for my weakness; but I expire with the consolation of knowing you are free. I adored you whilst I betrayed you, and I adore you in bidding you an eternal adieu."

She did not make a parade of a ridiculous fortitude; she did not understand that miserable glory of having some of her neighbors say, "she died with courage." Who, at twenty, can be at once torn from her lover, from life, and what is called honor, without regret, without some pangs? She felt all the horror of her situation, and made it felt by those expiring looks and accents which speak with so much energy. In a word, she shed tears like other people at those intervals that she was capable of giving vent to them.

Let others strive to celebrate the pompous deaths of those who insensibly rush into destruction. This is the lot of all animals. We die like them only when age or disorders make us resemble them by the paralysis of our organs. Whoever suffers a great loss must feel great regrets. If they are stifled, it is nothing but vanity that is pursued, even in the arms of death.

When the fatal moment came, all around her most feelingly expressed their grief by incessant tears and lamentations. The Huron was senseless. Great souls feel more violent sensations than those of less tender dispositions. The good old Gordon knew enough of his companion to dread that when he came to himself he would be guilty of suicide. All kinds of arms were put out of his way, which the unfortunate young man perceived. He said to his relations and Gordon, without shedding any tears, without a groan, or the least emotion:

"Do you then think that any one upon earth hath the right and power to prevent my putting an end to my life?"

Gordon took care to avoid making a parade of those commonplace declamations and arguments which are relied on to prove that we are not allowed to exercise our liberty in ceasing to be when we are in a wretched situation; that we should not leave the house when we can no longer remain in it; that a man is like a soldier at his post; as if it signified to the Being of beings whether the conjunction of the particles of matter were in one spot or another. Impotent reasons, to which a firm and concentrated despair disdains to listen, and to which Cato replied only with the use of a poniard.

The Huron's sullen and dreadful silence, his doleful aspect, his trembling lips, and the shivering of his whole frame, communicated to every spectator's soul that mixture of compassion and terror, which fetters all our powers, precludes discourse, or compels us to speak only in faltering accents. The hostess and her family were excited. They trembled to behold the state of his desperation, yet all kept their eyes upon him, and attended to all his motions. The ice-cold corpse of the beautiful Miss St. Yves had already been carried into a lower hall out of the sight of her lover, who seemed still in search of it, though incapable of observing any object.

In the midst of this spectacle of death, whilst the dead body was exposed at the door of the house; whilst two priests by the side of the holy water-pot were repeating prayers with an air of distraction; whilst some passengers, through idleness, sprinkled the bier with some drops of holy water, and others went their ways quite indifferent; whilst her relations were drowned in tears, and every one thought the lover would not survive his loss;—in this situation St. Pouange arrived with his female Versailles friend.

He alighted from his coach; and the first object that presented itself was a bier: he turned away his eyes with that simple distaste of a man bred up in pleasures, and who thinks he should avoid a spectacle which might recall him to the contemplation of human misery. He is inclined to go up stairs, whilst his female friend enquires through curiosity whose funeral it is. The name of Miss St. Yves is pronounced. At this name she turned, and gave a piercing shriek. St. Pouange now returns, whilst surprise and grief possess his soul. The good old Gordon stood with streaming eyes. He for a moment ceased his lamentations, to acquaint the courtier with all the circumstances of this melancholy catastrophe. He spoke with that authority which is the companion to sorrow and virtue. St. Pouange was not naturally wicked. The torrent of business and amusements had hurried away his soul, which was not yet acquainted with itself. He did not border upon that grey age which usually hardens the hearts of ministers. He listened to Gordon with a downcast look, and some tears escaped him, which he was surprised to shed. In a word, he repented.

"I will," said he, "absolutely see this extraordinary man you have mentioned to me. He affects me almost as much as this innocent victim, whose death I have occasioned."

Gordon followed him as far as the chamber in which the Prior Kerkabon, the Abbé St. Yves, and some neighbors, were striving to recall to life the young man, who had again fainted.

"I have been the cause of your misfortunes," said the deputy minister, when the Huron had regained consciousness, "and my whole life shall be employed in making reparation for my error."

The first idea that struck the Huron was to kill him and then destroy himself. But he was without arms, and closely watched. St. Pouange was not repulsed with refusals accompanied with reproach, contempt, and the insults he deserved, which were lavished upon him. Time softens everything. Mons. de Louvois at length succeeded in making an excellent officer of the Huron, who has appeared under another name at Paris and in the army, respected by all honest men, being at once a warrior and an intrepid philosopher.

He never mentioned this adventure without being greatly affected, and yet his greatest consolation was to speak of it. He cherished the memory of his beloved Miss St. Yves to the last moment of his life.[1]

The Abbé St. Yves and the Prior were each provided with good livings. The good Kerkabon rather chose to see his nephew invested with military honors than in the sub-deaconry. The devotee of Versailles kept the diamond earrings, and received besides a handsome present. Father *Tout-à-tous* had presents of chocolate, coffee, and confectionery, with the *Meditations of the Reverend Father Croiset*, and the *Flower of the Saints*, bound in Morocco. Good old Gordon lived with the Huron till his death, in the most friendly intimacy: he had also a benefice, and forgot, forever, essential grace, and the concomitant concourse. He took for his motto, "Misfortunes are of some use." How many worthy people are there in the world who may justly say, "Misfortunes are good for nothing?"

[1] In the Play, *Civilization*, the Huron musingly soliloquizes:

"And what is love to man? An only gift
Too precious to be idly thrown away!
For is it not as precious as our land,
Which, heeding not another's golden sky—
Soft airs, sweet flowers, hill and dale conjoin'd
By nature's cunning past comparison—
Is still our land; and, as our land, surpasses
Far such fairy worlds?

"There are some dreams that last a life—mine
Is one of these. I shall dream on till death
Shall end the vision!

"It is not hard to die! And life is but
A shadow on the wall—a falling leaf
Toy'd with by autumn winds—a flower—a star
Among the infinite, infinitesimal!
We are but breath whispering against the wind,—
Sand in the desert!—dew upon the sea!"—E.

MICROMEGAS:

A SATIRE ON THE PHILOSOPHY, IGNORANCE. AND SELF-CONCEIT OF MANKIND.

A medieval exploring vessel. [1]

I.

A VOYAGE TO THE PLANET SATURN, BY A NATIVE OF SIRIUS.

In one of the planets that revolve round the star known by the name of Sirius, was a certain young gentleman of promising parts, whom I had the honor to be acquainted with in his last voyage to this our little ant-hill. His name was Micromegas, an appellation admirably suited to all great men, and his stature amounted to eight leagues in height, that is, twenty-four thousand geometrical paces of five feet each.

Some of your mathematicians, a set of people always useful to the public, will, perhaps, instantly seize the pen, and calculate that Mr. Micromegas, inhabitant of the country of Sirius, being from head to foot four and twenty thousand paces in length, making one hundred and twenty thousand royal feet, that we, denizens of this earth, being at a medium little more than five feet high, and our globe nine thousand leagues in circumference: these things being premised, they will then conclude that the periphery of the globe which produced him must be exactly one and twenty millions six hundred thousand times greater than that of this our tiny ball. Nothing in nature is more simple and common. The dominions of some sovereigns of Germany or Italy, which may be compassed in half an hour, when compared with the empires of Ottoman, Russia, or China, are no other than faint instances of the prodigious difference that nature hath made in the scale of beings. The stature of his excellency being of these extraordinary dimensions, all our artists will agree that the measure around his body might amount to fifty thousand royal feet—a very agreeable and just proportion.

His nose being equal in length to one-third of his face, and his jolly countenance engrossing one-seventh part of his height, it must be owned that the nose of this same Sirian was six thousand three hundred and thirty-three royal feet to a hair, which was to be demonstrated. With regard to his understanding, it is one of the best cultivated I have known. He is perfectly well acquainted with abundance of things, some of which are of his own invention; for, when his age did not exceed two hundred and fifty years, he studied, according to the custom of the country, at the most celebrated university of the whole planet, and by the force of his genius discovered upwards of fifty propositions of Euclid, having the advantage by more than eighteen of Blaise Pascal, who, (as we are told by his own sister,) demonstrated two and thirty for his amusement and then left off, choosing rather to be an indifferent philosopher than a great mathematician.

About the four hundred and fiftieth year of his age, or latter end of his childhood, he dissected a great number of small insects not more than one hundred feet in diameter, which are not perceivable by ordinary microscopes, of which he composed a very curious treatise, which involved him in some trouble. The mufti of the nation, though very old and very ignorant, made shift to discover in his book certain lemmas that were suspicious, unseemly, rash, heretic, and unsound, and prosecuted him with great animosity, for the subject of the author's inquiry was whether, in the world of Sirius, there was any difference between the substantial forms of a flea and a snail.

Micromegas defended his philosophy with such spirit as made all the female sex his proselytes; and the process lasted two hundred and twenty years; at the end of which time, in consequence of the mufti's interest, the book was condemned by judges who had never read it, and the author expelled from court for the term of eight hundred years.

Not much affected at his banishment from a court that teemed with nothing but turmoils and trifles, he made a very humorous song upon the mufti, who gave himself no trouble about the matter, and set out on his travels from planet to planet, in order (as the saying is) to improve his mind and finish his education. Those who never travel but in a post-chaise or berlin, will, doubtless, be astonished at the equipages used above; for we that strut upon this little mole hill are at a loss to conceive anything that surpasses our own customs. But our traveler was a wonderful adept in the laws of gravitation, together with the whole force of attraction and repulsion, and made such seasonable use of his knowledge, that sometimes by the help of a sunbeam, and sometimes by the convenience of a comet, he and his retinue glided from sphere to sphere, as the bird hops from one bough to another. He in a very little time posted through the milky way, and I am obliged to own he saw not a twinkle of those stars supposed to adorn that fair empyrean, which the illustrious Dr. Derham brags to have observed through his telescope. Not that I pretend to say the doctor was mistaken. God forbid! But Micromegas was upon the spot, an exceeding good observer, and I have no mind to contradict any man. Be that as it may, after many windings and turnings, he arrived at the planet Saturn; and, accustomed as he was to the sight of novelties, he could not for his life repress a supercilious and conceited smile, which often escapes the wisest philosopher, when he perceived the smallness of that globe, and the diminutive size of its inhabitants; for really Saturn is but about nine hundred times larger than this our earth, and the people of that country mere dwarfs, about a thousand fathoms high. In short, he at first derided those poor pigmies, just as an Indian fiddler laughs at the music of Lully, at his first arrival in Paris: but as this Sirian was a person of good sense, he soon perceived that a thinking being may not be altogether ridiculous, even though he is not quite six thousand feet high; and therefore he became familiar with them, after they had ceased to wonder at his extraordinary appearance. In particular, he contracted an intimate friendship with the secretary of the Academy of Saturn, a man of good understanding, who, though in truth he had invented nothing of his own, gave a very good account of the inventions of others, and enjoyed in peace the reputation of a little poet and great calculator. And here, for the edification of the reader, I will repeat a very singular conversation that one day passed between Mr. Secretary and Micromegas.

[1] The Gazettes record that this vessel ran ashore on the coast of Bothnia, when returning from the polar circle with a party of philosophers on board who had been making observations, for which nobody has hitherto been the wiser; but, according to this romance, the vessel was illegally captured in the Baltic sea by the Sirian giant Micromegas and the Saturnian dwarf.—E.

II.

THE CONVERSATION BETWEEN MICROMEGAS AND THE INHABITANT OF SATURN.

His excellency having laid himself down, and the secretary approached his nose:

"It must be confessed," said Micromegas, "that nature is full of variety."

"Yes," replied the Saturnian, "nature is like a parterre, whose flowers—"

"Pshaw!" cried the other, "a truce with your parterres."

"It is," resumed the secretary, "like an assembly of fair and brown women, whose dresses—"

"What a plague have I to do with your brunettes?" said our traveler.

"Then it is like a gallery of pictures, the strokes of which—"

"Not at all," answered Micromegas, "I tell you once for all, nature is like nature, and comparisons are odious."

"Well, to please you," said the secretary—

"I won't be pleased," replied the Sirian, "I want to be instructed; begin, therefore, without further preamble, and tell me how many senses the people of this world enjoy."

"We have seventy and two," said the academician, "but we are daily complaining of the small number, as our imagination transcends our wants, for, with the seventy-two senses, our five moons and ring, we find ourselves very much restricted; and notwithstanding our curiosity, and the no small number of those passions that result from these few senses, we have still time enough to be tired of idleness."

"I sincerely believe what you say," cried Micromegas "for, though we Sirians have near a thousand different senses, there still remains a certain vague desire, an unaccountable inquietude incessantly admonishing us of our own unimportance, and giving us to understand that there are other beings who are much our superiors in point of perfection. I have traveled a little, and seen mortals both above and below myself in the scale of being, but I have met with none who had not more desire than necessity, and more want than gratification. Perhaps I shall one day arrive in some country where nought is wanting, but hitherto I have had no certain information of such a happy land."

The Saturnian and his guest exhausted themselves in conjectures upon this subject, and after abundance of argumentation equally ingenious and uncertain, were fain to return to matter of fact.

"To what age do you commonly live?" said the Sirian.

"Lack-a-day! a mere trifle," replied the little gentleman.

"It is the very same case with us," resumed the other, "the shortness of life is our daily complaint, so that this must be an universal law in nature."

"Alas!" cried the Saturnian, "few, very few on this globe outlive five hundred great revolutions of the sun; (these, according to our way of reckoning, amount to about fifteen thousand years.) So, you see, we in a manner begin to die the very moment we are born: our existence is no more than a point, our duration an instant, and our globe an atom. Scarce do we begin to learn a little, when death intervenes before we can profit by experience. For my own part, I am deterred from laying schemes when I consider myself as a single drop in the midst of an immense ocean. I am particularly ashamed, in your presence, of the ridiculous figure I make among my fellow-creatures."

To this declaration, Micromegas replied.

"If you were not a philosopher, I should be afraid of mortifying your pride by telling you that the term of our lives is seven hundred times longer than the date of your existence: but you are very sensible that when the texture of the body is resolved, in order to reanimate nature in another form, which is the consequence of what we call death—when that moment of change arrives, there is not the least difference betwixt having lived a whole eternity, or a single day. I have been in some countries where the people live a thousand times longer than with us, and yet they murmured at the shortness of their time. But one will find every where some few persons of good sense, who know how to make the best of their portion, and thank the author of nature for his bounty. There is a profusion of variety scattered through the universe, and yet there is an admirable vein of uniformity that runs through the whole: for example, all thinking beings are different among themselves, though at bottom they resemble one another in the powers and passions of the soul. Matter, though interminable, hath different properties in every sphere. How many principal attributes do you reckon in the matter of this world?"

"If you mean those properties," said the Saturnian, "without which we believe this our globe could not subsist, we reckon in all three hundred, such as extent, impenetrability, motion, gravitation, divisibility, et cætera."

"That small number," replied the traveler, "probably answers the views of the creator on this your narrow sphere. I adore his wisdom in all his works.

I see infinite variety, but every where proportion. Your globe is small: so are the inhabitants. You have few sensations; because your matter is endued with few properties. These are the works of unerring providence. Of what color does your sun appear when accurately examined?"

"Of a yellowish white," answered the Saturnian, "and in separating one of his rays we find it contains seven colors."

"Our sun," said the Sirian, "is of a reddish hue, and we have no less than thirty-nine original colors. Among all the suns I have seen there is no sort of resemblance, and in this sphere of yours there is not one face like another."

After divers questions of this nature, he asked how many substances, essentially different, they counted in the world of Saturn; and understood that they numbered but thirty: such as God; space; matter; beings endowed with sense and extension; beings that have extension, sense, and reflection; thinking beings who have no extension; those that are penetrable; those that are impenetrable, and also all others. But this Saturnian philosopher was prodigiously astonished when the Sirian told him they had no less than three hundred, and that he himself had discovered three thousand more in the course of his travels. In short, after having communicated to each other what they knew, and even what they did not know, and argued during a complete revolution of the sun, they resolved to set out together on a small philosophical tour.

III.

THE VOYAGE OF THESE INHABITANTS OF OTHER WORLDS.

Our two philosophers were just ready to embark for the atmosphere of Saturn, with a large provision of mathematical instruments, when the Saturnian's mistress, having got an inkling of their design, came all in tears to make her protests. She was a handsome brunette, though not above six hundred and threescore fathoms high; but her agreeable attractions made amends for the smallness of her stature.

"Ah! cruel man," cried she, "after a courtship of fifteen hundred years, when at length I surrendered, and became your wife, and scarce have passed two hundred more in thy embraces, to leave me thus, before the honeymoon is over, and go a rambling with a giant of another world! Go, go, thou art a mere virtuoso, devoid of tenderness and love! If thou wert a true Saturnian, thou wouldst be faithful and invariable. Ah! whither art thou going? what is thy design? Our five moons are not so inconstant, nor our ring so changeable as thee! But take this along with thee, henceforth I ne'er shall love another man."

The little gentleman embraced and wept over her, notwithstanding his philosophy; and the lady, after having swooned with great decency, went to console herself with more agreeable company.

Meanwhile our two virtuosi set out, and at one jump leaped upon the ring, which they found pretty flat, according to the ingenious guess of an illustrious inhabitant of this our little earth. From thence they easily slipped from moon to moon; and a comet chancing to pass, they sprang upon it with all their servants and apparatus. Thus carried about one hundred and fifty million of leagues, they met with the satellites of Jupiter, and arrived upon the body of the planet itself, where they continued a whole year; during which they learned some very curious secrets, which would actually be sent to the press, were it not for fear of the gentlemen inquisitors, who have found among them some corollaries very hard of digestion. Nevertheless, I have read the manuscript in the library of the illustrious archbishop of —— who, with that generosity and goodness which should ever be commended, has granted me permission to peruse his books; wherefore I promise he shall have a long article in the next edition of Moreri, and I shall not forget the young gentlemen, his sons, who give us such pleasing hopes of seeing perpetuated the race of their illustrious father. But to return to our travelers. When they took leave of Jupiter, they traversed a space of about one hundred millions of leagues, and coasting along the planet Mars, which is well known to be five times smaller than our little earth, they descried two moons subservient to that orb, which have escaped the observation of all our astronomers. I know father Castel will write, and that pleasantly enough, against the existence of these two moons; but I entirely refer myself to those who reason by analogy. Those worthy philosophers are very sensible that Mars, which is at such a distance from the sun, must be in a very uncomfortable situation, without the benefit of a couple of moons. Be that as it may, our gentlemen found the planet so small, that they were afraid they should not find room to take a little repose; so that they pursued their journey like two travelers who despise the paltry accommodation of a village, and push forward to the next market town. But the Sirian and his companion soon repented of their delicacy, for they journeyed a long time without finding a resting place, till at length they discerned a small speck, which was the Earth. Coming from Jupiter, they could not but be moved with compassion at the sight of this miserable spot, upon which, however, they resolved to land, lest they should be a second time disappointed. They accordingly moved toward the tail of the comet, where, finding an Aurora Borealis ready to set sail, they embarked, and arrived on the northern coast of the Baltic on the fifth day of July, new style, in the year 1737.

IV.

WHAT BEFELL THEM UPON THIS OUR GLOBE.

Having taken some repose, and being desirous of reconnoitering the narrow field in which they were, they traversed it at once from north to south. Every step of the Sirian and his attendants measured about thirty thousand royal feet: whereas, the dwarf of Saturn, whose stature did not exceed a thousand fathoms, followed at a distance quite out of breath; because, for every single stride of his companion, he was obliged to make twelve good steps at least. The reader may figure to himself, (if we are allowed to make such comparisons,) a very little rough spaniel dodging after a captain of the Prussian grenadiers.

As those strangers walked at a good pace, they compassed the globe in six and thirty hours; the sun, it is true, or rather the earth, describes the same space in the course of one day; but it must be observed that it is much easier to turn upon an axis than to walk a-foot. Behold them then returned to the spot from whence they had set out, after having discovered that almost imperceptible sea, which is called the Mediterranean; and the other narrow pond that surrounds this mole-hill, under the denomination of the great ocean; in wading through which the dwarf had never wet his mid-leg, while the other scarce moistened his heel. In going and coming through both hemispheres, they did all that lay in their power to discover whether or not the globe was inhabited. They stooped, they lay down, they groped in every corner, but their eyes and hands were not at all proportioned to the small beings that crawl upon this earth; and, therefore, they could not find the smallest reason to suspect that we and our fellow-citizens of this globe had the honor to exist.

The dwarf, who sometimes judged too hastily, concluded at once that there was no living creatures upon earth; and his chief reason was, that he had seen nobody. But Micromegas, in a polite manner, made him sensible of the unjust conclusion:

"For," said he, "with your diminutive eyes you cannot see certain stars of the fiftieth magnitude, which I easily perceive; and do you take it for granted that no such stars exist?"

"But I have groped with great care?" replied the dwarf.

"Then your sense of feeling must be bad," said the other.

"But this globe," said the dwarf, "is ill contrived; and so irregular in its form as to be quite ridiculous. The whole together looks like a chaos. Do but observe these little rivulets; not one of them runs in a straight line; and these ponds which are neither round, square, nor oval, nor indeed of any regular figure, together with these little sharp pebbles, (meaning the mountains,) that roughen the whole surface of the globe, and have torn all the skin from my feet. Besides, pray take notice of the shape of the whole, how it flattens at the poles, and turns round the sun in an awkward oblique manner, so as that the polar circles cannot possibly be cultivated. Truly, what makes me believe there is no inhabitant on this sphere, is a full persuasion that no sensible being would live in such a disagreeable place."

"What then?" said Micromegas, "perhaps the beings that inhabit it come not under that denomination; but, to all appearance, it was not made for nothing. Everything here seems to you irregular; because you fetch all your comparisons from Jupiter or Saturn. Perhaps this is the very reason of the seeming confusion which you condemn; have I not told you, that in the course of my travels I have always met with variety?"

The Saturnian replied to all these arguments; and perhaps the dispute would have known no end, if Micromegas, in the heat of the contest, had not luckily broken the string of his diamond necklace, so that the jewels fell to the ground; they consisted of pretty small unequal karats, the largest of which weighed four hundred pounds, and the smallest fifty. The dwarf, in helping to pick them up, perceived, as they approached his eye, that every single diamond was cut in such a manner as to answer the purpose of an excellent microscope. He therefore took up a small one, about one hundred and sixty feet in diameter, and applied it to his eye, while Micromegas chose another of two thousand five hundred feet. Though they were of excellent powers, the observers could perceive nothing by their assistance, so they were altered and adjusted. At length, the inhabitant of Saturn discerned something almost imperceptible moving between two waves in the Baltic. This was no other than a whale, which, in a dexterous manner, he caught with his little finger, and, placing it on the nail of his thumb, showed it to the Syrian, who laughed heartily at the excessive smallness peculiar to the inhabitants of this our globe. The Saturnian, by this time convinced that our world was inhabited, began to imagine we had no other animals than whales; and being a mighty debater, he forthwith set about investigating the origin and motion of this small atom, curious to know whether or not it was furnished with ideas, judgment, and free will. Micromegas was very much perplexed upon this subject. He examined the animal with the most patient attention, and the result of his inquiry was, that he could see no reason to believe a soul was lodged in such a body. The two travelers were actually inclined to think there was no such thing as mind in this our habitation, when, by the help of their microscope, they perceived something as large as a whale floating upon the surface of the sea. It is well known that, at this period, a flight of philosophers were upon their return from the polar circle, where they had been making observations, for which nobody has hitherto been the wiser. The gazettes record, that their vessel ran ashore on the coast of Bothnia and that they with great difficulty saved their lives; but in this world one can never dive to the bottom of things. For my own part, I will ingenuously recount the transaction just as it happened, without any addition of my own; and this is no small effort in a modern historian.

V.

THE TRAVELERS CAPTURE A VESSEL.

Micromegas stretched out his hand gently toward the place where the object appeared, and advanced two fingers, which he instantly pulled back, for fear of being disappointed, then opening softly and shutting them all at once, he very dexterously seized the ship that contained those gentlemen, and placed it on his nail, avoiding too much pressure, which might have crushed the whole in pieces.

"This," said the Saturnian dwarf, "is a creature very different from the former."

Upon which the Sirian placing the supposed animal in the hollow of his hand, the passengers and crew, who believed themselves thrown by a hurricane upon some rock, began to put themselves in motion. The sailors having hoisted out some casks of wine, jumped after them into the hand of Micromegas: the mathematicians having secured their quadrants, sectors, and Lapland servants, went overboard at a different place, and made such a bustle in their descent, that the Sirian at length felt his fingers tickled by something that seemed to move. An iron bar chanced to penetrate about a foot deep into his forefinger; and from this prick he concluded that something had issued from the little animal he held in his hand; but at first he suspected nothing more: for the microscope, that scarce rendered a whale and a ship visible, had no effect upon an object so imperceptible as man.

I do not intend to shock the vanity of any person whatever; but here I am obliged to beg your people of importance to consider that, supposing the stature of a man to be about five feet, we mortals make just such a figure upon the earth, as an animal the sixty thousandth part of a foot in height, would exhibit upon a bowl ten feet in circumference. When you reflect upon a being who could hold this whole earth in the palm of his hand, and is provided with organs proportioned to those we possess, you will easily conceive that there must be a great variety of created substances;—and pray, what must such beings think of those battles by which a conqueror gains a small village, to lose it again in the sequel?

Micromegas captures a ship.

I do not at all doubt, but if some captain of grenadiers should chance to read this work, he would add two large feet at least to the caps of his company; but I assure him his labor will be in vain; for, do what he will, he and his soldiers will never be other than infinitely diminutive and inconsiderable.

What wonderful address must have been inherent in our Sirian philosopher, that enabled him to perceive those atoms of which we have been speaking. When Leuwenhoek and Hartsoecker observed the first rudiments of which we are formed, they did not make such an astonishing discovery. What pleasure, therefore, was the portion of Micromegas, in observing the motion of those little machines, in examining all their pranks, and following them in all their operations! With what joy did he put his microscope into his companion's hand; and with what transport did they both at once exclaim:

"I see them distinctly,—don't you see them carrying burdens, lying down and rising up again?"

So saying, their hands shook with eagerness to see, and apprehension to lose such uncommon objects. The Saturnian, making a sudden transition from the most cautious distrust to the most excessive credulity, imagined he saw them engaged in their devotions and cried aloud in astonishment.

Nevertheless, he was deceived by appearances: a case too common, whether we do or do not make use of microscopes.

VI.

WHAT HAPPENED IN THEIR INTERCOURSE WITH MEN.

Micromegas being a much better observer than the dwarf, perceived distinctly that those atoms spoke; and made the remark to his companion, who was so much ashamed of being mistaken in his first suggestion, that he would not believe such a puny species could possibly communicate their ideas: for, though he had the gift of tongues, as well as his companion, he could not hear those particles speak; and therefore supposed they had no language.

"Besides, how should such imperceptible beings have the organs of speech? and what in the name of Jove can they say to one another? In order to speak, they must have something like thought, and if they think, they must surely have something equivalent to a soul. Now, to attribute anything like a soul to such an insect species appears a mere absurdity."

"But just now," replied the Sirian, "you believed they were engaged in devotional exercises; and do you think this could be done without thinking, without using some sort of language, or at least some way of making themselves understood? Or do you suppose it is more difficult to advance an argument than to engage in physical exercise? For my own part, I look upon all faculties as alike mysterious."

"I will no longer venture to believe or deny," answered the dwarf. "In short I have no opinion at all, let us endeavor to examine these insects, and we will reason upon them afterward."

"With all my heart," said Micromegas, who, taking out a pair of scissors which he kept for paring his nails, cut off a paring from his thumb nail, of which he immediately formed a large kind of speaking trumpet, like a vast tunnel, and clapped the pipe to his ear: as the circumference of this machine included the ship and all the crew, the most feeble voice was conveyed along the circular fibres of the nail; so that, thanks to his industry, the philosopher could distinctly hear the buzzing of our insects that were below. In a few hours he distinguished articulate sounds, and at last plainly understood the French language. The dwarf heard the same, though with more difficulty.

The astonishment of our travelers increased every instant. They heard a nest of mites talk in a very sensible strain: and that *Lusus Naturæ?* seemed to them inexplicable. You need not doubt but the Sirian and his dwarf glowed with impatience to enter into conversation with such atoms. Micromegas being afraid that his voice, like thunder, would deafen and confound the mites, without being understood by them, saw the necessity of diminishing the sound; each, therefore, put into his mouth a sort of small toothpick, the slender end of which reached to the vessel. The Sirian setting the dwarf upon his knees, and the ship and crew upon his nail, held down his head and spoke softly. In fine, having taken these and a great many more precautions, he addressed himself to them in these words:

"O ye invisible insects, whom the hand of the Creator hath deigned to produce in the abyss of infinite littleness! I give praise to his goodness, in that he hath been pleased to disclose unto me those secrets that seemed to be impenetrable."

If ever there was such a thing as astonishment, it seized upon the people who heard this address, and who could not conceive from whence it proceeded. The chaplain of the ship repeated exorcisms, the sailors swore, and the philosophers formed a system; but, notwithstanding all their systems, they could not divine who the person was that spoke to them. Then the dwarf of Saturn, whose voice was softer than that of Micromegas, gave them briefly to understand what species of beings they had to do with. He related the particulars of their voyage from Saturn, made them acquainted with the rank and quality of Monsieur Micromegas; and, after having pitied their smallness, asked if they had always been in that miserable state so near akin to annihilation; and what their business was upon that globe which seemed to be the property of whales. He also desired to know if they were happy in their situation? if they were inspired with souls? and put a hundred questions of the like nature.

A certain mathematician on board, braver than the rest, and shocked to hear his soul called in question, planted his quadrant, and having taken two observations of this interlocutor, said: "You believe then, Mr., what's your name, that because you measure from head to foot a thousand fathoms—"

"A thousand fathoms!" cried the dwarf, "good heavens! How should he know the height of my stature? A thousand fathoms! My very dimensions to a hair. What, measured by a mite! This atom, forsooth, is a geometrician, and knows exactly how tall I am; while I, who can scarce perceive him through a microscope, am utterly ignorant of his extent!"

"Yes, I have taken your measure," answered the philosopher, "and I will now do the same by your tall companion."

The proposal was embraced: his excellency reclined upon his side; for, had he stood upright, his head would have reached too far above the clouds. Our mathematicians planted a tall tree near him, and then, by a series of triangles joined together, they discovered that the object of their observation was a strapping youth, exactly one hundred and twenty thousand royal feet in length. In consequence of this calculation, Micromegas uttered these words:

"I am now more than ever convinced that we ought to judge of nothing by its external magnitude. O God! who hast bestowed understanding upon such seemingly contemptible substances, thou canst with equal ease produce that which is infinitely small, as that which is incredibly great: and if it be possible, that among thy works there are beings still more diminutive than these, they may nevertheless, be endued with understanding superior to the intelligence of those stupendous animals I have seen in heaven, a single foot of whom is larger than this whole globe on which I have alighted."

One of the philosophers assured him that there were intelligent beings much smaller than men, and recounted not only Virgil's whole fable of the bees, but also described all that Swammerdam hath discovered, and Réaumur dissected. In a word, he informed him that there are animals which bear the same proportion to bees, that bees bear to man; the same as the Sirian himself compared to those vast beings whom he had mentioned; and as those huge animals are to other substances, before whom they would appear like so many particles of dust. Here the conversation became very interesting, and Micromegas proceeded in these words:

"O ye intelligent atoms, in whom the Supreme Being hath been pleased to manifest his omniscience and power, without all doubt your joys on this earth must be pure and exquisite: for, being unincumbered with matter, and, to all appearance, little else than soul, you must spend your lives in the delights of pleasure and reflection, which are the true enjoyments of a perfect spirit. True happiness I have no where found; but certainly here it dwells."

At this harangue all the philosophers shook their heads, and one among them, more candid than his brethren, frankly owned, that excepting a very small number of inhabitants who were very little esteemed by their fellows, all the rest were a parcel of knaves, fools, and miserable wretches.

"We have matter enough," said he, "to do abundance of mischief, if mischief comes from matter; and too much understanding, if evil flows from understanding. You must know, for example, that at this very moment, while I am speaking, there are one hundred thousand animals of our own species, covered with hats, slaying an equal number of their fellow-creatures, who wear turbans; at least they are either slaying or being slain; and this hath usually been the case all over the earth from time immemorial."

The Sirian, shuddering at this information, begged to know the cause of those horrible quarrels among such a puny race; and was given to understand that the subject of the dispute was a pitiful mole-hill [called Palestine,] no larger than his heel. Not that any one of those millions who cut one another's throats pretends to have the least claim to the smallest particle of that clod. The question is, whether it shall belong to a certain person who is known by the name of Sultan, or to another whom (for what reason I know not) they dignify with the appellation of Pope. Neither the one nor the other has seen or ever will see the pitiful corner in question; and probably none of these wretches, who so madly destroy each other, ever beheld the ruler on whose account they are so mercilessly sacrificed!

"Ah, miscreants!" cried the indignant Sirian, "such excess of desperate rage is beyond conception. I have a good mind to take two or three steps, and trample the whole nest of such ridiculous assassins under my feet."

"Don't give yourself the trouble," replied the philosopher, "they are industrious enough in procuring their own destruction. At the end of ten years the hundredth part of those wretches will not survive; for you must know that, though they should not draw a sword in the cause they have espoused, famine, fatigue, and intemperance, would sweep almost all of them from the face of the earth. Besides, the punishment should not be inflicted upon them, but upon those sedentary and slothful barbarians, who, from their palaces, give orders for murdering a million of men and then solemnly thank God for their success."

Our traveler was moved with compassion for the entire human race, in which he discovered such astonishing contrasts. "Since you are of the small number of the wise," said he, "and in all likelihood do not engage yourselves in the trade of murder for hire, be so good as to tell me your occupation."

"We anatomize flies," replied the philosopher, "we measure lines, we make calculations, we agree upon two or three points which we understand, and dispute upon two or three thousand that are beyond our comprehension."

"How far," said the Sirian, "do you reckon the distance between the great star of the constellation Gemini and that called Caniculæ?"

To this question all of them answered with one voice: "Thirty-two degrees and a half."

"And what is the distance from hence to the moon?"

"Sixty semi-diameters of the earth."

He then thought to puzzle them by asking the weight of the air; but they answered distinctly, that common air is about nine hundred times specifically lighter than an equal column of the lightest water, and nineteen hundred times lighter than current gold. The little dwarf of Saturn, astonished at their answers, was now tempted to believe those people sorcerers, who, but a quarter of an hour before, he would not allow were inspired with souls.

"Well," said Micromegas, "since you know so well what is without you, doubtless you are still more perfectly acquainted with that which is within. Tell me what is the soul, and how do your ideas originate?"

Here the philosophers spoke altogether as before; but each was of a different opinion. The eldest quoted Aristotle; another pronounced the name of Descartes; a third mentioned Mallebranche; a fourth Leibnitz; and a fifth Locke. An old peripatecian lifting up his voice, exclaimed with an air of confidence. "The soul is perfection and reason, having power to be such as it is, as Aristotle expressly declares, page 633, of the Louvre edition:

"Ἐντελεχεῖά τις ἐστι, καὶ λόγος τοῦ δύναμιν ἔχοντος τοιοῦδι εἶ ταῖ."

"I am not very well versed in Greek," said the giant.

"Nor I either," replied the philosophical mite.

"Why then do you quote that same Aristotle in Greek?" resumed the Sirian.

"Because," answered the other, "it is but reasonable we should quote what we do not comprehend in a language we do not understand."

Here the Cartesian interposing: "The soul," said he, "is a pure spirit or intelligence, which hath received before birth all the metaphysical ideas; but after that event it is obliged to go to school and learn anew the knowledge which it hath lost."

"So it was necessary," replied the animal of eight leagues, "that thy soul should be learned before birth, in order to be so ignorant when thou hast got a beard upon thy chin. But what dost thou understand by spirit?"

"I have no idea of it," said the philosopher, "indeed it is supposed to be immaterial."

"At least, thou knowest what matter is?" resumed the Sirian.

"Perfectly well," answered the other. "For example: that stone is gray, is of a certain figure, has three dimensions, specific weight, and divisibility."

"I want to know," said the giant, "what that object is, which, according to thy observation, hath a gray color, weight, and divisibility. Thou seest a few qualities, but dost thou know the nature of the thing itself?"

"Not I, truly," answered the Cartesian.

Upon which the Sirian admitted that he also was ignorant in regard to this subject. Then addressing himself to another sage, who stood upon his thumb, he asked "what is the soul? and what are her functions?"

"Nothing at all," replied this disciple of Mallebranche; "God hath made everything for my convenience. In him I see everything, by him I act; he is the universal agent, and I never meddle in his work."

"That is being a nonentity indeed," said the Sirian sage; and then, turning to a follower of Leibnitz, he exclaimed: "Hark ye, friend, what is thy opinion of the soul?"

"In my opinion," answered this metaphysician, "the soul is the hand that points at the hour, while my body does the office of the clock; or, if you please, the soul is the clock, and the body is the pointer; or again, my soul is the mirror of the universe, and my body the frame. All this is clear and uncontrovertible."

A little partisan of Locke who chanced to be present, being asked his opinion on the same subject, said: "I do not know by what power I think; but well I know that I should never have thought without the assistance of my senses. That there are immaterial and intelligent substances I do not at all doubt; but that it is impossible for God to communicate the faculty of thinking to matter, I doubt very much. I revere the eternal power, to which it would ill become me to prescribe bounds. I affirm nothing, and am contented to believe that many more things are possible than are usually thought so."

The Sirian smiled at this declaration, and did not look upon the author as the least sagacious of the company: and as for the dwarf of Saturn, he would have embraced this adherent of Locke, had it not been for the extreme disproportion in their respective sizes. But unluckily there was another animalcule in a square cap, who, taking the word from all his philosophical brethren, affirmed that he knew the whole secret, which was contained in the abridgment of St. Thomas. He surveyed the two celestial strangers from top to toe, and maintained to their faces that their persons, their fashions, their suns and their stars, were created solely for the use of man. At this wild assertion our two travelers were seized with a fit of that uncontrollable laughter, which (according to Homer) is the portion of the immortal gods: their bellies quivered, their shoulders rose and fell, and, during these convulsions, the vessel fell from the Sirian's nail into the Saturnian's pocket, where these worthy people searched for it a long time with great diligence. At length, having found the ship and set everything to rights again, the Sirian resumed the discourse with those diminutive mites, and promised to compose for them a choice book of philosophy which would demonstrate the very essence of things. Accordingly, before his departure, he made them a present of the book, which was brought to the Academy of Sciences at Paris, but when the old secretary came to open it he saw nothing but blank paper, upon which:—

"Ay, ay," said he, "this is just what I suspected."

THE WORLD AS IT GOES.

THE VISION OF BABOUC.

The spiritual rulers of Persepolis. [1]

Among the genii who preside over the empires of the earth, Ithuriel held one of the first ranks, and had the department of Upper Asia. He one morning descended into the abode of Babouc, the Scythian, who dwelt on the banks of the Oxus, and said to him:

"Babouc, the follies and vices of the Persians have drawn upon them our indignation. Yesterday an assembly of the genii of Upper Asia was held, to consider whether we would chastise Persepolis or destroy it entirely. Go to that city; examine everything; return and give me a faithful account; and, according to thy report, I will then determine whether to correct or extirpate the inhabitants."

"But, my lord," said Babouc with great humility, "I have never been in Persia, nor do I know a single person in that country."

"So much the better," said the angel, "thou wilt be the more impartial: thou hast received from heaven the spirit of discernment, to which I now add the power of inspiring confidence. Go, see, hear, observe, and fear nothing. Thou shalt everywhere meet with a favorable reception."

Babouc mounted his camel, and set out with his servants. After having traveled some days, he met, near the plains of Senaar, the Persian army, which was going to attack the forces of India. He first addressed himself to a soldier, whom he found at a distance from the main army, and asked him what was the occasion of the war?

"By all the gods," said the soldier, "I know nothing of the matter. It is none of my business. My trade is to kill and to be killed, to get a livelihood. It is of no consequence to me whom I serve. To-morrow, perhaps, I may go over to the Indian camp; for it is said that they give their soldiers nearly half a copper drachma a day more than we have in this cursed service of Persia. If thou desirest to know why we fight, speak to my captain."

Babouc, having given the soldier a small present, entered the camp. He soon became acquainted with the captain, and asked him the cause of the war.

"How canst thou imagine that I should know it?" said the captain, "or of what importance is it to me? I live about two hundred leagues from Persepolis: I hear that war is declared. I instantly leave my family, and, having nothing else to do, go, according to our custom, to make my fortune, or to fall by a glorious death."

"But are not thy companions," said Babouc, "a little better informed than thee?"

"No," said the officer, "there are none but our principal satraps that know the true cause of our cutting one another's throats."

Babouc, struck with astonishment, introduced himself to the generals, and soon became familiarly acquainted with them. At last one of them said:

"The cause of this war, which for twenty years past hath desolated Asia, sprang originally from a quarrel between a eunuch belonging to one of the concubines of the great king of Persia, and the clerk of a factory belonging to the great king of India. The dispute was about a claim which amounted nearly to the thirtieth part of a daric. Our first minister, and the representative of India, maintained the rights of their respective masters with becoming dignity. The dispute grew warm. Both parties sent into the field an army of a million of soldiers. This army must be recruited every year with upwards of four hundred thousand men. Massacres, burning of houses, ruin and devastation, are daily multiplied; the universe suffers; and their mutual animosity still continues. The first ministers of the two nations frequently protest that they have nothing in view but the happiness of mankind; and every protestation is attended with the destruction of a town, or the desolation of a province."

Next day, on a report being spread that peace was going to be concluded, the Persian and Indian generals made haste to come to an engagement. The battle was long and bloody. Babouc beheld every crime, and every abomination. He was witness to the arts and stratagems of the principal satraps, who did all that lay in their power to expose their general to the disgrace of a defeat. He saw officers killed by their own troops, and soldiers stabbing their already expiring comrades in order to strip them of a few bloody garments torn and covered with dirt. He entered the hospitals to which they were conveying the wounded, most of whom died through the inhuman negligence of those who were well paid by the king of Persia to assist these unhappy men.

"Are these men," cried Babouc, "or are they wild beasts? Ah! I plainly see that Persepolis will be destroyed."

Full of this thought, he went over to the camp of the Indians, where, according to the prediction of the genii, he was as well received as in that of the Persians; but he saw there the same crimes which had already filled him with horror.

"Oh!" said he to himself, "if the angel Ithuriel should exterminate the Persians, the angel of India must certainly destroy the Indians."

But being afterward more particularly informed of all that passed in both armies, he heard of such acts of generosity, humanity, and greatness of soul, as at once surprised and charmed him:

"Unaccountable mortals! as ye are," cried he, "how can you thus unite so much baseness and so much grandeur, so many virtues and so many vices?"

Meanwhile the peace was proclaimed; and the generals of the two armies, neither of whom had gained a complete victory, but who, for their own private interest, had shed the blood of so many of their fellow-creatures, went to solicit their courts for rewards. The peace was celebrated in public writings which announced the return of virtue and happiness to the earth.

"God be praised," said Babouc, "Persepolis will now be the abode of spotless innocence, and will not be destroyed, as the cruel genii intended. Let us haste without delay to the capital of Asia."

He entered that immense city by the ancient gate, which was entirely barbarous, and offended the eye by its disagreeable rusticity. All that part of the town savored of the time when it was built; for, notwithstanding the obstinacy of men in praising ancient at the expense of modern times, it must be owned that the first essays in every art are rude and unfinished.

Babouc mingled in a crowd of people composed of the most ignorant, dirty and deformed of both sexes, who were thronging with a stupid air into a large and gloomy inclosure. By the constant hum; by the gestures of the people; by the money which some persons gave to others for the liberty of sitting down, he imagined that he was in a market, where chairs were sold: but observing several women fall down on their knees with an appearance of looking directly before them, while in reality they were leering at the men by their sides, he was soon convinced that he was in a temple. Shrill, hoarse, savage and discordant voices made the vault re-echo with ill articulated sounds, that produced the same effect as the braying of asses, when, in the plains of Pictavia, they answer the cornet that calls them together. He stopped his ears; but he was ready to shut his mouth and hold his nose, when he saw several laborers enter into the temple with picks and spades, who removed a large stone, and threw up the earth on both sides, from whence exhaled a pestilential vapor. At last some others approached, deposited a dead body in the opening, and replaced the stone upon it.

"What!" cried Babouc, "do these people bury their dead in the place where they adore the deity? What! are their temples paved with carcasses? I am no longer surprised at those pestilential diseases that frequently depopulate Persepolis. The putrefaction of the dead, and the infected breath of such numbers of the living, assembled and crowded together in the same place, are sufficient to poison the whole terrestial globe. Oh! what an abominable city is Persepolis! The angels probably intend to destroy it in order to build a more beautiful one in its place, and to people it with inhabitants who are more virtuous and better singers. Providence may have its reasons for so doing; to its disposal let us leave all future events."

Burying the dead in churches.—"*What!*" cried Babouc, "*do these people bury their dead in the place where they adore the deity? What! are their temples paved with carcasses?*"

Meanwhile the sun approached his meridian height. Babouc was to dine at the other end of the city with a lady for whom her husband, an officer in the army, had given him some letters: but he first took several turns in Persepolis, where he saw other temples, better built and more richly adorned, filled with a polite audience, and resounding with harmonious music. He beheld public fountains, which, though ill-placed, struck the eye by their beauty; squares where the best kings that had governed Persia seemed to breathe in bronze, and others where he heard the people crying out:

"When shall we see our beloved master?"

He admired the magnificent bridges built over the river; the superb and commodious quays; the palaces raised on both sides; and an immense house, where thousands of old soldiers, covered with scars and crowned with victory, offered their daily praises to the god of armies. At last he entered the house of the lady, who, with a set of fashionable people, waited his company to dinner. The house was neat and elegant; the repast delicious; the lady young, beautiful, witty, and engaging; and the company worthy of her; and Babouc every moment said to himself:

"The angel Ithuriel has little regard for the world, or he would never think of destroying such a charming city."

In the meantime he observed that the lady, who had begun by tenderly asking news about her husband, spoke more tenderly to a young magi, toward the conclusion of the repast. He saw a magistrate, who, in presence of his wife, paid his court with great vivacity to a widow, while the indulgent widow held out her hand to a young citizen, remarkable for his modesty and graceful appearance.

Babouc then began to fear that the genius Ithuriel had but too much reason for destroying Persepolis. The talent he possessed of gaining confidence let him that same day into all the secrets of the lady. She confessed to him her affection for the young magi, and assured him that in all the houses in Persepolis he would meet with similar examples of attachment. Babouc concluded that such a society could not possibly survive: that jealousy, discord, and vengeance must desolate every house; that tears and blood must be daily shed; and, *in fine*, that Ithuriel would do well to destroy immediately a city abandoned to continual disasters.

Such were the gloomy ideas that possessed his mind, when a grave man in a black gown appeared at the gate and humbly begged to speak to the young magistrate. Phis stripling, without rising or taking the least notice of the old gentleman, gave him some papers with a haughty and careless air, and then dismissed him. Babouc asked who this man was. The mistress of the house said to him in a low voice:

"He is one of the best advocates in the city, and hath studied the law these fifty years. The other, who is but twenty-five years of age, and has only been a satrap of the law for two days, hath ordered him to make an extract of a process he is going to determine, though he has not as yet examined it."

"This giddy youth acts wisely," said Babouc, "in asking counsel of an old man. But why is not the old man himself the judge?"

"Thou art surely in jest," said they; "those who have grown old in laborious and inferior posts are never raised to places of dignity. This young man has a great post, because his father is rich; and the right of dispensing justice is purchased here like a farm."

"O unhappy city!" cried Babouc, "this is surely the height of anarchy and confusion. Those who have thus purchased the right of judging will doubtless sell their judgments; nothing do I see here but an abyss of iniquity!"

While he was thus expressing his grief and surprise, a young warrior, who that very day had returned from the army, said to him:

"Why wouldst thou not have seats in the courts of justice offered for sale? I myself purchased the right of braving death at the head of two thousand men who are under my command. It has this year cost me forty daracs of gold to lie on the earth thirty nights successively in a red dress, and at last to receive two wounds with an arrow, of which I still feel the smart. If I ruin myself to serve the emperor of Persia, whom I never saw, the satrap of the law may well pay something for enjoying the pleasure of giving audience to pleaders."

Babouc was filled with indignation, and could not help condemning a country, where the highest posts in the army and the law were exposed for sale. He at once concluded that the inhabitants must be entirely ignorant of the art of war, and the laws of equity; and that, though Ithuriel should not destroy them, they must soon be ruined by their detestable administration.

He was still further confirmed in his bad opinion by the arrival of a fat man, who, after saluting all the company with great familiarity, went up to the young officer and said:

"I can only lend thee fifty thousand darics of gold; for indeed the taxes of the empire have this year brought me in but three hundred thousand."

Babouc inquired into the character of this man who complained of having gained so little, and was informed that in Persepolis there were forty plebian kings who held the empire of Persia by lease, and paid a small tribute to the monarch.

After dinner he went into one of the most superb temples in the city, and seated himself amidst a crowd of men and women, who had come thither to pass away the time. A magi appeared in a machine elevated above the heads of the people, and talked a long time of vice and virtue. He divided into several parts what needed no division at all: he proved methodically what was sufficiently clear, and he taught what everybody knew. He threw himself into a passion with great composure, and went away perspiring and out of breath. The assembly then awoke and imagined they had been present at a very instructive discourse. Babouc said:

"This man had done his best to tire two or three hundred of his fellow-citizens; but his intention was good, and there is nothing in this that should occasion the destruction of Persepolis."

Upon leaving the assembly he was conducted to a public entertainment, which was exhibited every day in the year. It was in a kind of great hall, at the end of which appeared a palace. The most beautiful women of Persepolis and the most considerable satraps were ranged in order, and formed so fine a spectacle that Babouc at first believed that this was all the entertainment. Two or three persons, who seemed to be kings and queens, soon appeared in the vestibule of their palace. Their language was very different from that of the people; it was measured, harmonious, and sublime. Nobody slept. The audience kept a profound silence which was only interrupted by expressions of sensibility and admiration. The duty of kings, the love of virtue, and the dangers arising from unbridled passions, were all described by such lively and affecting strokes, that Babouc shed tears. He doubted not but that these heroes and heroines, these kings and queens whom he had just heard, were the preachers of the empire; he even purposed to engage Ithuriel to come and hear them, being content that such a spectacle would forever reconcile him to the city.

As soon as the entertainment was finished, he resolved to visit the principal queen, who had recommended such pure and noble morals in the palace. He desired to be introduced to her majesty, and was led up a narrow staircase to an ill-furnished apartment in the second story, where he found a woman in a mean dress, who said to him with a noble and pathetic air:

"This employment does not afford me a sufficient maintenance. I want money, and without money there is no comfort."

Babouc gave her an hundred darics of gold, saying:

"Had there been no other evil in the city but this, Ithuriel would have been to blame for being so much offended."

From thence he went to spend the evening at the house of a tradesman who dealt in magnificent trifles. He was conducted thither by a man of sense, with whom he had contracted an acquaintance. He bought whatever pleased his fancy; and the toy man with great politeness sold him everything for more than it was worth. On his return home his friends showed him how much he had been cheated. Babouc set down the name of the tradesman in his pocket-book, in order to point him out to Ithuriel as an object of peculiar vengeance on the day when the city should be punished. As he was writing, he heard somebody knock at the door: this was the toy man himself, who came to restore him his purse, which he had left by mistake on the counter.

"How canst thou," cried Babouc, "be so generous and faithful, when thou hast had the assurance to sell me these trifles for four times their value?"

"There is not a tradesman," replied the merchant, "of ever so little note in the city, that would not have returned thee thy purse; but whoever said that I sold thee these trifles for four times their value is greatly mistaken: I sold them for ten times their value; and this is so true, that wert thou to sell them again in a month hence, thou wouldst not get even this tenth part. But nothing is more just. It is the variable fancies of men that set a value on these baubles; it is this fancy that maintains an hundred workmen whom I employ; it is this that gives me a fine house and a handsome chariot and horses; it is this, in fine, that excites industry, encourages taste, promotes circulation, and produces abundance.

"I sell the same trifles to the neighboring nation at a much higher rate than I have sold them to thee, and by these means I am useful to the empire."

Babouc, after having reflected a moment, erased the tradesman's name from his tablets.

Babouc, not knowing as yet what to think of Persepolis, resolved to visit the magi and the men of letters; for, as the one studied wisdom and the other religion, he hoped that they in conjunction would obtain mercy for the rest of the people. Accordingly, he went next morning into a college of magi. The archimandrite confessed to him, that he had an hundred thousand crowns a year for having taken the vow of poverty, and that he enjoyed a very extensive empire in virtue of his vow of humility; after which he left him with an inferior brother, who did him the honors of the place.

While the brother was showing him the magnificence of this house of penitence, a report was spread abroad that Babouc was come to reform all these houses. He immediately received petitions from each of them, the substance of which was, "Preserve us and destroy all the rest." On hearing their apologies, all these societies were absolutely necessary: on hearing their mutual accusations, they all deserved to be abolished. He was surprised to find that all the members of these societies were so extremely desirous of edifying the world, that they wished to have it entirely under their dominion.

Soon after a little man appeared, who was a demi-magi, and who said to him:

"I plainly see that the work is going to be accomplished: for Zerdust is returned to earth; and the little girls prophecy, pinching and whipping themselves. We therefore implore thy protection against the great lama."

"What!" said Babouc, "against the royal pontiff, who resides at Tibet?"

"Yes, against him, himself."

"What! you are then making war upon him, and raising armies!"

"No, but he says that man is a free agent, and we deny it. We have written several pamphlets against him, which he never read. Hardly has he heard our name mentioned. He has only condemned us in the same manner as a man orders the trees in his garden to be cleared from caterpillars."

Babouc was incensed at the folly of these men who made profession of wisdom; and at the intrigues of those who had renounced the world; and at the ambition, pride and avarice of such as taught humility and a disinterested spirit: from all which he concluded that Ithuriel had good reason to destroy the whole race.

On his return home, he sent for some new books to alleviate his grief, and in order to exhilarate his spirits, invited some men of letters to dine with him; when, like wasps attracted by a pot of honey, there came twice as many as he desired. These parasites were equally eager to eat and to speak; they praised two sorts of persons, the dead and themselves; but none of their contemporaries, except the master of the house. If any of them happened to drop a smart and witty expression, the rest cast down their eyes and bit their lips out of mere vexation that it had not been said by themselves. They had less dissimulation than the magi, because they had not such grand objects of ambition. Each of them behaved at once with all the meanness of a valet and all the dignity of a great man. They said to each other's face the most insulting things, which they took for strokes of wit. They had some knowledge of the design of Babouc's commission; one of them entreated him in a low voice to extirpate an author who had not praised him sufficiently about five years before; another requested the ruin of a citizen who had never laughed at his comedies; and the third demanded the destruction of the academy because he had not been able to get admitted into it. The repast being ended, each of them departed by himself; for in the whole crowd there were not two men that could endure the company or conversation of each other, except at the houses of the rich, who invited them to their tables. Babouc thought that it would be no great loss to the public if all these vermin were destroyed in the general catastrophe.

Having now got rid of these men of letters, he began to read some new books, where he discovered the true spirit by which his guests had been actuated. He observed with particular indignation those slanderous gazettes, those archives of bad taste, dictated by envy, baseness, and hunger; those ungenerous satires, where the vulture is treated with lenity, and the dove torn in pieces; and those dry and insipid romances, filled with characters of women to whom the author was an utter stranger.

All these detestable writings he committed to the flames, and went to pass the evening in walking. In this excursion he was introduced to an old man possessed of great learning, who had not come to increase the number of his parasites. This man of letters always fled from crowds; he understood human nature, availed himself of his knowledge, and imparted it to others with great discretion. Babouc told him how much he was grieved at what he had seen and read.

"Thou hast read very despicable performances," said the man of letters; "but in all times, in all countries, and in all kinds of literature, the bad swarm and the good are rare. Thou hast received into thy house the very dregs of pedantry. In all professions, those who are least worthy of appearing are always sure to present themselves with the greatest impudence. The truly wise live among themselves in retirement and tranquillity; and we have still some men and some books worthy of thy attention."

While he was thus speaking, they were joined by another man of letters; and the conversation became so entertaining and instructive, so elevated above vulgar prejudices, and so conformable to virtue, that Babouc acknowledged he had never heard the like.

"These are men," said he to himself, "whom the angel Ithuriel will not presume to touch, or he must be a merciless being indeed."

Though reconciled to men of letters, he was still enraged against the rest of the nation.

"Thou art a stranger," said the judicious person who was talking to him; "abuses present themselves to thy eyes in crowds, while the good, which lies concealed, and which is even sometimes the result of these very abuses, escapes thy observation."

He then learned that among men of letters there were some who were free from envy; and that even among the magi themselves there were some men of virtue. In fine, he concluded that these great bodies, which by their mutual shocks seemed to threaten their common ruin, were at bottom very salutary institutions; that each society of magi was a check upon its rivals; and that though these rivals might differ in some speculative points, they all taught the same morals, instructed the people, and lived in subjection to the laws; not unlike to those preceptors who watch over the heir of a family while the master of the house watches over them. He conversed with several of these magi, and found them possessed of exalted souls. He likewise learned that even among the fools who pretended to make war on the great lama there had been some men of distinguished merit; and from all these particulars he conjectured that it might be with the manners of Persepolis as it was with the buildings; some of which moved his pity, while others filled him with admiration.

He said to the man of letters:

"I plainly see that these magi, whom I at first imagined to be so dangerous, are in reality extremely useful; especially when a wise government hinders them from rendering themselves too necessary; but thou wilt at least acknowledge that your young magistrates, who purchase the office of a judge as soon as they can mount a horse, must display in their tribunals the most ridiculous impertinence and the most iniquitous perverseness. It would doubtless be better to give these places gratuitously to those old civilians who have spent their lives in the study of the law."

The man of letters replied:

"Thou hast seen our army before thy arrival at Persepolis; thou knowest that our young officers fight with great bravery, though they buy their posts; perhaps thou wilt find that our young magistrates do not give wrong decisions, though they purchase the right of dispensing justice."

He led him next day to the grand tribunal, where an affair of great importance was to be decided. The cause was known to all the world. All the old advocates that spoke on the subject were wavering and unsettled in their opinions. They quoted an hundred laws, none of which were applicable to the question. They considered the matter in a hundred different lights, but never in its true point of view. The judges were more quick in their decisions than the advocates in raising doubts. They were unanimous in their sentiments. They decided justly, because they followed the light of reason. The others reasoned falsely because they only consulted their books.

Babouc concluded that the best things frequently arose from abuses. He saw the same day that the riches of the receivers of the public revenue, at which he had been so much offended, were capable of producing an excellent effect; for the emperor having occasion for money, he found in an hour by their means what he could not have procured in six months by the ordinary methods. He saw that those great clouds, swelled with the dews of the earth, restored in plentiful showers what they had thence derived. Besides, the children of these new gentlemen, who were frequently better educated than those of the most ancient families, were sometimes more useful members of society; for he whose father hath been a good accountant may easily become a good judge, a brave warrior, and an able statesman.

Babouc was insensibly brought to excuse the avarice of the farmer of the revenues, who in reality was not more avaricious than other men, and besides was extremely necessary. He overlooked the folly of those who ruined themselves in order to obtain a post in the law or army; a folly that produces great magistrates and heroes. He forgave the envy of men of letters, among whom there were some that enlightened the world; and he was reconciled to the ambitious and intriguing magi, who were possessed of more great virtues than little vices. But he had still many causes of complaint. The gallantries of the ladies especially, and the fatal effects which these must necessarily produce, filled him with fear and terror.

As he was desirous of prying into the characters of men of every condition, he went to wait on a minister of state; but trembled all the way, lest some wife should be assassinated by her husband in his presence. Having arrived at the statesman's, he was obliged to remain two hours in the anti-chamber before his name was sent in, and two hours more after that was done. In this interval, he resolved to recommend to the angel Ithuriel both the minister and his insolent porters. The anti-chamber was filled with ladies of every rank, magi of all colors, judges, merchants, officers, and pedants, and all of them complained of the minister. The miser and the usurer said:

"Doubtless this man plunders the provinces."

The capricious reproached him with fickleness; the voluptuary said:

"He thinks of nothing but his pleasure."

The factious hoped to see him soon ruined by a cabal; and the women flattered themselves that they should soon have a younger minister.

Babouc heard their conversation, and could not help saying:

"This is surely a happy man; he hath all his enemies in his anti-chamber; he crushes with his power those that envy his grandeur; he beholds those who detest him groveling at his feet."

At length he was admitted into the presence-chamber, where he saw a little old man bending under the weight of years and business, but still lively and full of spirits.

The minister was pleased with Babouc, and to Babouc he appeared a man of great merit. The conversation became interesting. The minister confessed that he was very unhappy; that he passed for rich, while in reality he was poor; that he was believed to be all-powerful, and yet was constantly contradicted; that he had obliged none but a parcel of ungrateful wretches; and that, in the course of forty years labor, he had hardly enjoyed a moment's rest. Babouc was moved with his misfortunes; and thought that if this man had been guilty of some faults, and Ithuriel had a mind to banish him, he ought not to cut him off, but to leave him in possession of his place.

While Babouc was talking to the minister, the beautiful lady with whom he had dined entered hastily, her eyes and countenance showing all the symptoms of grief and indignation. She burst into reproaches against the statesman; she shed tears; she complained bitterly that her husband had been refused a place to which his birth allowed him to aspire, and which he had fully merited by his wounds and his service. She expressed herself with such force; she uttered her complaints with such a graceful air; she overthrew objections with so much address, and enforced her arguments with so much eloquence, that she did not leave the chamber till she had made her husband's fortune.

Babouc gave her his hand, and said: "Is it possible, madam, that thou canst take so much pains to serve a man whom thou dost not love, and from whom thou hast everything to fear?"

"A man whom I do not love!" cried she "know, sir, that my husband is the best friend I have in the world; and there is nothing I would not sacrifice for him, except my own inclinations."

The lady conducted Babouc to her own house. The husband, who had at last arrived overwhelmed with grief, received his wife with transports of joy and gratitude. He embraced by turns his wife, the little magi, and Babouc. Wit, harmony, cheerfulness, and all the graces, embellished the repast.

Babouc, though a Scythian, and sent by a geni, found, that should he continue much longer in Persepolis, he would forget even the angel Ithuriel. He began to grow fond of a city, the inhabitants of which were polite, affable, and beneficent, though fickle, slanderous, and vain. He was much afraid that Persepolis would be condemned. He was even afraid to give in his account.

This, however, he did in the following manner. He caused a little statue, composed of different metals, of earth, and stones, the most precious and the most vile, to be cast by one of the best founders in the city, and carried it to Ithuriel.

"Wilt thou break," said he, "this pretty statue, because it is not wholly composed of gold and diamonds?"

Ithuriel immediately understood his meaning, and resolved to think no more of punishing Persepolis, but to leave "The world as it goes."

"For," said he, "if all is not well, all is passable."

Thus Persepolis was suffered to remain; nor did Babouc complain like Jonas, who, [according to the scriptures,] was highly incensed at the preservation of Nineveh.

[1] When Babouc visited the college of the magi, "the archimandrite [the chief of the monks] confessed to him, that he had an hundred thousand crowns a year for having taken the vow of poverty, and that he enjoyed a very extensive empire in virtue of his vow of humility." (See page 365.)—E.

THE BLACK AND THE WHITE.

Procession of Souls to Judgment with Good and Evil Genii. From Frieze in the Grotto del Cardinale.

The adventure of the youthful Rustan is generally known throughout the whole province of Candahar. He was the only son of a Mirza of that country. The title of Mirza there is much the same as that of Marquis among us, or that of Baron among the Germans. The mirza, his father, had a handsome fortune. Young Rustan was to be married to a mirzasse, or young lady of his own rank. The two families earnestly desired their union. Rustan was to become the comfort of his parents, to make his wife happy, and to live blest in her possession.

But he had unfortunately seen the princess of Cachemire at the fair of Kaboul, which is the most considerable fair in the world, and much more frequented than those of Bassora and Astracan. The occasion that brought the old prince of Cachemire to the fair with his daughter was as follows:

He had lost the two most precious curiosities of his treasury; one of them was a diamond as thick as a man's thumb, upon which the figure of his daughter was engraved by an art which was then possessed by the Indians, and has since been lost; the other was a javelin, which went of itself wherever its owner thought proper to send it. This is nothing very extraordinary among us, but it was thought so at Cachemire.

A fakir belonging to his highness stole these two curiosities; he carried them to the princess:

"Keep these two curiosities with the utmost care; your destiny depends upon them;" said he, and then departed.

The Duke of Cachemire, in despair, resolved to visit the fair of Kaboul, in order to see whether there might not, among the merchants who go thither from all quarters of the world, be some one possessed of his diamond and his weapon. The princess carried his diamond well fastened to her girdle; but the javelin, which she could not so easily hide, she had carefully locked up at Cachemire, in a large chest.

Rustan and she saw each other at Kaboul. They loved one another with all the sincerity of persons of their age, and all the tenderness of affection natural to those of their country. The princess gave Rustan her diamond as a pledge of her love, and he promised at his departure to go incognito to Cachemire, in order to pay her a visit.

The young mirza had two favorites, who served him as secretaries, grooms, stewards, and valets de chambre. The name of one was Topaz; he was handsome, well-shaped, fair as a Circassian beauty, as mild and ready to serve as an Armenian, and as wise as a Gueber. The name of the other was Ebene; he was a very beautiful negro, more active and industrious than Topaz, and one that thought nothing difficult. The young mirza communicated his intention of traveling to these. Topaz endeavored to dissuade him from it, with the circumspect zeal of a servant who was unwilling to offend him. He represented to him the great danger to which he exposed himself. He asked him how he could leave two families in despair? how he could pierce the hearts of his parents? He shook the resolution of Rustan; but Ebene confirmed it anew, and obviated all his objections.

The young man was not furnished with money to defray the charge of so long a voyage. The prudent Topaz would not have lent him any; Ebene supplied him. He with great address stole his master's diamond, made a false one exactly like it which he put in its place, and pledged the true one to an Armenian for several thousand rupees.

As soon as the marquis possessed these rupees, all things were in readiness for his departure. An elephant was loaded with his baggage. His attendants mounted on horseback.

Topaz said to his master: "I have taken the liberty to expostulate with you upon your enterprise, but after expostulating it is my duty to obey. I am devoted to you, I love you, I will follow you to the extremity of the earth; but let us by the way consult the oracle that is but two parasongs distant from here."

Rustan consented. The answer returned by the oracle, was:

"If you go to the east you will be at the west."

Rustan could not guess the meaning of this answer. Topaz maintained that it boded no good. Ebene, always complaisant to his master, persuaded him that it was highly favorable.

There was another oracle at Kaboul; they went to it. The oracle of Kaboul made answer in these words:

"If you possess, you will cease to possess; if you are conqueror, you will not conquer, if you are Rustan, you will cease to be so."

This oracle seemed still more unintelligible than the former.

"Take care of yourself," said Topaz.

"Fear nothing," said Ebene; and this minister, as may well be imagined, was always thought in the right by his master, whose passions and hopes he encouraged. Having left Kaboul, they passed through a vast forest. They seated themselves upon the grass in order to take a repast, and left their horses grazing. The attendants were preparing to unload the elephant which carried the dinner, the table, cloth, plates, &c., when, all on a sudden, Topaz and Ebene were perceived by the little caravan to be missing. They were called, the forest resounded with the names of Topaz and Ebene; the lackeys seek them on every side, and fill the forest with their cries; they return without having seen anything, and without having received any answer.

"We have," said they to Rustan, "found nothing but a vulture that fought with an eagle, and stripped it of all its feathers."

The mention of this combat excited the curiosity of Rustan; he went on foot to the place; he perceived neither vulture nor eagle; but he saw his elephant, which was still loaded with baggage, attacked by a huge rhinoceros: one struck with its horn, the other with its proboscis. The rhinoceros desisted upon seeing Rustan; his elephant was brought back, but his horses were not to be found.

"Strange things happen in forests to travelers," cried Rustan.

The servants were in great consternation, and the master in despair from having at once lost his horse, his dear negro, and the wise Topaz, for whom he still entertained a friendship, though always differing from him in opinion.

The hope of being soon at the feet of the beautiful princess still consoled the mirza, who, journeying on, now met with a huge streaked ass, which a vigorous two-handed country clown beat with an oaken cudgel. The asses of this sort are extremely beautiful, very scarce, and beyond comparison swift in running. The ass resented the repeated blows of the clown by kicks which might have rooted up an oak. The young mirza, as was reasonable, took upon him the defence of the ass, which was a charming creature, the clown betook himself to flight, crying to the ass, "You shall pay for this."

The ass thanked her deliverer in her own language, and approaching him, permitted his caresses and caressed him in her turn. After dinner, Rustan mounted her, and took the road to Cachemire with his servants, who followed him, some on foot and some upon the elephant. Scarce had he mounted his ass, when that animal turned toward Kaboul, instead of proceeding to Cachemire. It was to no purpose for her master to turn the bridle, to kick, to press the sides of the beast with his knees, to spur, to slacken the bridle, to pull toward him, to whip both on the right and the left. The obstinate animal persisted in running toward Kaboul.

Rustan in despair fretted and raved, when he met with a dealer in camels, who said to him:

"Master, you have there a very malicious beast, that carries you where you do not choose to go. If you will give it to me, I will give you the choice of four of my camels."

Rustan thanked providence for having thrown so good a bargain in the way.

"Topaz was very much in the wrong," said he, "to tell me that my journey would prove unprosperous."

He mounts the handsome camel, the others follow; he rejoins his caravan and fancies himself on the road to happiness.

Scarce had he journeyed four parasongs, when he was stopped by a deep, broad, and impetuous torrent, which rolled over huge rocks white with foam. The two banks were frightful precipices which dazzled the sight and made the blood run cold. To pass was impracticable; to go to the right or to the left was impossible.

"I am beginning to be afraid," said Rustan, "that Topaz was in the right in blaming my journey, and that I was in the wrong in undertaking it. If he were still here he might give me good advice. If I had Ebene with me, he would comfort me and find expedients; but everything fails me."

This perplexity was increased by the consternation of his attendants. The night was dark, and they passed it in lamentations. At last fatigue and dejection made the amorous traveler fall asleep. He awoke at day-break, and saw, spanning the torrent, a beautiful marble bridge which reached from shore to shore.

Nothing was heard but exclamations, cries of astonishment and joy. Is it possible? Is this a dream? What a prodigy is this! What an enchantment! Shall we venture to pass? The whole company kneeled, rose up, went to the bridge, kissed the ground, looked up to heaven, stretched out their hands, set their feet on it with trembling, went to and fro, fell into ecstasies; and Rustan said:

"At last heaven favors me. Topaz did not know what he was saying. The oracles were favorable to me. Ebene was in the right, but why is he not here?"

Scarce had the company got beyond the torrent, when the bridge sunk into the water with a prodigious noise.

"So much the better, so much the better," cried Rustan. "Praised be God, blessed be heaven; it would not have me return to my country, where I should be nothing more than a gentleman. The intention of heaven is, that I should wed her I love. I shall become prince of Cachemire; thus in possessing my mistress I shall cease to possess my little marquisate at Candahar. 'I shall be Rustan, and I shall not be Rustan,' because I shall have become a great prince: thus is a great part of the oracle clearly explained in my favor. The rest will be explained in the same manner. I am very happy. But why is not Ebene with me? I regret him a thousand times more than Topaz."

He proceeded a few parasongs farther with the greatest alacrity imaginable; but, at the close of day, a chain of mountains more rugged than a counterscarp, and higher than the tower of Babel would have been had it been finished, stopped the passage of the caravan, which was again seized with dread.

All the company cried out: "It is the will of God that we perish here! he broke the bridge merely to take from us all hopes of returning; he raised the mountain for no other reason than to deprive us of all means of advancing. Oh, Rustan! oh, unhappy marquis! we shall never see Cachemire; we shall never return to the land of Candahar."

The most poignant anguish, the most insupportable dejection, succeeded in the soul of Rustan, to the immoderate joy which he had felt, to the hopes with which he had intoxicated himself. He was no longer disposed to interpret the prophecies in his favor.

"Oh, heavens! oh, God of my fathers!" said he, "must I then lose my friend Topaz!"

As he pronounced these words, fetching deep sighs and shedding tears in the midst of his disconsolate followers, the base of the mountain opened, a long gallery appeared to the dazzled eyes in a vault lighted with a hundred thousand torches. Rustan immediately begins to exult, and his people to throw themselves upon their knees and to fall upon their backs in astonishment, and cry out, "A miracle! a miracle! Rustan is the favorite of Witsnow, the well-beloved of Brahma. He will become the master of mankind."

Rustan believed it; he was quite beside himself; he was raised above himself.

"Alas, Ebene," said he, "my dear Ebene, where are you? Why are you not witness of all these wonders? How did I lose you? Beauteous princess of Cachemire, when shall I again behold your charms!"

He advances with his attendants, his elephants, and his camels, under the hollow of the mountain; at the end of which he enters into a meadow enameled with flowers and encompassed with rivulets. At the extremity of the meadows are walks of trees to the end of which the eye cannot reach, and at the end of these alleys is a river, on the sides of which are a thousand pleasure houses with delicious gardens. He everywhere hears concerts of vocal and instrumental music; he sees dances; he makes haste to go upon one of the bridges of the river; he asks the first man he meets what fine country that is?

He whom he addressed himself to answered:

"You are in the province of Cachemire; you see the inhabitants immersed in joy and pleasure. We celebrate the marriage of our beauteous princess, who is going to be married to the lord Barbabou, to whom her father promised her. May God perpetuate their felicity!"

At these words Rustan fainted away, and the Cachemirian lord thought he was troubled with the falling sickness. He caused him to be carried to his house, where he remained a long time insensible. He sent in search of the two most able physicians in that part of the country. They felt the patient's pulse, who having somewhat recovered his spirits, sobbed, rolled his eyes, and cried from time to time, "Topaz, Topaz, you were entirely in the right!"

One of the two physicians said to the Cachemirian lord:

"I perceive, by this young man's accent, that he is from Candahar, and that the air of this country is hurtful to him. He must be sent home. I perceive by his eyes that he has lost his senses. Entrust me with him, I will carry him back to his own country, and cure him."

The other physician maintained that grief was his only disorder; and that it was proper to carry him to the wedding of the princess, and make him dance. Whilst they were in consultation, the patient recovered his health. The two physicians were dismissed, and Rustan remained along with his host.

"My lord," said he, "I ask your pardon for having been so free as to faint in your presence. I know it to be a breach of politeness. I entreat you to accept of my elephant, as an acknowledgment of the kindness you have shown me."

He then related to him all his adventure, taking particular care to conceal from him the occasion of his journey.

"But, in the name of Witsnow and Brahma," said he to him, "tell me who is this happy Barbabou, who is to marry the princess of Cachemire? Why has her father chosen him for his son-in-law, and why has the princess accepted of him for an husband?"

"Sir," answered the Cachemirian, "the princess has by no means accepted of Barbabou. She is, on the contrary, in tears, whilst the whole province joyfully celebrates her marriage. She has shut herself up in a tower of her palace. She does not choose to see any of the rejoicings made upon the occasion."

Rustan, at hearing this, perceived himself revived. The bloom of his complexion, which grief had caused to fade, appeared again upon his countenance.

"Tell me, I entreat you," continued he, "why the prince of Cachemire is obstinately bent upon giving his daughter to lord Barbabou whom she does not love?"

"This is the fact," answered the Cachemirian. "Do you know that our august prince lost a large diamond and a javelin which he considered as of great value?"

"Ah! I very well know that," said Rustan.

"Know then," said his host, "that our prince, being in despair at not having heard of his two precious curiosities, after having caused them to be sought for all over the world, promised his daughter to whoever should bring him either the one or the other. A lord Barbabou came who had the diamond, and he is to marry the princess to-morrow."

Rustan turned pale, stammered out a compliment, took leave of his host, and galloped upon his dromedary to the capital city, where the ceremony was to be performed. He arrives at the palace of the prince, he tells him he has something of importance to communicate to him, he demands an audience. He is told that the prince is taken up with the preparations for the wedding.

"It is for that very reason," said he, "that I am desirous of speaking to him." Such is his importunity, that he is at last admitted.

"Prince," said he, "may God crown all your days with glory and magnificence! Your son-in-law is a knave."

"What! a knave! how dare you speak in such terms? Is that a proper way of speaking to a duke of Cachemire of a son-in-law of whom he has made choice?"

"Yes, he is a knave," continued Rustan; "and to prove it to your highness, I have brought you back your diamond."

The duke, surprised at what he heard, compared the two diamonds; and as he was no judge of precious stones, he could not determine which was the true one.

"Here are two diamonds," said he, "and I have but one daughter, I am in a strange perplexity."

He sent for Harbabou, and asked him if he had not imposed upon him, Harbabou swore he had bought his diamond from an Armenian; the other did not tell him who he had his from; but he proposed an expedient, which was that he should engage his rival in single combat.

"It is not enough for your son-in-law to give a diamond," said he, "he should also give proofs of valor. Do not you think it just that he who kills his rival should marry the princess?"

"Undoubtedly," answered the prince. "It will be a fine sight for the court. Fight directly. The conqueror shall take the arms of the conquered according to the customs of Cachemire, and he shall marry my daughter."

The two pretenders to the hand of the princess go down into the court. Upon the stairs there was a jay and a raven. The raven cried, "Fight, fight." The jay cried, "Don't fight."

This made the prince laugh; the two rivals scarce took any notice of it. They begin the combat. All the courtiers made a circle round them. The princess, who kept herself constantly shut up in her tower, did not choose to behold this sight. She never dreampt that her lover was at Cachemire, and she hated Barbabou to such a degree, that she could not bear the sight of him. The combat had the happiest result imaginable. Barbabou was killed outright; and this greatly rejoiced the people, because he was ugly and Rustan was very handsome. The favor of the public is almost always determined by this circumstance.

The conqueror put on the coat of mail, scarf, and the casque of the conquered, and came, followed by the whole court, to present himself under the windows of his mistress. The multitude cried aloud: "Beautiful princess, come and see your handsome lover, who has killed his ugly rival." These words were re-echoed by her women. The princess unluckily looked out of the window, and seeing the armor of a man she hated, she ran like one frantic to her strong box and took out the fatal javelin, which flew to pierce Rustan, notwithstanding his cuirass. He cried out loudly, and at this cry the princess thought she again knew the voice of her unhappy lover.

She ran down stairs, with her hair disheveled, and death in her eyes as well as her heart. Rustan had already fallen, all bloody, into the arms of his attendants. She sees him. Oh, moment! oh, sight! oh, discovery of inexpressible grief, tenderness and horror! She throws herself upon him, and embraces him.

"You receive," said she, "the first and last kisses of your mistress and your murderer."

She pulls the dart from the wound, plunges it in her heart, and dies upon the body of the lover whom she adores. The father, terrified, in despair, and ready to die like his daughter, tries in vain to bring her to life. She was no more. He curses the fatal dart, breaks it to pieces, throws away the two fatal diamonds; and whilst he prepared the funeral of his daughter instead of her marriage, he caused Rustan, who weltered in his blood and had still some remains of life, to be carried to his palace.

He was put into bed. The first objects he saw on each side of his deathbed were Topaz and Ebene. This surprise made him in some degree recover his strength.

"Cruel men," said he, "why did you abandon me? Perhaps the princess would still be alive if you had been with the unhappy Rustan."

"I have not forsaken you a moment," said Topaz.

"I have always been with you," said Ebene.

"Ah! what do you say? why do you insult me in my last moments?" answered Rustan, with a languishing voice.

"You may believe me," said Topaz. "You know I never approved of this fatal journey, the dreadful consequences of which I foresaw. I was the eagle that fought with the vulture and stripped it of its feathers; I was the elephant that carried away the baggage, in order to force you to return to your own country; I was the streaked ass that carried you, whether you would or no, to your father; it was I that made your horses go astray; it was I that caused the torrent that prevented your passage; it was I that raised the mountain which stopped up a road so fatal to you; I was the physician that advised you to return to your own country; I was the jay that cried to you not to fight."

"And I," said Ebene, "was the vulture that he stripped of his feathers, the rhinoceros who gave him a hundred strokes with the horn, the clown that beat the streaked ass, the merchant who made you a present of camels to hasten you to your destruction; I dug the cavern that you crossed, I am the physician that encouraged you to walk, the raven that cried out to you to combat."

"Alas!" said Topaz, "remember the oracles: 'If you go to the east you will be at the west.'"

"Yes," said Ebene, "here the dead are buried with their faces turned to the west. The oracle was plain enough, though you did not understand it. You possessed, and you did not possess; for though you had the diamond, it was a false one, and you did not know it. You are conqueror, and you die; you are Rustan, and you cease to be so: all has been accomplished."

Whilst he spoke thus, four white wings covered the body of Topaz, and four black ones that of Ebene.

"What do I see?" cried Rustan.

Topaz and Ebene answered together: "You see your two geniuses."

"Good gentlemen," cried the unhappy Rustan, "how came you to meddle; and what occasion had a poor man for two geniuses?"

"It is a law," answered Topaz; "every man has too geniuses. Plato was the first man who said so, and others have repeated it after him. You see that nothing can be more true. I who now speak to you, am your good genius. I was charged to watch over you to the last moment of your life. Of this task I have faithfully acquitted myself."

"But," said the dying man, "if your business was to serve me, I am of a nature much superior to yours. And then how can you have the assurance to say you are my good genius, since you have suffered me to be deceived in everything I have undertaken, and since you suffer both my mistress and me to die miserably?"

"Alas!" said Topaz, "it was your destiny."

"If destiny does all," answered the dying man, "what is a genius good for? And you, Ebene, with your four black wings, you are, doubtless, my evil genius."

"You have hit it," answered Ebene.

"Then I suppose you were the evil genius of my princess likewise," said Rustan.

"No," replied Ebene, "she had an evil genius of her own, and I seconded him perfectly."

"Ah! cursed Ebene," said Rustan, "if you are so malicious, you don't belong to the same master with Topaz: you have been formed by two different principles, one of which is by nature good, the other evil."

"That does not follow," said Ebene, "this is a very knotty point."

"It is not possible," answered the dying man, "that a benevolent being could create so destructive a genius."

"Possible or not possible," replied the genius, "the thing is just as I say."

"Alas!" said Topaz, "my poor unfortunate friend, don't you see that that rogue is so malicious as to encourage you to dispute, in order to inflame your blood and hasten your death?"

"Get you gone," said the melancholy Rustan, "I am not much better satisfied with you than with him. He at least acknowledges that it was his intention to hurt me; and you, who pretended to defend me, have done me no service at all."

"I am very sorry for it," said the good genius.

"And I too," said the dying man; "there is something at the bottom of all this which I cannot comprehend."

"Nor I neither," said the good genius.

"I shall know the truth of the matter in a moment," said Rustan. "We shall see that," said Topaz.

The whole scene then vanished. Rustan again found himself in the house of his father, which he had not quitted, and in his bed, where he had slept an hour.

He awakes in astonishment, perspiring all over, and quite wild. He rubs himself, he calls, he rings the bell. His valet de chambre, Topaz, runs in, in his nightcap, and yawning.

"Am I dead or alive?" cried out Rustan, "shall the beauteous princess of Cachemire escape?

"Does your lordship rave?" answered Topaz, coldly.

"Ah!" cried Rustan, "what then is become of this barbarous Ebene, with his four black wings! It is he that makes me die by so cruel a death."

"My lord," answered Topaz, "I left him snoring up stairs. Would you have me bid him come down?"

"The villain," said Rustan, "has persecuted me for six months together. It was he who carried me to the fatal fair of Kaboul; it is he that cheated me of the diamond which the princess presented me; he is the sole cause of my journey, of the death of my princess, and of the wound with a javelin, of which I die in the flower of my age."

"Take heart," said Topaz, "you were never at Kaboul; there is no princess of Cachemire; her father never had any children but two boys, who are now at college; you never had a diamond; the princess cannot be dead, because she never was born; and you are in perfect health."

"What! is it not then true that you attended me whilst dying, and in the bed of the prince of Cachemire? Did you not acknowledge to me, that, in order to preserve me from so many dangers, you were an eagle, an elephant, a streaked ass, a physician, and a jay?"

"My lord, you have dreamt all this," answered Topaz; "our ideas are no more of our own creating whilst we are asleep than whilst we are awake. God has thought proper that this train of ideas should pass in your head, most probably to convey some instruction to you, of which you may make a good use."

"You make a jest of me," replied Rustan, "how long have I slept?"

"My lord," said Topaz, "you have not yet slept an hour."

"Cursed reasoner," returned Rustan, "how is it possible that I could be in the space of an hour at the fair of Kaboul six months ago; that I could have returned from thence, have traveled to Cachemire, and that Barbabou, the princess, and I, should have died?"

"My lord," said Topaz, "nothing can be more easy and more common; and you might have traveled around the world, and have met with a great many more adventures in much less time. Is it not true that you can, in an hour's time, read the abridgment of the Persian history, written by Zoroaster? yet this abridgment contains eight hundred thousand years. All these events pass before your eyes one after another, in an hour's time. Now you must acknowledge, that it is as easy to Brahma to confine them to the space of an hour, as to extend them to the space of eight hundred thousand years. It is exactly the same thing. Imagine to yourself that time turns upon a wheel whose diameter is infinite. Under this vast wheel is a numerous multitude of wheels one within another. That in the centre is imperceptible, and goes round an infinite number of times, whilst the great wheel performs but one revolution. It is evident that all the events which have happened from the beginning of the world, to its end, might have happened in much less time than the hundred thousandth part of a second; and one may even go so far as to assert that the thing is so."

"I cannot comprehend all this," said Rustan.

"If you want information," said Topaz, "I have a parrot that will easily explain it to you. He was born some time before the deluge; he has been in the ark; he has seen a great deal; yet he is but a year and a half old. He will relate to you his history, which is extremely interesting."

"Go fetch your parrot," said Rustan, "it will amuse me till I again find myself disposed to sleep."

"It is with my sister, the nun," said Topaz: "I will go and fetch it. It will please you; its memory is faithful, it relates in a simple manner, without endeavoring to show wit at every turn."

"So much the better," said Rustan, "I like that manner of telling stories."

The parrot being brought to him, spoke in this manner:

N.B. Mademoiselle Catherine Vade could never find the history of the parrot in the commonplace-book of her late cousin Anthony Vade, author of that tale. This is a great misfortune, considering what age that parrot lived in.

Young Memnon.

MEMNON THE PHILOSOPHER.

Memnon one day took it into his head to become a great philosopher. "To be perfectly happy," said he to himself, "I have nothing to do but to divest myself entirely of passions; and nothing is more easy, as everybody knows. In the first place, I will never be in love; for, when I see a beautiful woman, I will say to myself, these cheeks will one day grow sallow and wrinkled, these eyes be encircled with vermilion, that bosom become lean and emaciated, that head bald and palsied. Now I have only to consider her at present in imagination as she will afterwards appear in reality, and certainly a fair face will never turn my head.

"In the second place, I shall always be temperate. It will be in vain to tempt me with good cheer, with delicious wines, or the charms of society, I will have only to figure to myself the consequences of excess—an aching head, a loathing stomach, the loss of reason, of health, and of time: I will then only eat to supply the waste of nature; my health will be always equal, my ideas pure and luminous. All this is so easy that there is no merit in accomplishing it."

"But," says Memnon, "I must think a little of how I am to regulate my fortune: why, my desires are moderate, my wealth is securely placed with the Receiver General of the finances of Nineveh. I have wherewithal to live independent; and that is the greatest of blessings. I shall never be under the cruel necessity of dancing attendance at court. I will never envy any one, and nobody will envy me. Still all this is easy. I have friends, and I will preserve them, for we shall never have any difference. I will never take amiss anything they may say or do; and they will behave in the same way to me. There is no difficulty in all this."

Having thus laid this little plan of philosophy in his closet, Memnon put his head out of the window. He saw two women walking under the plane-trees near his house. The one was old, and appeared quite at her ease. The other was young, handsome, and seemingly much agitated. She sighed, she wept, and seemed on that account still more beautiful. Our philosopher was touched, not, to be sure, with the lady, (he was too much determined not to feel any uneasiness of that kind) but with the distress which he saw her in. He came down stairs, and accosted the young Ninevite, designing to console her with philosophy. That lovely person related to him, with an air of the greatest simplicity, and in the most affecting manner, the injuries she sustained from an imaginary uncle—with what art he had deprived her of some imaginary property, and of the violence which she pretended to dread from him.

"You appear to me," said she, "a man of such wisdom, that if you will come to my house and examine into my affairs, I am persuaded you will be able to relieve me from the cruel embarrassment I am at present involved in."

Memnon did not hesitate to follow her, to examine her affairs philosophically, and to give her sound counsel.

The afflicted lady led him into a perfumed chamber, and politely made him sit down with her on a large sofa, where they both placed themselves opposite to each other, in the attitude of conversation; the one eager in telling her story, the other listening with devout attention. The lady spoke with downcast eyes, whence there sometimes fell a tear, and which, as she now and then ventured to raise them, always met those of the sage Memnon. Their discourse was full of tenderness, which redoubled as often as their eyes met. Memnon took her affairs exceedingly to heart, and felt himself every instant more and more inclined to oblige a person so virtuous and so unhappy. By degrees, in the warmth of conversation they drew nearer. Memnon counseled her with great wisdom, and gave her most tender advice.

At this interesting moment, as may easily be imagined, who should come in but the uncle. He was armed from head to foot, and the first thing he said was, that he would immediately sacrifice, as was just, both Memnon and his niece. The latter, who made her escape, knew that he was disposed to pardon, provided a good round sum were offered to him. Memnon was obliged to purchase his safety with all he had about him. In those days people were happy in getting so easily quit. America was not then discovered, and distressed ladies were not then so dangerous as they are now.

Memnon, covered with shame and confusion, got home to his own house. He there found a card inviting him to dinner with some of his intimate friends.

"If I remain at home alone," said he, "I shall have my mind so occupied with this vexatious adventure, that I shall not be able to eat a bit, and I shall bring upon myself some disease. It will therefore be prudent in me to go to my intimate friends and partake with them of a frugal repast. I shall forget, in the sweets of their society, the folly I have this morning been guilty of."

Accordingly he attends the meeting; he is discovered to be uneasy at something, and he is urged to drink and banish care.

"A little wine, drank in moderation, comforts the heart of God and man:" so reasoned Memnon the philosopher, and he became intoxicated. After the repast, play is proposed.

"A little play, with one's intimate friends, is a harmless pastime." He plays and loses all in his purse, and four times as much on his word. A dispute arises on some circumstance in the game, and the disputants grow warm. One of his intimate friends throws a dice-box at his head, and strikes out one of his eyes. The philosopher Memnon is carried home drunk and penniless, with the loss of an eye.

He sleeps out his debauch, and, when his head becomes clear, he sends his servant to the Receiver General of the finances of Nineveh, to draw a little money to pay his debt of honor to his intimate friends. The servant returns and informs him, that the Receiver General had that morning been declared a fraudulent bankrupt, and that by this means an hundred families are reduced to poverty and despair. Memnon, almost beside himself, puts a plaster on his eye and a petition in his pocket, and goes to court to solicit justice from the king against the bankrupt. In the saloon he meets a number of ladies, all in the highest spirits, and sailing along with hoops four-and-twenty feet in circumference. One of them, slightly acquainted with him, eyed him askance, and cried aloud: "Ah! what a horrid monster!"

Another, who was better acquainted with him, thus accosts him: "Good-morrow, Mr. Memnon, I hope you are well, Mr. Memnon. La! Mr. Memnon, how did you lose your eye?" and turning upon her heel, she tripped unconcernedly away.

Memnon hid himself in a corner, and waited for the moment when he could throw himself at the feet of the monarch. That moment at last arrived. Three times he kissed the earth, and presented his petition. His gracious majesty received him very favorably, and referred the paper to one of his satraps. The satrap takes Memnon aside, and says to him with a haughty air and satirical grin:

"Hark ye, you fellow with the one eye, you must be a comical dog indeed, to address yourself to the king rather than to me: and still more so, to dare to demand justice against an honest bankrupt, whom I honor with my protection, and who is also a nephew to the waiting-maid of my mistress. Proceed no further in this business, my good friend, if you wish to preserve the eye you have left."

Memnon having thus, in his closet, resolved to renounce women, the excess of the table, play, and quarreling, but especially having determined never to go to court, had been in the short space of four-and-twenty hours duped and robbed by a gentle dame, had got drunk, had gamed, had been engaged in a quarrel, had got his eye knocked out, and had been at court, where he was sneered at and insulted.

Petrified with astonishment, and his heart broken with grief, Memnon returns homeward in despair. As he was about to enter his house, he is repulsed by a number of officers who are carrying off his furniture for the benefit of his creditors. He falls down almost lifeless under a plane-tree. There he finds the fair dame of the morning, who was walking with her dear uncle; and both set up a loud laugh on seeing Memnon with his plaster. The night approached, and Memnon made his bed on some straw near the walls of his house. Here the ague seized him, and he fell asleep in one of the fits, when a celestial spirit appeared to him in a dream.

It was all resplendent with light: it had six beautiful wings, but neither feet, nor head, and could be likened to nothing.

"What art thou?" said Memnon.

"Thy good genius," replied the spirit.

"Restore me then my eye, my health, my fortune, my reason," said Memnon; and he related how he had lost them all in one day. "These are adventures which never happen to us in the world we inhabit," said the spirit.

"And what world do you inhabit?" said the man of affliction.

"My native country," replied the other, "is five hundred millions of leagues distant from the sun, in a little star near Sirius, which you see from hence."

"Charming country!" said Memnon. "And are there indeed with you no jades to dupe a poor devil, no intimate friends that win his money and knock out an eye for him, no fraudulent bankrupts, no satraps, that make a jest of you while they refuse you justice?"

"No," said the inhabitant of the star, "we have nothing of the kind. We are never duped by women, because we have none among us; we never commit excesses at table, because we neither eat nor drink; we have no bankrupts, because with us there is neither silver nor gold; our eyes cannot be knocked out, because we have not bodies in the form of yours; and satraps never do us injustice, because in our world we are all equal."

"Pray my lord," said Memnen, "without women and without eating how do you spend your time?"

"In watching, over the other worlds that are entrusted to us; and I am now come to give you consolation."

"Alas!" replied Memnon, "why did you not come yesterday to hinder me from committing so many indiscretions?"

"I was with your elder brother Hassan," said the celestial being. "He is still more to be pitied than you are. His most gracious majesty, the sultan of the Indies, in whose court he has the honor to serve, has caused both his eyes to be put out for some small indiscretion; and he is now in a dungeon, his hands and feet loaded with chains."

"'Tis a happy thing, truly," said Memnon, "to have a good genius in one's family, when out of two brothers, one is blind of an eye, the other blind of both; one stretched upon straw, the other in a dungeon."

"Your fate will soon change," said the spirit of the star. "It is true you will never recover your eye; but, except that, you may be sufficiently happy if you never again take it into your head to be a perfect philosopher."

"Is it then impossible?" said Memnon.

"As impossible as to be perfectly wise, perfectly strong, perfectly powerful, perfectly happy. We ourselves are very far from it. There is a world indeed where all this takes place; but, in the hundred thousand millions of worlds dispersed over the regions of space, everything goes on by degrees. There is less philosophy and less enjoyment in the second than in the first, less in the third than in the second, and so forth till the last in the scale, where all are completely fools."

"I am afraid," said Memnon, "that our little terraqueous globe here is the madhouse of those hundred thousand millions of worlds, of which your lordship does me the honor to speak."

"Not quite," said the spirit, "but very nearly; everything must be in its proper place."

"But are those poets and philosophers wrong, then, who tell us that everything is for the best?"

"No, they are right, when we consider things in relation to the gradation of the whole universe."

"Oh! I shall never believe it till I recover my eye again," said the unfortunate Memnon.

Memnon and the distressed Ninevite.—"The afflicted lady led him into a perfumed chamber, where they both placed themselves opposite to each other, in the attitude of conversation; the one eager in telling her story, the other listening with devout attention."

[1] The above engraving from Chamber's Guide to the British Museum, represents a head and bust of Memnon, "formed of a single block of fine syene granite, one piece of which is red, while the rest is blue or grayish. The sculptor, with admirable taste, used the red part for the head, and the darker part for the breast. Although the statue has all the characteristics of Egyptian sculpture—the projecting eyes, thick lips, high ears, and small chin—yet such is the beauty of the execution, so much sweetness and mildness is there in the expression of the countenance, that the effect is, on the whole, extremely pleasing. Here, in short, we have the masterpiece of some Egyptian sculptor of superior genius, whose name has perished. Here also, if we are to accept the statue as a genuine likeness, we behold the features of the great Egyptian Pharaoh, at whose name, some fourteen centuries before Christ, the Mediterranean nations trembled. Doubtless on such a subject the sculptor

would do his best; striving, while transmitting the features of the hero to posterity, to produce also a countenance that would be the ideal of Egyptian beauty."—E.

ANDRÉ DES TOUCHES AT SIAM.

André Des Touches was a very agreeable musician in the brilliant reign of Louis XIV. before the science of music was perfected by Rameau; and before it was corrupted by those who prefer the art of surmounting difficulties to nature and the real graces of composition.

Before he had recourse to these talents he had been a musketeer, and before that, in 1688, he went into Siam with the Jesuit Tachard, who gave him many marks of his affection, for the amusement he afforded on board the ship; and Des Touches spoke with admiration of father Tachard for the rest of his life.

At Siam he became acquainted with the first commissary of Barcalon, whose name was Croutef; and he committed to writing most of those questions which he asked of Croutef, and the answers of that Siamese. They are as follows:

DES TOUCHES.—How many soldiers have you?

CROUTEF.—Fourscore thousand, very indifferently paid.

DES TOUCHES.—And how many Talapolins?

CROUTEF.—A hundred and twenty thousand, very idle and very rich. It is true that in the last war we were beaten, but our Talapolins have lived sumptuously, and built fine houses.

DES TOUCHES.—Nothing could have discovered more judgment. And your finances, in what state are they?

CROUTEF.—In a very bad state. We have, however, about ninety thousand men employed to render them prosperous, and if they have not succeeded, it has not been their fault; for there is not one of them who does not honorably seize all that he can get possession of, and strip and plunder those who cultivate the ground for the good of the state.

DES TOUCHES.—Bravo! And is not your jurisprudence as perfect as the rest of your administration?

CROUTEF.—It is much superior. We have no laws, but we have five or six thousand volumes on the laws. We are governed in general by customs; for it is known that a custom, having been established by chance, is the wisest principle that can be imagined. Besides, all customs being necessarily different in different provinces, the judges may choose at their pleasure a custom which prevailed four hundred years ago, or one which prevailed last year. It occasions a variety in our legislation, which our neighbors are forever admiring. This yields a certain fortune to practitioners. It is a resource for all pleaders who are destitute of honor, and a pastime of infinite amusement for the judges, who can with safe consciences decide causes without understanding them.

DES TOUCHES.—But in criminal cases—you have laws which may be depended upon.

CROUTEF.—God forbid! We can condemn men to exile, to the galleys, to be hanged; or we can discharge them, according to our own fancy. We sometimes complain of the arbitrary power of the Barcalon; but we choose that all our decisions should be arbitrary.

DES TOUCHES.—That is very just. And the torture—do you put people to the torture?

CROUTEF.—It is our greatest pleasure. We have found it an infallible secret to save a guilty person, who has vigorous muscles, strong and supple hamstrings, nervous arms, and firm loins; and we gaily break on the wheel all those innocent persons to whom nature has given feeble organs. It is thus we conduct ourselves with wonderful wisdom and prudence. As there are half proofs, I mean half truths, it is certain there are persons who are half innocent and half guilty. We commence, therefore, by rendering them half dead; we then go to breakfast; afterwards ensues entire death, which gives us great consideration in the world, which is one of the most valuable advantages of our offices.

DES TOUCHES.—It must be allowed that nothing can be more prudent and humane. Pray tell me what becomes of the property of the condemned?

CROUTEF.—The children are deprived of it. For you know that nothing can be more equitable than to punish the single fault of a parent on all his descendants.

DES TOUCHES.—Yes. It is a great while since I have heard of this jurisprudence.

CROUTEF.—The people of Laos, our neighbors, admit neither the torture, nor arbitrary punishments, nor the different customs, nor the horrible deaths which are in use among us; but we regard them as barbarians who have no idea of good government. All Asia is agreed that we dance the best of all its inhabitants, and that, consequently, it is impossible they should come near us in jurisprudence, in commerce, in finance, and, above all, in the military art.

DES TOUCHES.—Tell me, I beseech you, by what steps men arrive at the magistracy in Siam.

CROUTEF.—By ready money. You perceive that it may be impossible to be a good judge, if a man has not by him thirty or forty thousand pieces of silver. It is in vain a man may be perfectly acquainted with all our customs; it is to no purpose that he has pleaded five hundred causes with success—that he has a mind which is the seat of judgment, and a heart replete with justice; no man can become a magistrate without money. This, I say, is the circumstance which distinguishes us from all Asia, and particularly from the barbarous inhabitants of Laos, who have the madness to recompense all kinds of talents, and not to sell any employment.

André des Touches, who was a little off his guard, said to the Siamese, that most of the airs which he had just sung sounded discordant to him; and wished to receive information concerning real Siamese music. But Croutef, full of his subject, and enthusiastic for his country, continued in these words:

"What does it signify that our neighbors, who live beyond our mountains, have better music than we have, or better pictures; provided we have always wise and humane laws? It is in that circumstance we excel. For example:

"If a man has adroitly stolen three or four hundred thousand pieces of gold, we respect him, and we go and dine with him. But if a poor servant gets awkwardly into his possession three or four pieces of copper out of his mistress's box, we never fail of putting that servant to a public death; first, lest he should not correct himself; secondly, that he may not have it in his power to produce a great number of children for the state, one or two of whom might possibly steal a few little pieces of copper, or become great men; thirdly, because it is just to proportion the punishment to the crime, and that it would be ridiculous to give any useful employment in a prison to a person guilty of so enormous a crime.

"But we are still more just, more merciful, more reasonable in the chastisements which we inflict on those who have the audacity to make use of their legs to go wherever they choose. We treat those warriors so well who sell us their lives, we give them so prodigious a salary, they have so considerable a part in our conquests, that they must be the most criminal of all men to wish to return to their parents on the recovery of their reason, because they had been enlisted in a state of intoxication. To oblige them to remain in one place, we lodge about a dozen leaden balls in their heads; after which they become infinitely useful to their country.

"I will not speak of a great number of excellent institutions, which do not go so far as to shed the blood of men, but which render life so pleasant and agreeable that it is impossible the guilty should avoid becoming virtuous. If a farmer has not been able to pay promptly a tax which exceeds his ability, we sell the pot in which he dresses his food; we sell his bed, in order that, being relieved of all his superfluities, he may be in a better condition to cultivate the earth."

DES TOUCHES.—That is extremely harmonious!

CROUTEF.—To comprehend our profound wisdom, you must know that our fundamental principle is to acknowledge in many places as our sovereign, a shaven-headed foreigner who lives at the distance of nine hundred miles from us. When we assign some of our best territories to any of our Talapolins, which it is very prudent in us to do, that Siamese Talapolin must pay the revenue of his first year to that shaven-headed Tartar, without which it is clear our lands would be unfruitful.

But the time, the happy time, is no more, when that tonsured priest induced one half of the nation to cut the throats of the other half, in order to decide whether Sammonocodom had played at leap-frog or at some other game; whether he had been disguised in an elephant or in a cow; if he had slept three hundred and ninety days on the right side, or on the left. Those grand questions, which so essentially affect morality, agitated all minds; they shook the world; blood flowed plentifully for it; women were massacred on the bodies of their husbands; they dashed out the brains of their little infants on the stones, with a devotion, with a grace, with a contrition truly angelic. Woe to us! degenerate offspring of pious ancestors, who never offer such holy sacrifices! But, heaven be praised, there are yet among us at least a few good souls, who would imitate them if they were permitted.

DES TOUCHES.—Tell me, I beseech you, sir, if at Siam you divide the tone major into two commas, or into two semi-commas; and if the progress of the fundamental sounds are made by one, three, and nine?

CROUTEF. By Sammonocodom, you are laughing at me. You observe no bounds. You have interrogated me on the form of our government, and you speak to me of music!

DES TOUCHES.—Music is everything. It was at the foundation of all the politics of the Greeks. But I beg your pardon; you have not a good ear; and we will return to our subject. You said, that in order to produce a perfect harmony—

CROUTEF.—I was telling you, that formerly the tonsured Tartar pretended to dispose of all the kingdoms of Asia; which occasioned something very different from perfect harmony. But a very considerable benefit resulted from it; for people were then more devout toward Sammonocodom and his elephant than they are now; for, at the present time, all the world pretends to common sense, with an indiscretion truly pitiable. However, all things go on; people divert themselves, they dance, they play, they dine, they sup, they make love; this makes every man shudder who entertains good intentions.

DES TOUCHES.—And what would you have more? You only want good music. If you had good music, you might call your nation the happiest in the world.

THE BLIND PENSIONERS AT QUINZE VINGT.

A SHORT DIGRESSION.—When the hospital of the Quinze Vingt was first founded, the pensioners were all equal, and their little affairs were concluded upon by a majority of votes. They distinguished perfectly by the touch between copper and silver coin; they never mistook the wine of Brie for that of Burgundy. Their sense of smelling was finer than that of their neighbors who had the use of two eyes. They reasoned very well on the four senses; that is, they knew everything they were permitted to know, and they lived as peaceably and as happily as blind people could be supposed to do. But unfortunately one of their professors pretended to have clear ideas in respect to the sense of seeing, he drew attention; he intrigued; he formed enthusiasts; and at last he was acknowledged chief of the community. He pretended to be a judge of colors, and everything was lost.

This dictator of the Quinze Vingt chose at first a little council, by the assistance of which he got possession of all the alms. On this account, no person had the resolution to oppose him. He decreed, that all the inhabitants of the Quinze Vingt were clothed in white. The blind pensioners believed him; and nothing was to be heard but their talk of white garments, though, in fact, they possessed not one of that color. All their acquaintance laughed at them. They made their complaints to the dictator, who received them very ill; he rebuked them as innovators, freethinkers, rebels, who had suffered themselves to be seduced by the errors of those who had eyes, and who presumed to doubt that their chief was infallible. This contention gave rise to two parties.

To appease the tumult, the dictator issued a decree, importing that all their vestments were red. There was not one vestment of that color in the Quinze Vingt. The poor men were laughed at more than ever. Complaints were again made by the community. The dictator rushed furiously in; and the other blind men were as much enraged. They fought a long time; and peace was not restored until the members of the Quinze Vingt were permitted to suspend their judgments in regard to the color of their dress.

A deaf man, reading this little history, allowed that these people, being blind, were to blame in pretending to judge of colors; but he remained steady to his own opinion, that those persons who were deaf were the only proper judges of music.

Boodh resting "upon the face of the waters," supported by serpents.[1]

BABABEC.

When I was in the city of Benarez, on the borders of the Ganges, the country of the ancient Brahmins, I endeavored to instruct myself in their religion and manners. I understood the Indian language tolerably well. I heard a great deal, and remarked everything. I lodged at the house of my correspondent Omri, who was the most worthy man I ever knew. He was of the religion of the Brahmins: I have the honor to be a Mussulman. We never exchanged one word higher than another about Mahomet or Brahma. We performed our ablutions each on his own side; we drank of the same sherbet, and we ate of the same rice, as if we had been two brothers.

One day we went together to the pagoda of Gavani. There we saw several bands of Fakirs. Some of whom were Janguis, that is to say, contemplative Fakirs; and others were disciples of the ancient Gymnosophists, who led an active life. They all have a learned language peculiar to themselves; it is that of the most ancient Brahmins; and they have a book written in this language, which they call the *Shasta*. It is, beyond all contradiction, the most ancient book in all Asia, not excepting the *Zend*.

I happened by chance to cross in front of a Fakir, who was reading in this book.

"Ah! wretched infidel!" cried he, "thou hast made me lose a number of vowels that I was counting, which will cause my soul to pass into the body of a hare instead of that of a parrot, with which I had before the greatest reason to flatter myself."

I gave him a rupee to comfort him for the accident. In going a few paces farther, I had the misfortune to sneeze. The noise I made roused a Fakir, who was in a trance.

"Heavens!" cried he, "what a dreadful noise. Where am I? I can no longer see the tip of my nose,—the heavenly light has disappeared."

"If I am the cause," said I, "of your not seeing farther than the length of your nose, here is a rupee to repair the great injury I have done you. Squint again, my friend, and resume the heavenly light."

Having thus brought myself off discreetly enough, I passed over to the side of the Gymnosophists, several of whom brought me a parcel of mighty pretty nails to drive into my arms and thighs, in honor of Brahma. I bought their nails, and made use of them to fasten down my boxes. Others were dancing upon their hands, others cut capers on the slack rope, and others went always upon one foot. There were some who dragged a heavy chain about with them, and others carried a packsaddle; some had their heads always in a bushel—the best people in the world to live with. My friend Omri took me to the cell of one of the most famous of these. His name was Bababec: he was as naked as he was born, and had a great chain about his neck, that weighed upwards of sixty pounds. He sat on a wooden chair, very neatly decorated with little points of nails that penetrated into his flesh; and you would have thought he had been sitting on a velvet cushion. Numbers of women flocked to him to consult him. He was the oracle of all the families in the neighborhood; and was, truly speaking, in great reputation. I was witness to a long conversation that Omri had with him.

[1] Boodhism, is described in *Webster's Dictionary* as "a system of religion in Eastern Asia, embraced by more than one third of the human race. It teaches that, at distant intervals, a Boodh, or deity, appears, to restore the world from a state of ignorance and decay, and then sinks into a state of entire non-existence, or rather, perhaps, of bare existence without attributes, action, or consciousness. This state, called *Nirvana*, or *Nicban*, is regarded as the ultimate supreme good, and the highest reward of virtue among men. Four Boodhs have thus appeared in the world, and passed into *Nirvana*, the last of whom, Gaudama, became incarnate about 500 years before Christ, from his death, in 543 B.C., many thousand years will elapse before the appearance of another; so that the system, in the mean time, is practically one of pure atheism."

The serpent has ever been a significant emblem in religion and mythology. Being "the most subtle beast of the field," it was naturally accepted as the emblem of wisdom. With its tail in its mouth it formed a circle, which was regarded by the ancients as the emblem of eternity. Moses set up a brazen serpent on a cross in the wilderness as an emblem of healing. Æsculapius, the god of medicine, is seen on ancient statues with a serpent twining around a staff by his side, symbolizing health, prudence and foresight. Hygiea, the goddess of health, is represented in works of art as a virgin dressed in a long robe and feeding a serpent from a cup. Mercury is always shown holding in his right hand a wand with two twined serpents. The nine coiled serpents in the above engraving, correspond with the nine muses in the Grecian mythology. The cobra, whose poison is death, is an emblem of the destroying power, and destruction, or rather change, symbolizes new formation, renovation or creation. Thus eternal formation, proceeds from eternal destruction. The serpent also figures in a beautiful allegory concerning the introduction of knowledge among mankind, *i.e.*, "the knowledge of good and evil."—E.

The Fakir.

RELIGIOUS ZEAL.

The most earnest and zealous advocates of modern Christianity are, undoubtedly, to be found in the ranks of that grotesque organization known as the "Salvation Army"; but the wildest efforts of these misguided propagandists fall far short of the intense religious fervor displayed by the zealous followers of Brahma.

A contributor to Cassell's *Illustrated Travels* describes a religious festival which he witnessed a few years ago at Hurdwar on the Ganges, while on an elephant shooting expedition in the Dehra Dhoon, Northern India, which vividly illustrates the folly and fanaticism of these degraded religious devotees, and which is only second in repulsiveness to the horrible ceremonies of Juggernaut.

"There is," says this writer, "a religious festival every year at Hurdwar, but every sixth year the ceremonies are more holy and the crowd of pilgrims larger. The *Koom Mela*, a religious feast of great holiness in native eyes, occurs every eleven years, and the pilgrims on such occasions arrive from every part of India. The crowd usually numbers over two millions. But it is when the festivals occurring at intervals of six years and at intervals of eleven years happen to meet in the same year that the crowd is the largest, the importance of the fair greatest, and the concourse of fanatic fakirs and holy Brahmins, from every hole and corner of India, the most striking and remarkable. Merchants arrive from the most distant countries; not from different parts of India only, but from Persia, Thibet, China, Afghanistan, and even from Russia. It was one of these festivals and giant fairs that we had the good fortune to see.

"As the day of the great festival approaches, the fakirs—who by the way are always stark naked, and generally as disgusting specimens of humanity as it is possible to conceive—and the Brahmins, excite their hearers by increasingly-fervent speeches, by self-applied tortures, frightful contortions, and wild dances and gestures, to which the crowd loudly responds by shouts and wild yells. Early on the morning of the day which to their mind is more holy than any other in their whole lifetime, the assembled people to the number of two or even three millions, repair to the ghauts and patiently wait for the signal, to begin their work of regeneration and salvation. This desirable end is attained by each and every individual who within a certain time, during the tinkling of a well-known bell, precipitates himself into the river, washes himself thoroughly, and repeats a short prayer. This done, the pilgrim must leave the river again, and if he has not entered it until the bell began to tinkle, and has succeeded in going through his performance and left the water again before the sound of the bell has ceased, his sins from his birth are remitted and washed away, and his happy future after death is assured, unless he commits some specifically named and very enormous sins. The other pilgrims, who by reason of the great crowd cannot reach the water in time to go through the whole performance as required by the Brahmins, receive blessings commensurate with the length of their stay in the water while the bell was ringing. Even the unfortunate pilgrims who altogether fail to enter the water at the right moment, are consoled by the partial removal of their load of wickedness; but the blessings which accompany a full performance of what the Brahmins require, are so superior to the favors following an incomplete or tardy immersion, that it is not strange extraordinary efforts are made to enter the water at the first sound of the bells and gongs.

"The crowd was made up of men and women of half-a-hundred tribes of nations, in every variety of dress and partial nakedness. Many men wore their loincloths only; the women's hair was loose and flying to the wind; all were newly and hideously painted; many were intoxicated, not only with opium and spirits, but with religious frenzy and impatient waiting. As the exciting moment approached shouts rent the air; the priests harangued louder and louder; the fakirs grew wilder and more incoherent; then gradually the great noise subsided, when suddenly a single bell, immediately followed by a hundred more, broke the silence, and with one accord, shouting like madmen, the people rushed forward and the foremost ranks threw themselves into the water. Then there arose a mighty shout, the many gongs joined in, and the bells redoubled their efforts. But the confusion, the crushing, the struggling for very life, the surging of the mad masses at the water's edge, defy all description.

"As the first rows of men and women reached the water they were upset and overturned by the people in their rear, who passed over them into still deeper water, and in their turn suffered the same fate at the bands of the on-rushing crowd behind them, until deep water was reached.... The shouts of excitement were changed to shrieks and passionate cries for help; the men under water struggled with those above them: weak women were carried out by the stream or trampled on; men pulled each other down, and in their mad fear exerted their utmost strength without object or purpose. Then the survivors, trying to escape from the water, met the yet dry crowd still charging down to death, and this increased the dire confusion. It was a horrid sight, and one I was quite unprepared for, notwithstanding all I had heard before."—E.

"Do you think, father," said my friend, "that after having gone through seven metempsichoses, I may at length arrive at the habitation of Brahma?"

"That is as it may happen," said the Fakir. "What sort of life do you lead?"

"I endeavor," answered Omri, "to be a good subject, a good husband, a good father, and a good friend. I lend money without interest to the rich who want it, and I give it to the poor: I always strive to preserve peace among my neighbors."

"But have you ever run nails into your flesh?" demanded the Brahmin.

"Never, reverend father."

"I am sorry for it," replied the father; "very sorry for it, indeed. It is a thousand pities; but you will certainly not reach above the nineteenth heaven."

"No higher!" said Omri. "In truth, I am very well contented with my lot. What is it to me whether I go into the nineteenth or the twentieth, provided I do my duty in my pilgrimage, and am well received at the end of my journey? Is it not as much as one can desire, to live with a fair character in this world, and be happy with Brahma in the next? And pray what heaven do you think of going to, good master Bababec, with your chain?"

"Into the thirty-fifth," said Bababec.

"I admire your modesty," replied Omri, "to pretend to be better lodged than me. This is surely the result of an excessive ambition. How can you, who condemn others that covet honors in this world, arrogate such distinguished ones to yourself in the next? What right have you to be better treated than me? Know that I bestow more alms to the poor in ten days, than the nails you run into your flesh cost for ten years? What is it to Brahma that you pass the whole day stark naked with a chain about your neck? This is doing a notable service to your country, doubtless! I have a thousand times more esteem for the man who sows pulse or plants trees, than for all your tribe, who look at the tips of their noses, or carry packsaddles, to show their magnanimity."

Having finished this speech, Omri softened his voice, embraced the Brahmin, and, with an endearing sweetness, besought him to throw aside his nails and his chain, to go home with him, and live with decency and comfort.

The Fakir was persuaded, he was washed clean, rubbed with essences and perfumes, and clad in a decent habit; he lived a fortnight in this manner, behaved with prudence and wisdom, and acknowledged that he was a thousand times happier than before; but he lost his credit among the people, the women no longer crowded to consult him; he therefore quitted the house of the friendly Omri, and returned to his nails and his chain, *to regain his reputation.*

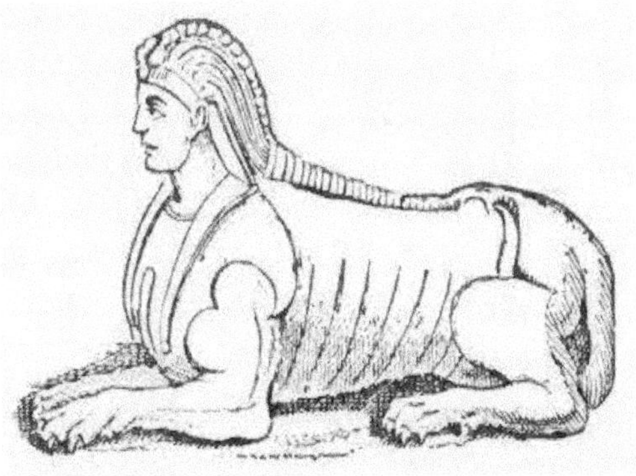

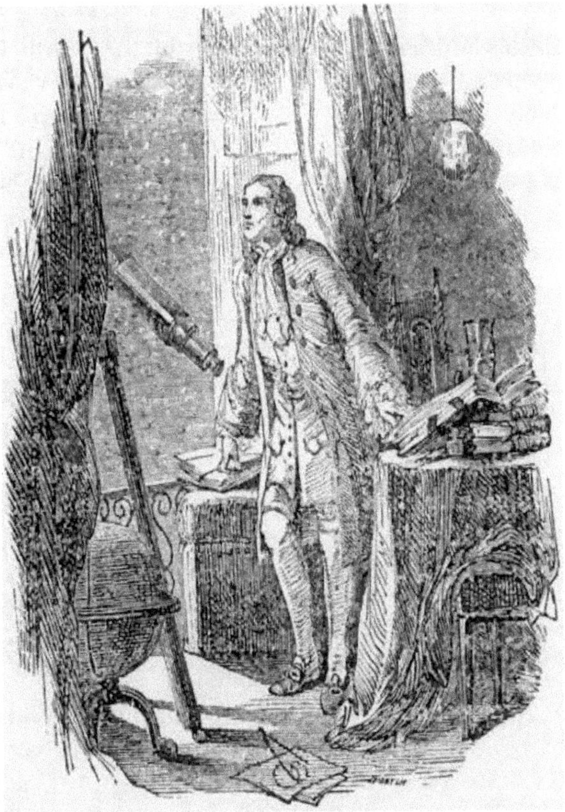

THE STUDY OF NATURE.

I.

INTRODUCTION.

There can be no doubt that everything in the world is governed by fatality. My own life is a convincing proof of this doctrine. An English lord, with whom I was a great favorite, had promised me that I should have the first living that fell to his gift. An old incumbent of eighty happened to die, and I immediately traveled post to London to remind the earl of his promise. I was honored with an immediate interview, and was received with the greatest kindness. I informed his lordship of the death of the rector, and of the hope I cherished relative to the disposal of the vacant living. He replied that I really looked very ill. I answered that, thanks to God, my greatest affliction was poverty. I am sorry for you, said his lordship, and he politely dismissed me with a letter of introduction to a Mr. Sidrac, who dwelt in the vicinity of Guildhall. I ran as fast as I could to this gentleman's house, not doubting but that he would immediately install me in the wished for living. I delivered the earl's letter, and Mr. Sidrac, who had the honor to be my lord's surgeon, asked me to sit down, and, producing a case of surgical instruments, began to assure me that he would perform an operation which he trusted would very soon relieve me.

You must know, that his lordship had understood that I was suffering from some dreadful complaint, and that he generously intended to have me cured at his own expense. The earl had the misfortune to be as deaf as a post, a fact with which I, alas! had not been previously acquainted.

During the time which I lost in defending myself against the attacks of Mr. Sidrac, who insisted positively upon curing me, whether I would or no, one out of the fifty candidates who were all on the lookout, came to town, flew to my lord, begged the vacant living—and obtained it.

I was deeply in love with an interesting girl, a Miss Fidler, who had promised to marry me upon condition of my being made rector. My fortunate rival not only got the living, but also my mistress into the bargain!

My patron, upon being told of his mistake, promised to make me ample amends, but alas! he died two days afterwards.

Mr. Sidrac demonstrated to me that, according to his organic structure, my good patron could not have lived one hour longer. He also clearly proved that the earl's deafness proceeded entirely from the extreme dryness of the drums of his ears, and kindly offered, by an application of spirits of wine, to harden both of my ears to such a degree that I should, in one month only, become as deaf as any peer of the realm.

I discovered Mr. Sidrac to be a man of profound knowledge. He inspired me with a taste for the study of nature, and I could not but be sensible of the valuable acquisition I had made in acquiring the friendship of a man who was capable of relieving me, should I need his services. Following his advice, I applied myself closely to the study of nature, to console myself for the loss of the rectory and of my enchanting Miss Fidler.

II.

THE STUDY OF NATURE.

After making many profound observations upon nature, (having employed in the research, my five senses, my spectacles, and a very large telescope,) I said one day to Mr. Sidrac, unless I am much deceived, philosophy laughs at us. I cannot discover any trace of what the world calls nature; on the contrary, everything seems to me to be the result of art. By art the planets are made to revolve around the sun, while the sun revolves on its own axis. I am convinced that some genius has arranged things in such a manner, that the square of the revolutions of the planets is always in proportion to the cubic root from their distance to their centre, and one had need be a magician to find out how this is accomplished. The tides of the sea are the result of art no less profound and no less difficult to explain.

All animals, vegetables and minerals are arranged with due regard to weight and measure, number and motion. All is performed by springs, levers, pullies, hydraulic machines, and chemical combinations, from the insignificant flea to the being called man, from the grass of the field to the far spreading oak, from a grain of sand to a cloud in the firmament of heaven. Assuredly, everything is governed by art, and the word *nature* is but a chimera.

What you say, answered Mr. Sidrac, has been said many years ago, and so much the better, for the probability is greater that your remark is true. I am always astonished when I reflect, that a grain of wheat cast into the earth will produce in a short time above a handful of the same corn. Stop, said I, foolishly, you forget that wheat must die before it can spring up again, at least so they say at college. My friend Sidrac, laughing heartily at this interruption, replied. That assertion went down very well a few years ago, when it was first published by an apostle called Paul; but in our more enlightened age, the meanest laborer knows that the thing is altogether too ridiculous even for argument.

My dear friend, said I, excuse the absurdity of my remark, I have hitherto been a theologian, and one cannot divest one's self in a moment of every silly opinion.

III.

GOOD ADVICE.

Some time after this conversation between the disconsolate person, whom we shall call Goodman, and the clever anatomist, Mr. Sidrac, the latter, one fine morning, observed his friend in St. James's Park, standing in an attitude of deep thought. What is the matter? said the surgeon. Is there anything amiss? No, replied Goodman, but I am left without a patron in the world since the death of my friend, who had the misfortune to be so deaf. Now supposing there be only ten thousand clergymen in England, and granting these ten thousand have each two patrons, the odds against my obtaining a bishopric are twenty thousand to one; a reflection quite sufficient to give any man the blue-devils. I remember, it was once proposed to me, to go out as cabin-boy to the East Indies. I was told that I should make my fortune. But as I did not think I should make a good admiral, whenever I should arrive at the distinction, I declined; and so, after turning my attention to every profession under the sun, I am fixed for life as a poor clergyman, good for nothing.

Then be a clergyman no longer! cried Sidrac, and turn philosopher: what is your income? Only thirty guineas a year, replied Goodman; although at the death of my mother, it will be increased to fifty. Well, my dear Goodman, continued Sidrac, that sum is quite sufficient to support you in comfort. Thirty guineas are six hundred and thirty shillings, almost two shillings a day. With this fixed income, a man need do nothing to increase it, but is at perfect liberty to say all he thinks of the East India Company, the House of Commons, the king and all the royal family, of man generally and individually, and lastly, of God and his attributes; and the liberty we enjoy of expressing our thoughts upon these most interesting topics, is certainly very agreeable and amusing.

Come and dine at my table every day. That will save you some little money. We will afterwards amuse ourselves with conversation, and your thinking faculty will have the pleasure of communicating with mine by means of speech, which is certainly a very wonderful thing, though its advantages are not duly appreciated by the greater part of mankind.

The poor clergyman.—"*I remember, it was once proposed to me, to go out as cabin-boy to the East Indies. I was told that I should make my fortune. But as I did not think I should make a good admiral, whenever I should arrive at the distinction, I declined; and so, after turning my attention to every profession under the sun, I am fixed for life as a poor clergyman, good for nothing.*"

IV.

DIALOGUE UPON THE SOUL AND OTHER TOPICS.

GOODMAN.—But my dear Sidrac, why do you always say *my thinking faculty* and not *my soul?* If you used the latter term I should understand you much better.

SIDRAC.—And for my part, I freely confess, I should not understand myself. I *feel,* I *know,* that God has endowed me with the faculties of thinking and speaking, but I can neither *feel* nor *know* that God has given me a thing called a soul.

GOODMAN.—Truly upon reflection, I perceive that I know as little about the matter as you do, though I own that I have, all my life, been bold enough to believe that I knew. I have often remarked that the eastern nations apply to the soul the same word they use to express life. After their example, the Latins understood the word *anima* to signify the life of the animal. The Greeks called the breath the soul. The Romans translated the word breath by *spiritus,* and thence it is that the word spirit or soul is found in every modern nation. As it happens that no one has ever seen this spirit or breath, our imagination has converted it into a being, which it is impossible to see or touch. The learned tell us, that the soul inhabits the body without having any place in it, that it has the power of setting our different organs in motion without being able to reach and touch them, indeed, what has not been said upon the subject? The great Locke knew into what a chaos these absurdities had plunged the human understanding. In writing the only reasonable book upon metaphysics that has yet appeared in the world, he did not compose a single chapter on the soul; and if by chance he now and then makes use of the word, he only introduces it to stand for intellect or mind.

In fact, every human being, in spite of Bishop Berkeley, is sensible that he has a mind, and that this mind or intellect is capable of receiving ideas; but no one can feel that there is another being—a soul,—within him, which gives him motion, feeling and thought. It is, in fact, ridiculous to use words we do not understand, and to admit the existence of beings of whom we cannot have the slightest knowledge.

SIDRAC.—We are then agreed upon a subject which, for so many centuries, has been a matter of dispute.

GOODMAN.—And I must observe that I am surprised we should have agreed upon it so soon.

SIDRAC. Oh! that is not so astonishing. We really wish to know what is truth. If we were among the Academies, we should argue like the characters in Rabelais. If we had lived in those ages of darkness, the clouds of which so long enveloped Great Britain, one of us would very likely have burned the other. We are so fortunate as to be born in an age comparatively reasonable; we easily discover what appears to us to be truth, and we are not afraid to proclaim it.

GOODMAN.—You are right, but I fear, that, after all, the truth we have discovered is not worth much. In mathematics, indeed, we have done wonders; from the most simple causes we have produced effects that would have astonished Apollonius or Archimedes: but what have we proved in metaphysics? Absolutely nothing but our own ignorance.

SIDRAC.—And do you call that nothing? You grant the supreme Being has given you the faculties of feeling and thinking, he has in the same manner given your feet the faculty of walking, your hands their wonderful dexterity, your stomach the capability of digesting food, and your heart the power of throwing arterial blood into all parts of your body. Everything we enjoy is derived from God, and yet we are totally ignorant of the means by which he governs and conducts the universe. For my own part, as Shakespeare says, I thank him for having taught me that, of the principles of things, I know absolutely nothing. It has always been a question, in what manner the soul acted upon the body. Before attempting to answer this question, I must be convinced that I have a soul. Either God has given us this wonderful spark of intellect, or he has gifted us with some principle that answers equally well. In either case, we are still the creatures of his divine will and goodness, and that is all I know about the matter.

GOODMAN.—But if you do not know, tell me at least, what you are inclined to think upon the subject. You have opened skulls, and dissected the human fœtus. Have you ever, in these, dissections, discovered any appearance of a soul?

SIDRAC.—Not the least, and I have not been able to understand how an immortal and spiritual essence, could dwell for months together in a membrane. It appears to me difficult to conceive that this pretended soul existed before the foundation of the body; for in what could it have been employed during the many ages previous to its mysterious union with flesh? Again! how can we imagine a spiritual principle waiting patiently in idleness during a whole eternity, in order to animate a mass of matter for a space of time, which, compared with eternity, is less than a moment?

It is worse still, when I am told that God forms immortal souls out of nothing, and then cruelly dooms them to an eternity of flames and torments. What? burn a spirit, in which there can be nothing capable of burning; how can he burn the sound of a voice, or the wind that blows? though both the sound and wind were material during the short time of their existence; but a pure spirit—a thought—a doubt—I am lost in the labyrinth; on whichever side I turn, I find nothing but obscurity and absurdity, impossibility and contradiction. But I am quite at ease when I say to myself God is master of all. He who can cause each star to hold its particular course through the broad expanse of the firmament, can easily give to us sentiments and ideas, without the aid of this atom, called the soul. It is certain that God has endowed all animals, in a greater or lesser degree, with thought, memory, and judgment; he has given them life; it is demonstrated that they have feeling, since they possess all the organs of feeling; if then they have all this without a soul, why is it improbable that we have none? and why do mankind flatter themselves that they alone are gifted with a spiritual and immortal principle?

GOODMAN.—Perhaps this idea arises from their inordinate vanity. I am persuaded that if the peacock could speak, he would boast of his soul, and would affirm that it inhabited his magnificent tail. I am very much inclined to believe with you, that God has created us thinking creatures, with the faculties of eating, drinking, feeling, &c., without telling us one word about the matter. We are as ignorant as the peacock I just mentioned, and he who said that we live and die without knowing how, why, or wherefore, spoke nothing but the truth.

SIDRAC.—A celebrated author, whose name I forget, calls us nothing more than the puppets of Providence, and this seems to me to be a very good definition. An infinity of movements are necessary to our existence, but we did not ourselves invent and produce motion. There is a Being who has created light, caused it to move from the sun to our eyes in about seven minutes. It is only by means of motion that my five senses are put in action, and it is only by means of my senses that I have ideas, hence it follows that my ideas are derived from the great author of motion, and when he informs me how he communicates these ideas to me, I will most sincerely thank him.

GOODMAN.—And so will I. As it is I constantly thank him for having permitted me, as Epictetus says, to contemplate for a period of some years this beautiful and glorious world. It is true that he could have made me happier by putting me in possession of Miss Fidler and a good rectory; but still, such as I am, I consider myself as under a great obligation to God's parental kindness and care.

SIDRAC.—You say that it is in the power of God to give you a good living, and to make you still happier than you are at present. There are many persons who would not scruple flatly to contradict this proposition of yours. Do you forget that you yourself sometimes complain of fatality? A man, and particularly a priest, ought never to contradict one day an assertion he has perhaps made the day before. All is but a succession of links, and God is wiser than to break the eternal chain of events, even for the sake of my dear friend Goodman.

GOODMAN.—I did not foresee this argument when I was speaking of fatality; but to come at once to the point, if it be so, God is as much a slave as myself.

SIDRAC.—He is the slave of his will, of his wisdom, and of the laws which he has himself instituted; and it is impossible that he can infringe upon any of them; because it is impossible that he can become either weak or inconsistent.

GOODMAN.—But, my friend, what you say would tend to make us irreligious, for, if God cannot change any of the affairs of the world, what is the use of teasing him with prayers, or of singing hymns to his praise?

SIDRAC.—Well! who bids you worship or pray to God? We praise a man because we think him vain; we entreat of him when we think him weak and likely to change his purpose on account of our petitions. Let us do our duty to God, by being just and true to each other. In that consists our real prayers, and our most heartfelt praises.

Kwan-yin, the goddess of mercy.—Burmese Buddha.—Chinese figure in ivory.[1]

A CONVERSATION WITH A CHINESE.

In the year 1723, there was a Chinese in Holland, who was both a learned man and a merchant, two things that ought by no means to be incompatible; but which, thanks to the profound respect that is shown to money, and the little regard that the human species pay to merit, have become so among us.

This Chinese, who spoke a little Dutch, happened to be in a bookseller's shop at the same time that some literati were assembled there. He asked for a book; they offered him Bossuet's *Universal History*, badly translated. At the title *Universal History*—

"How pleased am I," cried the Oriental, "to have met with this book. I shall now see what is said of our great empire; of a nation that has subsisted for upwards of fifty thousand years; of that long dynasty of emperors who have governed us for such a number of ages. I shall see what these Europeans think of the religion of our literati, and of that pure and simple worship we pay to the Supreme Being. What a pleasure will it be for me to find how they speak of our arts, many of which are of a more ancient date with us than the eras of all the kingdoms of Europe! I fancy the author will be greatly mistaken in relation to the war we had about twenty-two thousand five hundred and fifty-two years ago, with the martial people of Tonquin and Japan, as well as the solemn embassy that the powerful emperor of Mogulitian sent to request a body of laws from us in the year of the world 00000000000079123450000."

"Lord bless you," said one of the literati, "there is hardly any mention made of that nation in this world, the only nation considered is that marvelous people, the Jews."

"The Jews!" said the Chinese, "those people then must certainly be masters of three parts of the globe at least."

"They hope to be so some day," answered the other; "but at present they are those pedlars you see going about here with toys and nicknacks, and who sometimes do us the honor to clip our gold and silver."

"Surely you are not serious," exclaimed the Chinese. "Could those people ever have been in possession of a vast empire?"

Here I joined in the conversation, and told him that for a few years they were in possession of a small country to themselves; but that we were not to judge of a people from the extent of their dominions, any more than of a man by his riches.

"But does not this book take notice of some other nations?" demanded the man of letters.

"Undoubtedly," replied a learned gentleman who stood at my elbow; "it treats largely of a small country about sixty leagues wide, called Egypt, in which it is said that there is a lake of one hundred and fifty leagues in circumference, made by the hands of man."

"My God!" exclaimed the Chinese, "a lake of one hundred and fifty leagues in circumference within a spot of ground only sixty leagues wide! This is very curious!"

"The inhabitants of that country," continued the doctor, "were all sages."

"What happy times were those!" cried the Chinese; "but is that all?"

"No," replied the other, "there is mention made of those famous people the Greeks."

"Greeks! Greeks!" said the Asiatic, "who are those Greeks?"

"Why," replied the philosopher, "they were masters of a little province, about the two hundredth part as large as China, but whose fame spread over the whole world."

"Indeed!" said the Chinese, with an air of openness and ingenuousness; "I declare I never heard the least mention of these people, either in the Mogul's country, in Japan, or in Great Tartary."

"Oh, the barbarian! the ignorant creature!" cried out our sage very politely. "Why then, I suppose you know nothing of Epaminondas the Theban, nor of the Pierian Heaven, nor the names of Achilles's two horses, nor of Silenus's ass? You have never heard speak of Jupiter, nor of Diogenes, nor of Lais, nor of Cybele, nor of—"

"I am very much afraid," said the learned Oriental, interrupting him, "that you know nothing of that eternally memorable adventure of the famous Xixofon Concochigramki, nor of the masteries of the great Fi-psi-hi-hi! But pray tell me what other unknown things does this *Universal History* treat of?"

Upon this my learned neighbor harangued for a quarter of an hour together about the Roman republic, and when he came to Julius Cæsar the Chinese stopped him, and very gravely said.

"I think I have heard of him, was he not a Turk?"

"How!" cried our sage in a fury, "don't you so much as know the difference between Pagans, Christians, and Mahometans? Did you never hear of Constantine? Do you know nothing of the history of the popes?"

"We have heard something confusedly of one Mahomet," replied the Asiatic.

"It is surely impossible," said the other, "but that you must have heard at least of Luther, Zuinglius, Bellarmin, and Œcolampadius."

"I shall never remember all those names," said the Chinese, and so saying he quitted the shop, and went to sell a large quantity of Pekoa tea, and fine calico, and then after purchasing what merchandise he required, set sail for his own country, adoring *Tien*, and recommending himself to Confucius.

As to myself, the conversation I had been witness to plainly discovered to me the nature of vain glory; and I could not forbear exclaiming:

"Since Cæsar and Jupiter are names unknown to the finest, most ancient, most extensive, most populous, and most civilized kingdom in the universe, it becomes ye well, O ye rulers of petty states! ye pulpit orators of a narrow parish, or a little town! ye doctors of Salamanca, or of Bourges! ye trifling authors, and ye heavy commentators!—it becomes you well, indeed, to aspire to fame and immortality."

[1] According to Chambers' work on *The British Museum*, from which the above cuts are copied, "the Chinese, are a vast nation of some 300,000,000 of souls, nearly a third part of the whole human race. The entire population is subject to the supreme and despotic authority of a single hereditary ruler who resides at Pekin, the chief city of the whole empire. Under him the government is administered by a descending hierarchy of officials or mandarins, who are chosen from all ranks of the people, according to their talents as displayed in the course, first of their education at school and college, and afterwards of their public life. The officials are, in short, the men in highest repute for scholarship and accomplishments in the empire; and the whole system of the government is that of promotion upwards from the ranks of the people, according to merit. The Chinese generally are remarkable for common sense, orderliness, and frugal prudential habits. Printing and paper being cheap among them, and education universal, they have an immense literature, chiefly in the departments of the drama, the novel, and the moral essay; their best writers of fiction are said to resemble Richardson in style, and their best moralists Franklin. The greatest name in their literature, or indeed in their history, is that of Confucius, a philosopher and religious teacher who lived about 500 years B.C., and who left a number of books expounding and enforcing the great maxims of morality. During all the revolutions that have since elapsed, the doctrines of Confucius have retained their hold of the Chinese mind, and the religion of China consists in little more than an attachment to these doctrines, and a veneration for their founder. With abstract notions of the Deity, and of the destiny of man when he quits this life, the Chinese do not trouble themselves; a moral, correct life, and especially an honorable discharge of the duties of a son and a citizen, is the whole aim of their piety. There are, however, some voluntary

sects among them, who superinduce articles of speculative belief on the prosaic code of morality established by Confucius; and forms of religious worship are practised over the whole country under the direct sanction of the government. There are a number of figures, larger and smaller, of Chinese divinities, some of which are very neatly carved in ivory, wood, and stone. With what precise feelings the more educated Chinese address these images in prayer—whether they look upon them as symbols, or whether, like Polytheists generally, they actually view the carved figures themselves as gifted with powers—it would be difficult to say; the mass of the people, however, probably never ask the question, but, from the mere force of custom, come to regard such objects as the figure of Kwan-yin, the goddess of mercy, and the larger gilt figures of the god and goddess, precisely as the Polytheistic Greeks or Romans regarded their statues in their temples; that is, as real divinities with power for good or evil. The religious sentiment, however, sits very lightly on the Chinese. Absence of any feeling of the supernatural is perhaps the most remarkable feature of the Chinese character.

"Buddhism, was founded, as is generally believed, some centuries before Christ by a Hindoo prince and sage named Gautama. As originally propounded, Buddhism is supposed to have been a purer and more reasonable form of faith than Brahminism, recognising more clearly the spiritual and moral aims of religion; but, having been expelled from Hindostan during the early centuries of our era, after having undergone severe persecution from the Brahmins—at whose power it struck, by proscribing the system of castes—it sought refuge in the eastern peninsula, Ceylon, Thibet, Japan, and China, where it has been modified and corrupted into various forms."—E.

The birth of Minerva from the brain Of Jove.

The birth of Eve from the side of Adam.

ANDROGYNOUS DEITIES.

The ancients ascribed the existence of the universe to the fiat of omnipotence. Almighty power conjoined with infinite wisdom had produced the world and all that it inhabits. Man, the head of visible creation, was formed in the image of the gods, but the gods only were endowed with generative or creative power. These gods were androgynous—that is, male and female—containing in one person both the paternal and maternal attributes. Plato taught that mankind, like the gods, were originally androgynous, and Moses tells us that Eve, in matured wisdom and beauty, sprang forth from the side of Adam, even as

"From great Jove's head, the armed Minerva sprung
With awful shout."

"The thought of God as the Divine Mother," says a sincere and intelligent clergyman in a sermon recently published, "is a very ancient one, found in the most early nature worships." "We thank Thee O God," says the Rev. Theodore Parker, "that Thou art our Father and our Mother." "O God," says St. Augustine, "Thou art the Father, Thou the Mother of Thy children."

The preceding illustration of the birth of Minerva,—the goddess of wisdom,—*i.e. wisdom issuing from the brain of Jove*, is from Falkener's *Museum of Classical Antiquities*. It is taken from an ancient Etruscan patera (mirror), now in the Museum at Bologna, and is supposed to have been copied from the pediment of the eastern or main entrance to the Parthenon, or temple of Minerva. This pediment was the work of Phidias, and, like so many of the former monuments of ancient art and civilization, is now forever lost to mankind.

"The goddess," says the distinguished architect and antiquary M. De Quincy, "is shown issuing from the head of Jupiter. She has a helmet on her head, buckler on her arm, and spear in her hand. Jupiter is seated, holding a sceptre in one hand and a thunderbolt in the other. On the right of the new born goddess is Juno, whose arms are elevated, and who seems to have assisted at the extraordinary childbirth. On the left of Jupiter is Venus, recognizable by a sprig of myrtle and a dove. Behind Juno is Vulcan, still armed with the axe which has cleft the head of the god, and seeming to regard with admiration the success of his operations."

The engraving representing the birth of Eve, is from the *Speculum Salutis, or the Mirror of Salvation*, of which many manuscript copies were issued, for the instruction of the mendicant friars, between the twelfth and fifteenth centuries. "Heineken describes a copy in the imperial library of Vienna, which he attributes to the twelfth century. He says, such was the popularity of the work with the Benedictines that almost every monastery possessed a copy of it. Of the four manuscript copies owned by the British Museum, one is supposed to have been written in the thirteenth century, another copy is in the Flemish writing of the fifteenth century." This work, which contains several engravings and forty-five chapters of barbarous Latin rhymes, presents a good illustration of Christian art as it existed during the period immediately preceding the revival of letters, when the barbarism and ignorance of the dark ages had supplanted the artistic culture of ancient Greece and Rome.

Unprejudiced readers will doubtless admit that the birth of Minerva from the brain of Jove greatly resembles the birth of Eve from the side of Adam, and these myths show the analogy existing between the Jewish and Pagan mythologies; but the design and execution of the respective engravings, show the retrogression in art that had taken place between the time of the immortal Phidias and that of Pope Innocent III.[1]—between Pagan civilization as it existed prior to the Christian era, and the medieval barbarism of the successors of St. Peter.

"God created man in his own image," says Godfrey Higgins in the *Anacalypsis*, (vol. 2, p. 397.) "Everything was supposed to be in the image of God; and thus man was created double—the male and female in one person, or androgynous like God. By some uninitiated Jews, of about the time of Christ, this double being was supposed to have been created back to back [see the bearded Bacchus and Ariadne on the following page]; but I believe, from looking at the twins in all ancient zodiacs, it was side by side; precisely as we have seen the Siamese boys,—but still *male* and *female*. Besides, the book of Genesis implies that they were side by side, by the woman being taken from the *side* of man. Among the Indians the same doctrine is found, as we might expect."

"We must rise to man," says the eloquent clergyman previously referred to, "in order to know rightly what God is. Humanity plainly images a power which is at once the source and pattern of the womanly as well as of the manly qualities, inasmuch as woman as well as man is needed to fill out the idea of humanity. The womanly traits—pity, forgiveness, gentleness, patience, sympathy, unselfishness—are as worthy of the Divine Being as the manly traits."—E.

[1] "It was," says Gibbon, "at the feet of his legate that John of England surrendered his crown; and Innocent may boast of the two most signal triumphs over sense and humanity, the establishment of transsubstantiation, and the origin of the inquisition."

Bacchus and Ariadne.

PLATO'S DREAM.

Plato was a great dreamer, as many others have been since his time. He dreampt that mankind were formerly double; and that, as a punishment for their crimes, they were divided into male and female.

He undertook to prove that there can be no more than five perfect worlds, because there are but five regular mathematical bodies. His Republic was one of his principal dreams. He dreampt, moreover, that watching arises from sleep, and sleep from watching; and that a person who should attempt to look at an eclipse, otherwise than in a pail of water, would surely lose his sight. Dreams were, at that time, in great repute.

Here follows one of his dreams, which is not one of the least interesting. He thought that the great Demiurgos, the eternal geometer, having peopled the immensity of space with innumerable globes, was willing to make a trial of the knowledge of the genii who had been witnesses of his works. He gave to each of them a small portion of matter to arrange, nearly in the same manner as Phidias and Zeuxis would have given their scholars a statue to carve, or a picture to paint, if we may be allowed to compare small things to great.

Envy.

Demogorgon had for his lot the lump of mould, which we call the Earth; and having formed it, such as it now appears, he thought he had executed a masterpiece. He imagined he had silenced Envy herself, and expected to receive the highest panegyrics, even from his brethren; but how great was his surprise, when, at his next appearing among them, they received him with a general hiss.

One among them, more satirical than the rest, accosted him thus:

"Truly you have performed mighty feats! you have divided your world into two parts; and, to prevent the one from having communication with the other, you have carefully placed a vast collection of waters between the two hemispheres. The inhabitants must perish with cold under both your poles, and be scorched to death under the equator. You have, in your great prudence, formed immense deserts of sand, so that all who travel over them may die with hunger and thirst. I have no fault to find with your cows, your sheep, your cocks, and your hens; but can never be reconciled to your serpents and your spiders. Your onions and your artichokes are very good things, but I cannot conceive what induced you to scatter such a heap of poisonous plants over the face of the earth, unless it was to poison its inhabitants. Moreover, if I am not mistaken, you have created about thirty different kinds of monkeys, a still greater number of dogs, and only four or five species of the human race. It is true, indeed, you have bestowed on the latter of these animals a faculty by you called Reason; but, in truth, this same reason is a very ridiculous thing, and borders very near upon folly. Besides, you do not seem to have shown any very great regard to this two-legged creature, seeing you have left him with so few means of defense; subjected him to so many disorders, and provided him with so few remedies; and formed him with such a multitude of passions, and so small a portion of wisdom or prudence to resist them. You certainly was not willing that there should remain any great number of these animals on the earth at once; for, without reckoning the dangers to which you have exposed them, you have so ordered matters that, taking every day through the year, the small pox will regularly carry off the tenth part of the species, and sister maladies will taint the springs of life in the nine remaining parts; and then, as if this was not sufficient, you have so disposed things, that one-half of those who survive will be occupied in going to law with each other, or cutting one another's throats.

"Now, they must doubtless be under infinite obligations to you, and it must be owned you have executed a masterpiece."

Demogorgon blushed. He was sensible there was much moral and physical evil in this affair; but still he insisted there was more good than ill in it.

"It is an easy matter to find fault, good folks," said the genii; "but do you imagine it is so easy to form an animal, who, having the gift of reason and free-will, shall not sometimes abuse his liberty? Do you think that, in rearing between nine and ten thousand different plants, it is so easy to prevent some few from having noxious qualities? Do you suppose that, with a certain quantity of water, sand, and mud, you could make a globe that should have neither seas nor deserts?"

"As for you, my sneering friend, I think you have just finished the planet Jupiter. Let us see now what figure you make with your great belts, and your long nights, with four moons to enlighten them. Let us examine your worlds, and see whether the inhabitants you have made are exempt from follies or diseases."

Accordingly the genii fell to examining the planet Jupiter, when the laugh went strongly against the laugher. The serious genii who had made the planet Saturn, did not escape without his share of the censure, and his brother operators, the makers of Mars, Mercury, and Venus, had each in his turn some reproaches to undergo.

Several large volumes, and a great number of pamphlets, were written on this occasion; smart sayings and witty repartees flew about on all sides; they railed against and ridiculed each other; and, in short, the disputes were carried on with all the warmth of party heat, when the eternal Demiurgos thus imposed silence on them all:

"In your several performances there is both good and bad, because you have a great share of understanding, but at the same time fall short of perfection. Your works will not endure above an hundred millions of years, after which you will acquire more knowledge, and perform much better. It belongs to me alone to create things perfect and immortal."

This was the doctrine Plato taught his disciples. One of them, when he had finished his harangue, cried out, "*And so you then awoke?*"

[1] The above representation of a bearded Bacchus and Ariadne is from Falkener's *Museum of Classical Antiquities*. The statue was found at Pompeii in 1847.—E.

Plato.

Visiting Seignior Pococurante.

PLEASURE IN HAVING NO PLEASURE.

"Hitherto," said Candide to Martin, "I have met with none but unfortunate people in the whole habitable globe, except in El Dorado, but, observe those gondoliers, are they not perpetually singing?"

"You do not see them," answered Martin, "at home with their wives and brats. The doge has his chagrin, gondoliers theirs. Nevertheless, in the main, I look upon the gondolier's life as preferable to that of the doge; but the difference is so trifling, that it is not worth the trouble of examining into."

"I have heard great talk," said Candide, "of the Senator Pococurante, who lives in that fine house at the Brenta, where, they say, he entertains foreigners in the most polite manner. They pretend this man is a perfect stranger to uneasiness."

"I should be glad to see so extraordinary a being," said Martin.

Candide thereupon sent a messenger to Seignior Pococurante, desiring permission to wait on him the next day.

Accordingly, Candide and his friend Martin went in a gondola on the Brenta, and arrived at the palace of the noble Pococurante. The gardens were laid out in elegant taste, and adorned with fine marble statues; his palace was built after the most approved rules in architecture. The master of the house, who was a man of sixty, and very rich, received our two travelers with great politeness, but without much ceremony, which somewhat disconcerted Candide, but was not at all displeasing to Martin.

As soon as they were seated, two very pretty girls, neatly dressed, brought in chocolate, which was extremely well frothed. Candide could not help making encomiums upon their beauty and graceful carriage.

"The creatures are well enough," said the senator, "but I am heartily tired of women, of their coquetry, their jealousy, their quarrels, their humors, their vanity, their pride, and their folly; I am weary of making sonnets, or of paying for sonnets to be made on them; and, after all, those two girls begin to grow very indifferent to me."

After having refreshed himself, Candide walked into a large gallery, where he was struck with the sight of a fine collection of paintings.

"Pray," said Candide, "by what master are the first two of these?"

"They are Raphael's," answered the senator. "I gave a great deal of money for them seven years ago, purely out of curiosity, as they were said to be the finest pieces in Italy; but I cannot say they please me: the coloring is dark and heavy; the figures do not swell nor come out enough, and the drapery is very bad. In short, notwithstanding the encomiums lavished upon them, they are not, in my opinion, a true representation of nature. I approve of no paintings but where I think I behold nature herself; and there are very few, if any, of that kind to be met with. I have what is called a fine collection, but it affords me no delight."

While dinner was getting ready, Pococurante ordered a concert. Candide praised the music to the skies.

"This noise," said the noble Venetian, "may amuse one for a little time, but if it were to last above half an hour, it would grow very tiresome, though perhaps no one would care to own it. Music has become the art of executing that which is difficult. Now whatever is difficult cannot long continue pleasing. I might take more pleasure in an opera if they had not made that species of dramatic entertainment so shockingly monstrous; and I am amazed that people can bear to see wretched tragedies set to music, where the scenes are contrived for no other purpose than to lug in, as it were by the ears, three or four ridiculous songs, to give a favorite actress an opportunity of exhibiting her voice. Let who will or can die away in raptures at the trills of an eunuch quavering the majestic part of Cæsar or Cato, and strutting in a foolish manner on the stage; for my part, I have long ago renounced these paltry entertainments, which constitute the glory of modern Italy, and are so dearly purchased by crowned heads."

Candide opposed these sentiments; but he did it in a discreet manner; as for Martin, he was entirely of the old senator's opinion.

Dinner being served up, they sat down to table, and after a very hearty repast returned to the library. Candide observing Homer richly bound, commended the noble Venetian's taste.

"This," said he, "is a book that was once the delight of the great Pangloss, the best philosopher in Germany."

"Homer is no favorite of mine," answered Pococurante, very coolly: "I was made to believe once that I took a pleasure in reading him; but his continual repetitions of battles have all such a resemblance with each other; his gods, that are forever in a hurry and bustle without ever doing anything; his Helen, that is the cause of the war, and yet hardly acts in the whole performance; his Troy, that holds out so long, without being taken; in short, all these things together make the poem very insipid to me. I have asked some learned men, whether they are not in reality as much tired as myself with reading this poet? Those who spoke ingenuously, assured me that he had made them fall asleep; and yet, that they could not well avoid giving him a place in their libraries; but it was merely as they would do an antique, or those rusty medals which are kept only for curiosity, and are of no manner of use in commerce."

"But your excellency does not surely form this same opinion of Virgil?" said Candide.

"Why, I grant," replied Pococurante, "that the second, third, fourth, and sixth book, of his Æneid are excellent; but as for his pious Æneas, his strong Cloanthus, his friendly Achates, his boy Ascanius, his silly King Latinus, his ill-bred Amata, his insipid Lavinia, and some other characters much in the same strain, I think there cannot be in nature anything more flat and disagreeable. I must confess, I much prefer Tasso to him; nay, even that sleepy tale-teller Ariosto."

"May I take the liberty to ask if you do not receive great pleasure from reading Horace?" said Candide.

"There are maxims in this writer," replied Pococurante, "from whence a man of the world may reap some benefit; and the short measure of the verse makes them more easy to retain in the memory. But I see nothing extraordinary in his journey to Brundusium, and his account of his bad dinner; nor in his dirty low quarrel between one Rupilius, whose words, as he expresses it, were full of poisonous filth; and another, whose language was dipped in vinegar. His indelicate verses against old women and witches have frequently given me great offense; nor can I discover the great merit of his telling his friend Mecænas, that if he will but rank him in the class of lyric poets, his lofty head shall touch the stars. Ignorant readers are apt to praise everything by the lump in a writer of reputation. For my part, I read only to please myself. I like nothing but that which makes for my purpose."

Candide, who had been brought up with a notion of never making use of his own judgment, was astonished at what he had heard; but Martin found there was a good deal of reason in the senator's remarks.

"O! here is a Tully," said Candide: "this great man, I fancy, you are never tired of reading?"

"Indeed, I never read him at all," replied Pococurante. "What is it to me whether he pleads for Rabirius or Cluentius? I try causes enough myself. I had once some liking for his philosophical works; but when I found he doubted of everything, I thought I knew as much as himself, *and had no need of a guide to learn ignorance.*

"Ha!" cried Martin, "here are fourscore volumes of the *Memoirs of the Academy of Sciences*. Perhaps there may be something curious and valuable in this collection."

"Yes," answered Pococurante, "so there might, if any one of these compilers of this rubbish had only invented the art of pin-making; but all these volumes are filled with mere chimerical systems, without one single article conducive to real utility."

"I see a prodigious number of plays," said Candide, "in Italian, Spanish, and French."

"Yes," replied the Venetian, "there are, I think, three thousand, and not three dozen of them good for anything. As to these huge volumes of divinity, and those enormous collections of sermons, they are not altogether worth one single page in Seneca; and I fancy you will readily believe that neither myself, nor any one else, ever looks into them."

Martin, perceiving some shelves filled with English books, said to the senator:

"I fancy that a republican must be highly delighted with those books, which are most of them written with a noble spirit of freedom."

"It is noble to write as we think," said Pococurante; "it is the privilege of humanity. Throughout Italy we write only what we do not think; and the present inhabitants of the country of the Cæsars and Antoninuses dare not acquire a single idea without the permission of a father dominican. I should be enamoured of the spirit of the English nation, did it not utterly frustrate the good effects it would produce, by passion and the spirit of party."

Candide, seeing a Milton, asked the senator if he did not think that author a great man?

"Who?" said Pococurante, sharply; "that barbarian who writes a tedious commentary in ten books of rambling verse on the first chapter of Genesis? that slovenly imitator of the Greeks, who disfigures the creation by making the Messiah take a pair of compasses from heaven's armory to plan the world; whereas Moses represented the Deity as producing the whole universe by his fiat? Can I, think you, have any esteem for a writer who has spoiled Tasso's hell and the devil? who transforms Lucifer sometimes into a toad, and at others, into a pigmy? who makes him say the same thing over again an hundred times? who metamorphoses him into a school-divine? and who, by an absurdly serious imitation of Ariosto's comic invention of fire-arms, represents the devils and angels cannonading each other in heaven? Neither I nor any other Italian can possibly take pleasure in such melancholy reveries; but the marriage of sin and death, and snakes issuing from the womb of the former, are enough to make any person sick that is not lost to all sense of delicacy. This obscene, whimsical, and disagreeable poem, met with the neglect it deserved at its first publication; and I only treat the author now as he was treated in his own country by his contemporaries."

Candide was sensibly grieved at this speech, as he had a great respect for Homer, and was very fond of Milton.

"Alas!" said he softly to Martin, "I am afraid this man holds our German poets in great contempt."

"There would be no such great harm in that," said Martin.

"O, what a surprising man!" said Candide still to himself; "what a genius is this Pococurante! nothing can please him."

After finishing their survey of the library, they went down into the garden, when Candide commended the several beauties that offered themselves to his view.

"I know nothing upon earth laid out in such bad taste," said Pococurante; "everything about it is childish and trifling; but I shall soon have another laid out upon a nobler plan."

"Well," said Candide to Martin, as soon as our two travelers had taken leave of his excellency: "I hope you will own, that this man is the happiest of all mortals, for he is above everything he possesses."

"But do you not see," said Martin, "that he likewise dislikes everything he possesses? It was an observation of Plato, long since, that those are not the best stomachs that reject, without distinction, all sorts of aliments."

"True," said Candide; "but still there must certainly be a pleasure in criticising everything, and in perceiving faults where others think they see beauties."

"That is," replied Martin, "there is a pleasure in having no pleasure."

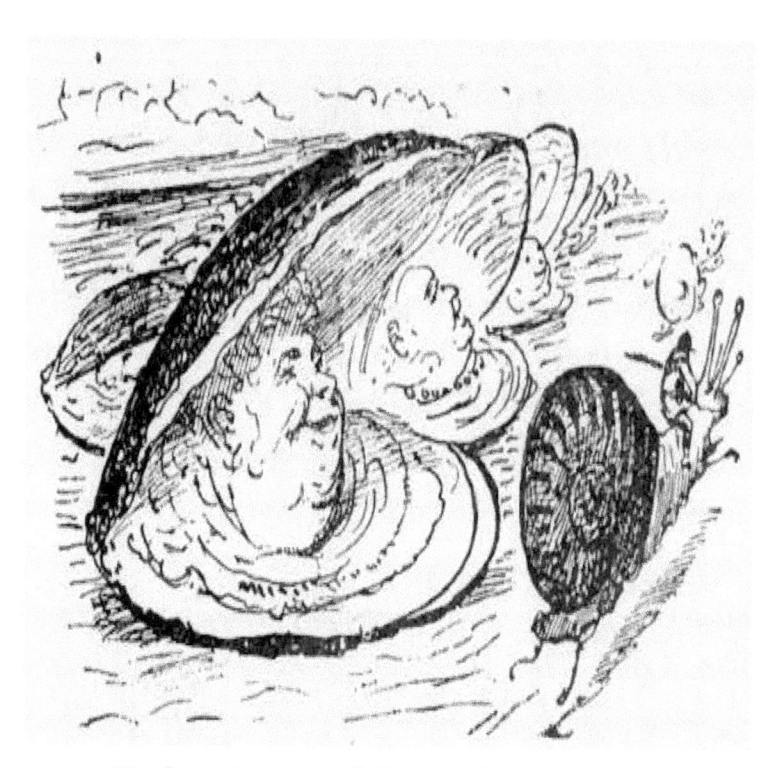

The "yawning oysters" discovered by Pythagoras.

AN ADVENTURE IN INDIA.

All the world knows that Pythagoras, while he resided in India, attended the school of the Gymnosophists, and learned the language of beasts and plants.[1] One day, while he was walking in a meadow near the seashore, he heard these words:

"How unfortunate that I was born an herb! I scarcely attain two inches in height, when a voracious monster, an horrid animal, tramples me under his large feet; his jaws are armed with rows of sharp scythes, by which he cuts, then grinds, and then swallows me. Men call this monster a sheep. I do not suppose there is in the whole creation a more detestable creature."

Pythagoras proceeded a little way and found an oyster yawning on a small rock. He had not yet adopted that admirable law, by which we are enjoined not to eat those animals which have a resemblance to us.[2] He had scarcely taken up the oyster to swallow it, when it spoke these affecting words:

"O, Nature, how happy is the herb, which is, as I am, thy work! though it be cut down, it is regenerated and immortal; and we, poor oysters, in vain are defended by a double cuirass: villains eat us by dozens at their breakfast, and all is over with us forever. What an horrible fate is that of an oyster, and how barbarous are men!"

Pythagoras shuddered; he felt the enormity of the crime he had nearly committed; he begged pardon of the oyster with tears in his eyes, and replaced it very carefully on the rock.

As he was returning to the city, profoundly meditating on this adventure, he saw spiders devouring flies; swallows eating spiders, and sparrow-hawks eating swallows. "None of these," said he, "are philosophers."

On his entrance, Pythagoras was stunned, bruised, and thrown down by a lot of tatterdemalions, who were running and crying: "Well done, he fully deserved it." "Who? What?" said Pythagoras, as he was getting up. The people continued running and crying: "O how delightful it will be to see them boiled!"

Pythagoras supposed they meant lentiles, or some other vegetables: but he was in an error; they meant two poor Indians. "Oh!" said Pythagoras, "these Indians, without doubt, are two great philosophers weary of their lives, they are desirous of regenerating under other forms; it affords pleasure to a man to change his place of residence, though he may be but indifferently lodged: there is no disputing on taste."[3]

He proceeded with the mob to the public square, where he perceived a lighted pile of wood, and a bench opposite to it, which was called a tribunal.

On this bench judges were seated, each of whom had a cow's tail in his hand, and a cap on his head, with ears resembling those of the animal which bore Silenus when he came into that country with Bacchus, after having crossed the Erytrean sea without wetting a foot, and stopping the sun and moon; as it is recorded with great fidelity in the Orphicks.

Among these judges there was an honest man with whom Pythagoras was acquainted. The Indian sage explained to the sage of Samos the nature of that festival to be given to the people of India.

"These two Indians," said he, "have not the least desire to be committed to the flames. My grave brethren have adjudged them to be burnt; one for saying, that the substance of Xaca is not that of Brahma; and the other for supposing, that the approbation of the Supreme Being was to be obtained at the point of death without holding a cow by the tail; 'Because,' said he, 'we may be virtuous at all times, and we cannot always have a cow to lay hold of just when we may have occasion.' The good women of the city were greatly terrified at two such heretical opinions; they would not allow the judges a moment's peace until they had ordered the execution of those unfortunate men."

Pythagoras was convinced that from the herb up to man, there were many causes of chagrin. However, he obliged the judges and even the devotees to listen to reason, which happened only at that time.

He went afterwards and preached toleration at Crotona; but a bigot set fire to his house, and he was burnt—the man who had delivered the two Hindoos from the flames? Let those save themselves who can![1]

[1] Perhaps it would be impossible at the present day to convince scientists that oysters formerly conversed intelligibly with mankind and protested eloquently against human injustice; but all men are not scientists, and there are many worthy people who still have implicit faith in ancient Semitic records—who firmly believe in miracles and prodigies—and who would consider it rank heresy to doubt that the serpent, though now as mute as an oyster, formerly held a very animated conversation, in the original Edenic language, with the inexperienced and confiding female who then graced with her charming presence the bowers of Paradise; and this sacred narrative of the "maiden and the reptile" is quite as repugnant to modern science as the sentimental fish story of "Pythagoras and the oyster".

As a matter of fact, the doctrine of the metempsichosis, as taught by the Samian sage, was formerly held in great repute by the most civilized nations of antiquity, and it is surely as easy to credit the assertion of our author, that the ancient Gymnosophists "had learned the language of beasts and plants" as to believe the unquestioned and orthodox statement that a certain quadruped, (*Asinus vulgaris,*) —whose romantic history is recorded in the twenty-second chapter of Numbers,—was once upon a time able to converse in very good Hebrew with Monsieur Balaam, an ancient prophet of great merit and renown.—E.

[2] The resemblance of oysters to mankind, here implied, can only be apparent to the "eye of faith," and lovers of these delicious bivalves will fail to recognize the family likeness.—E.

[3] Pythagoras was born at Samos, about 590 years before the Christian era. He received an education well calculated to enlighten his mind and invigorate his body. He studied poetry, music, eloquence and astronomy, and became so proficient in gymnastic exercises, that in his eighteenth year he won the prize for wrestling at the Olympic games. He then visited Egypt and Chaldea, and gaining the confidence of the priests, learned from them the artful policy by which they governed the people. On his return to Samos he was saluted by the name of *Sophist*, or wise man, but he declined the name, and was satisfied with that of philosopher, or the *friend of wisdom*. He ultimately fixed his residence in Magna Græcia, in the town of Crotona, where he founded the school called *the Italian*.

This school became very prosperous, and hundreds of pupils received the *secret instructions* of Pythagoras, who taught by the use of ciphers or numbers, and hieroglyphic writings. His pupils were thus enabled to correspond together in unknown characters; and, by the signs and words employed, they could discover among strangers those who had been educated in the Pythagorean school. All the pupils of the philosopher greatly reverenced their teacher, and deemed it a crime to dispute his word. One of their expressions "*thus saith the Master*," has been adopted by modern sects.

The Samian sage taught the doctrine of the metempsichosis, or the transmigration of the soul into different bodies, which he had probably learned from the Brahmins; who believed that, in these various peregrinations, the soul or thinking principle was purged from all evil, and was ultimately absorbed into the Divine substance from which it was supposed to have emanated.

Godfrey Higgins in the *Anacalypsis* cites authorities to prove that the doctrine of the metempsichosis was held by "many of the early fathers of the Christians, which they defended on several texts of the New Testament. It was held by Origin, Calcidius, Synesius, and by the Simonians, Basilidians, Valentiniens, Marcionites, and the Gnostics in general. It was also held by the Pharisees among the Jews, and by the most learned of the Greeks, and by many Chinese, Hindoos and Indians.

"When all the circumstances relating to Pythagoras and to his doctrines, both in moral and natural philosophy, are considered," continues Higgins, "nothing can be more striking than the exact conformity of the latter to the received opinions of the moderns, and of the former to the moral doctrines of Jesus Christ."

"The pupils of Pythagoras," says Eschenburg, *Manual of Classical Literature*, "soon amounted to 600, dwelt in one public building, and held their property in common. Under philosophy, the Italic school included every object of human knowledge. But Pythagoras considered music and astronomy of special value. He is supposed to have had some very correct views of astronomy, agreeing with the true Copernican system. The beautiful fancy of the music of the spheres is attributed to him. The planets striking on the ether, through which they pass, must produce a sound; this must vary according to their different magnitudes, velocities, and relative distances; these differences were all adjusted with perfect regularity and exact proportions, so that the movements of the bodies produced the richest tones of harmony; not heard, however, by mortal ears."

Pythagoras taught, and his followers maintained, the absolute equality of property, "all their worldly possessions being brought into a common store". The early Christians had also "all things in common," and the doctrines of Jesus and Pythagoras have many points of resemblance. Both were reformers, both sought to benefit the poor and the oppressed, both taught and practised the doctrines now known as Communism, and both, for their love to the human race, suffered a cruel martyrdom from an orthodox and vindictive priesthood.

In obedience to an oracle, the Romans, long after the death of Pythagoras, erected a statue to his memory as the wisest of mankind.—E.

[4] Godfrey Higgins in the *Anacalypsis* draws aside the veil of Isis, and explains in a satisfactory manner the reason why Pythagoras, like Socrates and Jesus, was condemned to death by the established priesthood. Each of these great reformers had been initiated into the *sacred mysteries*, and each taught his followers by secret symbols or parables that contained a hidden meaning; so "that seeing the *uninitiated* might see and not perceive, and hearing might hear and not understand." The reason that Jesus gave for following this method was "because it is given unto you (*i.e.* the initiated) to know the mysteries of the kingdom of heaven, but to them (*i.e.* the people) it is not given." (Matt. XIII: II.) The mass of mankind, being excluded from this secret knowledge, were kept in a state of debasement as compared with the favored few who were acquainted with the jealously guarded secrets of the Cabala; and the earnest desire of these great reformers—of these noble men who cheerfully gave their lives to benefit their race—was, without

divulging the secrets of their initiation, to teach mankind to partake of the forbidden fruit of the tree of knowledge, and to learn "that a virtuous life would secure eternal happiness." Such philanthropic doctrines were denounced as wicked and heretical by the orthodox priesthood, who instinctively oppose human progress, and who, like the silversmith of Ephesus, described by St. Paul, felt that "this our craft is in danger" should the people become enlightened. They therefore, excited a popular clamor, and aroused the worst passions and prejudices of their followers; who, inspired with fanatic zeal, cruelly and wickedly burned Pythagoras of Crotona, poisoned Socrates of Athens, and crucified Jesus of Nazareth.—E.

The school at Issoire.

JEANNOT AND COLIN.

Many persons, worthy of credit, have seen Jeannot and Colin at school in the town of Issoire, in Auvergne, France,—a town famous all over the world for its college and its caldrons.

Jeannot was the son of a dealer in mules of great reputation; and Colin owed his birth to a good substantial farmer in the neighborhood, who cultivated the land with four mules; and who, after he had paid all taxes and duties at the rate of a sol per pound, was not very rich at the year's end.

Jeannot and Colin were very handsome, considering they were natives of Auvergne; they dearly loved each other. They had many enjoyments in common, and certain little adventures of such a nature as men always recollect with pleasure when they afterwards meet in the world.

Their studies were nearly finished, when a tailor brought Jeannot a velvet suit of three colors, with a waistcoat from Lyons, which was extremely well fancied. With these came a letter addressed to Monsieur de la Jeannotière.

Colin admired the coat, and was not at all jealous; but Jeannot assumed an air of superiority, which gave Colin some uneasiness. From that moment Jeannot abandoned his studies; he contemplated himself in a glass, and despised all mankind.

Soon after, a valet-de-chambre arrived post-haste, and brought a second letter to the Marquis de la Jeannotière; it was an order from his father, who desired the young marquis to repair immediately to Paris. Jeannot got into his chaise, giving his hand to Colin with a smile, which denoted the superiority of a patron. Colin felt his littleness, and wept. Jeannot departed in all the pomp of his glory.

Such readers as take a pleasure in being instructed should be informed that Monsieur Jeannot the father, had, with great rapidity, acquired an immense fortune by business. You will ask how such great fortunes are made? My answer is, by luck. Monsieur Jeannot had a good person, so had his wife; and she had still some freshness remaining. They went to Paris on account of a law-suit, which ruined them; when fortune, which raises and depresses men at her pleasure, presented them to the wife of an undertaker belonging to one of the hospitals for the army. This undertaker, a man of great talents, might make it his boast, that he had buried more soldiers in a year than cannons destroy in ten. Jeannot pleased the wife; the wife of Jeannot interested the undertaker. Jeannot was employed in the undertaker's business; this introduced him to other business. When our boat runs with wind and stream, we have nothing to do but let it sail on. We then make an immense fortune with ease. The poor creatures who from the shore see you pursue your voyage with full sail, stare with astonishment; they cannot conceive to what you owe your success; they envy you instinctively, and write pamphlets against you which you never read.

This is just what happened to Jeannot the father, who soon became Monsieur de la Jeannotière; and who having purchased a marquisate in six months time, took the young marquis, his son, from school, in order to introduce him to the polite world at Paris.

Colin, whose heart was replete with tenderness, wrote a letter of compliments to his old companion, and congratulated him on his good fortune. The little marquis did not reply. Colin was so much affected at this neglect that he was taken ill.

The father and mother immediately consigned the young marquis to the care of a governor. This governor, who was a man of fashion, and who knew nothing, was not able to teach his pupil anything.

The marquis would have had his son learn Latin; this his lady opposed. They then referred the matter to the judgment of an author, who had at that time acquired great reputation by his entertaining writings. This author was invited to dinner. The master of the house immediately addressed him thus:

"Sir, as you understand Latin, and are a man acquainted with the court,—"

"I understand Latin! I don't know one word of it," answered the wit, "and I think myself the better for being unacquainted with it. It is very evident that a man speaks his own language in greater perfection when he does not divide his application between it and foreign languages. Only consider our ladies; they have a much more agreeable turn of wit than the men, their letters are written with a hundred times the grace of ours. This superiority they owe to nothing else but their not understanding Latin."

"Well, was I not in the right?" said the lady. "I would have my son prove a notable man, I would have him succeed in the world; and you see that if he was to understand Latin he would be ruined. Pray, are plays and operas performed in Latin? Do lawyers plead in Latin? Do men court a mistress in Latin?"

The marquis, dazzled by these reasons, gave up the point, and it was resolved, that the young marquis should not misspend his time in endeavoring to become acquainted with Cicero, Horace and Virgil.

"Then," said the father, "what shall he learn? For he must know something. Might not one teach him a little geography?"

"Of what use will that be?" answered the governor. "When the marquis goes to his estate, won't the postillion know the roads? They certainly will not carry him out of his way. There is no occasion for a quadrant to travel thither; and one can go very commodiously from Paris to Auvergne without knowing what latitude one is in."

"You are in the right," replied the father; "but I have heard of a science, called astronomy, if I am not mistaken."

"Bless me!" said the governor, "do people regulate their conduct by the influence of the stars in this world? And must the young gentleman perplex himself with the calculation of an eclipse, when he finds it ready calculated to his hand in an almanac, which, at the same time, shows him the movable feasts, the age of the moon, and also that of all the princesses in Europe?"

The lady agreed perfectly with the governor; the little marquis was transported with joy; the father remained undetermined. "What then is my son to learn?" said he.

"To become amiable," answered the friend who was consulted, "and if he knows how to please, he will know all that need be known. This art he will learn in the company of his mother, without either he or she being at any trouble."

The lady, upon hearing this, embraced the ignorant flatterer, and said: "It is easy to see, sir, that you are the wisest man in the world. My son will be entirely indebted to you for his education. I think, however, it would not be amiss if he was to know something of history."

"Alas, madam, what is that good for," answered he; "there certainly is no useful or entertaining history but the history of the day; all ancient histories, as one of our wits has observed, are only fables that men have agreed to admit as true. With regard to modern history, it is a mere chaos, a confusion which it is impossible to make anything of. Of what consequence is it to the young marquis, your son, to know that Charlemagne instituted the twelve peers of France, and that his successor stammered?"

"Admirably said," cried the governor; "the genius of young persons is smothered under a heap of useless knowledge; but of all sciences, the most absurd, and that which, in my opinion, is most calculated to stifle genius of every kind, is geometry. The objects about which this ridiculous science is conversant, are surfaces, lines, and points, that have no existence in nature. By the force of imagination, the geometrician makes a hundred thousand curved lines pass between a circle and a right line that touches it, when, in reality, there is not room for a straw to pass there. Geometry, if we consider it in its true light, is a mere jest, and nothing more."

The marquis and his lady did not well understand the governor's meaning, yet they were entirely of his opinion.

"A man of quality, like the young marquis," continued he, "should not rack his brains with useless sciences. If he should ever have occasion for a plan of the lands of his estate, he may have them correctly surveyed without studying geometry. If he has a mind to trace the antiquity of his noble family, which leads the inquirer back to the most remote ages, he will send for a Benedictine. It will be the same thing with regard to all other wants. A young man of quality, endowed with a happy genius, is neither a painter, a musician, an architect, nor a graver; but he makes all these arts flourish by generously encouraging them. It is, doubtless, better to patronize than to practice them. It is enough for the young marquis to have a taste; it is the business of artists to exert themselves for him; and it is in this sense that it is said very justly of people of quality, (I mean those who are very rich), that they know all things without having learnt anything; for they, in fact, come at last to know how to judge concerning whatever they order or pay for."

The ignorant man of fashion then spoke to this purpose:

"You have very justly observed, madam, that the grand end which a man should have in view is to succeed in the world. Can it possibly be said that this success is to be obtained by cultivating the sciences? Did anybody ever so much as think of talking of geometry in good company? Does anyone ever inquire of a man of the world, what star rises with the sun? Who enquires at supper, whether the long-haired Clodio passed the Rhine?"

"No, doubtless," cried the marchioness, whom her charms had in some measure initiated into the customs of the polite world; "and my son should not extinguish his genius by the study of all this stuff. But what is he, after all, to learn? for it is proper that a young person of quality should know how to shine upon an occasion, as my husband observes. I remember to have heard an abbé say, that the most delightful of all the sciences, is something that begins with a *B*."

"With a B, madam? Is it not botany you mean?"

"No, it was not botany he spoke of; the name of the science he mentioned began with *B*, and ended with *on*."

"Oh, I comprehend you, madam," said the man of fashion; "it is *Blason* you mean. It is indeed a profound science; but it is no longer in fashion, since the people of quality have ceased to cause their arms to be painted upon the doors of their coaches. It was once the most useful thing in the world, in a well regulated state. Besides, this study would be endless. Now-a-days there is hardly a barber that has not his coat of arms; and you know that whatever becomes common is but little esteemed."

In fine, after they had examined the excellencies and defects of all the sciences, it was determined that the young marquis should learn to dance.

Nature, which does all, had given him a talent that quickly displayed itself surprisingly; it was that of singing ballads agreeably. The graces of youth, joined to this superior gift, caused him to be looked upon as a young man of the brightest hopes. He was admired by the women; and having his head full of songs, he composed some for his mistress. He stole from the song "*Bacchus and Love*" in one ballad; from that of "*Night and Day*" in another; from that of "*Charms and Alarms*" in a third. But as there were always in his verses some superfluous feet, or not enough, he had them corrected for twenty louis-d'ors a song; and in the annals of literature he was put upon a level with the La Fares, Chaulieus, Hamiltons, Sarrazins, and Voitures.

The marchioness then looked upon herself as the mother of a wit, and gave a supper to the wits of Paris. The young man's brain was soon turned; he acquired the art of speaking without knowing his own meaning, and he became perfect in the habit of being good for nothing. When his father found he was so eloquent, he very much regretted that his son had not learned Latin; for he would have bought him a lucrative place among the gentry of the long robe. The mother, who had more elevated sentiments, undertook to procure a regiment for her son; and in the meantime, courtship was his occupation. Love is sometimes more expensive than a regiment. He was very improvident, whilst his parents exhausted their finances still more, by expensive living.

A young widow of fashion, their neighbor, who had but a moderate fortune, had an inclination to secure the great wealth of Monsieur and Madame de la Jeannotière, and appropriating it to herself, by a marriage with the young marquis. She allured him to visit her; she admitted his addresses; she showed that she was not indifferent to him; she led him on by degrees; she enchanted and captivated him without much difficulty. Sometimes she lavished praises upon him, sometimes she gave him advice. She became the most intimate friend of both the father and mother.

An elderly lady, who was their neighbor, proposed the match. The parents, dazzled by the glory of such an alliance, accepted the proposal with joy. They gave their only son to their intimate friend.

The young marquis was now on the point of marrying a woman whom he adored, and by whom he was beloved; the friends of the family congratulated them; the marriage articles were just going to be drawn up, whilst wedding clothes were being made for the young couple, and their epithalamium composed.

The young marquis was one day upon his knees before his charming mistress, whom love, esteem, and friendship were going to make all his own. In a tender and spirited conversation, they enjoyed a foretaste of their coming happiness, they concerted measures to lead a happy life. When all on a sudden a valet-de-chambre belonging to the old marchioness, arrived in a great fright.

"Here is sad news," said he, "officers have removed the effects of my master and mistress; the creditors have seized upon all by virtue of an execution; and I am obliged to make the best shift I can to have my wages paid."

"Let's see," said the marquis, "what is this? What can this adventure mean?"

"Go," said the widow, "go quickly, and punish those villains."

He runs, he arrives at the house; his father is already in prison; all the servants have fled in different ways, each carrying off whatever he could lay his hands upon. His mother is alone, without assistance, without comfort, drowned in tears. She has nothing left but the remembrance of her fortune, of her beauty, her faults, and her extravagant living.

After the son had wept a long time with his mother, he at length said to her:

"Let us not give ourselves up to despair. This young widow loves me to excess; she is more generous than rich, I can answer for her; I will go and bring her to you."

He returns to his mistress, and finds her in company with a very amiable young officer.

"What, is it you, M. de la Jeannotière," said she; "what brings you here? Is it proper to forsake your unhappy mother in such a crisis? Go to that poor, unfortunate woman, and tell her that I still wish her well. I have occasion for a chamber-maid, and will give her the preference."

"My lad," said the officer, "you are well shaped. Enlist in my company; you may depend on good usage."

The marquis, thunderstruck, and with a heart enraged, went in quest of his old governor, made him acquainted with his misfortune, and asked his advice. The governor proposed that he should become a tutor, like himself.

"Alas!" said the marquis, "I know nothing; you have taught me nothing, and you are the first cause of my misfortunes." He sobbed when he spoke thus.

"Write romances," said a wit who was present; "it is an admirable resource at Paris."

The young man, in greater despair than ever, ran to his mother's confessor. This confessor was a Theatin of great reputation, who directed the consciences only of women of the first rank. As soon as he saw Jeannot, he ran up to him:

"My God, Mr. Marquis," said he, "where is your coach? How is the good lady your mother?"

The poor unfortunate young man gave him an account of what had befallen his family. In proportion as he explained himself the Theatin assumed an air more grave, more indifferent, and more defiant.

"My son," said he, "it is the will of God that you should be reduced to this condition; riches serve only to corrupt the heart. God, in his great mercy, has then reduced your mother to beggary?"

Jeannot and Colin.

"Yes, sir," answered the marquis.

"So much the better," said the confessor, "her election is the more certain."

"But father," said the marquis, "is there in the mean time no hopes of some assistance in this world?"

"Farewell, my son," said the confessor; "a court lady is waiting for me."

The marquis was almost ready to faint. He met with much the same treatment from all; and acquired more knowledge of the world in half a day than he had previously learned in all the rest of his life.

Being quite overwhelmed with despair, he saw an old-fashioned chaise advance, which resembled an open wagon with leather curtains; it was followed by four enormous carts which were loaded. In the chaise there was a young man, dressed in the rustic manner, whose fresh countenance was replete with sweetness and gaiety. His wife, a little woman of a brown complexion and an agreeable figure, though somewhat stout, sat close by him. As the carriage did not move on like the chaise of a petit-maître, the traveler had sufficient time to contemplate the marquis, who was motionless and immersed in sorrow.

"Good God," cried he, "I think that is Jeannot." Upon hearing this name, the marquis lifts up his eyes, the carriage stops, and Colin cries out, "'Tis Jeannot, 'tis Jeannot himself."

The little fat bumpkin gave but one spring from the chaise and ran to embrace his old companion. Jeannot recollected his friend Colin, while his eyes were blinded with tears of shame.

"You have abandoned me," said Colin; "but, though you are a great man, I will love you forever."

Jeannot, confused and affected, related to him with emotion a great part of his history.

"Come to the inn where I lodge, and tell me the rest of it," said Colin; "embrace my wife here, and let us go and dine together." They then went on foot, followed by their baggage.

"What is all this train," said Jeannot; "is it yours?"

"Yes," answered Colin, "it all belongs to me and to my wife. We have just come in from the country. I am now at the head of a large manufactory of tin and copper. I have married the daughter of a merchant well provided with all things necessary for the great as well as the little. We work a great deal; God blesses us; we have not changed our condition; we are happy; we will assist our friend Jeannot. Be no longer a marquis; all the grandeur in the world is not to be compared to a good friend. You shall return with me to the country. I will teach you the trade; it is not very difficult; I will make you my partner, and we will live merrily in the remote corner where we were born."

Jeannot, quite transported, felt emotions of grief and joy, tenderness and shame; and he said within himself: "My fashionable friends have betrayed me, and Colin, whom I despised, is the only one who comes to relieve me." What instruction does not this narrative afford!

Colin's goodness of heart caused the seeds of a virtuous disposition, which the world had not quite stifled in Jeannot, to revive. He was sensible that he could not forsake his father and mother.

"We will take care of your mother," said Colin; "and as to the good man your father, who is now in jail, his creditors, seeing he has nothing, will compromise matters for a trifle. I know something of business, and will take the whole affair upon myself."

Colin found means to procure the father's enlargement. Jeannot returned to the country with his relatives, who resumed their former way of life. He married a sister of Colin, and she, being of the same temper with her brother, made him completely happy.

Jeannot the father, Jeannote the mother, and Jeannot the son, were thus convinced that happiness is not the result of vanity.

THE HISTORY OF THE TRAVELS OF SCARMENTADO. [1]

I was born in Candia, in the year 1600. My father was governor of the city; and I remember that a poet of middling parts, and of a most unmusical ear, whose name was Iro, composed some verses in my praise, in which he made me to descend from Minos in a direct line; but my father being afterwards disgraced, he wrote some other verses, in which he derived my pedigree from no nobler an origin than the amours of Pasiphæ and her gallant. This Iro was a most mischievous rogue, and one of the most troublesome fellows in the island.

My father sent me at fifteen years of age to prosecute my studies at Rome. There I arrived in full hopes of learning all kinds of truth; for I had hitherto been taught quite the reverse, according to the custom of this lower world from China to the Alps. Monsignor Profondo, to whom I was recommended, was a man of a very singular character, and one of the most terrible scholars in the world. He was for teaching me the categories of Aristotle; and was just on the point of placing me in the category of his minions; a fate which I narrowly escaped. I saw processions, exorcisms, and some robberies.

It was commonly said, but without any foundation, that la Signora Olympia, a lady of great prudence, had deceived many lovers, she being both inconstant and mercenary. I was then of an age to relish such comical anecdotes.

A young lady of great sweetness of temper, called la Signora Fatelo, thought proper to fall in love with me. She was courted by the reverend father Poignardini, and by the reverend father Aconiti,[2] young monks of an order now extinct; and she reconciled the two rivals by declaring her preference for me; but at the same time I ran the risk of being excommunicated and poisoned. I left Rome highly pleased with the architecture of St. Peter.

I traveled to France. It was during the reign of Louis the Just. The first question put to me was, whether I chose to breakfast on a slice of the Marshal D'Ancre,[3] whose flesh the people had roasted and distributed with great liberality to such as chose to taste it.

This kingdom was continually involved in civil wars, sometimes for a place at court, sometimes for two pages of theological controversy. This fire, which one while lay concealed under the ashes, and at another burst forth with great violence, had desolated these beautiful provinces for upwards of sixty years. The pretext was, defending the liberties of the Gallican church. "Alas!" said I, "these people are nevertheless born with a gentle disposition. What can have drawn them so far from their natural character? They joke and keep holy days.[4] Happy the time when they shall do nothing but joke!"

I went over to England, where the same disputes occasioned the same barbarities. Some pious Catholics had resolved, for the good of the church, to blow up into the air with gunpowder the king, the royal family, and the whole parliament, and thus to deliver England from all these heretics at once. They showed me the place where Queen Mary of blessed memory, the daughter of Henry VIII., had caused more than five hundred, of her subjects to be burnt. An Irish priest assured me that it was a very good action; first, because those who were burnt were Englishmen; and secondly, because they did not make use of holy water, nor believe in St. Patrick. He was greatly surprised that Queen Mary was not yet canonized; but he hoped she would receive that honor as soon as the cardinal should be a little more at leisure.

From thence I went to Holland, where I hoped to find more tranquillity among a people of a more cold and phlegmatic temperament. Just as I arrived at the Hague, the people were cutting off the head of a venerable old man. It was the bald head of the prime minister Barnevelt; a man who deserved better treatment from the republic. Touched with pity at this affecting scene, I asked what was his crime, and whether he had betrayed the state.

"He has done much worse," replied a preacher in a black cloak; "he believed that men may be saved by good works as well as by faith. You must be sensible," adds he, "that if such opinions were to gain ground, a republic could not subsist; and that there must be severe laws to suppress such scandalous and horrid blasphemies."

A profound politician said to me with a sigh: "Alas! sir, this happy time will not last long; it is only by chance that the people are so zealous. They are naturally inclined to the abominable doctrine of toleration, and they will certainly at last grant it." This reflection set him a groaning. For my own part, in expectation of that fatal period when moderation and indulgence should take place, I instantly quitted a country where severity was not softened by any lenitive, and embarked for Spain.

The court was then at Seville, the galleons had just arrived; and everything breathed plenty and gladness, in the most beautiful season of the year. I observed at the end of an alley of orange and citron trees, a kind of large ring, surrounded with steps covered with rich and costly cloth. The king, the queen, the infants, and the infantas, were seated under a superb canopy. Opposite to the royal family was another throne, raised higher than that on which his majesty sat. I said to a fellow-traveler: "Unless this throne be reserved for God, I don't see what purpose it can serve."

This unguarded expression was overheard by a grave Spaniard, and cost me dear. Meanwhile, I imagined we were going to a carousal, or a match of bull-baiting, when the grand inquisitor appeared in that elevated throne, from whence he blessed the king and the people.

Then came an army of monks, who led off in pairs, white, black, grey, shod, unshod, bearded, beardless, with pointed cowls, and without cowls. Next followed the hangman; and last of all were seen, in the midst of the guards and grandees, about forty persons clad in sackcloth, on which were painted the figures of flames and devils. Some of these were Jews, who could not be prevailed upon to renounce Moses entirely; others were Christians, who had married women with whom they had stood sponsors to a child; who had not adored our Lady of Atocha; or who had refused to part with their ready money in favor of the Hieronymite brothers. Some pretty prayers were sung with much devotion, and then the criminals were burnt at a slow fire; a ceremony with which the royal family seemed to be greatly edified.

As I was going to bed in the evening, two members of the inquisition came to my lodging with a figure of St. Hermandad. They embraced me with great tenderness, and conducted me in solemn silence to a well-aired prison, furnished with a bed of mat, and a beautiful crucifix. There I remained for six weeks; at the end of which time the reverend father, the Inquisitor, sent for me. He pressed me in his arms for some time with the most paternal affection, and told me that he was sorry to hear that I had been so ill lodged; but that all the apartments of the house were full, and hoped I should be better accommodated the next time. He then asked me with great cordiality if I knew for what reason I was imprisoned.

I told the reverend father that it was evidently for my sins.

"Very well," said he, "my dear child; but for what particular sin? Speak freely."

I racked my brain with conjectures, but could not possibly guess. He then charitably dismissed me. At last I remembered my unguarded expression. I escaped with a little bodily correction, and a fine of thirty thousand reals. I was led to make my obeisance to the grand Inquisitor, who was a man of great politeness. He asked me how I liked his little feast. I told him it was a most delicious one; and then went to press my companions to quit the country, beautiful as it was.

They had, during my imprisonment, found time to inform themselves of all the great things which the Spaniards had done for the interest of religion. They had read the memoirs of the famous bishop of Chiapa, by which it appears that they had massacred, or burnt, or drowned, about ten millions of infidels in America, in order to convert them. I believe the accounts of the bishop are a little exaggerated; but suppose we reduce the number of victims to five millions, it will still be a most glorious achievement.

The impulse for traveling still possessed me. I had proposed to finish the tour of Europe with Turkey, and thither we now directed our course. I made a firm resolution not to give my opinion of any public feasts I might see in the future. "These Turks," said I to my companions, "are a set of miscreants that have not been baptized, and therefore will be more cruel than the reverend fathers the inquisitors. Let us observe a profound silence while we are among the Mahometans." When we arrived there, I was greatly surprised to see more Christian churches in Turkey than in Candia. I saw also numerous troops of monks, who were allowed to pray to the virgin Mary with great freedom, and to curse Mahomet—some in Greek, some in Latin, and others in Armenian. "What good-natured people are these Turks," cried I.

The Greek christians, and the Latin christians in Constantinople were mortal enemies. These sectarians persecuted each other in much the same manner as dogs fight in the streets, till their masters part them with a cudgel.

The grand vizier was at that time the protector of the Greeks. The Greek patriarch accused me of having supped with the Latin patriarch; and I was condemned in full divan to receive an hundred blows on the soles of my feet, redeemable for five hundred sequins. Next day the grand vizier was strangled. The day following his successor, who was for the Latin party, and who was not strangled till a month after, condemned me to suffer the same punishment, for having supped with the Greek patriarch. Thus was I reduced to the sad necessity of absenting myself entirely from the Greek and Latin churches.

In order to console myself for this loss, I frequently visited a very handsome Circassian. She was the most entertaining lady I ever knew in a private conversation, and the most devout at the mosque. One evening she received me with tenderness and sweetly cried, "Alla, Illa, Alla."

These are the sacramental words of the Turks. I imagined they were the expressions of love, and therefore cried in my turn, and with a very tender accent, "Alla, Illa, Alla."

"Ah!" said she, "God be praised, thou art then a Turk?"

I told her that I was blessing God for having given me so much enjoyment, and that I thought myself extremely happy.

In the morning the inman came to enroll me among the circumcised, and as I made some objection to the initiation, the cadi of that district, a man of great loyalty, proposed to have me impaled. I preserved my freedom by paying a thousand sequins, and then fled directly into Persia, resolved for the future never to hear Greek or Latin mass, nor to cry "Alla, Illa, Alla," in a love encounter.

On my arrival at Ispahan, the people asked me whether I was for white or black mutton? I told them that it was a matter of indifference to me, provided it was tender. It must be observed that the Persian empire was at that time split into two factions, that of the white mutton and that of the black. The two parties imagined that I had made a jest of them both; so that I found myself engaged in a very troublesome affair at the gates of the city, and it cost me a great number of sequins to get rid of the white and the black mutton.

I proceeded as far as China, in company with an interpreter, who assured me that this country was the seat of gaiety and freedom. The Tartars had made themselves masters of it, after having destroyed everything with fire and sword.

The reverend fathers, the Jesuits, on the one hand, and the reverend fathers, the Dominicans, on the other, alleged that they had gained many souls to God in that country, without any one knowing aught of the matter. Never were seen such zealous converters. They alternately persecuted one another; they transmitted to Rome whole volumes of slander; and treated each other as infidels and prevaricators for the sake of one soul. But the most violent dispute between them was with regard to the manner of making a bow. The Jesuits would have the Chinese to salute their parents after the fashion of China, and the Dominicans would have them to do it after the fashion of Rome.

I happened unluckily to be taken by the Jesuits for a Dominican. They represented me to his Tartarian majesty as a spy of the pope. The supreme council charged a prime mandarin, who ordered a sergeant, who commanded four shires of the country, to seize me and bind me with great ceremony. In this manner I was conducted before his majesty, after having made about an hundred and forty genuflections. He asked me if I was a spy of the pope's, and if it was true that that prince was to come in person to dethrone him. I told him that the pope was a priest of seventy years of age; that he lived at the distance of four thousand leagues from his sacred Tartaro-Chinese majesty; that he had about two thousand soldiers, who mounted guard with umbrellas; that he never dethroned anybody; and that his majesty might sleep in perfect security.

Of all the adventures of my life this was the least fatal. I was sent to Macao, and there I took shipping for Europe.

My ship required to be refitted on the coast of Golconda. I embraced this opportunity to visit the court of the great Aureng-Zeb, of whom such wonderful things have been told, and which was then in Delphi. I had the pleasure to see him on the day of that pompous ceremony in which he receives the celestial present sent him by the Sherif of Mecca. This was the besom with which they had swept the holy house, the Caaba, and the Beth Alla. It is a symbol that sweeps away all the pollutions of the soul.

Aureng-Zeb seemed to have no need of it. He was the most pious man in all Indostan. It is true, he had cut the throat of one of his brothers, and poisoned his father. Twenty Rayas, and as many Omras, had been put to death; but that was a trifle. Nothing was talked of but his devotion. No king was thought comparable to him, except his sacred majesty Muley Ismael, the most serene emperor of Morocco, who always cut off some heads every Friday after prayers.

I spoke not a word. My travels had taught me wisdom. I was sensible that it did not belong to me to decide between these august sovereigns. A young Frenchman, a fellow-lodger of mine, was, however, greatly wanting in respect to both the emperor of the Indies and to that of Morocco. He happened to say very imprudently, that there were sovereigns in Europe who governed their dominions with great equity, and even went to church without killing their fathers or brothers, or cutting off the heads of their subjects.

This indiscreet discourse of my young friend, the interpreter at once translated. Instructed by former experience, I instantly caused my camels to be saddled, and set out with my Frenchman. I was afterwards informed that the officers of the great Aureng-Zeb came that very night to seize me, but finding only the interpreter, they publicly executed him; and the courtiers all claimed, very justly, that his punishment was well deserved.

I had now only Africa to visit in order to enjoy all the pleasures of our continent; and thither I went to complete my voyage. The ship in which I embarked was taken by the Negro corsairs. The master of the vessel complained loudly, and asked why they thus violated the laws of nations. The captain of the Negroes thus replied:

"You have a long nose and we have a short one. Your hair is straight and ours is curled; your skin is ash-colored and ours is of the color of ebon; and therefore we ought, by the sacred laws of nature, to be always at enmity. You buy us in the public markets on the coast of Guinea like beasts of burden, to make us labor in I don't know what kind of drudgery, equally hard and ridiculous. With the whip held over our heads, you make us dig in mines for a kind of yellow earth, which in itself is good for nothing, and is not so valuable as an Egyptian onion. In like manner wherever we meet you, and are superior to you in strength, we make you slaves, and oblige you to cultivate our fields, or in case of refusal we cut off your nose and ears."

To such a learned discourse it was impossible to make any answer. I submitted to labor in the garden of an old negress, in order to save my nose and ears. After continuing in slavery for a whole year, I was at length happily ransomed.

As I had now seen all that was rare, good, or beautiful on earth, I resolved for the future to see nothing but my own home. I took a wife, and soon suspected that she deceived me; but, notwithstanding this doubt, I still found that of all conditions of life this was much the happiest.

[1] The reader will perceive that this is a spirited satire on mankind in general, and particularly on persecution for conscience sake.—*Trans.*

[2] Alluding to the infamous practice of poisoning and assassination at that time prevalent in Rome.—*Trans.*

[3] This was the famous Concini, who was murdered on the draw-bridge of the Louvre, by the intrigues of De Luines, not without the knowledge of the king, Louis XIII. His body, which had been secretly interred in the church of St. Germain de l'Auxerrois, was next day dug up by the populace, who dragged it through the streets, then burned the flesh, and threw the bones into the river. The marshal's greatest crime was his being a foreigner.—*Tr.*

[4] Referring to the massacre of Protestants, on the eve of St. Bartholomew.—*Tr.*

Brahma, the Creator.—Vishnu, the Preserver.—Siva, the Destroyer.

THE GOOD BRAMIN.

DOES HAPPINESS RESULT FROM IGNORANCE OR FROM KNOWLEDGE?

In my travels I once happened to meet with an aged Bramin. This man had a great share of understanding and prudence, and was very learned. He was also very rich, and his riches added greatly to his popularity; for, wanting nothing that wealth could procure, he had no desire to defraud any one. His family was admirably managed by three handsome wives, who always studied to please him; and when he was weary of their society, he had recourse to the study of philosophy.

Not far from his house, which was handsome, well-furnished and embellished with delightful gardens, dwelt an old Indian woman who was a great bigot, ignorant, and withall very poor.

"I wish," said the Bramin to me one day, "I had never been born!"

"Why so?" said I.

"Because," replied he, "I have been studying these forty years, and I find it has been so much time lost. While I teach others I know nothing myself. The sense of my condition is so humiliating, it makes all things so distasteful to me, that life has become a burden. I have been born, and I exist in time, without knowing what time is. I am placed, as our wise men say, in the confines between two eternities, and yet I have no idea of eternity. I am composed of matter, I think, but have never been able to satisfy myself what it is that produces thought. I even am ignorant whether my understanding is a simple faculty I possess, like that of walking and digesting, or if I think with my head in the same manner as I take hold of a thing with my hands. I am not only thus in the dark with relation to the principles of thought, but the principles of my motions are entirely unknown to me. I do not know why I exist, and yet I am applied to every day for a solution of the enigma. I must return an answer, but can say nothing satisfactory on the the subject. I talk a great deal, and when I have done speaking remain confounded and ashamed of what I have said."

"I am in still greater perplexity when I am asked if Brama was produced by Vishnu, or if they have both existed from eternity. God is my judge that I know nothing of the matter, as plainly appears by my answers. 'Reverend father,' says one, 'be pleased to inform me how evil is spread over the face of the earth.' I am as much at a loss as those who ask the question. Sometimes I tell them that every thing is for the best; but those who have the gout or the stone—those who have lost their fortunes or their limbs in the wars—believe as little of this assertion as I do myself. I retire to my own house full of curiosity, and endeavor to enlighten my ignorance by consulting the writings of our ancient sages, but they only serve to bewilder me the more. When I talk with my brethren upon this subject, some tell me we ought to make the most of life and laugh at the world. Others think they know something, and lose themselves in vain and chimerical hypotheses. Every effort I make to solve the mystery adds to the load I feel. Sometimes I am ready to fall into despair when I reflect that, after all my researches, I neither know from whence I came, what I am, whither I shall go, or what is to become of me."

The condition in which I saw this good man gave me real concern. No one could be more rational, no one more open and honest. It appeared to me that the force of his understanding and the sensibility of his heart were the causes of his misery.

The same day I had a conversation with the old woman, his neighbor. I asked her if she had ever been unhappy for not understanding how her soul was made? She did not even comprehend my question. She had not, for the briefest moment in her life, had a thought about these subjects with which the good Bramin had so tormented himself. She believed from the bottom of her heart in the metamorphoses of her god Vishnu, and, provided she could get some of the sacred water of the Ganges in which to make her ablutions, she thought herself the happiest of women.

Struck with the happiness of this poor creature, I returned to my philosopher, whom I thus addressed:

"Are you not ashamed to be thus miserable when, not fifty yards from you, there is an old automaton who thinks of nothing and lives contented?"

"You are right," he replied. "I have said to myself a thousand times that I should be happy if I were but as ignorant as my old neighbor, and yet it is a happiness I do not desire."

This reply of the Bramin made a greater impression on me than any thing that had passed. I consulted my own heart and found that I myself should not wish to be happy on condition of being ignorant.

I submitted this matter to some philosophers, and they were all of my opinion: and yet, said I, there is something very contradictory in this manner of thinking; for, after all, what is the question? Is it not to be happy? What signifies it then whether we have understandings or whether we are fools? Besides, there is this to be said: those who are contented with their condition are sure of that content; while those who have the faculty of reasoning are not always sure of reasoning right. It is evident then, I continued, that we ought rather to wish not to have common sense, if that common sense contributes to our being either miserable or wicked.

They were all of my opinion, and yet not one of them could be found, to accept of happiness on the terms of being ignorant. From hence I concluded, that although we may set a great value upon happiness, we set a still greater upon reason.

But after mature reflection upon this subject I still thought there was great madness in preferring reason to happiness. How is this contradiction to be explained? Like all other questions, a great deal may be said about it.

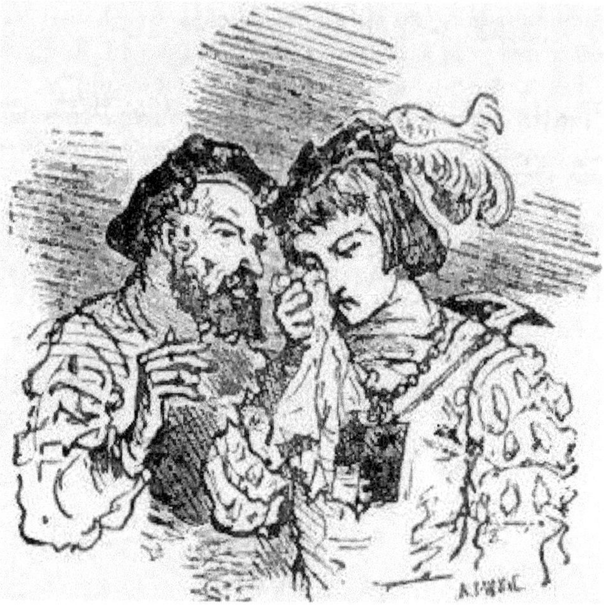

THE TWO COMFORTERS.

The great philosopher Citosile once said to a woman who was disconsolate, and who had good reason to be so: "Madame, the queen of England, daughter to Henry IV., was as wretched as you. She was banished from her kingdom, was in great danger of losing her life at sea, and saw her royal spouse expire on a scaffold."

"I am sorry for her," said the lady, and began again to lament her own misfortunes.

"But," said Citosile, "remember the fate of Mary Stuart. She loved, (but with a most chaste and virtuous affection,) an excellent musician, who played admirably on the bass-viol. Her husband killed her musician before her face; and in the sequel, her good friend and relative, queen Elizabeth, who called herself a virgin, caused her head to be cut off on a scaffold covered with black, after having confined her in prison for the space of eighteen years."

"That was very cruel," replied the lady, and presently relapsed into her former melancholy.

"Perhaps," said the comforter, "you have heard of the beautiful Joan of Naples, who was taken prisoner and strangled."

"I have a dim remembrance of her," said the afflicted lady.

"I must relate to you," continued the other, "the adventure of a sovereign princess who, within my recollection, was dethroned after supper, and who died in a desert island."

"I know her whole history," replied the lady.

"Well, then," said Citosile, "I will tell you what happened to another great princess whom I instructed in philosophy. She had a lover as all great and beautiful princesses have. Her father surprised this lover in her company, and was so displeased with the young man's confused manner and excited countenance, that he gave him one of the most terrible blows that had ever been given in his province. The lover seized a pair of tongs and broke the head of the angry parent, who was cured with great difficulty, and who still bears the marks of the wound. The lady in a fright leaped out of the window and dislocated her foot, in consequence of which she habitually halts, though still possessed in other respects of a very handsome person. The lover was condemned to death for having broken the head of a great prince. You can imagine in what a deplorable condition the princess must have been when her lover was led to the gallows. I have seen her long ago when she was in prison, and she always spoke to me of her own misfortunes."

"And why will you not allow me to think of mine?" said the lady.

"Because," said the philosopher, "you ought not to think of them; and since so many great ladies have been so unfortunate, it ill becomes you to despair. Think of Hecuba, —think of Niobe."

"Ah!" said the lady, "had I lived in their time, or in that of so many beautiful princesses, and had you endeavored to console them by a relation of my misfortunes, would they have listened to you, do you imagine?"

Next day the philosopher lost his only son, and was entirely prostrated with grief. The lady caused a catalogue to be drawn up of all the kings who had lost their children, and carried it to the philosopher. He read it—found it very exact—and wept nevertheless.

Three months afterwards they chanced to renew their acquaintance, and were mutually surprised to find each other in such a gay and sprightly humor. To commemorate this event, they caused to be erected a beautiful statue to Time, with this inscription: "TO HIM WHO COMFORTS."

The winged dragon.

ANCIENT FAITH AND FABLE.

In order to be successful in their efforts to govern the multitude, rulers have endeavored to instill all the visionary notions possible into the minds of their subjects.

The good people who read *Virgil*, or the *Provincial Letters*, do not know that there are twenty times more copies of the *Almanac of Liège* and of the *Courier Boiteux* printed, than of all the ancient and modern books together. No one can have a greater admiration than myself for the illustrious authors of these *Almanacs* and their brethren. I know that ever since the time of the ancient Chaldeans there have been fixed and stated days for taking physic, paring our nails, giving battle, and cleaving wood. I know that the best part of the revenue of an illustrious academy consists in the sale of these *Almanacs*. May I presume to ask, with all possible submission, and a becoming diffidence of my own judgment, what harm it would do to the world if some powerful astrologer were to assure the peasants and the good inhabitants of little villages that they might safely pare their nails when they please, provided it be done with a good intention? The people, I shall be told, would not buy the *Almanacs* of this new astrologer. On the contrary, I will venture to affirm, that there would be found among your great geniuses many who would make a merit in following this novelty. Should it be alleged, however, that these geniuses, in their new born zeal, would form factions and kindle a civil war, I would have nothing farther to say on the subject, but readily give up for the sake of peace my too radical and dangerous opinion.

Every body knows the king of Boutan. He is one of the greatest princes in the universe. He tramples under his feet the thrones of the earth; and his shoes (if he has any) are provided with sceptres instead of buckles. He adores the devil, as is well known, and his example is followed by all his courtiers. He one day sent for a famous sculptor of my country, and ordered him to make a beautiful statue of Beelzebub. The sculptor succeeded admirably. Never before was there seen such an interesting and handsome devil. But, unhappily, our Praxiteles had only given five clutches to his statue, whereas the devout Boutaniers always gave him six. This serious blunder of the artist was aggravated by the grand master of ceremonies to the devil with all the zeal of a man justly jealous of his master's acknowledged rights, and also of the established and sacred customs of the kingdom of Boutan. He insisted that the sculptor should be punished for his thoughtless innovation by the loss of his head. The anxious sculptor explained that his five clutches were exactly equal in weight to six ordinary clutches; and the king of Boutan, who was a prince of great clemency, granted him a pardon. From that time the people of Boutan no longer believed the dogma relating to the devil's six clutches.

The same day it was thought necessary that his majesty should be bled, and a surgeon of Gascony, who had come to his court in a ship belonging to our East India Company, was appointed to take from him five ounces of his precious blood. The astrologer of that quarter cried out that the king would be in danger of losing his life if the surgeon opened a vein while the heavens were in their present state. The Gascon might have told him that the only question was about the king's health; but he prudently waited a few moments and then, taking an *Almanac* in his hand, thus addressed the astrologer.

"You was in the right, great man! The king would have died held he been bled at the instant you mentioned; but the heavens have since changed their aspect, and now is the favorable moment."

The astrologer assented to the surgeon's observation. The king was cured; and by degrees it became an established custom among the Boutaniers to bleed their kings whenever it was considered necessary.

Although the Indian astronomers understood the method of calculating eclipses, yet the common people obstinately held to the old belief that the sun, when obscured, had fallen into the throat of a great dragon, and that the only way to free him from thence was by standing naked in the water and making a hideous noise to frighten away the monster, and oblige him to release his hold.[2] This notion, which is quite prevalent among the orientals, is an evident proof how much the symbols of religion and natural philosophy have at all times been perverted by the common people. The astronomers of all ages have been wont to distinguish the two points of intersection, upon which every eclipse happens, and which are called the Lunar Nodes, by marking them with a dragon's head and tail. Now the vulgar, who are equally ignorant in every part of the world, took the symbol or sign for the thing itself. Thus, when the astronomers said the sun is in the dragon's head, the common people said the dragon is going to swallow up the sun; and yet these people were remarkable for their fondness for astrology. But while we laugh at the ignorance and credulity of the Indians, we do not reflect that there are no less than 300,000 *Almanacs* sold yearly in Europe, all of them filled with observations and predictions equally as false and absurd as any to be met with among the Indians. It is surely as reasonable to say that the sun is in the mouth or the claws of a dragon, as to tell people every year in print that they must not sow, nor plant, nor take physic, nor be bled, but on certain days of the moon. It is high time, in an age like ours, that some men of learning should think it worth their while to compose a calendar that might be of use to the industrious classes by instructing instead of deceiving them.

A blustering Dominican at Rome said to an English philosopher with whom he was disputing:

"You are a dog; you say that it is the earth that turns round, never reflecting that Joshua made the sun to stand still!"

"Well! my reverend father," replied the philosopher, "ever since that time hath not the sun been immovable?"

The dog and the Dominican embraced each other, and even the devout Italians were at length convinced that the earth turns round.

An augur and a senator lamented, in the time of Cæsar, the declining state of the republic.

"The times, indeed, are very bad," said the senator, "we have reason to tremble for the liberty of Rome."

"Ah!" said the augur, "that is not the greatest evil; the people now begin to lose the respect which they formerly had for our order. We seem barely to be tolerated—we cease to be necessary. Some generals have the assurance to give battle without consulting us. And, to complete our misfortunes, even those who sell us the sacred pullets begin to reason."

"Well, and why don't you reason likewise?" replied the senator, "and since the dealers in pullets in the time of Cæsar are more knowing than they were in the time of Numa, ought not you modern augurs to be better philosophers than those who lived in former ages?"

[1] This dragon was of the same species, *Draco Volans*, as the savage reptile slain by St. George, the patron saint of England, or the sleepless dragon at Colchis, from which Jason rescued the *golden fleece*. The bible history abounds with allusions to dragons, and with prophecies of their coming exploits in the stellar spheres. These marvels may be considered, however, as more strange than credible, and more ancient than authentic—E.

[2] In Rev. XII: 3, 4, the Dragon is represented as deftly seizing one-third of the stars of heaven with his tail, and rudely wresting them in dire confusion from the celestial spheres.—E.